Sensual Philosophy

For Michelle—
Don't neglect
Michel in your
studies.
Best,
Alan Levine

Sensual Philosophy

Toleration, Skepticism, and Montaigne's Politics of the Self

Alan Levine

LEXINGTON BOOKS
Lanham • Boulder • New York • Oxford

LEXINGTON BOOKS

Published in the United States of America
by Lexington Books
4720 Boston Way, Lanham, Maryland 20706

12 Hid's Copse Road
Cumnor Hill, Oxford OX2 9JJ, England

British Library Cataloguing in Publication Information Available

Library of Congress Cataloging-in-Publication Data

Levine, Alan, 1961–
  Sensual philosophy : toleration, skepticism, and Montaigne's politics of the self /
Alan Levine.
    p. cm. — (Applications of political theory)
  Includes bibliographical references (p.) and index.
  ISBN 0-7391-0246-X (cloth : alk. paper) — ISBN 0-7391-0247-8 (pbk. : alk. paper)
    1. Montaigne, Michel de, 1533–1592. 2. Religious tolerance—History.
  3. Skepticism—History. 4. Self—History. I. Title. II. Series.

B785.M74 L48 2001
194–dc21

                                                                  2001029124
Printed in the United States of America

♾™ The paper used in this publication meets the minimum requirements of American
National Standard for Information Sciences—Permanence of Paper for Printed Library
Materials, ANSI/NISO Z39.48–1992.

To My Parents

Contents

Preface

Although this book is about Montaigne, it is haunted by Nietzsche. This is true both in the book's question and its answer. The question concerns the ground and justification of morality. It is as old as political philosophy itself, but since Nietzsche's announcement of the death of God (which, like Heidegger, I take to mean a lack of ground for all religious and secular values), it has taken on a particular shape and urgency. Nietzsche's challenge to morality is the following: if there is no moral truth that transcends an individual's subjective will—and we today are hard pressed to articulate any such truth—why should one act morally? According to Nietzsche and his followers, there is no such absolute truth, and anyone who restrains him- or herself in the name of morality is merely the brainwashed dupe of a view instituted to serve the interests of others. Few people want to be anyone's dupe, and many twentieth-century thinkers fashionably trumpet Nietzsche's radical rejection of metaphysics, emphasizing the liberation and joy accompanying it. But they neglect to think through the moral implications of this view. What passes for philosophy today is full of both liberal democratic assertions and a joyful play and irony befitting a wide-open world, but the moral visions espoused do not adequately confront the terrible possibilities of Nietzsche's thought. Liberal and postmodern thinkers today argue against domination, repression, and inequalities of all sorts—but Nietzsche himself favors varieties of each of these. The question remains: if there is no truth, on what ground can these moral preferences be justified? The failure to address this aspect of Nietzsche's thought is a failure to take morality seriously. Few, if any, thinkers want to encourage cruel or illiberal behavior, but their fundamentally Nietzschean description of the world cannot give a principled reason not to act as Nietzsche recommends. In a more general way, this problem characterizes all of the so-called skeptical and non-foundational approaches of turn-of-the-century political theory.

The answer offered in this book involves Nietzsche as well, for I was first directed to Montaigne by Nietzsche's own writing. Nietzsche praises Montaigne and his joyfulness. Based on his descriptions of Montaigne, I began to think that perhaps Montaigne's skepticism might offer a more fruitful answer to the question that Nietzsche poses. Indeed, this is what I found. Montaigne offers a profoundly sane and humane vision of the world, one that argues for morality without appealing to metaphysics or mere custom. For Montaigne, self-interest properly understood and the toleration of others are complementary, not contradictory, phenomena. Whether this book adequately describes Montaigne's thought, whether the features I find in it adequately address the problems, or whether I sufficiently understand the problems of modernity are for the reader to decide. This is what I found, and how the idea for this book was born.

The shape of my thought in general and on Montaigne in particular has benefitted from many people. As an undergraduate, I was fortunate to have attended the University of Chicago, a school that takes ideas more seriously than any other I have come across. A freshman course called Human Being and Citizen, team-taught by Herman Sinaiko and Rob McKay, changed my life. In Plato, Aristotle, and the other authors we read, I discovered questions I had always wanted to ask but had never been able to articulate. Later courses with Joseph Cropsey, Allan Bloom, and Nathan Tarcov cultivated this interest. I am particularly grateful to Nathan Tarcov for his guidance both inside and outside of the classroom.

At Harvard, I was lucky enough to have a trio of readers who supported my work even as they challenged it. When I first began working on Montaigne, I had no idea that he was Judith Shklar's favorite thinker, so it is perhaps fitting that the dissertation from which this book grew was the last to have Shklar's name attached to it. Although the final product was not subjected to her scrutiny, my ideas on Montaigne weathered her onslaughts through two independent study classes on him. As those who have sat in the wooden chair across from her desk know, I was subject class after class to the tempests of her mind, bending like a palm tree in a storm, fortunate never to snap or become unrooted. To her credit, she never insisted that my Montaigne had to be hers. Harvey Mansfield was a gentle reader and advisor, supportive of me and this project throughout. His analysis of and questions on the ground of liberalism helped shape my understanding of the fundamental problems addressed in this book. Stephen Macedo was a teacher and a colleague and is as good a professional friend as they come. Peter Berkowitz joined the committee after Shklar's death, but we had long since been discussing the nature of skepticism. Thanks also to Patrick Riley, present at my prospectus defense, for insisting on the importance of the unity of self-interest and morality that I find in Montaigne and for encouraging me to focus on it.

Numerous friends and colleagues read all or part of different versions of the manuscript. Along the way, I benefitted from conversations with and comments from Ahmad Baig, Christine Foureau, Michael Gillespie, Maryanne Horowitz, Daryl Koehn, Chris Laursen, Pierre Manent, Joshua Mitchell, Cary Nederman, Joel Schwartz, Adam Shulman, and Ken Weinstein. Ingrid Creppell, Philip Lyons, and David Schaefer read a near-final version of the manuscript and offered consistently helpful comments above and beyond what could be reasonably expected. Schaefer's detailed comments were particularly helpful, and I will always be grateful to him for inviting me to present my first academic conference paper. The comments by the readers for Lexington Books, Adam Wolfson and Aurelian Craiutu, were poignant and encouraging, and Wolfson's insights led me to change the book's title. Finally, I owe a debt of gratitude to Marianne Noble, who read the whole manuscript—and parts of it several times. Her compassionate probing and depth helped get me through the most difficult phases of rewriting, and she shaved away numerous difficulties. While the arguments and interpretations advanced here benefitted from all of the above, I alone, needless to say, am responsible for all remaining errors.

This book also benefitted from the material support of several different organizations and individuals. A version of chapter 2 appears in the *Review of Metaphysics* and is reprinted here with their permission. Fellowships from Harvard University's Program on Constitutional Government supported research trips to France. The Earhart Foundation supported the writing phase of this book, as did a grant from the Dean of the School of Public Affairs at American University. I have also been fortunate to have benefitted from a number of talented undergraduate and graduate students. Joanne Molina checked references to Montaigne, Brian Della Torre helped codify the endnotes and bibliography, Jeffrey Edwards proofread, and Michael Schmidt prepared the Index and numerous other things. Lexington Books' Serena Leigh, Jason Proetorius, Jason Hallman, and, especially, Steven Wrinn were helpful throughout. I am grateful to all of the above.

Finally, my sister, Zahavah, and my parents, Richard and Nessa Levine, were lovingly supportive throughout the years it took to write my dissertation and the years spent transforming it into this book. Their love helped get me through. With love and respect, this book is gratefully dedicated to my parents.

Introduction

This book aims to shed light on the fundamental question of the ground of liberalism, with which we so struggle. In addressing this problem, it operates within the skeptical paradigm dominant in political philosophy today by presenting the political thought of the modern era's first great skeptic, Michel de Montaigne (1533-1592).[1] Montaigne is no liberal and does not defend liberalism as we know it. He does not insist on a democratic form of government, advocate the separation of powers, or assert the various political and civil rights that liberals deem essential for a society to be humane and just. However, he provides something even more important: a ground for the liberal *weltanschauung*, upon which all of our political institutions are based. Institutions cannot take root without a mind-set to support them; one need only consider the intractable difficulties encountered in the post-World War II attempts to transplant liberalism to parts of the world where it did not have historical roots to see how important such a foundation is. Historically speaking, Montaigne's thought played a significant role in establishing the liberal ethos in the West, and it is the aim of this book to consider how his philosophy is still relevant in terms of a particular intellectual problem from which the West now suffers. Today the *political* institutions of liberalism exist and are (more or less) thriving in the Western world; it is their *theoretical* justification that is problematic.

Montaigne is a particularly good figure in whom to find arguments for theoretical justification, because he offered his arguments for toleration and the separation of the public and private spheres, two of the most fundamental ideas of liberalism, at a time when liberalism's political institutions, upon which post-World War II theorists so often rely, were not yet conceived. Given this historical context, he is more aware of fundamental alternatives and necessarily argues for toleration without the benefit of a tradition to which he can appeal, and he does this without relying on custom, habit, or rights of any kind. While Montaigne's arguments are not entirely *ex nihilo*, they are largely so; he was forced to plumb the depths of issues that are often taken for granted by those thinking after liberalism had achieved its considerable worldly success. In short, he makes exactly the kind of argument for the justification of liberalism that is wanting today. This is not to say that Montaigne has completely resolved our current problems about justifying toleration. But his thought processes illuminate key problems in contemporary thought and pose appealing answers to questions with which we still wrestle.

This book aims to do two things. First, it aims to articulate and assess Montaigne's skeptically based arguments for toleration, which can serve as an alternative or supplementary justification for liberalism. In doing this, the book both analyzes the nature and extent of Montaigne's skepticism and specifies the other factors on which his arguments for toleration depend. For skepticism does not necessarily lead to toleration, so it must be limited or supplemented by some other concept, idea, or aim if a tolerant conclusion is to be reached. Secondarily, this book also aims to put Montaigne's thought in the context of the history of political philosophy, both because his historical importance is underappreciated today, and because the unique way he bridges ancient and modern thought remains philosophically compelling. Indeed, his thought is attractive precisely because he celebrates the individual freedom characteristic of modernity while articulating limits that echo the limits/concerns of the ancients. It is this balance that enables Montaigne to avoid many of the problems that characterize liberalism as it was later to develop.

I. Montaigne's Main Argument for Toleration

The main source of intolerance, according to Montaigne, lies not in the economic system or the political regime but in an unruliness of or imbalance in the human mind. With the very act of thinking itself comes the seeds of discontent, as people's minds and imaginations conceive how their lot in life or the world as a whole could be better. Reflection on the unavoidable questions of where human beings have come from and where they are going also makes people anxious and afraid. To pursue their positive desires and to allay their fears, humans come up with ideas and doctrines—and worldly institutions to support them. However, Montaigne fears that such ideas and institutions often cause more harm than good. For intolerance and physical cruelty, he argues, most commonly result from the zealous application of such ideas and from the ambitious who cynically manipulate them. Although Montaigne argued this primarily with respect to the wars of religion between Catholics and Protestants that were plaguing the times through which he lived, a similar argument might be made about the ideologically driven horrors of the twentieth century.

Although he sometimes describes all human beings as inevitably discontented with their condition, he often embodies this discontent in ideologues and intellectuals. In trying to remake the world and in attempting to institute new ideas, he thinks, these people either purposely overlook and willingly rationalize the suffering that they cause, or they are so blinded by their one idea that they tend to muck everything else up. As opposed to both those who accept the traditions and opinions of the place in which they live and those who transcend these myths and truly achieve wisdom, Montaigne considers most of the tumults and man-made troubles in the world to result from the innovations and unruly minds of half-baked intellectuals and fanatics. They have rejected or lost their original innocence and contentment without having achieved the wisdom necessary for a sophisticated person to be happy. It is "the middle region" that "harbors the tempests; the two extremes, philosophers and rustics, concur in tranquility and happiness" (III.10, 997-98 [780]); "The half-breeds who have disdained the first seat, ignorance of letters, and have not been able to reach the other [wisdom]—their rear between two saddles, like me and so many others—are dangerous, inept, and importunate: these men trouble the world" (I.54, 300 [227]). What is charming about Montaigne's self-presentation is that he often, as he does here, lists himself among the troublemakers. Montaigne does not, in the end, consider himself to be a troublemaker, but he is aware of the seeds of the problem in himself. Indeed, insofar as the problem is coeval with the faculties of reason and imagination themselves, the seeds of the problem are in every human being. Montaigne's acknowledgment of his own vices encourages readers to acknowledge theirs. This open mode of self-description breaks down the barrier between author and reader.[2] It allows Montaigne to speak directly to these troublemakers—and to the troublemaking tendencies in every human being.

Montaigne's political project is to a large degree an attempt to tame and control the unruliness of the human mind in general and of these troublemakers in particular, who have freed their minds from conventions but have not yet found a solid and stable alternative to pursue. Montaigne's *Essays* are an attempt to educate, persuade, dissuade, and tame the troublemaking people who are half-ignorant and half-wise. His irony, wit, and nose for hypocrisy are tools he employs to humble the proud, fell the hubristic, and swat the overreaching innovators. Sometimes he pleads, sometimes he tries to persuade, sometimes he angrily exposes. Should his words fail, which he fears is certain, he suggests institutional constraints. They must be tamed. This is not to say that intellectuals are the sole source of political problems or that there are not times when they need to speak out; Montaigne himself was an intellectual, and he—almost alone in his century—condemned the cruelty of the religious wars, the Spanish Inquisition, and the horrible treatment of the natives of the New World. Insofar as the seeds of the problem of the unruliness of the mind are sown in the human condition itself, one might see but a scant possibility for permanent change. But there is some reason for optimism; whereas tyrants like Hitler and Stalin are not amenable to moral arguments of any kind, intellectuals, although they have helped pave the way for the rise of intolerant movements, are (sometimes) open to moral suasion and to new ideas.

Montaigne's solution to the problem of the unruliness of the human mind is to make people more content with the human condition as it is. Montaigne's main approach to taming the unruly is a powerful two pronged, carrot-and-stick, argument. The stick is his skepticism, which allows him to attack and swat down all sorts of claims as unreal imaginings. Part of his skepticism is based on his claims about the limits of human abilities. He offers systematic critiques of the means by which human beings can attain knowledge, reason and the sense organs, in order to show that they cannot consciously provide knowledge of transcendent essences, those things that are always and everywhere true. Human beings might hold some opinions that are in fact true, but they lack the means definitively to distinguish these true opinions from false ones. To live a life based on unverifiable ideas, such as those that often serve as the basis for customs, religions, and philosophies, might to some extent be unavoidable if one is to act in the world. But to persecute others in the name of them strikes Montaigne as absurd and imprudent. It is absurd because one does not really know if one is right; it is imprudent because if one cannot be sure, it is better to act moderately and because the zealous pursuit or application of any metaphysical idea often involves sacrificing more tangible, real goods in the here and now. But Montaigne's skepticism does not rely on logical and analytical arguments alone. Rather, Montaigne is a master psychologist, and he parades himself before the reader to illustrate the unhealthy but all-too-human tendencies of the mind to run away with itself. By calling attention to and demonstrating this process before the reader's mind's eye, he makes the reader feel how his or her own mind tends to do the same thing. Montaigne hopes to bring about a self-awareness that can combat the mind's immodest zeal. For example, Montaigne explains that he began to write his book in order to control his own mind, which:

> like a runaway horse . . . gives itself a hundred times more trouble than it took for others, and gives birth to so many chimeras and fantastic monsters, one after another, without order or purpose, that in order to contemplate their ineptitude and strangeness at my pleasure, I have begun to put them in writing, hoping in time to make my mind ashamed of itself. (I.8, 34 [21])

As much as anything else, Montaigne's skepticism is based on introspection. He aims to focus the self on itself in order to combat itself.

It is precisely here that one sees the limits to Montaigne's skepticism—for to critique oneself, one must have some knowledge of oneself. If Montaigne doubts that human beings can know any transcendent truth about the eternal essence of things, he does think that human beings have access to a certain kind of self-knowledge. He argues that human beings can have knowledge only of themselves, of how the phenomena of the body and mind operate in themselves. This "knowledge" is experiential and only of subjective phenomena as felt by a particular person at a particular moment in time. Since this experiential or phenomenological knowledge of the self and how it experiences the world is all that a human being can know, according to Montaigne, anyone who lives on another basis is much less grounded in a verifiable understanding of reality.

Montaigne's conception of experiential or phenomenological knowledge allows him to avoid two opposite epistemological claims that underlie the main threats to liberalism in the twentieth century—that human beings can possess the essence of moral truth and that they cannot know anything at all. Indeed, it is in part due to such claims that the traditional grounds for toleration have become unhinged. The dogmatic self-certainty of the former view buttressed the political experiments of communism and fascism, which were undertaken to realize visions of a "new politics" and a "new man." Given the horrors that ensued, skepticism emerges as an attractive alternative, except that skepticism is prone to its own excesses. The nihilistic doubting of Nietzsche and his postmodern followers, which claims that there is no moral truth or criteria by which to judge human lives, has undermined the ground not only of the principles that support liberalism but also of the possibility of any principled action or belief. Because he articulates limits to his skepticism, Montaigne avoids slipping into nihilism; but because these limits are not based on claims of transcendent truth, he avoids dogmatism.

The knowledge that Montaigne advocates is self-knowledge. A wise individual will be fully aware of his ignorance of all transcendent matters and understand what can be known, while appreciating its merely phenomenological status. It is for this reason that Montaigne approves of the tale told of the Milesian "wench" who tripped the philosopher Thales, who was spending all his time gazing upward in contemplation of the heavens. "She gave him good counsel," says Montaigne, "to look rather to himself [*à soy*] than to the sky" (II.12, 519 [402]).[3] With this quotation, Montaigne echoes Cicero's famous praise of Socrates as the first to bring philosophy down from the heavens. What Montaigne praises in Socrates—that he always brings everything back to the "conditions of his present and past life, which he examined and judged, considering any other learning subordinate to that and superfluous" (II.12, 488-89 [376-77])—becomes his normative recommendation for everyone. Montaigne emphasizes the importance of knowing one's limits. Referring to Socrates, Montaigne writes: "The wisest man that ever was, when they asked him what he knew, answered that he knew this much, that he knew nothing" (II.12, 480-81 [370]). He was able to do this because he had some self-knowledge: "Ignorance that knows itself, that judges itself and condemns itself, is not complete ignorance: to be that it must be ignorant of itself [*s'ignore soy-mesme*]" (II.12, 482 [372]). Knowing nothing is a function of self-knowledge, and a knowledge of ignorance strips away many of the causes—metaphysical and religious truth claims—that cause intolerance and persecution.

The carrot that Montaigne offers is his alluring conception of the self. If self-knowledge is the only kind of knowledge that can be had, Montaigne would have everyone turn inwards, to explore and essay themselves; and this call for self-exploration serves as the positive pivot on which his moral and political views are based. Unlike the conceptions of the self that underlie passion-driven modernity, Montaigne's conception is not primarily of a self whose strong desires lead one out into the world in a never-ending search to acquire, whether it be glory, power, or wealth. Nor does he find a single ineluctable will that needs to be willed. He finds the self, paradoxically, to contain everything and nothing. He sees a human being as an integral unity of body and mind, and he encourages individuals to explore both aspects of themselves. But he also finds the self to be a rich assortment of beautiful and horrifying wills, impulses, and desires. Being aware of the multiplicities in oneself creates the basis for a dialogue within oneself. When should one pursue one thing, when another? And what are these impulses that one finds in oneself and from where do they come? On the one hand, analysis reveals depth and never-ending layers. Wills and desires turn out to be derivative from and influenced by all sorts of other wills and desires. And because these things are questionable, unsteady, and often dissolve under the analytical gaze, when we explore ourselves, "test [*essaye*] our common impressions," we find a "natural weakness" (II.12, 521 [403] and II.12, 486 [375]). This weakness is the self's uncertainty about itself. It is based on a kind of ultimate emptiness. And here we see the ultimate attraction and frustration of the human self as Montaigne sees it: for if the self is bottomless, according to Montaigne, one can get immense and never-ending pleasure in the searches of oneself for oneself. It is this activity in itself, Montaigne argues, that is the most enjoyable activity for a human being—and it is also the most real, because people have access to the phenomena of themselves more than they do to abstract questions about universal essences. However, not finding a final, ultimate self is sometimes frustrating—and this explains why people flee themselves. But for Montaigne, this failure to stay in oneself, to stay "home" [*chez soi*], means to privilege one part of oneself and make that one's all. Montaigne is not against this on a temporary basis, for one must act on one's desires and wills in order to explore them, but one must never lose sight of the rest of oneself. To do that is to cheat oneself, to rob oneself of one's possibilities.

This phenomenological conception of the self and its self-interest properly understood leads him to powerful and original arguments for one of liberalism's key tenets—toleration—and for one of its key political ideas—the separation of the public sphere from the private sphere. For if the human good is the self-exploration of the essaying process, exploring the phenomena of oneself in myriad and never-ending ways, then the self-knowing self is happy and content "at home." Unlike conceptions of the self which envision the good as the satisfaction of material desires or willing one's will, in Montaigne's conception, the self has no interest in violating others. Moreover, since what the self finds in itself is a kind of ultimate emptiness, the self has nothing to force. And finally, Montaigne argues that self-aware people feel others' pain. When individuals become aware of the weaknesses in themselves, Montaigne argues, this forms an identification, a mutual identification through empathy, with other equally vulnerable selves. This creates an affirmative desire for every self to be able to explore itself and form itself free from external violation. Whereas the traditional argument for a private sphere free from government interference is based on the claim that people have "rights"—and thus has to justify the ground of these rights—Montaigne reaches the same endpoint not by appealing to rights but only to the self-interest, properly understood, of an individual. Toleration for Montaigne is grounded not on self-denial, as Nietzsche says, but on self-knowledge. Tolerating others and self-interest are united. Indeed, Montaigne's conception of self-interest is not only compatible with toleration, it demands it.

II. Montaigne's Argument for Toleration versus the Main Contemporary Views

Toleration is one of the most attractive and widespread ideals of our day. It is a cornerstone of liberalism, a key protection for both individual citizens and minority groups, and the predominant ethos of all moral civilizations in the modern world. But what is the justification for toleration? Is toleration a moral imperative based on natural or divine rights? Is it a pragmatic way of dealing with pluralistic conflict? Or does it somehow just seem obvious? Since toleration has not been the standard moral policy throughout the world during most of recorded history, nor indeed even throughout most of the world today, some more compelling justification must be offered for it. Justifying toleration is an important philosophical and political issue, because if we cannot explain why it is necessary and good, the institutions that uphold it cannot help being weakened. The problem is that while toleration has never been more widely applied than in the Western world today, the grounds upon which it is defended are becoming difficult to justify philosophically.

Montaigne's arguments for toleration are based on his skepticism and the conception of the self that survives his skeptical doubting. The success of his project depends on attracting readers to his self-portrayal and persuading them to choose to emulate him. Insofar as Montaigne's offering does not move readers, and is unlikely to do so, his project is doomed to fail. Indeed, it can be argued that the simpler conceptions of the human good based on satisfying one's (especially materialistic) desires, described by Hobbes, Locke, and Montesquieu, for example, were inevitably going to triumph over Montaigne's more complicated and less accessible conception. However, insofar as Montaigne has influenced many of the most important thinkers of modernity (as will be described in the next section), one can argue that his ideas, although unlikely to succeed on a mass scale, are nonetheless powerful and appealing to more intellectual readers. For example, Pascal testifies eloquently about Montaigne's success in provoking introspection when he writes that "it is not in Montaigne, but in me, that I find all that I see there."[4] And this testimony is legion. As Nannerl Keohane has argued, "More than any other writer, Montaigne succeeded in making such a self-centered life attractive."[5] Even if Montaigne's conception of the self never has mass appeal, it continues to appeal to intellectuals—who are, as we have seen, Montaigne's target audience to begin with. Indeed, liberal skeptics today often desire toleration and the creation of a private sphere but cannot justify it theoretically. Montaigne's thought helps with this process while at the same time avoiding the danger of nihilism. For this group especially, Montaigne's conception has the supreme benefit of being an *internal* justification for toleration (appealing only to one's own self-interest), thus avoiding the problems associated with the traditional rights-based conceptions which appeal to rights *external* to the individual.

Montaigne's unification of toleration and self-interest is critical because liberals typically conceive these as in tension, if not contradiction, with each other. Toleration is usually defined as an acceptance of difference. Originally, and still often today, toleration implied an only grudging acceptance of these differences, a *principled* rejection of the thing to be tolerated and an acceptance of it only as a *practical* expedient. Toleration was the second-best policy for those who practiced it; the ideal was having things completely ordered one's own way. One might dislike, distrust, even detest some idea or practice but tolerate it because one cannot eliminate it at an acceptable price.[6] As liberalism developed historically, toleration has been secured through political institutions that guarantee rights. To the extent that others possess them, rights serve as a check, a limit, on one's actions toward those others. The possession of rights entitles one to a certain sphere in which one is not to be denied, repressed, or victimized by others. Thought and action within this protected sphere, no matter how objectionable, cannot legitimately be subjected to political interference and are to be tolerated by both the state and other citizens. However, by describing toleration as an externally enforced limitation on one's will, the individual pursuit of self-interest is in fundamental tension with the principle of toleration; practically speaking, toleration is reduced to an area in which one cannot pursue one's will. Far from being an immediate good for the tolera*tor*, according to this account it is only a good for the tolera*ted*. Although everyone wants to be tolerated by others, this gap between self-interest and morality constantly threatens to destabilize liberalism, for people often prefer their self-interest to someone else's good.

The difficulty caused by the gap between self-interest and morality results from the fact that the political philosophy of liberalism functions according to what Isaiah Berlin defines as negative liberty.[7] In describing some liberty as "negative," Berlin is not making a value judgment. Rather, he is stating that freedom and happiness are achieved by the absence (hence the negative) of external constraints. As Hobbes, Locke, and most liberals argue, freedom and happiness are understood as the pursuit of self-interest, although prudence demands that some self-interest be sacrificed for the sake of securing the rest of it. According to this view, toleration emerges not as an internal ingredient of one's own self-interest but as a limit on it. By contrast, thinkers who subscribe to views that Berlin calls positive liberty argue that one is only truly free and happy if one meets—that is to say, conforms to—some clearly articulated standard (e.g., following God's will, the general will, reason, or the categorical imperative). Under positive liberty, there is a necessary interconnection between self-interest and morality.

However, the demands of many of the most famous doctrines of "positive" liberty are not compatible with toleration or liberalism. For example, pursuit of the general will, it is sometimes argued, might require forcing people against their stated wishes even if they are not harming anyone else.[8] In Rousseau's phrase, this means that individuals might have to be "forced to be free,"[9] which is both a contradiction and a chilling violation of an individual's autonomy from the point of view of negative liberty. Frightened of the possible abuse of positive liberty, Berlin—and all liberals—prefers negative liberty, but in doing so they theoretically cement the conflict between the self and others, leading to the numerous criticisms of liberalism as overly individualistic. Toleration under this guise might be acceptable as a long-term strategy, to reap the gains of being tolerated, but since self-interest holds sway, if one could break the law with impunity, it would be a tempting thing to do.

Montaigne fits into Berlin's conceptions of liberty in a unique way: he advances negative conditions as the positive criteria to which one must conform. Montaigne argues that toleration follows from self-interest properly understood, which is based on what he deems proper to a healthy self; to this extent he thus conceives of liberty as positive. However, since he also focuses on the interest of individual selves and argues that key parts of a healthy self are radically subjective, the "positive" criterion to be met is not universal, as it is in most conceptions of positive liberty, but is in some sense relative to each individual. Montaigne's limiting conditions on this sphere of subjectivity, however, do not require affirmative knowledge about metaphysical or transcendent truth of any kind. Rather, they are based on knowing human limits. The key to Montaigne's concept of toleration and to his humane political vision is for human beings to know what they cannot know. Montaigne's moral and political wisdom is based on negatives, that is to say human inabilities, human lacks. Toleration, he argues, can be secured by—and only reliably by—knowing humanity's limits, humanity's ignorance. Montaigne shares the fears of today's ultra-sober pluralists that any positive conception can lead to zealous crusading and cruelty. But Montaigne also knows that without any grounding at all, morality will wither away. He gambles that the acceptance of human ignorance is hardly a banner under which one can fight a crusade. In this way, Montaigne avoids what Berlin and the other realists fear but still provides a grounding for his conception of toleration.

To appreciate fully the kinds of problems that Montaigne's arguments for toleration avoid, it is helpful to compare his views to the five kinds of grounds on which toleration is most commonly defended today: toleration is grounded in metaphysical rights (natural and divine); it is grounded on rights set up by a prudential calculation; it is grounded in political rights that by now have become customary; it is grounded in the postmodern belief that self-fashioning is a good; or it is grounded in a gut sense that people are by nature tolerant. However, each of these five kinds of justification is problematic, and Montaigne sidesteps some of the main problems with each.

Montaigne does not appeal to metaphysics, thus avoiding the problem of justifying the metaphysical basis of rights which is difficult, if not impossible, to prove. For example, while America's Declaration of Independence asserts that it is "self-evident" that human beings naturally possess rights, and grounds this claim in appeals to nature and nature's God, this claim is no longer "self-evident." The scientific and historicist revolutions of the past 150 years, signified by the names Darwin, Einstein, Hegel, Marx, Nietzsche, and Freud, have thoroughly rendered the original liberal conception of rights problematic. Many theorists consider both God and nature to be historical constructions. Others consider appeals to God to be too divisive and controversial. In a pluralistic society, whose God justifies rights? How is God known? And by whom? Similarly, the Enlightenment idea that scientific progress would reveal a natural basis for morality now seems quaint and hopelessly naive. The progress of the natural sciences has led them to muteness on the question of human rights, not to definitive answers. Science is silent on moral issues. A convincing case for toleration must either refute historicism and science or avoid metaphysical justification. By proceeding on a skeptical basis, Montaigne does the latter, avoiding the quagmires of the former.

Similarly, Montaigne's broad conception of the self allows him to avoid a key problem with the prudential argument for toleration. The prudential argument for toleration is simple: prudence dictates that one restrict one's pursuit of self-interest to secure the rest of it. Without appealing to natural or divine rights, it argues that one should relinquish one's right to victimize others because not to do so would risk being subject to victimization oneself. A restatement of the golden rule on prudential (not moral) grounds, it is most famously captured by Hobbes' attempt to overcome the fear and horrors of the state of nature. To secure stability, peace, and the goods that come with them, individuals, with no metaphysical pretenses, do, have, or would institute government and set up recognized punishments to keep citizens law-abiding.[10] The conventionally created law thus determines individuals' "rights" and the extent to which toleration of others' views, property, and honors must be respected. The contractarians who make this prudential argument tend, however, to have a narrow definition of self-interest which is not happily compatible with toleration—or with the contractual argument itself. If self-interest is one's only guide, and self-interest is, as they argue, understood as acquisition (of either power, glory, or property), the optimal position for a person might be for everyone else to follow the law while violating it with impunity oneself. Why shouldn't one steal or kill if one could get away with it? There is no reason not to—except fear of external authority. Most people, according to Glaucon's challenge in Plato's *Republic,* might judge that it is better to give up the greatest good (unlimited pursuit of self-interest) in order to avoid the greatest evil (suffering at the hands of others), but this prudential (not moral) calculation might not persuade everyone, as indeed it does not persuade Glaucon.[11] Why should the strong or powerful, who might not be overwhelmed by Hobbes' fear of violent death, tolerate others instead of repressing or inflicting cruelty on them? Why should they care about others at all? The prudential argument alone not only cannot answer these questions, but an argument based on this conception of self-interest also plays into the hands of people like Nietzsche and his followers who argue for the pursuit of one's interest unlimited by concern for others. Disparities in power—real or perceived—whether based on natural or social factors, mitigate the effect of the prudential argument. With his broader and, I think, more appealing appreciation of the subtleties of the self, Montaigne endeavors to show that true self-interest and toleration are consistent.

Moreover, even though Montaigne takes an earthly view of politics—as do the contractarians—he understands that the prudential argument for toleration might not only fail to persuade the strong, those who are in a position to be intolerant, but it might actually increase everyone's propensity toward harming others by emphasizing the pursuit of earthly goods. To the extent that liberalism tries to inculcate toleration by undermining people's religious convictions, it opens new avenues for victimizing others. The taming and debunking of religion is desirable to prevent such religious persecution as the horrible wars of religion that wracked France in the sixteenth century and out of which both Montaigne's thought and the liberal tradition of toleration originally grew. But by directing people's attention to the pursuit of earthly goods, the prudential argument lifts the self-restraints that religion teaches. After all, the Ten Commandments not only privilege a particular God, but they categorically condemn murder and covetousness. Montaigne understands that instability is likely to occur when existing customs are stripped bare, and he takes this into account when making his political recommendations. But more importantly, his conception of the self guides thoughtful individuals toward a tolerant life even in the absence of external restraints.

As much as any thinker who ever wrote, Montaigne recognizes the power of belief, habit, and custom and is sensitive to the fact that they need to be politically upheld lest anarchy and violence erupt, but other than this one—admittedly large—*prudential* concession, he does not appeal to tradition, habit, or custom to justify his *theoretical* recommendations. Like Montaigne, contemporary America's two leading political theorists, John Rawls and Richard Rorty, reject metaphysical justifications for toleration; but, unlike Montaigne, their proposed theoretical positions rely primarily on what they call "political" justifications.[12] Rather than justify their views on first principles, they choose to appeal to "our" contemporary political intuitions and preferences. By "our" intuitions, Rorty and Rawls refer to the beliefs of Western, democratic capitalists at the end of the twentieth century. Far from attempting to justify liberalism to outsiders or on first principles, Rorty and Rawls do not take up the challenge. Instead, they strive only to harmonize our preexisting opinions and do not address the fundamental challenges that Nietzsche, for example, poses.[13] They rely instead on political traditions, and they thus rely excessively on tradition and convention when articulating their normative visions. Their work is compelling to the extent that one accepts their premises. They supply *political* arguments that might work in a polity where everyone shares their views (if a place without debate could be called a polity at all). However, their views are not compelling *philosophically* insofar as they do not even try to justify the presuppositions or intuitions of "our" age. Even if all citizens of twenty-first-century liberal democracies agree with Rawls and Rorty, cultural consensus does not make a view true. No one knew this more than Montaigne, who repeatedly acknowledges the power of custom. But even as he upholds existing customs to insure political stability, he debunks rather than validates their authority on philosophical and moral grounds. Some deeper argument, such as he offers with his conception of the self, is necessary.

Like today's postmodern thinkers, Montaigne rejects metaphysical truth as the basis for a good political order and promotes self-fashioning as the most important human activity, but he does this in a way that avoids problems that characteristically plague postmodern arguments for toleration. Postmodern thinkers who reject the existence of "objective truth" criticize the idea of "rights" as totalitarian, because to be forced to follow any "truth" is considered too restrictive, too confining, and a mere mask for political, religious, economic, or cultural domination. Nietzsche, Foucault, and other postmoderns argue against the "totalized," "dominating" visions of the past in order to liberate totally the subjectivity of the self, be it expressed by "will," "instinct," or "the body."[14] Several liberal political theorists have attempted to build on this understanding of the self by arguing that if everyone were to privilege self-realization, as the postmoderns propose, we could live fruitful, flourishing, and diverse lives side by side with no one condemning or squelching anyone else's individuality. In other words, they attempt to justify liberalism and toleration based on the postmodern view of self-fashioning.[15] Montaigne craves self-fashioning, but unlike the postmoderns, he delineates limits based on his conception of what the self can and cannot know, for total subjectivity alone cannot justify toleration either. If nothing is true, why shouldn't one follow one's subjective drives regardless of whether or not they hurt other people? As Dostoyevsky is often credited for stating in *The Brothers Karamazov*: "If nothing is true, everything is permitted."[16] The oft articulated liberal response to this problem is insufficient. All values and all ways of life, it is argued, should be tolerated, because if none is "right," neither is any wrong. No view, it is said, is more true, more just, or better than any other, so all should be accepted. According to this argument, total moral skepticism leads to toleration. Indeed, moral skepticism is characteristic of most post-World War II attempts to justify toleration. This argument, however, cannot in principle exclude the toleration of intolerance. The views of a passionately committed intolerant person would be just as valid as the views of a tolerant person. Moral skepticism thus does not necessarily lead to toleration. Moral skeptics must be able to give a *non-transcendent* reason why one should not follow one's will wherever it may take one. Montaigne's conception of the self does just that.

There have been other attempts to justify toleration based on assertions of a natural attachment to community, virtue, or caring. These movements argue for tolerance and morality by making assumptions about human behavior, past and present, that are totally devoid of historical reality and knowledge of the history of philosophy. Their proponents are skeptical of universal truth but nonetheless seem to think that everyone basically thinks like them. What Amy Gutmann has said of communitarianism (the communitarian critics want us to live in Salem, but not to believe in witches) is even truer for contemporary "care" and "virtue" theory.[17] They attempt to draw general conclusions about virtue or caring without fully exploring the ramifications of their views. It is almost as if these theoreticians had never confronted Nietzsche or believe that sincerely motivated people could never have taken the Spanish Inquisition or Nazism seriously. By contrast, Montaigne avoids simplistic assumptions about human nature. He knows that there are many people who do not possess tolerant impulses. Indeed, he not only repeatedly refers to the bloody civil war through which he lived and to the Inquisition and the horrible slaughter of the New World that were occurring at the same time, but he feels the need to grapple with and explain these worst aspects of human nature. He thus avoids the naive and historically uninformed errors that characterize these recent movements in moral and political thought. While the connection between skepticism and toleration is à la mode, Montaigne knew that this connection depends not on shallow hope about human nature but on carefully and realistically considered assessments of human nature, which these movements do not supply.

In short, a convincing defense of toleration must avoid the problems associated with arguments based on both metaphysical "truth" and its opposite, complete subjectivity. It also cannot unduly appeal to the conventions, habits, or opinions of a particular place and time. And it would need to state limits that can show an individual why it would not be in his or her self-interest to violate others, even if he or she could get away with it. Montaigne offers just such a defense of toleration.

III. Montaigne's Place in the History of Political Thought

The second aim of this book is to demonstrate Montaigne's important but underappreciated influence on modern thought as a whole and his role in the origins of liberalism in particular. Consistent with my claims on Montaigne's behalf, he has been influential and admired in every age since his book was first published four hundred years ago—except for most of the twentieth century. Prominent contemporaries praised him as another Plutarch, another Seneca, and another Thales.[18] In the next generation, Montaigne influenced both Bacon and Descartes, the great early moderns who built their philosophical systems in part to overcome the skeptical crisis that Montaigne both crystallized and provoked.[19] Indeed, one scholar says that Montaigne endeavored "before the great Bacon, to reform human understanding" and that together with Bacon and Descartes, he is "the restorer or the founder of philosophy in Europe."[20] Shakespeare's borrowings from Montaigne are well documented, including some of his memorable psychological musings and the idea that all the world's a stage.[21] Montaigne's influence on Pascal has been well chronicled, and although Pascal ultimately strongly rejects Montaigne as an atheist, many scholars have noted how in the course of wrestling with Montaigne's skepticism, he became more and more like him.[22] Montaigne's influence on Locke and Rousseau has also been traced, and Rousseau especially borrowed Montaigne's critique of culture, his idea that modern people vainly live for appearances, and his idealization of "natural man."[23] Voltaire refers to Montesquieu as "Montaigne as legislator," meaning that the two *bordelais* shared the same sensibility excepting only Montesquieu's addition of political institutions to secure the vision which they shared.[24] Voltaire himself both praises and has been compared to Montaigne,[25] and Hume's skepticism was certainly informed by many of Montaigne's ideas.[26] Nineteenth-century philosophers as disparate as Nietzsche[27] and Emerson[28] laud Montaigne, and in an age of "Top Ten" lists, Montaigne has made several notable short lists of his own: he is on Montesquieu's list of the "four great poets," Emerson's list of the six representative lives, and Nietzsche's list of the eight people from whom he thinks he can learn and to whom he must answer.[29] Thus, until the end of the nineteenth century Montaigne was very much a part of philosophical and political discourse. Seemingly forgotten during much of the twentieth century, Montaigne has recently reemerged in France, becoming a darling of the deconstructionists and called postmodern by one of postmodernity's leading lights.[30]

With this history of praise by and influence on so many important philosophers, it is surprising that Montaigne should have dropped out of the philosophical and political discourses during much of the twentieth century. Indeed, he has been nearly omitted from the standard histories of philosophy and political philosophy in the English speaking world,[31] and the first, and until now only, comprehensive book in English on Montaigne's political thought was published only in 1990.[32] The neglect of Montaigne in the field of political science is a reflection of a larger neglect. Since the creation and separation of the social and human science disciplines at the end of the nineteenth century, Montaigne has been largely relegated to the field of literature, barely being considered a philosopher at all, let alone a political philosopher. This artificial and lamentable division of the disciplines cast Montaigne out of the limelight of the history of political and philosophical ideas[33] and almost exclusively into departments of romance languages and literature, where his style of writing is still much discussed. To the extent that he is taught in American universities today, it is usually only in these departments (and in occasional surveys of Western civilization where his two essays containing his radical views on the recently discovered peoples of the New World might be assigned). Montaigne is rarely taught in departments of philosophy or political science. Montaigne's absence from political philosophy is a twentieth-century phenomenon, the result of the overly rigid demarcation of the academic disciplines, and is inconsistent with his historical renown.

In the past twenty years, however, Montaigne has begun to get his historical due from political theorists. A wave of interest in Montaigne has washed into political theory, figuring in books by such leading political theorists as Judith Shklar, Charles Taylor, Quentin Skinner, Richard Tuck, Richard Flathman, and John Christian Laursen.[34] Although none has written on Montaigne exclusively, these theorists have recognized Montaigne's central place in the history of toleration. Before this wave of scholarship, Montaigne's arguments for toleration had been noted in only two areas of scholarship: by a handful of Montaigne scholars and by historians chronicling the history of toleration, albeit inadequately by both. A few Montaigne scholars have recognized the role of toleration in Montaigne's thought, but they have treated it only in passing.[35] Similarly, until recently most scholars of the history of toleration focused on the religious origins of toleration, and thus even the most comprehensive of these studies have had difficulty fitting Montaigne into their categories. Joseph Lecler, in his monumental two-volume study *Toleration and the Reformation,* frankly admits this difficulty. He says that Montaigne's ideas on toleration "do not strictly belong to any particular school; his own personality and mind left too strong a mark on them."[36] He rightly concludes that Montaigne's thoughts on this subject "demand a study by themselves," but no one has as yet produced this study.[37] Similarly, Henry Kamen's short but useful *The Rise of Toleration* notes Montaigne's influence on the Enlightenment conception of toleration, but he mentions Montaigne only in passing, because his is a view "in which toleration was supported not because it was essential to religion but because religion itself was unessential. Such a toleration, based ultimately on unbelief," Kamen acknowledges, "we are not immediately concerned with."[38] It was not until scholars began to focus on the secular arguments for toleration—as political theorists trained since World War II have been doing largely for the first time—that Montaigne began to get his due.

The main research into the secular arguments for toleration has been done by what might be called the "Cambridge" school of historical scholarship lead by Quentin Skinner and Richard Tuck. Indeed, one of the best works on the secular arguments for toleration begins with Richard Tuck's famous essay "Skepticism and Toleration in the Seventeenth Century," thus omitting Montaigne's century altogether.[39] Tuck, however, dwells on the sixteenth-century origins of the tradition of toleration that interests him, focusing on two thinkers, whom he apparently places at the tradition's beginning: Montaigne and Justus Lipsius. Tuck perhaps unfairly emphasizes Lipsius, but on Lipsius' relation to Montaigne he writes that "When Lipsius read Montaigne's *Essayes*, he wrote to their author that he was the one man in Europe who shared his own ideas, while he described him elsewhere as 'the French Thales'—implying that Montaigne was the first of a new kind of thinker."[40] Nonetheless, Tuck underemphasizes Montaigne's historical importance relative to Lipsius, I believe, because Montaigne does not completely fit into the neo-stoical story that Tuck wants to tell. In his neo-stoical interpretation of Montaigne, Tuck follows Quentin Skinner, excepting only that unlike Tuck, Skinner considers Montaigne to be even more tolerant than Lipsius: "he was certainly far more tolerant—by comparison not merely with Lipsius, but with the most learned political writers of his age."[41] But Montaigne is more complex than Skinner and Tuck allow.[42] By emphasizing what Montaigne has in common with others of his time period, they lose something of his unique character, especially concerning his radically new conception of the subjective self, and thus miss out on what I think is the key aspect of his argument for toleration. Thus, while Montaigne's importance in the history of toleration in the West has been acknowledged by both the religious and secular accounts of toleration's history, his just due has not yet been given.

More than anyone else, however, Judith Shklar in *Ordinary Vices* and "The Liberalism of Fear" has brought Montaigne into the mainstream of current philosophical discourse. Like Skinner and Tuck, Shklar emphasizes Montaigne's tolerance: "Montaigne was surely tolerant and humanitarian," but because he does not describe political institutions, she also rightly notes that "he was no liberal." Nonetheless, Shklar considers Montaigne to be "the most notable" of a group of thinkers who first articulated the mental attitude of liberalism, its psychology, which she considers "to go very far indeed toward liberalism." Indeed, she goes further: "It is, I think, the *core* of its historical development" so that "liberalism's *deepest grounding* is in place from the first" (emphasis added).[43] Shklar shares Montaigne's skepticism and admires his non- or antimetaphysical stance, which allows a vision of tolerant politics to take shape on nonmetaphysical grounds. To serve as her foundation, she elaborates on Montaigne's condemnation of cruelty to articulate a minimal liberalism in which the main aim is not to promote virtue, community, or do anything but protect personal freedom, which, she argues, is jeopardized above all by terror and cruelty. Her self-styled Montaignian, hardheaded, no-nonsense approach to politics has influenced many political theorists, especially Richard Rorty, who has adopted what Shklar considers to be the Montaignian core of being a liberal (one who sees politics as the prevention of cruelty).[44]

This book agrees with Shklar's assessment that in Montaigne one finds "liberalism's deepest grounding"; however, it argues that Shklar's characterization of this grounding is too narrow. The negative argument for toleration (to prevent cruelty), which Shklar rightly finds in Montaigne, depends on the object upon which the cruelty is being inflicted. If one violently "tortured" a rock, slowly hacking it over and over again with a pickax until it was completely shattered, there would be no moral problem. Montaigne is horrified by cruelty and torture to human beings—because of his conception of the self.[45] It is this conception of the self—which Shklar does not emphasize and that Rorty wants to eliminate from philosophical speculation altogether[46]—that underlies and makes possible the negative argument for toleration that they emphasize. Thus, for all the good that Shklar has done in boosting Montaigne's place in (and adding sobriety to) current philosophical discourse, she neglects the substantive strand that I believe underlies everything in Montaigne's thought, but which she, given her oft stated aversion to theories of virtue or notions of self-perfection, probably considers unnecessary or potentially dangerous.[47] The way that Montaigne's conception of the self leads to a positive argument for toleration, that relies neither on metaphysical conceptions of rights nor merely on custom, habit, or convention, is the linchpin of this book.

Finally, if Judith Shklar has done more than anyone else to bring Montaigne into the mainstream of contemporary political theory, David Schaefer has done more than anyone else in exploring Montaigne's political thought systematically. In his 1990 book *The Political Philosophy of Montaigne*, Schaefer shows the consistent and systematic nature of Montaigne's thought and rightly highlights its anti-Christian implications. However, Schaefer goes too far in interpreting Montaigne as a "bourgeois individualist" and in asserting that "Montaigne is, in short, one of the earliest philosophic advocates of the modern liberal regime."[48] Montaigne neither advocates core political institutions of liberalism, such as a separation of powers and democratic representation, nor is his normative ethos about commerce and consumption. Schaefer astutely notes Montaigne's elevation of the body—and Montaigne's emphasis on the body and on the individual self may well have devolved into bourgeois materialism—but in stressing Montaigne's attachment to the body alone, Schaefer captures only one half of Montaigne's account of human life, which Montaigne encapsulates as "the general human law—intellectually sensual, sensually intellectual" (III.13, 1087 [850]). Schaefer loses sight of the intellectual aspects of Montaigne's vision, going so far as to say that Montaigne does not favor exploration of oneself, but rather that he advocates that people "plunge oneself anew into the 'diversions' of life."[49] Schaefer ascribes Montaigne's emphasis on the body to "a kind of philosophic propaganda directed at the multitude," and he calls Montaigne a philosopher, so he does not think that Montaigne recommends this course for reflective individuals.[50] However, Schaefer not only does not emphasize Montaigne's philosophical calls for self-exploration and self-essaying, but he emphasizes the opposite, writing: "since the soul needs to be occupied with the pursuit of some object *outside itself*, the closest we can come to tranquility is to immerse ourselves in the pursuit of harmless *sensual* pleasures."[51] Schaefer is right that Montaigne says the soul needs an object on which to focus, but is not the main point of the *Essays* that the most proper object upon which the soul should fix is itself? Montaigne does not seek *divertissement* but self-knowledge. Schaefer makes Montaigne more modern than he is, blaming Montaigne for *consciously* ushering in many of the excesses of modernity. Like Schaefer, I argue that Montaigne helped usher in modernity, but, unlike Schaefer, I think Montaigne recognizes natural limits to desires, limits based on Montaigne's understanding of what human beings can and cannot know about themselves.[52]

It is exactly these human limits, consistent with Classical and Hellenistic Academic skepticism but with Montaigne's own unique twist, that my book aims to articulate. Knowing these limits is of critical importance for two reasons. First, it differentiates Montaigne's worldview from the passion-driven modernity that is associated with Machiavelli, Hobbes, and bourgeois individualism. Rather than embodying the excesses of modernity, Montaigne represents a unique and appealing historical position: half ancient, half modern. Because he conceives of natural limits to which a healthy self must conform, he has one foot planted firmly in the ancients' camp. But because his moral vision is also based on the phenomenological knowledge of a subjective self, he has one foot planted firmly in modernity. Second, this combination of modern subjectivity limited by an ancient conception of nature is exactly what is so worth recovering about Montaigne, because the kind of self-knowledge that he seeks enables him—and possibly us, too—to reject metaphysics while avoiding nihilism. He stops from plunging full speed into total relativism, because he insists that the realm in which the human good is subjective, though large, is not total. It must be limited by a proper understanding of what human beings can and cannot know and the fundamental need to dialogue with oneself, to essay oneself and one's thoughts. Schaefer and several other scholars have shrewdly recognized the centrality of freedom of conscience and toleration in Montaigne both substantively and architecturally—"Of Freedom of Conscience" is the central essay of the central book of the *Essays*—yet they don't adequately explain why this is or should be the case.[53] They do not adequately link this theme to the *Essays'* other main themes. Supplying that link is my aim.

IV. Montaigne's Times and Our Times

The two goals of this book—demonstrating the power of Montaigne's arguments for toleration and a private sphere and showing his importance in the history of political philosophy—are related. Montaigne was so important in the past for the same reason that he should be important today: because his ideas are powerful and provocative. But after a long period of neglect, how can one explain the renaissance of interest in this renaissance man just now?[54] Montaigne's writing appeals to each reader as a human being, but Montaigne's times, concerns, and themes particularly echo our own.[55] Both the sixteenth and the twentieth centuries have suffered from brutal ideologically driven wars and crises of authority. In Montaigne's time the wars were religious, Catholics versus Protestants over otherworldly concerns; the wars of the twentieth century were driven by political ideology. In both cases there was unprecedented cruelty and mass destruction exploited by cynics and opportunists, but the battles took their particular character due to the all-encompassing, theoretical visions at stake. Religious fervor inflamed civil wars in France, England, Holland, Germany, and Italy where Christian brother fratricidally slew Christian brother and was used to justify the mass slaughter of the inhabitants of the New World. Everyone except the lunatic fringe today acknowledges the barbarity of Hitler, Stalin, Pol-Pot, and the like; Montaigne was almost alone in his century in condemning the horror of Spanish imperial policy. While most of Europe was agitated and in arms, Montaigne was one of the few who spoke of toleration. Montaigne's response to chaos and cruelty is what is needed in our own times, and while we generally agree with his outcome, we are less clear about our intellectual rationale. Montaigne articulates it particularly well.

The similarity between our times and Montaigne's, however, is deeper: both suffer from a crisis of intellectual authority. The intellectual basis of sixteenth-century authority was undermined by numerous factors: political, economic, social, religious, and philosophical. The nascent rise of the nation-state, which was replacing the previous feudal organization, and the formation of trade-based towns and cities with their newly acquired wealth led to shifts of power with all the attendant jockeying and uncertainties. These changes in basic social organization were intensified, even dwarfed, by the ideological breakdown which they both engendered and were further inflamed by. For example, the recovery by Europe of the ancient world through the reentry of Greek and Roman pagan texts (due to the influx of scholars caused by the fall of Constantinople and to increased trade with the Islamic world) and the discovery of the New World exploded numerous intellectual assumptions. Renaissance scholars could not help noticing that both the "ancient" and "new" worlds were inhabited by seemingly healthy people (not to say profoundly wise in the case of Plato and Aristotle) despite (perhaps even because of) their lack of Biblical revelation. This was a problem that shook the very core of Christendom's self-understanding. Furthermore, the uncovering of natural phenomena based on scientific discoveries in the fields of astronomy, physics, and geography shook the foundations of medieval cosmology, according to which everything had its proper place in the cosmos. The challenges to one aspect of Christian cosmology, such as were posed by Copernicus' and Kepler's questioning of the earth being the center of the universe or by Giordano Bruno's inferring the improbability of the Biblical account of Noah's ark because of the numerous peoples living on disparate continents, called into question the entire cosmological edifice. Not only was Christian culture called into question, but so was its very understanding of the place of human beings in the cosmos—and the very nature of the cosmos itself. These cosmological shifts played their role in fomenting internal and external attacks on a corrupt Church, which together with the Reform movements, fostered a dramatic era of religious and political controversies. These ideas, discoveries, and actions provoked reason and tradition to be doubted in world-shattering ways, creating widespread change and intellectual uncertainty.[56]

The twentieth century's political and moral ideals have been undermined by different variations of some of the same reasons. The success of materialistic science has led to the separation between scientific and moral truth and to the idea that moral truth cannot be rationally justified. Science teaches that everything is matter and motion. It has no room for a divine soul, cannot state a fundamental difference between human beings and the other animals, and cannot give an explanation of morality at all. Science is value-free, leaving us to our own moral (de)vices. Indeed, it teaches that human beings evolved from the animals, after originally crawling out of the primordial muck. It teaches that we are not in the center of the universe but merely inhabiting a speck of dust after a big bang. Not only does science not offer moral guidance, but it undermines the status of any truth outside of human will, resulting in a kind of easygoing moral relativism. The moral relativism resulting from the physical sciences has been reinforced by the dominance of historicism in the human and social sciences. The "softer" sciences teach that all moral truths are mere values, relative to a particular age, culture, and place. Anyone claiming to possess a universal moral truth would be mocked in and laughed out of the academy. The world wars shattered illusions about progress and the evolution of man's moral nature. Whereas the Enlightenment had replaced religious truths with a belief in progress, the horrors of the twentieth century have marked it as among the most homicidal in history. Even technology, which was to bring the fruits of science to the relief of man's estate, and which has marked an important advance in fighting famine and disease, has given us the drudgeries of the assembly line, mass culture, pollution, and the atom bomb, so that modern-day Luddites abound. In short, far from meeting humanity's moral needs, science and technology have merely made the questions more pressing. Having undermined the basis for believing in natural and divine rights, they have no moral or political guidance to offer. Thus, twentieth-century individuals, just as those of the sixteenth century, suffered a difficulty in rationally justifying the moral and political beliefs they held dear. Fortunate to have political traditions of rights and separation of powers, liberalism is thriving throughout the West almost in proportion to our inability to explain the ground on which it stands.

Dissatisfaction with this intellectual malaise justifies renewed interest in the origins and grounds of liberalism in general and in Montaigne in particular. Montaigne participated in the unique creation of modernity in the West. Montaigne responded to the crisis of authority by powerfully articulating a vision of the good life based on self-exploration and a way to order social relations based on toleration and the creation of a private sphere. Without discussing the liberal democratic political institutions and constitutional protections that seem so essential to the preservation of a humane society today, Montaigne was instrumental in creating the moral and political world of liberalism.[57] He did so by powerfully articulating key elements of the liberal sensibility that people need to share for the political institutions to work. It is the contention of this book that Montaigne can help us think through these issues anew, to gain insight into the problems with which we struggle and will continue to struggle. Montaigne grapples deeply with timeless questions, and his grappling is particularly timely today.

Nonetheless, one may wonder whether intellectual justification is needed for an age which otherwise seems stable. Many thinkers argue that ideas do not matter at all. Conservatives, such as Oakeshott, who emphasize man's fundamental reliance on tradition, and radicals, such as Marx, who emphasize the dependence of ideas on material conditions, both minimize the importance of coherent, rationally defensible political and moral principles. Richard Rorty doubts whether philosophers should even attempt such justifications. Philosophy, it is argued, has little or nothing to do with the stability and preservation of a political regime, the morality of a society's conduct, or the ordinary life of normal citizens; people act based on habits, traditions, and material concerns, not ideas. On the other hand, philosophers like Carl Schmitt argue that ideas are everything and consequently that a regime is doomed to ruin the moment its principled justification is no longer believed.

I reject the extreme answers to this question; ideas matter but they are not everything. Many people never know, let alone understand, the intellectual basis of the rights that they enjoy without jeopardizing the preservation of those rights. This ignorance may be regrettable, but it is perhaps inevitable. Intellectual justification on the order of which we speak may not be accessible to most people, be it due to lack of interest, talent, time, or resources or to false ideological consciousness. To this extent, I agree with those who downplay the role of ideas in human life and concede that the lack of coherent, believable principles does not in the short term undermine a political regime.[58] But are ideas nothing? The lack of belief in a system surely contributes to its decay. Moral questions are forever debated in politics; and war, especially in liberal democracies, seems to require principled justification. Every society is weakened if it cannot provide justification for its actions and existence.

V. Montaigne's Book and This Book

Michel de Montaigne (1533-1592) lived the kind of life that is not lived anymore. His mother was born Jewish into a family that had several of its members burned at the stake during the Inquisition in Spain.[59] She, however, converted to Catholicism and became a fanatic. Several of Montaigne's siblings converted to Protestantism, a risky act during the religious wars of the sixteenth century, but Montaigne maintained good relations with all of them. He was a member of the Paris and Bordeaux parliaments, mayor of Bordeaux (in the four-hundred-year history of Bordeaux, Montaigne was only the third mayor to be reelected), and a confidant of kings. He advised both the Catholic Henry III and the Protestant Henry of Navarre, who as King Henry IV enacted the famous Edict of Nantes, one of the first acts of religious toleration in Europe. Before he was king, Henry IV stayed at Montaigne's chateau when he was in the area and asked Montaigne to come to Paris with him once he decided that "Paris is worth a mass."[60] Montaigne recurrently served as a negotiator between the Catholic and Huguenot factions, because he was one of the few people in France to have good relations with both sides in the conflict. Montaigne did have enemies, but Catherine de Medici, the power behind the Catholic throne for fifty years, personally intervened to free him when he was once imprisoned in the Bastille. He lived through an outbreak of the plague and had a niece who was canonized, made a Catholic saint. At her canonical hearings Montaigne was given official credit for keeping her in the Catholic fold, yet in 1676 his book was placed on the Church's *Index of Prohibited Books*, where it remained until the *Index* was abolished in 1961.

Just as Montaigne's life is full of change and upheaval, so is his style of writing. One reason Montaigne has been relegated to the academic discipline of literature can be found in his style of writing, which causes difficulty in locating his arguments. As I have already noted, numerous political theorists have claimed that Montaigne was very tolerant, including Skinner's claim that he was the most tolerant man of his age. However, Montaigne rarely uses the word *tolerance*, and he speaks of toleration as a political principle on only a few occasions.[61] Yet, the *Essays* as a whole are saturated in toleration, and his arguments persistently evoke the desirability of a private sphere of free individual judgment, such as his famous call for everyone to preserve for himself a back room, an *arrière boutique*, of independent thought and judgment (I.39, 235 [177]).[62] The intensely tolerant feeling of Montaigne's *Essays* combined with the lack of explicit statements about it is characteristic of Montaigne's style of writing. Instead of writing systematic treatises, the conventional mode of philosophical expression, characterized by sobriety and seriousness (to say clarity would be going too far), Montaigne's writing style is exactly the opposite. It is freewheeling, unsystematic, irreverent, and fun. In short, it is likely that many "serious" scholars have ignored him for precisely the reasons he has been loved by his readers.

Montaigne published only one book, which he wrote after having withdrawn from court life and secluded himself in the tower library of his chateau in the Perigord, just east of Bordeaux. His book, titled *Essais* in French and *Essays* in English, consists of a series of essays written over several years and organized in no apparent order. Montaigne coined the current usage of the word "*essai*" as a noun (from the French verb "*essaier*," to attempt or to try), and his essays are a series of explorations of various issues, in which he tries to refine his judgment by exploring human paradoxes and man's contradictory character. Just as Montaigne's unsystematic style makes him sometimes seem to say too little on a subject, he also sometimes seems to say too much about a subject, arguing opposite positions in different places or even back-to-back. In short, his style is a reflection of his dialectic. He explores several sides of every issue, although it is largely through self-exploration that he hones his judgment, formulates his problems, and finds his responses. By structuring his arguments in this dialectical manner, he forces his readers to essay themselves as they essay what Montaigne has written. This is the unique relation between Montaigne's method and substantive recommendations.

His unique style of self-exploration gives his book both a permanent and a whimsical character. The *Essays* seems weighty, because it is nothing if not an attempt to grapple with fundamental human questions, such as "what am I?" "what do I know?" and "how should I live?" At the same time, it lapses into meditations on some of his own frailties (his kidney stones, appetites, dreams), sources of human embarrassment (sexual impotency, burping, farting), and every kind of human inanity, triviality, frivolity, and vanity. Montaigne even goes so far as to create a humorous courtroom scene in which he defends his "member" against charges brought by other—jealous—body parts (I.21, 100-01 [72-73]). The presence of these seemingly frivolous passages—which are deadly serious in terms of making the reader confront a whole array of fears and anxieties—has, I fear, led many philosophers and political theorists to take him less seriously than those who write in a conventionally "serious" vein. This style of writing is why scholars (except for specialists only on Montaigne) often have a sense of what Montaigne says, but don't make a systematic exposition of it. When presenting Montaigne's ideas, I shall pay special attention to his mode of presenting them.

Essaying, however, implies much more than a mere means of presentation for Montaigne; it is a way of living. Indeed, he more often uses the word essay as a verb, as in to essay himself, to test himself, than as a noun referring to the product of his writing. Montaigne's style is inseparable from his substance. Just as he argues that the good life for a human being consists in essaying himself, so he writes that way. But in demonstrating it before the reader's mind's eye, the reader is forced to essay the *Essays*, to examine and reflect on the sometimes seeming incoherence of the pages in front of him or her. Montaigne's method makes the reader do what he thinks the reader ought. Is there any better way to affect one's audience then through such a self-performative style?

The heart of this book traces the movement of Montaigne's thought from his skepticism to his recommendations for tolerant political institutions. Chapter 1 analyzes Montaigne's epistemology by carefully examining Montaigne's longest, most systematic, and most skeptical essay, "The Apology for Raymond Sebond." In order to give the inquiry a firm foundation, this examination requires an immersion into the details of the argument, for the "Apology" is Montaigne's most important and most disputed essay. In the "Apology," Montaigne examines exactly what can and cannot be known by human beings, and his answers lay both the ground and the limits for his argument for toleration. Montaigne explores a multitude of human claims for knowledge, concluding (unlike the dogmatists) that human beings cannot self-consciously know metaphysical truths but (unlike the Pyrrhonists) that they can phenomenologically know things about the self. The limited nature of the kind of experiential or phenomenological knowledge that Montaigne says human beings can possess—not everything but more than nothing—determines the character of the kind of human life that Montaigne recommends.

In fact, two ways of life survive his skeptical attacks: a life of what I call "*habitude naturelle*," natural habit, and a life of sensual self-seeking that I call "sophisticated simplicity." Both of these ways of life represent different forms of a phenomenological existence, and both reconcile supposed opposites, habit with nature, body with mind. The former is purer and more natural; the latter more self-aware. The former must necessarily be achieved *en masse* and is thus a fundamentally political way of life; the latter is radically individualistic. These two possibilities structure the remainder of the book.

Chapter 2 examines Montaigne's conception of "*habitude naturelle*," which he ascribes to the Indians of the New World. It traces the utopian nature of this way of life, which Montaigne momentarily calls the best that ever was, real or imaginary, and examines the problems that lead Montaigne ultimately to reject it. These "natural men" have tranquility of soul and enjoy the sensual pleasures without guilt. In short, they are happy, but because they live according to custom, without a critical self-awareness, they do not maximize human potential and are vulnerable to outside influences. Their lack of self-awareness and their vulnerability to external factors mark this way of life, despite its benefits, as neither fully desirable nor fully stable.

Chapter 3 analyzes the life of sophisticated simplicity, which Montaigne ultimately considers to be the best way of life for a human being. Sophisticated simplicity accepts tranquility of soul as embodied in natural man as desirable and articulates a method by which sophisticated and corrupt peoples like ourselves, who are born so far from our natural state, might be able to attain tranquility. He suggests that we essay ourselves—explore and fight through both the opinions and customs that have been internalized and explore and tame the anxieties, fears, and longings that naturally cause human beings to flee from their natural condition. By essaying these imagined visions and the natural desires that are shaped and cultivated by social forces, Montaigne aims to induce the readers back to their "truer" selves at "home." What Montaigne finds at the core of the self is everything and nothing. There is a sphere, he says, within which each individual is unique, and he calls on each of us to explore, create, and indulge ourselves in this realm. Doing so, he argues, provides one with a never-ending source of wonder and delight. However, he also finds a general human inability to comprehend many of the things that we most seek to know, such as metaphysical truth and life after death. Montaigne emphasizes these human inabilities, because he thinks that a proper appreciation of fundamental human ignorance will encourage individuals to be tolerant.

Chapter 4 examines Montaigne's politics of the good life and shows how it is to secure the sensually intellectual life of sophisticated simplicity, the fullest and happiest life for a human being, that Montaigne suggests his practical political innovations. Because his conception of the good life is so private, he argues for toleration and for a private sphere of free conscience and free political judgment to secure it. Key to his political argument is the fact that he appeals only to self-interest, not to "rights" of any kind.

Chapter 5 concludes the book by assessing Montaigne's argument for toleration in light of the numerous worldly objections that can be raised against it. For example, insofar as he debunks metaphysics in order to eliminate the most common reason for intolerance, must not his skepticism inevitably lead to nihilism? And might not his emphasis on self-interest promote an excessive selfishness that would lead to the harming of others out of the extreme desire to acquire either wealth, power, or glory? I conclude that while being skeptical, Montaigne's conception of the self enables him to avoid the problems associated both with nihilism and excessive individualism. Montaigne's conception of the self shows how individuals have no interest in forcing anything on anyone else—and they have little to force. This chapter also examines a corollary of Montaigne's argument, showing how his conception of the self leads to an organic argument for compassion. He strives to show how self-aware individuals feel pain when aware of the suffering of others.

In short, Montaigne's conception of the self allows him to justify toleration while avoiding many of the problems that plague today's justifications. Most importantly, it allows him to argue that self-interest and toleration are united, not in tension as most liberal conceptions of the self depict. To do this, Montaigne appeals to an understanding of self-interest that is not the most ordinary conception, and this is both the genius and weakness of his views. But to see how these arguments work in Montaigne, his thought must be examined *in toto*. Philosophers have considered Montaigne's views on skepticism, historians have examined his views on the Indians, deconstructionists and other literary figures have examined Montaigne's view of the self, and political scientists have touched on his arguments for toleration, but because each of these projects has been done largely in isolation from the others, most previous scholars have failed to see the relations between the various aspects of his thought and have thus failed to appreciate their richness and implications. This book unites Montaigne's thought to show how self-knowledge and self-interest lead to toleration.

Chapter One

Montaigne's Skepticism

The core of Montaigne's thought, and the ground for his conception of toleration, is his skepticism. This chapter analyzes Montaigne's skepticism as he presents it in his most skeptical and most famous essay, "The Apology for Raymond Sebond," and attempts to put its teaching in the context of the history of ideas.[1] Taking issue with those who see this essay as a scattered, disunified meditation, this chapter argues that the entire essay functions as a coherent whole when read as an attack on human vanity that is integral to Montaigne's skepticism.[2] It also explores the limits of Montaigne's skepticism, for as we shall see, it is precisely those things which he cannot doubt that will come to serve as the basis from which the rest of his philosophy grows.

Montaigne's skeptical attack on human opinion is twofold: it is made on a psychological as well as on a logical basis. Montaigne is concerned with showing doctrinal gaps and logical fallacies in systems of thought, but he is perhaps even more interested in debunking the self-serving pride and hubris that he thinks lead many of these systems—and humanity—to absurd claims. The heart of the "Apology"—the heart of Montaigne's skepticism—is his attempt to combat presumptuousness by showing the self-serving way in which it emerges from human "imagination" and by revealing the shortcomings and uncertainty of the main attribute of which human beings are so proud, reason. To these ends, the "Apology" is brutally systematic. The main aim of the first half of the essay is to humble its readers in their own estimation. Montaigne does this by undermining claims that lead to human vanity. He damningly "defends" the essay's namesake, because he considers Sebond to be the epitome of vanity. From this exposé of the height of hubris, Montaigne moves on to a radical attack on all previously existing authority, including and especially the authority of his time, Christianity. Montaigne critiques Christianity both on the basis of its practice and on the basis of some of its central theoretical ideas, which he condemns as self-serving anthropocentrisms. The conclusion and final blow of Montaigne's attack on human presumption is his radical revaluation of humanity's place in the cosmos: he distances humanity from God and lowers it toward the animals. Like a lawyer covering all of his bases, Montaigne argues both that humans are the same as the animals in all important respects *and*, after conceding that humans uniquely possess reason and freedom of imagination, he argues that to the extent that we differ it is to man's disadvantage, because these attributes enable us to deviate from nature. In point of fact, Montaigne does not truly believe in and ultimately backs away from this argument, too; he engages in this not entirely sincere discussion because he deems human vanity to be profoundly strong and therefore misses no opportunity to denounce it. After this, Montaigne shifts his focus, making a systematic attack on the human faculties. He proceeds to "leave the people aside" and examine "man in his highest estate" in order to show that despite man's attempts over millennia, even the greatest human beings have achieved little in their quests for knowledge. This section argues that we have no knowledge of God or man and explains the motives behind the claims of possessing it that great human beings have made. The final section carries the argument to its logical conclusion. Just as he has shown that man *has* no knowledge, he then argues that man *cannot* have it. He does this by systematically critiquing our only possible means of acquiring it, reason and the human senses.[3]

Montaigne's withering skeptical doubting leads to the moral and political problem that every skeptic must confront: if human beings possess no knowledge and cannot possess it, how should we live? In the face of human ignorance, are there any moral criteria that can and should guide each individual and society as a whole? Or, if nothing is true, perhaps morality does not matter at all. Montaigne does not leave the reader empty-handed. Each of the two overall parts of his skeptical argument—his critique of the psychology underlying human vanity and his analytical critique of the human faculties—suggests a remedy (albeit two very different and mutually exclusive remedies) for the moral and political problems with which humanity wrestles. Because these remedies—living a life according to natural habits or a life of sensual philosophy—are Montaigne's most extensive and specific contributions to political theory, they are discussed at length in subsequent chapters. This chapter indicates how these remedies emerge from Montaigne's skepticism. But before we examine Montaigne's arguments themselves, let us briefly discuss their context and significance.

I. Context: Montaigne's Skepticism and the Crisis of Authority

The epistemological skepticism that has characterized much of modern philosophy has been used to reject the transcendent philosophies that had previously dominated Europe, both ancient and Christian. Early modern philosophers wanted to reject the ancients' idea—which they found naive—that nature is the foundation of human knowledge. But more importantly, they wanted to reject Christianity, the dominant authority of the time, as the benchmark and arbiter of truth. And these were not entirely separate projects: ancient thought and Christianity were entangled insofar as the various theological "schools" had incorporated ancient thought, especially Aristotle, into the Christian orthodoxies of the fourteenth, fifteenth, and sixteenth centuries. The questioning of Christianity from without had been under way for some time before Montaigne. Scholarship keeps pushing back the date of this rejection, but it happened at least as early as Marsilius of Padua and Machiavelli.[4] The Church was also being challenged from within. Luther, Calvin, Zwingli, and other reformers questioned the authority of Rome and led their followers out of its fold. Even earlier reformist attacks on the Church can also be cited, including those by Wycliffe, Jan Hus, and Erasmus. While the reformers' attacks might have been resolvable by political, social, or doctrinal adjustments, the attacks from without demanded more radical solutions. All in all, philosophical questioning during the fifteenth and sixteenth centuries contributed to the radical breakdown of authority—religious, political, social, economic, and intellectual—and served as the womb in which modern thought was to be conceived.[5]

Montaigne both responded to and further provoked this breakdown, weaving together several different threads of skeptical doubting and bringing them to a powerfully new head. At a time when the religious wars between Protestants and Catholics (and one Protestant sect versus another) were forcing most people to choose sides, Montaigne was left cold by theological debates and dismissed the combatants as fanatical partisans. He saw people arguing over questions to which they could not possibly know the answers and killing those who disagreed with what was nothing more than opinion. A few Christian humanists such as Sebastian Castellio condemned the cruelty of these murders, but they made their condemnations by arguing largely on Christian grounds.[6] Montaigne, almost alone, condemned the butchery from a more skeptical, human-centered position, reacting strongly against the religious zealots and cynical manipulators who exploited these religious differences by raising serious moral and epistemological questions to try to bring an end to the religious madness. Montaigne's skepticism was influenced not only by the lunacy around him, but also by several ancient sources, including Plato, Aristotle, Plutarch, Lucretius, Cicero, and the whole tradition of ancient Roman and Renaissance poetry that lamented the difficult and unknowable nature of the human condition. Some of the work of these thinkers had been known in Christendom, but it was hardly influential before the advent of the printing press.[7] Often it was co-opted and interpreted to fit in with Christian truths. For example, just as Aristotle was co-opted by Aquinas and the numerous schools of Christian theology, so Plato was incorporated into Christianity through the ecumenical Italian humanists, such as Ficino and Mirandola. Montaigne was among the first in modern times to emphasize the profoundly skeptical nature of the ancient pagan teachings and their fundamental incompatibility with Christianity. The fall of Constantinople and the influx of scholars from the Byzantine Empire to Western Europe multiplied the number of pagan sources; Montaigne knew these works well. Having had Latin as his first language, he was able to digest them as few others were able.[8]

Montaigne's sense of cultural contingency and his openness to science also had the effect of making his work an important part of the breakdown of traditional authority. He was almost uniquely sensitive to the challenge that the discovery of America posed to the typical Christian claim that Christianity and European civilization represented the essence of truth and human goodness. Unlike Vitoria, Las Casas, or Sepúlveda, who also wrote systematically about the discovery of the New World, Montaigne argued that the people of the New World were neither deviations from nor limited realizations of nature, but rather that they lived as close to nature as possible and thus embodied it in a pure form.[9] His radical openness to other ways of life, also manifested in his serious consideration of numerous and diverse cultures and peoples, enabled Montaigne to bring anthropological and historical evidence to support his skeptical arguments. Montaigne also took seriously Copernicus' theory that the Earth was not the center of the universe. Giordano Bruno would later be burned at the stake in 1600 for saying, among other things, some of what Montaigne said about the Indians. Galileo would be accused of heresy in 1632 for supporting Copernicus.

Montaigne was more prudent in his declarations; his work would not be put on *The Index of Prohibited Books* until 1676, well after his death. He nonetheless, before them, marshaled these and other ideas in his attack on traditional Christian cosmology. Montaigne combined all of these trends into a great skeptical synthesis that catalyzed the skeptical crisis of early modern times.

Montaigne advanced the skeptical crisis in another way as well: he introduced Pyrrhonism to a wide audience. While the authority of the Church was being attacked from within and without, an extraordinary work of antiquity was published in Latin, the international language of the learned, for the first time. This book, published in 1562 by the French scholar and publisher Stephanus,[10] is Sextus Empiricus' *Outlines of Pyrrhonism*. Sextus (around 200 AD) was a follower of the ancient Greek skeptic, Pyrrho of Elis (approximately 360-275 BC), and while his book probably does not present any arguments that were original to himself, it presents the most radically skeptical arguments that have come down to us from antiquity.[11] In fact, so crucial is this work to modern philosophy that many scholars, such as Annas and Barnes, and philosophers, such as Pierre Bayle, have dated the publication of Sextus' text as the beginning of modern philosophy.[12] Montaigne was the first great presenter of Sextus, and it was he who brought Sextus' arguments to a large audience for the first time.

Historians of ideas have appreciated Montaigne's pivotal role in the emergence of skepticism in modernity; but because they have focused more on Sextus than on Montaigne, they have often not done justice to Montaigne's originality. Historians of ideas often acknowledge Montaigne's role, but they have admired more than explored it. J. B. Schneewind says that Montaigne "opens up the modern era in moral thought," but explains this remark without once quoting him.[13] Richard Popkin, perhaps the most famous historian of modern skeptical thought, says that "Montaigne's genial 'Apologie' became the coup de grâce to an entire intellectual world," yet his interpretation merely scratches its surface.[14] Annas and Barnes, writing on the rediscovery of Sextus' work, note that "[Sextus'] first major literary manifestation is Montaigne's remarkable essay entitled *A Defense of Raymond Sebond*," but in addition to seeing it as literary, not philosophical, they feel compelled to add that it is "long, rambling," and unoriginal, saying it "assembles a mass of skeptical arguments, most of them lifted from the text of Sextus."[15] Montaigne does indeed use several of Sextus' arguments, but it seems not to occur to them that Montaigne might be using Sextus toward his own very original ends.

And, finally, M. F. Burnyeat patronizingly "honours" Montaigne by referring to his thought as "the country gentleman's interpretation" of Pyrrhonist skepticism.[16] Burnyeat makes Montaigne's skepticism seem shallow: "One advantage of the country gentleman's interpretation is that there is no great difficulty in understanding how he can walk about his estate making arrangements for next year's crops while proclaiming himself a skeptic about space and time."[17] Both parts of Burnyeat's assertion may be questioned. Montaigne gives little evidence of worrying about his crops but did take the skeptical challenge to his ordinary life extraordinarily seriously. In sum, many scholars recognize Montaigne's tremendous importance in the history of skepticism, but at the same time they tend not to engage his thought seriously or to dismiss it as derivative, confused, or shallow.

In a further irony that would have delighted Montaigne (and supported his point about the difficulty of knowing anything outside oneself), while Montaigne is most famous for his skepticism, the precise nature of his skepticism is also among the most debated aspect of his thought among scholars. Different scholars claim that Montaigne is a devout Catholic, a fideist, an atheist, and a Pyrrhonist.[18] Even when scholars agree on the label, they sometimes disagree on the reasons for it. For example, Frieda Brown and Jacob Zeitlin both claim that Montaigne is a Catholic, but Brown because he is a sincere believer,[19] whereas Zeitlin attributes it to Montaigne's respect for tradition and authority, that is to say, nonreligious reasons.[20] Herman Janssen, Donald Frame, and Hugo Friedrich, the leading Dutch, American, and German Montaigne scholars respectively, all consider Montaigne a fideist, someone who argues that no truth is available to human beings by *natural means* but only through the *revealed* word of God accepted by *faith*, but they assess his fideism differently. Janssen considers Montaigne's fideism to be "typical of [Montaigne's] whole age,"[21] whereas Friedrich states that Montaigne's fideism is not orthodox and is in fact noted by its "bizarrerie."[22] By complete contrast, Arthur Armaingaud and André Gide consider Montaigne a rationalist;[23] Zbigniew Gierczynski and Schaefer consider Montaigne an atheist.[24] Richard Popkin, Myles Burnyeat, and numerous others consider him a Pyrrhonist, a position which, due to its lack of any settled conviction, is obviously incompatible with all of the above.[25] The scholarship gives no consensus, let alone definitive answers about the nature of Montaigne's skepticism.

It is my argument that Montaigne's position differs from all of these. Montaigne does not hold any of these epistemological positions in their entirety but uses aspects of each as means toward advancing his own original goals. For example, fideistic declarations are often part of his rhetoric, not part of his bottom line. His argument has several impious features that are inconsistent with fideism. First, throughout Montaigne's discussions of religion there is a tension, sometimes even a contradiction, between pious assertions and a much less pious argument that is supposed to be proving them. The "Apology" and other essays are full of pious assertions that are contradicted by the meat of their arguments. Second, there is a tension between unconventional arguments and conventional conclusions which Montaigne (sometimes unwarrantably) draws from them. Third, Montaigne never invokes scripture authoritatively, and he is highly selective in his citations. He is much more likely to cite it to support a pagan's point revealing the nothingness of man than to affirm Christianity's distinctive tenets. Moreover, he quotes primarily pagan authors, even to prove points concerning the nature of God. He also moves easily back and forth between his quotations from scripture and from ancient pagans, as if both serve his purposes equally well. Fourth, while never calling much attention to this, he questions or dismisses many of the central tenets of Christianity, including the Garden of Eden version of natural man, the notion of a virgin birth, the doctrine of transubstantiation, and the possibility that God could have a human incarnation. Fifth, Montaigne often states that a matter needs treatment by a religious authority, which he admits he is not, but then proceeds to give his own (irreligious) interpretations of the phenomena in question. Sometimes he claims to defer to religious views, but then proceeds to undermine the basis for belief in the thing to which he allegedly surrendered. Since all of these irreligious tropes are found throughout Montaigne's writing, he cannot be a fideist in any straightforward understanding of the term.

Similarly, Montaigne is not a Pyrrhonist (let alone a simple popularizer of Sextus) in any of the most important senses. Rather, he uses Pyrrhonist arguments in support of his own aims. Unlike the Pyrrhonists, Montaigne has a clear agenda. Pyrrhonists don't judge any issue more important than any other, so to them all issues are equally important. By contrast, Montaigne does not doubt petty concerns such as the whiteness of snow, as Pyrrhonists do; all of his skeptical analyses focus on concerns of primary importance to human life, such as the nature of human opinion, the body, soul, and God. Montaigne's selective use of Sextus to shed light on psychological and moral questions makes his thought more politically useful than Pyrrhonism. Montaigne does not want to eliminate judgment, a faculty so critical to moral reasoning, as do strict Pyrrhonists; he wants to cultivate and refine it. But if Montaigne emphasizes moral reasoning, he is no rationalist. Reason is Montaigne's tool—all language and thought takes place within its bounds—but he aims to show the limits of what reason can achieve. He uses reason against itself, arguing that rational truth is impossible for human beings to achieve; better and more refined judgment is the best that humans can do. In sum, Montaigne is neither a fideist, Pyrrhonist, or rationalist.

In the end, Montaigne's epistemological position most closely resembles that of the Academic skeptics of the Hellenistic era.[26] Like the Academic skeptics, Montaigne argues that he knows he knows nothing. This is a troubling claim for a skeptic: if no knowledge is possible, how is this known? First, however, Montaigne sets out to make the reader ripe, i.e., receptive to his arguments; before we can know what we can know, we must be made much more conscious of those things which impel us to claim things beyond our grasp. An examination of vanity lays the ground of Montaigne's skepticism, so it is to an analysis of this that we now turn.

II. The Human Problem: Vanity

In order to understand Montaigne's skepticism, we must understand how he uses it. Montaigne does not trifle over the sweetness of honey, use skepticism to uphold religious faith, or doubt the world in order to put it back together again, as Descartes attempts to, on firm foundations. Montaigne's skepticism arises out of human needs and more political concerns.

Before systematically defining the kinds of skepticism and launching his systematic attack on the inadequacy of human faculties, Montaigne spends the first forty percent of the "Apology" attacking human vanity.[27] "Presumption is our natural and original malady. The most vulnerable and frail of all creatures is man, and at the same time the most arrogant" (II.12, 429 [330]). Montaigne attacks vanity because presumption is the source of much of what he hates in the world: arrogant know-it-alls who inflict cruelty and suffering in the name of their supposed goods. Montaigne's skepticism is, in the first place, an attempt to humble and tame rambunctious intellectuals and political and moral crusaders.

Montaigne uses skeptical doubt to expose the groundlessness of habit and opinion.[28] He claims that human beings are born so far from man's natural state that the world does not appear to us as it actually is. He despises the unnatural and corrupt "civilization" of which we are so proud. Everywhere one turns, one meets pomp and pretention. All people claim to be something that they are not. Princes claim grandeur; scholars claim wisdom; priests claim to know divine will; Europeans claim to be the quintessence of man.

Montaigne attacks such opinions not only in the pursuit of truth but also to overcome the anxiety and cruelty they provoke. We are taught to worry, to fear unseen things, and to desire all sorts of extraneous and questionable goods. We are led to wars, tempted to convert sinners, and forced to punish heretics. It is bad enough if the actors believe their claims to be true, but Montaigne thinks it is even worse. The ambitious, including monarchs, priests, and revolutionaries, are cynical, he believes; needing men to fight for their cause, they exploit human gullibility. Ordinary men are susceptible to these claims because of natural human weaknesses. The common inability to distinguish convention from truth, and man's unruly imagination, which can always be excited, make human beings mistake the appearance of things for the real things. Wherever anyone looks, triumphant impostors and satisfied dupes are to be found. "Any opinion is strong enough to make people espouse it at the price of life" (I.14, 52 [35]). In other words, his age sounds much like our own. The presumption and exploitation of "knowledge" would seem to be a problem coeval with humanity. And if presumption is claiming to know what one in fact does not know, skepticism is acknowledging what one does not know. Montaigne uses his skepticism as a club to compel his readers to acknowledge their ignorance, that what they think is true is most likely based on unsubstantiated presumptions.

So before systematically establishing the limits of human abilities and thus the limits of what can be known by human beings, Montaigne goes for the jugular, attacking the readers' sense of self-importance and self-certainty. This makes the reader much more receptive to the analytical attacks that come afterward. Montaigne attacks the hubris of ordinary human psychology and basic opinions almost universally held in the West. Many of the parts of his argument begin and end with pious affirmations of faith, but within this framework Montaigne makes a devastating three-part attack on human vanity and one of its main sources, Christianity. First, Montaigne discusses the essay's namesake, the fifteenth-century Christian philosopher, Raymond Sebond. He titles his essay after Sebond yet proceeds to attack him, I believe, because Sebond's epistemological position is the vainest possible. Second, Montaigne attacks the vanities inherent in the practice of Christianity, the authority of his day. Third, he attacks Christianity's anthropocentric theoretical conception of mankind's place in the cosmos. Montaigne disputes humanity's right to rule the earth, in the process distancing man from God and lowering it toward the animals.[29] Throughout this attack, Montaigne takes the reader through a series of humbling arguments, many of which are merely rhetorical since he proceeds to undermine or silently drop them. A highly ironic but self-conscious thinker, many of Montaigne's statements are provisional. The first among these provisionally assumed positions is his so-called "defense" of Raymond Sebond.

Vanity I: Sebond, Vainest of the Vain

As is his wont, Montaigne does not entitle his essay on skepticism "Of Skepticism," "Of Epistemology," or "On What Can Be Known By Human Beings." Nor does he entitle it, "why human weakness should turn men to faith." Rather, he names it after a then obscure and today forgotten fifteenth-century theologian named Raymond Sebond.[30] But despite the essay's title, Sebond is barely mentioned after the first ten pages of this 150-page essay. Different commentators have explained the curious relation between title and substance in different ways. Many have suggested that it has no significance. For example, Villey asserts that Montaigne proceeded capriciously and merely forgot his original project.[31] Norton says that Montaigne was "confused" and might not even have noticed: "it can easily be believed that he never cared to review his conclusions—all the more, because they took no formal or formulated shape to him."[32] Frame says that the "Apology" probably took its shape when Montaigne combined two originally unrelated pieces.[33] Friedrich sees Montaigne turn against Sebond, but he imagines that it happens accidentally: "Without expressly intending this or stating it, he becomes Sebond's opponent."[34] By contrast, other scholars such as Schaefer, Sainte-Beuve, Armaingaud, and Gierczynski more compellingly explain the gap by arguing that Montaigne was intentionally "betraying" Sebond, that he is condemning and not defending him.[35] Schaefer takes this argument the furthest, seeing Montaigne's use of Sebond not as accidental but as a shrewd cover; in subtly attacking Sebond, Schaefer claims, Montaigne is actually taking on St. Thomas Aquinas and the whole tradition of ancient and medieval thought, whose views are devastated by Montaigne's arguments just as Sebond's are.[36] But whereas explicitly attacking Aquinas would have gotten Montaigne into serious trouble with the Church's censors, Schaefer suggests, attacking Sebond would have raised nobody's ire. Schaefer's argument is shrewd insofar as Montaigne had no intention of defending his essay's namesake. But Schaefer too easily conflates Aquinas and Sebond (not to mention the whole history of ancient and medieval thought), and his interpretation begs the question "why Sebond?" Could any philosopher or theologian have taken Sebond's place in the title? I argue no, there is something about Sebond's claims that are crucial to Montaigne and that reveal the unity of the essay as a whole.[37] Explaining why Sebond is chosen for the title remedies a crucial gap in the literature.[38]

Montaigne's use of Sebond, I believe, is straightforwardly ironic: Sebond's claims about what human beings can know are the vainest imaginable (much more so than Aquinas', for example), and as such he deserves to be the poster-boy for human vanity, the subject of Montaigne's excoriation throughout the essay. Sebond's main work, the *Theologia naturalis sive Liber creaturarum, specialiter de homine* or *Natural Theology* (1484), which Montaigne translated into French (1569), stakes out the most extreme epistemological position imaginable. Sebond argues that all natural and divine phenomena, including the doctrines of the Trinity and the incarnation of God in which he wholeheartedly believed, can be known by unaided human reason by studying "God's book," the world.[39] Montaigne was probably genuinely attracted to the idea of turning to nature as a basis for theology, or as the basis for a secular way of living, since he translated the text. However this may be, he demolishes Sebond's claims as absurdly anthropocentric and presumptuous.

Indeed, after having chosen to put Sebond's name in the essay's title, Montaigne labors to separate himself from Sebond from the very beginning. Montaigne explains how Sebond was thrust on him, and how he was "commanded" (a word hated by one so jealous of his freedom as Montaigne) to work on it. His father, whom Montaigne describes as having "no knowledge of letters" and as "less qualified to judge them," happened to be given a copy of Sebond's work by one Pierre Bunel, "a man of great reputation for learning in his time" (II.12, 415 [319]). Montaigne's emphasis on Bunel's "reputation" as opposed to his true qualities makes us wonder about Montaigne's own opinion of him. Indeed, Montaigne notes unflattering similarities between Bunel and Sebond.[40] In any case, he says the book was forgotten until "some days before his death, my father, having by chance come across this book under a pile of other abandoned papers, commanded me to put it into French for him" (II.12, 416 [320]). Popkin considers this account "probably inaccurate" but fails to tell us why he thinks so or why Montaigne would begin his longest essay with such a falsehood.[41] Schaefer convincingly shows problems with this account and argues that the patent falsehood alerts the astute reader to the fact that something else is going on; Sebond is a less dangerous stand-in for Aquinas. This argument has merit: it makes a certain political sense for

Montaigne to attack a figure who is so much less well-known; Montaigne once suggests that Sebond's book may be a quintessence extracted from Aquinas; and Sebond was known as a Thomistic philosopher.[42] However, there is a fundamental difference between their theological positions: Sebond's epistemological claims are *more* extreme than Aquinas'.

To appreciate fully the extreme nature of Sebond's claim and the difference between his and Aquinas' positions, it would be helpful briefly to discuss the theological problem that both thinkers were addressing: the relation of reason to revelation. This debate was occasioned by the confrontation of the pagan philosophy of antiquity, such as Plato's and Aristotle's, that relied on reason alone in making its arguments, with the tradition of revealed religion in the forms of the various monotheistic religions of the Western world, Judaism, Christianity, and Islam. The fertile period of Islamic philosophy spanning roughly the ninth through twelfth centuries, which included thinkers such as Alfarabi, Avicenna, Avempace, Ibn Tufayl, and Averroes, was the first to deal philosophically with this problem of conflicting authorities.[43] This confrontation between natural and revealed truth happened first in the Arab world because pagan thought was preserved there, whereas Christendom had largely destroyed it shortly after it came to power in the Roman Empire.[44] The works of Aristotle made their way back to Christendom from the Arabic world and were translated into Latin in the thirteenth century, and Aquinas became the most successful Christian to establish the compatibility of the Biblical and pagan traditions. Aquinas argued that reason and revelation were consistent, but he deemed Biblical revelation to be the glorious and necessary crown for unassisted human reason. Reason alone, he argued, could not reveal all of the truths of the Bible. Faith was necessary for that.[45] However, Christian theorists also developed another way of dealing with these different traditions, one based on the works of Averroes. The so-called Latin Averroists argued in favor of the doctrine of the "double truth," according to which both religious and rational truths—even when contradictory—could each be accepted on their own terms (much as Max Weber was later to do with his radically separated realms of facts and values). But in the words of Hugo Friedrich:

> The consequences of this division [between reason and revelation] were dangerous. Irrationalized faith was no longer sufficiently safe from rationalized criticism. The method of "double truth" threatened to turn into a trick with which reason, under the protection of the assurance that it was merely speaking rationally, thus not accountably, could break down the article of faith as something nonsensical. Lack of faith settled into the gap

between faith and knowledge.[46]

It was to combat this doctrine of the "double truths" that, beginning with Raymond Lulle, a school arose claiming that the mysteries of the Christian religion, even the seemingly nonrational teachings such as those dealing with the Trinity or the incarnation of God, were accessible to unassisted human thought. This radical project claimed to demonstrate not only the *harmony* of reason with the mysteries of revealed religion, as Aquinas argued, but it also claimed rationally to *prove* revelation by human means. Raymond Sebond is an exemplar of this more radical school of thought. Aquinas argued that revealed religion is harmonious with but not identical to the teaching of natural reason. Sebond went further, arguing that natural reason, if properly employed, teaches exactly and fully what the Bible reveals. Unlike Sebond, Aquinas always thought faith necessary to supplement the inadequacy of natural human powers. Sebond's argument implies that Aquinas did not go far enough in reconciling the dictates of reason to the revealed truth of Christianity.

By putting Sebond's name in the title, Montaigne effectively raises, in order to dispose of, the most extreme epistemological position first—that ordinary human abilities can enable us to know everything in the cosmos and even provide knowledge of God Himself. A refutation of Sebond is not necessarily a refutation of Aquinas, although Montaigne's argument is so radical that it does in fact sweep both aside. The point is that Sebond's extreme views supply a substantive reason for Montaigne to use his name as the standard bearer for his attack on human vanity.

But even though he despises Sebond's arguments, Montaigne finds himself in the same difficult position that he attributes to every philosopher: trying to explore fundamental questions without undermining the beliefs that help hold their societies together.[47] Though Montaigne seriously doubts the claims of any religion to know the nature of God or what happens after death, he does not therefore wish too blatantly to strip Sebond—and the religious tradition he represents—bare. Montaigne believes that major attempts to change or eliminate a religion from a society in which it is dominant would lead to political and social chaos—such as the wars of religion were wreaking all around him; he wanted to avoid that at all costs. For political—not religious—reasons, Montaigne considers it imperative to support these beliefs. Montaigne's view echoes Bunel's fear that "the innovations of Luther" would undermine "our old belief" and lead to "an execrable atheism," and both worry about this because they fear that if "the common herd" [*le vulgaire*] have any of their beliefs shaken, they will overthrow them all (II.12, 416 [320]).[48] Like Plato and James Madison in *Federalist* 49, Montaigne believes that most people act based on custom; political prudence therefore demands that custom be respected.[49] Because ordinary people hold their beliefs by convention or faith, not reason, they lack the judgment to discern good versus bad customs, laws, and opinions. Once they start overthrowing authority, they will "shake off as a tyrannical yoke" all the opinions they have received only on "the authority of the laws or the reverence of ancient usage" (II.12, 416 [320]). It might sometimes be justifiable to overthrow such traditions, but Montaigne worries about the logistics of limiting such a process once it has begun. Once change begins, on what grounds can it be prevented from snowballing endlessly? Arguing that the basis of custom is irrational and so complex that when one aspect of it is tinkered with, unforeseen repercussions might be felt anywhere or everywhere, Montaigne repeatedly expresses doubts about the ability of human beings to alter custom in a rational manner. He fears that once authority is stripped bare, it will lead, as it later in fact did in the French Revolution, to *le déluge*. Therefore, Montaigne is generally skeptical of efforts of political and social reform.[50] But this is not to say that Montaigne thinks that political or religious authority is based on anything sacred. While Bunel fears that only ignorant people will conclude that all customs are tyrannical and arbitrary, Montaigne argues this exact position himself. For example, the main argument in his essay entitled "Of Custom" is that all habits are "violent and treacherous," establish themselves in human beings "little by little, stealthily," and tyrannize over our original natures so profoundly that "we no longer have the liberty of even raising our eyes" (I.23, 106 [77]). But Montaigne does not consider this fact alone to be a legitimate ground for overthrowing habits. While he advocates the relaxation of excessive laws insofar as is prudent, Montaigne, following Epicurus and anticipating Hobbes, also argues that we need groundless laws—and he says that they are all groundless—to prevent us from "eating ourselves."[51]

Just as Montaigne teaches, so he writes: he demolishes Sebond's claims but upholds Sebond's piety. This explains why Montaigne ostensibly claims to defend Sebond but proceeds to belittle him in almost every way possible. The "Apology," indeed all Montaigne's essays, has a rhetoric which praises piety, and at the same time it makes arguments that undermine the religious grounds upon which piety is based. This rhetoric was necessary, not only because Montaigne did not want to be burned at the stake, but also because it enabled him to criticize without advocating destruction, which is the most useful position that can be advanced by a philosopher who disagrees with the views of his society.[52] Montaigne insults Sebond's writing style, disparaging it as "Spanish scrambled up with Latin endings" and as lacking "grace" and "elegance of language" (II.12, 415-16 [319-20]). Montaigne rejects Sebond's central claim that reason can apprehend the truth. "It would be doing a wrong to divine goodness," Sebond asserts, "if the universe did not assent to our belief" (II.12, 424 [326]), which is a position that Montaigne fervently dismisses as hubristically anthropomorphic. The sky, the earth, the elements, our body, and our soul all instruct us about God, Sebond argues, if we only know how to read them.[53] But Montaigne cites two thinkers, St. Paul and the pagan Manilius, who used Sebond's method but reached radically different conclusions (II.12, 424 [326]). The world might teach those who inquire into it, but it does not teach everyone the same thing. Reason and imagination easily go off on their own paths.[54] And Montaigne thinks that Sebond is one of those thinkers who has gone astray, indicating this with what might seem to be praise. Montaigne says that he found Sebond's "plan full of piety" (II.12, 416 [320]), and that "Faith, coming to color and illumine Sebond's arguments, makes them firm and solid" (II.12, 425 [327]), which is a devastating criticism of Sebond, who explicitly claims to be proving his claims based on reason alone, without appealing to faith. According to Montaigne's way of characterizing the argument, Sebond would consider his entire project a failure. Indeed, Montaigne calls Sebond's ideas "imaginations," implying that they have no grounding in reality other than in Sebond's mind (II.12, 416 [320]). The vainest of the vain has been totally discredited.

But because Sebond's piety might be useful in certain limited circumstances, Montaigne proposes to defend him. Montaigne notes that Sebond is popular with the ladies, even calling Sebond's work "their book" (II.12, 417 [320]), and Sebond's chief recommender, Bunel, intended it to be beneficial for the masses to prevent them from falling into an "execrable atheism."[55] Since Sebond's arguments, "capable of serving as a start and a first guide to an apprentice" (II.12, 425 [327]), might be useful for these limited audiences, Montaigne "defends" Sebond from two unattributed charges, although his defenses are damning of Sebond's philosophical reasoning. The first criticism of Sebond is that Christians do themselves harm by trying to support their faith "by human reasons," since Christianity is conceived *only* by faith and by a particular inspiration of divine grace (II.12, 417 [321]).[56] Montaigne supports Sebond only insofar as he says that, as long as the arguer does not think that his faith depends on his rational proofs, such arguments do no harm.[57] For, contra Sebond, Montaigne here sides with the critics, saying that he "judges" that revealed truth is "so far surpassing human intelligence" that human beings will never understand it without God's help (II.12, 417 [321]).[58] The second charge from which Montaigne damningly "defends" Sebond is that his arguments do not achieve his objectives. Montaigne's defense against this charge is both brief (the explicit discussion of it is only one page) and long, insofar as the entire "Apology" can be construed as an elaboration of this response. Montaigne asserts that "to tell the truth, I find him so firm and felicitous that I do not think it is possible to do better in that argument [of proving Christian beliefs through reason], and I think that no one has equaled him" (II.12, 417 [320]). Sebond has pushed the argument to its limit; high praise indeed. But Montaigne's praise cannot be due to Sebond's unprecedented results; Montaigne has disparaged Sebond's arguments at every turn. Rather, the logical drift of his argument *in toto* is that Sebond has not been surpassed because all such arguments are equally vain. Montaigne proposes to prove this by showing how impotent man is in general, arguing that human reason cannot prove anything: "all subjects alike, and nature in general, disavow her jurisdiction and mediation" (II.12, 427 [328]). "It is for God alone to know himself and interpret his works," he says (II.12, 479 [369]). Montaigne makes this argument—the polar opposite of Sebond's—to support Sebond. In short, as one wit has aptly put it, "Montaigne supports Sebond as the rope supports the hanged man."[59]

Vanity II: Attack on Christian Practice

Woven into Montaigne's "defense" of Sebond is a withering critique of Christianity as practiced. Montaigne's attack on Sebond, his own pretend "authority," opens out to an attack on Christianity, the authority of his time. As realized in practice, Montaigne says, Christianity has little restraint upon its adherents. In Montaigne's eyes, Christianity, like all religions, lacks divine origins, but arises and is held as are all other customs. The one advantage of Christianity, as with other religions, for Montaigne, is that it is often comforting in a way that atheism is not. Far from offering a ringing endorsement of religion, Montaigne accepts it as of limited political and psychological usefulness but demolishes it philosophically. Montaigne proffers this critique not to "*ecrasez l'infame*" as Enlightenment *philosophes* will later demand, but rather to shake educated readers, the potential Sebonds of the world, out of their absurdly smug attachments to their own beliefs. Only by doing this, he suggests, will the readers be open to true learning.

Montaigne begins and ends his condemnation of Christian practice with pious fideistic statements in which he does not believe. Montaigne criticizes his contemporaries' ordinary religious behavior in the name of a purer kind of divine revelation, but since he will soon argue that there is no evidence of the purer kind existing, the high-minded pious pretense which he maintains throughout this discussion ultimately undermines itself. Distinguishing between faith held on an extraordinary, divine basis and faith held on a human basis, Montaigne, contra Sebond, proposes that faith is only in its glory and splendor when detached from reason: "If it does not enter into us by an extraordinary infusion; if it enters, I will not say only by reason, but by human means of any sort, it is not in us in its dignity or in its splendor" (II.12, 418 [321]). Similarly, at the end of this section, Montaigne calls Plato "great with human greatness only," because he did not know "our sacred truth" and for cynically suggesting that the old and the young are more susceptible to religion because of psychological vulnerabilities (II.12, 423-24 [325-26]). Montaigne here also similarly criticizes Socrates and Cato, who form an important pair, representing the peaks of pagan intellectual and practical virtue, respectively, and concludes this discussion of Christian practices by saying that because they are ignorant of God, the virtue of these pagans is "vain and useless" (II.12, 425 [326]). Very Christian sounding, indeed. Statements like these are why people claim that Montaigne is a sincerely believing fideist Christian.

However, these condemnations of pagan philosophers and statesmen on the grounds of their not possessing an "extraordinary infusion" of faith are problematic. All of these figures emerge as heroes elsewhere in the *Essays*. Indeed, in addition to Montaigne himself, Socrates emerges as *the* hero of the book. Could the virtue of his heroes be "vain and useless"? Montaigne might be simply contradicting himself, as Norton argues, in which case we readers are wasting our time in studying him. Villey explains such inconsistencies by proposing that Montaigne's thought went through stages, but according to Villey's chronology, Montaigne is supposed to be having a skeptical crisis in this essay, not piously upholding faith. Moreover, throughout the essay—and even in between these pious assertions in this very section—Montaigne upholds the wisdom of the ancient pagan thinkers.[60] Indeed, Montaigne's substantive arguments fundamentally undermine the basis of his pious assertions.

Montaigne operates according to Latin Averroism's radical separation of reason from revelation, but with one important difference: Montaigne impiously argues that there is no evidence that an "extraordinary infusion" of faith exists in this world. If Montaigne argues that views held by divine inspiration are more resplendent than those held by human means, he also argues that no actual human beings hold views on this basis.[61] In addition to (and in between) his pious affirmation of the value of faith, Montaigne denies that faith is ever held on the basis of an "extraordinary infusion." Rather, he argues that all religious opinion is held for and by *human* means: "I am afraid that we enjoy it only in this way" (II.12, 418 [321]). Montaigne argues that if faith were divinely inspired, human beings would not be easily swayed from their religious paths: "human accidents would not have the power to shake us as they do" (II.12, 418 [321]). The love of novelty, the good fortune of a particular political party, or a new argument, he says, would not lead to changes of actions and behaviors as Montaigne witnesses all around him. Furthermore, Montaigne seems to argue that divinely inspired faith has never existed. Montaigne takes seriously the effect that truly divine inspiration would necessarily, he thinks, have on someone. Such a revelation would be so powerful that it could not help coloring every aspect of an individual's life: "If this ray of divinity touched us at all, it would appear all over" (II.12, 418 [322]). Since no one has existed who did only good, Montaigne concludes that no one has ever been touched by the divine ray.[62] This is not to deny that there are people who genuinely "believe" or who do good actions. Nor is it an argument against the possibility of God's existence; God might reach out to human beings who, through their own inabilities or weaknesses, fail to hear His message. These are all possible, based on Montaigne's argument here. Montaigne's claim is that the belief and good action that can be observed in individuals cannot be attributed to *divine* inspiration, because if there were *divine* inspiration there would be *only* good action. Thus, if Montaigne says that fideism is the most divine position for human beings to hold, he also argues that there are no—and never have been—human beings who believe on such a divinely inspired basis. The consequence of Montaigne's separation of reason and revelation is to leave revelation behind.[63] Faith is held on human—not divine—grounds. Montaigne is not a pious thinker.

Given his claim that divinely inspired belief does not exist, it is not surprising to see Montaigne accuse the Christian community of corruption and ignorance of the true nature of belief. These faults each characterize a different type of person, corresponding to "the prelates and people," i.e., the religious rulers and ruled (II.12, 419 [322]).[64] Montaigne argues that both the religious and secular Christian leaders of his time are fundamentally corrupt. These Christians leaders—like the leaders of all "human sects" and every "partisan"—are marked only "by their words" (II.12, 419 [322]). With a condemnation that could have been penned by Machiavelli, Montaigne asserts that they "make the world believe that they believe what they do not believe" (II.12, 419 [322]).[65] But of all sects (he mentions the Muslims and pagans), the behavior of Christians is the worst. The hypocrisy was clear in the religious wars between the Protestants and Catholics that were raging at the time. Both sides used justice as an ornament; they mouthed it without practicing it or even believing what they said. And even more hypocritically, both sides used their avowals of piety to cover their cruel excesses and injustices, so much so that Montaigne doubts there is any difference between them. "Can one see conduct more uniform, more at one," he asks, "issue from the same school and teaching?" (II.12, 420 [323]). He complains that "we" burn people for saying that "truth must be made to endure the yoke of our need" but "how much worse France does than just say it!" (II.12, 420 [323]). Montaigne does not condemn attention to need; he advocates just such a position later in the essay, but he does condemn the hypocritical way in which his contemporaries pursue it. There is but a handful of men who act only out of "zeal of affection for religion" (II.12, 420 [323]). When the political winds change, both Catholics and Protestants change their supposedly sacred positions to exploit the situation. "Men are the leaders here, and make use of religion; it ought to be quite the contrary" (II.12, 420 [323]).[66] "Our religion is made to extirpate vices; it covers them, fosters them, incites them" (II.12, 421 [324]). Montaigne says that these Christian leaders act so badly because they believe neither in God nor in any of Christianity's teachings.[67] They are corrupt, self-interested opportunists—and Montaigne lambasts such corruption numerous times throughout the *Essays*. But this does not make Montaigne a pious thinker; he is simply turning the avowed principles of Christianity against its leadership.

After lambasting the corruption of Christian leaders, Montaigne laments a deeper problem, the nature of Christian belief. While the leaders do not believe but cynically manipulate their flocks, the flocks themselves do believe. According to Montaigne, however, their belief is problematic. The faithful flock to "make themselves believe [Christian teaching], being unable to penetrate what it means to believe" (II.12, 419 [322]). Montaigne explains this failure by probing the nature of Christian belief, asking what it means to believe in God and to live accordingly. "If we believed in him, I do not say by faith, but with a simple belief; in fact (and I say it to our great confusion), if we believed in him just as in any other history," Montaigne asserts, everything would be beautiful (II.12, 421 [324]). But human beings do not treat God like other "histories." Because He is not concrete, Montaigne argues, He is not valued as much as tangible, worldly goods: "riches, pleasures, glory, and our friends" (II.12, 421 [324]). Thus,

Christian faith, even of the sincerely motivated faithful, is often counteracted by human desires, which Montaigne interprets not as weakness of the
flesh but as weakness of faith. If people truly believed, they would not so
easily be swayed. If Montaigne had his way, it seems, we would believe in
God as we believe our senses. This kind of visceral and phenomenological
approach to the world recurs repeatedly throughout the *Essays* and emerges
as one of Montaigne's central desires.[68] However, it is doubtful whether
such a simple, phenomenological mode of being-in-the-world is religious.

Montaigne explains the problem of Christian belief by revealing what
he considers to be the true basis of Christianity: it is based on custom, not
revelation. The problems of Christian belief are not unique to Montaigne's
age nor due to problems with its authorities or power. Rather, Montaigne
argues that it has to do with why people believe what they believe.
Anticipating John Stuart Mill's argument of some 250 years later,[69]
Montaigne concludes that Christianity is embraced by its adherents just as
all other practices are. Christianity is no different from any other human
custom.

> [W]e receive our religion only in our own way and with our own hands, and
> not otherwise than as other religions are received. We happen to have been
> born in a country where it was in practice; or we regard its antiquity or the
> authority of the men who have maintained it; or we fear the threats it fastens
> upon unbelievers, or pursue its promises. Those considerations should be
> employed in our belief, but as subsidiaries; they are human ties. Another
> region, other witnesses, similar promises and threats, might imprint upon
> us in the same way a contrary belief.
>
> We are Christians by the same title that we are Perigordians[70] or
> Germans. (II.12, 422 [324-25])

On the one hand, Montaigne could be seen as chastising his readers for
treating Christianity just like any other custom: "we are Christians just as
we are Germans, but it should be otherwise," he could be seen to be saying.
This interpretation gains support from the phrase above that human
considerations should play a role in our lives, but only as subsidiaries, i.e.,
faith should be the main element of our lives.[71] On the other hand,
Montaigne has been vehemently arguing that faith is patently not the main
element of our lives. Even amidst the wars of religion that Montaigne was
suffering through, where individuals were willing to fight and die under the
banner of their faiths, Montaigne argues that much of the fighting is fanned
by opportunists and cynics, and he cannot seem to find anyone who believes
in God and who acts according to His precepts. Faith does not exert that

hold on human life. These statements taken *in toto* seem to offer a simple description of the human condition. It is evident, Montaigne says, that Christianity, exactly like every religion, is created and subscribed to for human reasons. "Subscribed to" is the way to put it, because human beings do not "believe" in it as they believe what they see with their eyes. We adopt one religion for the same accidental reasons that we adopt any habit. Indeed, Montaigne seems as though he would be happy if religion held as much power over his contemporaries as their other customs and opinions do. The former interpretation is consistent with fideism; the latter with atheism. The fact that Montaigne launches into a discussion of atheism in the very next sentence suggests that the latter interpretation is the correct one.[72] Christianity is a custom like any other.

Montaigne has shot his opening salvo: he has begun to tame human vanity by attacking the practice of one of its main sources, Christianity, the pre-eminent authority of his day. His argument is as follows: most Christian leaders are corrupt and do not believe; the flocks are sincere but do not understand what it means to believe, they merely act from habit; and there is truly nothing divinely revealed for them to believe in—Christianity is a human creation just as is every other human custom.

Vanity III: Attack on Christian Theory as Anthropocentric

After having decimated Sebond and Christian epistemological certitude, Montaigne launches the main prong of his skeptical attack on human vanity, which is aimed at the anthropocentric hubris that characterizes some of Christianity's key theoretical tenets. Later Montaigne will systematically analyze key concepts, such as God, human nature, reason, and the senses. But before making these systematic critiques, Montaigne attempts to unravel the psychology behind the views—and he does so in a manner devastating to the traditional Western opinions of the dignity of the human race. Montaigne attacks the important cosmological place that humanity, at least in the Western world, has traditionally assigned to itself: above the animals and akin to the gods. Montaigne attempts to put humanity in its proper place by attacking human pride from above and below, distancing humanity from the gods and lowering it toward the animals.

To humble his readers even more than he already has, Montaigne proposes to consider "man alone, without outside assistance, armed solely with his own weapons, and deprived of divine grace and knowledge" (II.12, 427 [328]). This move is not unique in the history of Western thought. The Latin Averroists made this move purportedly to support faith, although there is considerable scholarly disagreement whether this avowal was sincere. Rousseau made the same move, and when he casts the so-called facts of religion aside, he clearly disbelieves them despite his speaking of the "evident" truths of the "Holy Scriptures."[73] Montaigne separates reason and religion, saying that the realm of heavenly grace is man's "whole honor, his strength, and the foundation of his being" (II.12, 427 [328]), and, like Rousseau, he does not mean this. We have already seen that Montaigne considers religion to be a human construction. Accordingly, after detaching reason and revelation, Montaigne praises religion in only a qualified manner: because it is "useful" to particular societies, not because it is true. Montaigne's view of the natural status and natural abilities of human beings is far from the strand of Christianity that celebrates man's being as akin to God's. Rather, it is downright humbling, and to the extent that he cites any Christian authors at all, it is only to the strand of Christian thought that emphasizes man's debased state.[74] But rather than pointing to religion as humanity's saving grace, Montaigne goes in distinctly secular directions.

Insofar as Christianity preaches humility and meekness, one might think that it would be an excellent cure for natural human vanity. According to Montaigne, however, the contrary is true: the Christian religion epitomizes human conceit. Christianity praises humility, but it does so in a self-contradictory and anthropocentric manner, encouraging human pride even while condemning it. Pride results from some of the central tenets of Christianity: man is created in God's image and human beings are the lords and masters of earth and all its creatures. Montaigne explicitly attacks both of these notions as the height of unfounded pride. He asks:

> Is it possible to imagine anything so ridiculous as that this miserable and puny creature, who is not even master of himself, exposed to the attacks of all things, should call himself master and emperor of the universe, the least part of which it is not in his power to know, much less to command? And this privilege that he attributes to himself of being the only one in this great edifice who has this capacity to recognize its beauty and its parts, the only one who can give thanks for it to the architect and keep an account of the receipts and expenses of the world: who has sealed him this privilege? Let him show us his letters patent for this great and splendid charge. (II.12, 427 [329])

In blatant effrontery to the authority of the Bible, Montaigne questions humanity's "privilege" and "patent" to rule the earth, demands to know who gave mankind this authority, and demands to see the written proof—which is what the Bible claims to be! Montaigne's doubt that man is created in

God's image and has the authority to name, classify, and rule over the other animals clearly contradicts Genesis 1.26-31. But rather than try to disprove the biblical account, Montaigne dismisses it as the peak of anthropocentric vanity. The greatest human hubris would be to imagine ourselves as the creators of the universe. Because our power reveals itself as unable to do anything of the sort, i.e. create new universes, one supposes that no doctrine has ever maintained this.[75] But the biblical claims that human beings are created in God's image and that they are the lords and masters of the planet are perhaps the next most hubristic claims imaginable.[76] So when Montaigne laments that "of all vanities the vainest is man" (II.12, 427 [328]) and that "Presumption is our natural and original malady. The most vulnerable and frail of all creatures is man, and at the same time the most arrogant" (II.12, 429 [330]), he is not just decrying mankind's fallen state and original sin. The hubris of Christianity is part of the problem, not the solution. Montaigne's argument is not Christian. Revelation has no authority.

Just as Montaigne distances the human species from God, he lowers it toward the animals. He blames mankind's hubristic condemnation of the animals on the same source that leads humanity to view itself as created in God's image: its unruly imagination.

> It is by the vanity of this same imagination that he equals himself to God, attributes to himself divine characteristics, picks himself out and separates himself from the horde of other creatures, carves out their shares to his fellows and companions the animals, and distributes among them such portions of faculties and powers as he sees fit. How does he know, by the force of his intelligence, the secret internal stirrings of animals? By what comparison between them and us does he infer the stupidity that he attributes to them? (II.12, 429-30 [331])

Montaigne's lowering of humanity to the animals revolves around two questions: do the animals have the same abilities as we? And if so, why do we tell ourselves they do not? The first question is one of biology and anatomy, which Montaigne tries to answer with an unpersuasive but admittedly humbling narrative of examples purporting to show an equality among all living creatures. We will first consider these, and we will then proceed to the second question, which is one of psychology and is far more relevant to Montaigne's philosophical intentions.

Montaigne's humbling comparison of man and the animals is ironic. His principle of procedure is that "We must infer from like results like faculties"

(II.12, 437 [336]), which is surprising from someone whose first chapter is entitled "By Diverse Means We Arrive at the Same End." This juxtaposition implies that Montaigne may be less than fully committed to the argument he is advancing here. This suspicion is confirmed in three ways. First, there is little doubt that Montaigne does not believe many of the stories and the interpretations of animal behavior that he conveys. A typically outrageous claim is that elephants pray, since we see them, after many ablutions and purifications, raising their trunks like arms and keeping their eyes fixed toward the rising sun, standing still in meditation and contemplation at certain hours of the day (II.12, 446 [343]). But Montaigne does not claim that this interpretation of elephantine behavior is true, merely that "we can say" it. Later, Montaigne expresses doubt about the accuracy of his sources generally (II.12, 505-6 [390-91]). Second, it is clear that even the authors of Montaigne's sourcebooks on animal behavior, Cicero, Pliny, Herodotus, and Plutarch, are themselves skeptical of the stories they record. For example, Plutarch's stories are written in dialogues where the characters are engaged in a one-upmanship of animal stories. Finally, at the beginning of the next section of the "Apology," Montaigne drops the claim that the animals have the same abilities as humans, conceding that human beings have unique qualities, freedom of imagination and reason. Montaigne is not being duplicitous, but he misses no opportunity to humble humankind, even if he sometimes has to exaggerate his claims to do so.

Despite his exaggerations, Montaigne's assault on human self-centeredness is thought provoking and likely to have a humbling effect on the reader. He begins his comparison of man to the animals with an easily accessible example: "When I play with my cat," he asks, "who knows if I am not a pastime to her more than she is to me?" (II.12, 430 [331]). Just because we keep animals as pets does not mean we are superior to them. Force proves nothing; slaves are kept on these same grounds. And a case is to be made, as Diogenes did and Montesquieu and Hegel were to do, that the keeper is really more enslaved than the kept. Certainly, cat owners will acknowledge the truth of this. Montaigne also attacks man's claim of uniquely possessing speech and reason, the characteristics alleged as the basis of human privilege. Like humans, the animals communicate with their own kind through voice, motions, and signs. Humans cannot communicate with other species through speech, but whose fault is that? "This defect that hinders communication between them and us, why is it not just as much ours as theirs?" (II.12, 430 [331]). They cannot understand us any more than we understand them. By the same reasoning, they might consider us beasts just as we consider them beasts. Similarly, humans flatter themselves that they alone have reason and that they alone act based on reflection. But Montaigne asks if honeybees can have such an ordered community "without reason and foresight," how birds choose the most suitable place to build their nests and construct it, now adding clay, now water, without judging ("*jugement*") that hardness is softened by moistening, and why a spider varies the thickness of its webs and the type of its knots "unless she has the power of reflection, and thought, and inference" (II.12, 432 [332-3]). Humanity claims a superiority over the animals because it has reason, yet it cannot imitate many of the animals' works. There is a certain speciousness to these arguments, because, as Montaigne ultimately concedes, human beings are the unique possessors of reason and free imagination. But Montaigne hopes that his readers, when thinking about these arguments, will wonder at the animals' many accomplishments and see the animals—and themselves—from a different perspective.

Montaigne continues his attack on human vanity by arguing that animals are in many ways better than human beings. Some hear better, some see better. Many are stronger. Echoing Machiavelli, Montaigne notes that they hunt both by force, like the lion, and by subtlety and cleverness, like the fox. Moreover, the animals are nobler than man because none has ever let himself be enslaved to another of his species "for lack of heart" (II.12, 439 [338]). The animals have "science and knowledge" because many, such as certain goats and tortoises, out of the millions of herbs around them, know the exact one that can cure their illnesses and wounds (II.12, 440 [339]). Birds are taught to speak, many animals are taught tricks, dances, and to act. Furthermore, Democritus "concluded and proved, that the animals have taught us most of the arts, as the spider to weave and sew, the swallow to build, the swan and the nightingale music, and many animals, through imitation of them, to practice medicine" (II.12, 442 [340]).[77] Montaigne cites many other examples of animals engaged in friendship, fidelity, virtues (justice, courage, clemency, magnanimity), and vices (jealousy, envy, debauchery, trickery, war). But even though animals possess vices, he argues that human beings are in many ways the worst of all the animals. While animals and humans both kill, Montaigne argues that humans kill each other and are cruel to each other for frivolous reasons of vanity which do not plague the animals. Moreover, he asserts that "we are the only animal whose defectiveness offends our own fellows, and the only ones who have to hide, in our natural actions, from our own species" (II.12, 463 [356-57]). One might think that possessing shame is a sign of human superiority, but Montaigne finds it strange that mankind (at least in Christendom) is most ashamed of the act of procreation, the most natural and necessary act of the species, but not ashamed of its more horrendous behavior. And it is "a wonderful sign of our defectiveness that acquaintance and familiarity disgust us with one another" (II.12, 464 [357]). But in keeping with the polemical nature of the entire comparison to the animals, Montaigne's conclusion is not that human beings are worse than the animals, but that "We are neither above nor below the rest" (II.12, 436 [336]); "there is more difference between a given man and a given man than between a given animal and a given man" (II.12, 444 [342]). So while many of Montaigne's comparisons are absurd, the number of them and the spirit in which they are presented aim to make the readers reflect on their presumptuous presuppositions. In fact, we are animals too, even though we have distinctive abilities. And there is something wondrous and as yet unexplained about animal behavior.

The underlying psychological question in this section is why human beings consider the animals to be inferior. "Since animals are born, beget, feed, act, move, live, and die in a manner so close to our own," Montaigne argues, "all that we detract from their motive powers, and all that we add to ours to raise our state above theirs, can in no way proceed from the judgment of our reason" (II.12, 448-49 [345]). Despite all the similarities between us, we explain them by different causes. Why do we attribute to the animals a natural and servile inclination when we do not feel such an inclination ourselves and their works often exceed what we can do by either nature or art?

The answer, Montaigne says, is human vanity: "The vanity of our presumption makes us prefer to owe our ability to our powers [rather] than to nature's liberality; and we enrich the other animals with natural goods and renounce them in their favor, in order to honor and ennoble ourselves with goods acquired" (II.12, 437 [337]). We attribute the animals' deeds to instinct rather than reason. We assert that the animals do what they do out of compulsion, not out of choice, as a way to demean them. We, on the other hand, flatter ourselves that "goods acquired" make us nobler and better. We earned them. God gave us life, we tell ourselves, but we give ourselves the good life, thus ennobling ourselves even more than God does. Montaigne considers such vain distinctions to be the peak of pride, arguing that there is but one law and one nature for all living creatures and that our differences from the animals are only ones of "orders and degrees" (II.12, 436-37 [336]).[78] Throughout the *Essays* Montaigne refers to the human condition. Here he argues that our condition is fundamentally the same as the animals'.

To the extent that there is a difference between man and the animals, however, Montaigne argues that it is to man's disadvantage. Human beings often break away from the natural order because our "freedom of imagination" deceives us and makes us unruly and licentious. We are alienated from ourselves, says Montaigne, not because of the economic system or political regime; the problem is in our mind. Our imagination, a natural faculty, tempts us and leads us out of ourselves. Instead of pursuing natural desires—eating, drinking, and procreating—we pursue "superfluous and artificial" desires.[79] Our tendency to think about the future ruins the present. Our mind takes us away from the here and now, making us anxious and afraid about the future. "Fear, desire, hope, project us toward the future and steal from us the feeling and consideration of what is" (I.3, 18 [8]); "We are never at home, we are always beyond" (I.3, 18 [8]).

Human beings are, unfortunately, contradictory creatures. We have a natural state that includes a natural faculty, imagination, that tends to alienate us from ourselves. Freedom of imagination leads to "unruliness in thought" and "is an advantage that is sold [to man] very dear, and in which he has little cause to glory, for from it springs the principal source of the ills that oppress him: sin, disease, irresolution, confusion, despair" (II.12, 437 [336]).[80] Montaigne thus partially agrees with the Christian description of human beings as debased; Eden ends where the human faculties begin.[81]

But unlike Christianity, Montaigne does not lament our natural condition as a "fall," or despise our natural being. It is no reason to despise ourselves just because our natural condition does not accord with something that can be imagined. He writes:

> As for the opinion that disdains our life, it is ridiculous. For after all, life is our being, it is our all. Things that have a nobler and richer being may accuse ours; but it is against nature that we despise ourselves and care nothing about ourselves. It is a malady peculiar to man, and not seen in any other creature, to hate and disdain himself.
>
> It is by a similar vanity that we wish to be something other than we are. (II.3, 334 [254])

Rather than flagellate ourselves from some supposedly divine point of view, Montaigne wants human beings to accept themselves for what they are.

Montaigne's un-Christian analysis of the problem, contains an un-Christian remedy: imitate the animals. Rather than urging human beings to uplift themselves and follow God, he turns down toward the animals: "Animals are much more self-controlled than we are, and restrain themselves with more moderation within the limits that nature has prescribed to us" (II.12, 450 [346]). Montaigne, like Aristotle and unlike Hobbes, speaks of natural limits. Learning to remain within these natural limits, both in action and desire, he suggests, is the key to human happiness.

> We attribute to ourselves imaginary and fanciful goods, goods future and absent, for which human capacity by itself cannot answer, or goods which we attribute to ourselves falsely through the license of our opinion, like reason, knowledge, and honor. And to them for their share we leave essential, tangible, and palpable goods: peace, repose, security, innocence, and health—health, I say, the finest and richest present that nature can give to us. (II.12, 464 [357])

For Montaigne, health and the other goods of the animals are also beneficial for human beings. Health is mental as well as physical. Avoiding fear and anxiety is as important as avoiding pain and disease. Indeed, Montaigne emphasizes the mental aspect of this when he makes his standard concrete; our objective should be tranquility. Montaigne's ideal is a sensual and robust tranquility, happily compatible with bodily pleasures, a tranquility that more closely resembles the lusty, sensual tranquility recommended by Epicurus[82] than the know-nothing tranquility of Pyrrho or the asceticism of saints. This combination of inner peace and sensual satisfaction, free of the falsities produced by unruly minds, serves as a standard throughout the *Essays*.

Vanity IV: Obedience and Simplicity as Solutions to Human Vanity

The question arises, however: how is this tranquility to be achieved? The "Apology," taken with all of Montaigne's writings, suggests two very different answers to this question: follow external authority or follow oneself. By conforming to external standards, an individual is relieved of the anxiety entailed in choosing for oneself (and society is inoculated from the crazy opinions and deeds of misguided individuals). By following oneself an individual assumes the burden of choice, but is freer to uncover a truer impression of nature than the external authorities have been able to establish. Montaigne entertains both as serious possibilities, and recommends each for different people. Self-reliance is acceptable only for those few who can adequately fight through false opinions and false presumptions and regulate their behavior by themselves. For everyone else, who either cannot get beyond the customs in which they have been born or who can see through them but are unable to replace them with a truer standard for their behavior, it is better to conform to the external authorities of their time and place than to follow their own inadequate powers. Following his critique of human vanity, the solution that first emerges emphasizes obedience; indeed, this "solution" is the very next subject in the "Apology." But we must press the question: "obedience to what?" By pressing this question, we can see why Montaigne ultimately rejects blind obedience as a solution for thinking people.

Although Montaigne ultimately rejects obedience as a path to tranquility for thinking people, he nonetheless emphasizes it as the way to achieve tranquility for most people. Thus, it is important to follow this thread of his dialectic. Whereas he had previously derived tranquility to be the human good from his analysis of the animals, he now claims to derive it not from the animals but from philosophy. "On this there is general agreement among all the philosophers of all sects, that the sovereign good consists in tranquility of soul and body" (II.12, 468 [360]). It is doubtful that all philosophers have always held this position, and Montaigne offers no argument to support his claim but merely asserts it. Conveniently, this dictate of "all philosophers" coincides with what he deduced from his study of the animals. However, he here suggests a "solution" under which most philosophers would bridle. This solution emerges in the context of his doubting the extent to which most human beings can benefit from learning. Montaigne argues that tranquility is more effectively achieved for most people through simple obedience than through the rational pursuit of knowledge. Surprisingly for someone who spent his life reading and writing, Montaigne here says that he only moderately values learning. He ranks it no more "necessary for life" than glory, nobility, dignity, beauty, or riches, which he says are only remotely useful, "and a little more in fancy than in nature" (II.12, 466-67 [359]). Learning, while capable of producing only a slight reward, can however easily lead to disaster. Montaigne asserts, "The plague of man is the opinion of knowledge," by which he means that those presumptuous men, religious or secular, who think they know what is good and right for the world cause untold horrors by trying to rearrange it according to their vision (II.12, 467 [360]). This is so on several levels. Politically, their presumptuous actions can lead to intolerance, cruelty, and zealotry. Those who are certain of their beliefs are less likely to compromise and more likely to try to force them on others. Psychologically, opinions lead to new—and crazy—desires, fears, and anxieties. Opinions lead people to pursue imaginary goods at the expense of real ones, even to accept real ills in pursuit of fancies. On a practical level, Montaigne argues, knowledge does not necessarily relieve misfortune, and even if it sometimes does, misfortune is better dealt with by reliance on deeply ingrained customs. (He is criticizing the Stoics and other philosophical sects that claim that their "knowledge" relieves them from suffering.) Montaigne also criticizes learning because the subtlest minds are more liable to madness and because some sects, such as the Stoics, deal with ills by idiotically denying that they are bad.[83] In short, Montaigne does not here recommend the rational cultivation of the self as the solution for human ills: "humility and submissiveness alone can make a good man. The knowledge of his duty should not be left to each man's judgment; it should be prescribed to him, not left to the choice of his reason" (II.12, 467 [359]). "[T]o obey is the principal function of a reasonable soul. . . . From obeying and yielding spring all other virtues, as from presumption all sin" (II.12, 467 [359]). But it is important to emphasize the context of this discussion: most people, including most of the so-called "learned," are incapable of wisely regulating themselves. This lack of confidence in most human beings is what accounts for the anti-individualistic strand of thought that is woven throughout the "Apology." Tranquility is best achieved for these people by obedience.

Montaigne's emphasis on obedience parallels a powerful current of early-modern Christian fideism that was popular in the sixteenth century. Having proponents from within both the Catholic and Protestant camps, this strand of Christian thought argued that since human beings were fundamentally frail and unable to discern the best way to live based on their own unaided powers, they should surrender their judgment to that of the Church.[84] Like these Christian skeptics, Montaigne here emphasizes the inadequacy and dangers of unaided human thought and agrees that law is essential to combat the immodesty and unruliness of the human mind. Without law, he says, we would devour each other: "Judging by the imbecility and infinite variety of our reasons and opinions, we would finally forge for ourselves duties that would set us to eating one another, as Epicurus says" (II.12, 467 [359]).[85] Indeed, Montaigne's own experience has shown that the quickest minds of his time have been extraordinarily "incontinent in the license of their opinions and conduct" (II.12, 541 [419]). "Our mind is an erratic, dangerous, and heedless tool; it is hard to impose order and moderation upon it" (II.12, 541 [419]). He concludes, "People are right to give the tightest possible barriers to the human mind. In study, as in everything else, its steps must be counted and regulated for it" (II.12, 541 [419]), and "the principal qualities for the preservation of human society require a soul that is open, docile, and with little presumption" (II.12, 477 [368]). Montaigne's call for surrender of the self to an external authority is consistent with Christian fideistic critiques of human capacities.[86]

But Montaigne does not call for surrender to the Church simply. Unlike the Christian skeptics of early modern times, he does not think that Christianity, and it alone, possesses the truth or the sole means to bring about the fundamental tranquility of which he speaks. Preaching religious obedience alone is inconsistent with his claim about the human origins of religion, which he has made clear. Montaigne is just as clear that the prescribed Christian authorities are external to individuals: "It is not by reasoning or by our understanding that we have received our religion; it is by external authority and command" (II.12, 479-80 [369]). Montaigne does sometimes talk about obediently "recognizing a heavenly superior and benefactor" (II.12, 467 [359]), but he makes it clear that any kind of law will do, and that all law, even religious law, is artificial: "The limits of the chase must be *artificially* determined for it. They bridle and bind it with *religions*, laws, customs, science, precepts, mortal and immortal punishments and rewards" (II.12, 541 [419], my emphasis). Note Montaigne's impious boldness: all of these things—including religion, precepts, and the idea of "immortal punishments and rewards"—are human inventions. The calm psyche that Montaigne desires might be achieved by a pious obedience to Christianity, but it can also be achieved by being obedient to other authorities as well. The key point is that to the extent that Montaigne praises Christianity it is not on religious grounds but on the effect that it has on the follower—an effect available in many other, and perhaps just as good, ways.

The only way to reconcile the paradox of Montaigne's religious statements and his calls for obedience in itself—and do it consistently with the criteria he has set up—is to conclude that in making these arguments Montaigne is less concerned with the truth of the belief, i.e., its epistemological status, than with its effect on the believer. Conforming to beliefs that one accepts, he argues, can leave the mind at peace, the psyche healthy and whole. Montaigne echoes the tradition of surrender and obedience that was common at the time, but he develops it in another direction. To the extent that he upholds Christianity, it is because this is the dominant belief system of his day and preserving it will be beneficial in effect, not because he believes it to be true. For it to have the desired effect on the believers, they might need to think that it is true, but Montaigne does not want his thoughtful readers to be similarly deluded. This is consistent with Montaigne's well-known (although not decisive) conservative call to simply follow the authorities that exist in any given place and time.[87]

But there is, of course, a serious problem with simply obeying authority as a way of life: a follower of authority has no way of judging the truth, justice, or goodness of that to which he or she conforms. From the point of view of the *effects* produced in the believer's psyche, the substance of the belief is less important than the fact of believing. Conforming to any belief soothes the mind of the believer. This is analogous to Tocqueville's statement on the civic importance of religion to a society. From the point of view of the society, Tocqueville says, it does not matter whether the believed religion is in fact true, just that it moderates and regulates citizens' behavior in socially beneficial ways.[88] However, the substances of different beliefs have different political consequences; it matters to the tranquility of the world whether a society believes in Buddhism or Nazism. And as Tocqueville also notes, from the point of view of a thoughtful inquirer (let alone a genuine believer), it makes all the difference. One wants to follow not just any authority but a true, just, and good one. Montaigne's discussion of obedience is often left vague, so we might assume Montaigne refers to religious obedience. However, the standard Montaigne uses to judge is that which is "most useful and appropriate for his life" (II.12, 467 [359]), which recalls the first paragraph of the essay, and the discussion on religion, where utility was the standard.[89] Montaigne judges Christianity by its usefulness, and not what is useful by the extent to which it promotes Christianity.

While Montaigne judges obedience to the Church as acceptable because it relieves an individual's mind of stress and anxiety, he suggests a more useful authority to which an individual should conform: *habitude naturelle*. Picking up on the phenomenological simplicity that the animals represented, Montaigne suggests that one follow customs that more closely approximate a vision of nature that he deems naturally good. Although Montaigne uses the phrase *habitude naturelle* only one time (II.12, 470 [362]), I believe it expresses one of the key concepts of his entire political thought. The phrase "*habitude naturelle*," which translates as "natural habit," seems contradictory. By definition, nature and habit are usually seen to be opposed to one another. Montaigne gives three examples of what he means by this. None is religious. Montaigne's ideal of simplicity belongs to a plowman, the animals, and the native Brazilians of the New World.

> [A] plowman letting himself follow his natural appetites, measuring things only by the present sensation, without knowledge and without prognostica-tion . . . has pain only when he has it; whereas [an intellectual] often has the stone in his soul before he has it in his loins. As if he were not in time to suffer the pain when he is in it, he anticipates it in imagination and runs to meet it. (II.12, 470 [362])

The health of the animals shows how many human ills are caused by "the agitation of our mind" (II.12, 471 [362]). The Brazilians have "tranquility and serenity of their souls, unburdened with any tense or unpleasant passion or thought or occupation, as people who spent their life in admirable simplicity and ignorance, without letters, without law, without king, without religion of any kind" (II.12, 471 [362]). Not only does Montaigne not mention religion to illustrate his ideal of obedience and simplicity, but he praises people—and animals—who do without it. A pious Christian is not on the list, because, as we have seen, Montaigne argues that Christianity, perhaps because of the pridefulness built into it, ordinarily fails to bring about truly Christian behavior. The keys are simplicity and obedience as such—not religion or Christianity.

Montaigne's praise of the simplicity of *habitude naturelle* is ironic on at least two levels. On one level, it is the culmination of his attempt to humble the presumptions of his Christian readers. Just as his praise of Sebond and the animals is a rhetorical device to humble his readers, so too is his praise of such a non-Christian, indeed non-European, way of life. Nonetheless, because this image of obedience is left standing as the purest embodiment of this "solution" to a world in which knowledge is scarce, and because it recurs throughout the *Essays*, chapter 2 offers extensive and systematic analysis of its political ramifications. On a second level, Montaigne's anti-individualistic suggestion that obedience in any form can serve as a "solution" for human problems is ironic, because the entire tenor and tone of Montaigne's work is nothing if not a radical questioning of authority and a search for individual meaning. And insofar as the reader follows Montaigne's thought, the reader too is led through such questioning. Obedience is Montaigne's recommendation for those who are incapable of using reason well, those who get carried away by the unruliness of their minds and imaginations. Up until this point in the argument, he has been arguing that reason is harmful to most men: "Reason . . . is a plague to many and salutary only to a few" (II.12, 466 [358]).[90] It is these "many" that Montaigne has had in mind. There is a question as to whether "the many" represents the uneducated masses or an existential quality with which every human being must deal. In any case, this explains his preoccupation with upholding piety and why he suggests simple obedience as the solution for the problem created by human ignorance. But Montaigne is aware that this solution is inadequate for truly thinking people, so he does not leave it at that. He launches a whole new kind of skeptical inquiry that suggests an entirely different solution to the human problem. One inquiry is ending and another beginning; the questions concerning how one should live in a skeptical world cannot be fully answered until after Montaigne's second, and more systematic, critique.

III. A Systematic Critique of the Human Faculties

After having systematically attacked human presumption and suggesting that the happiest human beings possess the simplicity of the animals, Indians, and commoners by not developing their critical faculties and surrendering themselves to an external authority, the second part of the "Apology" embarks on an altogether different skeptical inquiry and arrives at an altogether different image of a good human life. The first part of the "Apology," concerned with most men, emphasizes simple obedience as the solution to human ills. The second part undermines the basis for believing in any kind of authority at all—Montaigne argues that human beings *do not* and *cannot* possess knowledge.

The second part of the "Apology," analyzed in the rest of this chapter, aims to show that human beings *do not* and *cannot* possess knowledge by providing a systematic critique of the human faculties. To show that human beings do not possess any knowledge, Montaigne explores what humanity has achieved in its millennia of attempting to acquire it. To do this, Montaigne shifts gears and proposes to "leave the people aside" and examine "man in his highest estate . . . that small number of excellent and select men" who have been born with and developed human capacities to their fullest extent, because "it is in them that the utmost height of human nature is found" (II.12, 481 [371]). Although the "Apology's" argument has until this point suggested that the best human life is more akin to the simplicity of the common people, their wisdom is in living, not in thinking. Their happiness is by habit, not by systematic thought. To show the limits of reason, Montaigne examines its most shining embodiments. But Montaigne does not leave it at that. He aims to prove that human beings cannot know anything by systematically examining reason and the senses, the only human faculties by which knowledge can be attained. But this radical skepticism has its limits, and just as the first part of the "Apology" suggests a way of living with skepticism, so too does the second. After rejecting all grounds for *transcendent* knowledge of any kind, Montaigne delineates the only acceptable realm of an alternative *phenomenological* kind of knowledge: the self. This leads Montaigne to suggest a solution to the human problem that is tolerant, indeed celebratory, of individual creativity.

Montaigne classifies thinkers by their epistemological positions.

Everyone who inquires, he says, must come to one of three positions: either we can know, we cannot know, or we cannot know whether we can know or not. These groups were called dogmatists, Academic skeptics, and Pyrrhonist skeptics, respectively (II.12, 482 [371]).[91] At first glance, this classification seems to cover all the possibilities, except it leaves out the one that most modern scholars ascribe to Montaigne, fideism.[92] Fideists agree with the Academics that no knowledge is possible by rational or human means, but they believe that truths have been revealed to us in the form of the Bible. These truths, they claim, are the only truths available to us and can be grasped only by faith. Thus, fideism is a particular kind of dogmatism. In order to define precisely Montaigne's skepticism, we shall analyze Montaigne's views in light of these possible positions.

Montaigne is not a dogmatist. When discussing the dogmatists, Montaigne's method resembles that of Sextus Empiricus, but with a unique twist. He examines philosophers in the fashion of Sextus, by cataloguing their different and conflicting opinions on an array of issues. All of the main discussions—on God, the soul, and the body—begin with long lists of the numerous opinions held on that topic. Montaigne also draws Sextus' conclusion, that faced with such conflicting opinions, there is no way to adjudicate between them. Unlike Sextus, however, Montaigne does not take the claims of philosophers at face value. Instead, he reveals what he considers to be their secret motives. This revelation greatly affects what we think of their views.

If any truth has been achieved by humanity, it would have been achieved by one of the famous so-called dogmatists. Not only is Montaigne not a dogmatist, but he does not think that the dogmatists are either. On the contrary, Montaigne claims that "most of them have put on the mask of assurance only to look better" (II.12, 487 [375]). Dogmatists only choose to *appear* dogmatic—in reality, they are not. Montaigne never discusses the minority that might have sincerely held their dogmatic convictions. Perhaps they are inferior thinkers unworthy of consideration, perhaps they do not fit his scheme, or perhaps they are the religious dogmatists like Sebond. Whatever the reason, the point of Montaigne's discussion is to humble human pretension. If these greatest, most celebrated embodiments of human intellectual achievement have not attained knowledge about the most pressing questions—and understand that they have not attained it—then it is unlikely that anyone else has either. To prove his claims, Montaigne discusses the most famous so-called dogmatists, Aristotle, Plato, and Cicero, at length. Let us analyze his interpretations.

Montaigne doubts that philosophers believe their doctrines for several reasons. First, he claims that if one reads them carefully, one will see that they claim only to give something plausible, not true. He points to various statements of Plato's and Cicero's where they explicitly say that "probability" is the best that human beings can achieve.[93] Second, Montaigne asserts that many philosophers are misinterpreted. Plato is considered by some to be a dogmatist, by others to be a doubter, and by yet others in some things the former and others the latter. Montaigne, however, knows exactly what he thinks: "in my opinion, never was teaching wavering and noncommittal if his is not" (II.12, 489 [377]). "The leader of his dialogues, Socrates, is always asking questions and stirring up discussion, never concluding, never satisfying; and says he has no other knowledge than that of opposing" (II.12, 489 [377]). Of "Anaxagoras, Democritus, Parmenides, Xenophanes, and others," Montaigne says, "their way of writing is doubtful in substance, and their plan is to inquire rather than to instruct, even though they sprinkle their style with dogmatic cadences. Do we not see this as well in both Seneca and Plutarch? How much they say now one way, now another, for those who study them closely!" (II.12, 489 [377]). Third, Montaigne cannot persuade himself that such obviously intelligent people believed such questionable doctrines as that of Epicurus' Atoms and Plato's Ideas. He writes,

> I cannot easily persuade myself that Epicurus, Plato, and Pythagoras gave us their Atoms, their Ideas, and their Numbers as good coin of the realm. They were too wise to establish their articles of faith on anything so uncertain and so debatable. But into the obscurity and ignorance of this world, each one of those great men labored to bring some semblance of light, such as it was; and they exercised their minds on such conceptions as had at least a pleasant and subtle appearance, provided that, false though they might be, they could hold their own against opposing ideas. "These are created by each man's imaginative genius, not by the power of his knowledge" [Seneca]. (II.12, 491-92 [379])

Self-consciously deployed imagination, not truth, underlies their discourses. Montaigne does not consider even Aristotle, the so-called prince of dogmatists, to be dogmatic. According to Montaigne, Aristotle knows that he does not know the truth about the things he discusses; he merely tries to outdo other philosophers in imagining their likenesses, "*la verisimilitude.*" "[W]e learn from him that knowing much gives occasion for doubting more. We see him often deliberately covering himself with such thick and inextricable obscurity that we cannot pick out anything of his opinion" (II,12, 487 [376]).[94] In short, Montaigne claims that none of the so-called dogmatists is truly dogmatic.

But if it is the case that philosophers are not dogmatic, why did they advance such unbelievable theoretical speculations? One answer that Montaigne acknowledges is that philosophers want to be recognized as superior to the rest. They seek glory. But Montaigne cites other reasons as the main ones. Philosophers philosophize primarily because it is pleasant. "It must not be thought strange if people despairing of the capture have yet taken pleasure in the chase; study being in itself a pleasant occupation" (II.12, 490 [378]). "They wanted to consider everything, to weigh everything, and they found that occupation suited to the natural curiosity in us" (II.12, 492 [379]). This seems to be the main motive of Montaigne himself. But this does not explain why philosophers write and publicly publish ideas in which they do not believe. "By profession," Montaigne says, "they do not always present their opinion openly and apparently; they have hidden it now in the fabulous shades of poetry, now under some other mask" (II.12, 527-28 [408]). They publicize *faux* ideas, according to Montaigne, as pedagogy—both for individuals and for their societies. Some of the philosophers, Aristotle for example, want us to think our way through their tangles. They arrange their arguments to show us their problems, thereby forcing us to think them through: "By the variety and instability of opinions they lead us as by the hand, tacitly, to this conclusion of their inconclusiveness" (II.12, 527 [408]). This is what Montaigne means when he says that Aristotle's philosophy is "in fact a Pyrrhonism in an affirmative form" (II.12, 487 [376]). Writers such as Aristotle, Montaigne argues, also write this way out of a playful sense of pedagogy, to lead the readers "as by the hand, tacitly," into the pleasure of thinking. Philosophers want to encourage philosophizing and evoke wonder in others. "[M]ost philosophers affect difficulty . . . to bring out the vanity of the subject and keep the curiosity of our mind amused" (II.12, 488 [376]). Montaigne writes:

> For myself, I prefer to believe that they treated knowledge casually, like a toy to play around with, and amused themselves with reason as with a vain and frivolous instrument, putting forward all sorts of notions and fancies, sometimes more studied, sometimes more loose. This same Plato who defines man as he would a chicken, says elsewhere, after Socrates, that in truth he does not know what man is, and that he is one part of the world as difficult as any to know. (II.12, 527-28 [408])

This playfulness applies to Montaigne's writing, too. Insofar as every reader must "essay" Montaigne's essays in order to make sense of them, the reader is forced to retrace and rethink Montaigne's own thought process, which he considers to be immensely pleasurable. And just as Montaigne describes philosophic arguments as consciously illustrating the "vanity" and "curiosity" of the human mind, so he describes the origin of his writing project as taming the "chimeras and fantastic monsters" of his own mind (I.8, 34 [21]). Philosophy is serious play. It illustrates and sheds light on the inner workings—and limits—of the human mind.

A final reason philosophers wrote dogmatically, according to Montaigne, was for the public benefit: "Some things they wrote for the needs of society, like their religions" (II.12, 492 [379]). Thus, they teach those who look carefully to doubt by showing the limits of inquiry. For those who look less carefully, they formulate doctrines that if believed, will benefit the believers, individual and society alike. The differences in their doctrines can be explained, in part, by historical circumstances. "They did not want to bare popular opinions to the skin, so as not to breed disorder in people's obedience to the laws and customs of their country" (II.12, 492 [379]).

> For our imperfection also provides this, that raw meat is not always fit for our stomach, it must be dried, altered, and corrupted. They do the same: they sometimes obscure their natural opinions and judgments and falsify them to accommodate themselves to public usage. They do not want openly to profess ignorance and the imbecility of human reason, so as not to frighten the children; but they reveal it to us clearly enough under the guise of a muddled and inconsistent knowledge. (II.12, 527-28 [408])[95]

Philosophers knowingly make up false doctrines to be useful; "It is the bane of our condition that often what appears to our imagination as most true does not appear to it as most useful for our life" (II.12, 492 [380]). Truth, at least as it is often conceived in human imagination, and utility do not simply accord; philosophers have tried to breach this gap by inventing doctrines that they deem "most useful for our life" (II.12, 492 [380]). Montaigne is not himself a myth-maker. He inquires into the truth about life. He finds that human life benefits from falsehood, but this claim about the utility of falsehood is the truth. While this assertion about what is useful for human life is a truth claim, it speaks only about human psychological needs, not epistemological reality.

From his discussion of useful falsehoods, Montaigne launches into a discussion of God. Montaigne is often described as a fideist, but the fact that his most systematic discussion of God happens in the context of the various insincere dogmatic views indicates that this is not the case. That Montaigne does not even mention this position among the epistemological possibilities alone should make one doubtful that he himself believes in it.[96] Moreover, despite numerous references to God, Montaigne never says that he *believes in* a God. To the contrary, he describes God as a human construction: "In short, the construction and the destruction of the deity, and its conditions, are wrought by man, on the basis of a relationship to himself. What a pattern and what a model" (II.12, 512 [396]). We are not created in God's image, he argues, but create God in our own. Montaigne's discussion of God begins and ends with an account of His human origins. In so doing, Montaigne reveals the psychological origins of the deities. We create gods to support us and calm us. Our views of God originate from "the utmost effort of our imagination toward perfection, each man amplifying the idea according to his capacity" (II.12, 494 [381]). To be useful in inspiring different peoples, God has been given a body "as necessity required" (II.12, 494 [381]); and Montaigne argues that if the animals have gods, they "certainly make them like themselves, and glorify themselves as we do" (II.12, 514 [397]).

When Montaigne does venture to offer a judgment, the conception of God that he describes as the "most excusable" is more Greek (philosophic, not Homeric) than Jewish or Christian (II.12, 493 [380]). Montaigne says God does not care about human beings, nor does He have anything to do with the cares that make up our lives (II.12, 493-517 [380-400]). Montaigne also questions the immortality of the soul and advises us not to concern ourselves with thoughts of an afterlife. He dismisses the Garden of Eden version of natural man,[97] the notion of a virgin birth (II.12, 513 [397]),[98] the doctrine of transubstantiation,[99] and the possibility that God could have a human incarnation. Montaigne further argues that God cannot be understood in human terms such as justice or goodness. These are but our attempts to create God out of our concerns.[100] Thus, even if Montaigne did believe in Christianity, unlike Thomas Jefferson, he does not tremble because he does not know that God is just.[101] Indeed, he argues that God has nothing to do with justice.[102] Montaigne concludes his most systematic account of God by saying that "In Socrates' opinion, and in mine too, the wisest way to judge heaven is not to judge it at all" (II.12, 517 [400]). Thus, at minimum, Montaigne argues that human beings can know nothing about God that is of any moral or political consequence. In this world, the world of the here and now, human beings must find their own way.

Montaigne upholds religion to the extent that he does, because religion is useful. The alternative to religion is atheism, which Montaigne criticizes not because it is untrue, but because it is "not easy to establish in the human mind" (II.12, 423 [325]). When atheists are about to die, he says, they panic and, fearing death, "let themselves be managed by the common faith and examples" (II.12, 423 [325]). Montaigne does not explicitly attack Christianity because it is the "common faith" of his time. Without it, people would have nothing. Montaigne seems to describe all religious and philosophical ideas as attempts by their authors to be useful as crutches. What he says of the ancient philosophers—"some things they wrote for the needs of society, like their religions" (II.12, 492 [379])—seems just as true for Christianity, whose customs Montaigne describes as "warm[ing] the souls of the people with religious emotion very beneficial in effect" (II.12, 494 [381]). And just as the ancients judged that "on that account it was reasonable that they did not want to bare popular opinions to the skin, so as not to breed disorder in people's obedience to the laws and customs of their country," so Montaigne upholds Christianity as a custom of his time and place.[103] If he lived in a different time and place, he would have upheld its customs instead. Montaigne seems not to be a believer—but even if he is, it would be a belief, as noted above, without any political consequences. This is important, because if Montaigne, like many of the thinkers of his time, thought that public policy should be guided by divine revelation, his views would be less useful to secular and skeptically oriented polities such as exist in the West at the dawn of the twenty-first century. It is Montaigne's differences from his time which make him potentially useful to ours.

Just as Montaigne is not a fideist nor a dogmatist of any kind, neither is he a Pyrrhonist.[104] Pyrrhonists are the most radical skeptics, that is to say the most doubting. They do not know whether they can know anything or not. They argue that there is insufficient evidence to determine if any knowledge is possible, and hence that one ought to suspend judgment on all questions concerning knowledge. If they convince an interlocutor of any position, they will immediately switch positions and argue the opposite, even when the subject is the possibility of knowledge. Montaigne does use Pyrrhonist arguments and the Pyrrhonist mode of procedure throughout the "Apology," and like the Pyrrhonists, Montaigne begins his analysis by noting the multiplicity of views on the subject under consideration. Unlike the Pyrrhonists, however, Montaigne focuses his inquiries on human things. Because the Pyrrhonists know nothing, no topic is inherently more important or more interesting to them than another. They will argue over the whiteness of snow or the sweetness of honey just as soon as they will argue about the nature of man. Montaigne, by contrast, focuses on human concerns. In the "Apology," for example, his longest discussions concern God, the soul, and the human body. Montaigne is not working the Pyrrhonist agenda. Instead, he uses Pyrrhonism to support his own agenda.[105] And whereas the Pyrrhonists argue that there is no way to determine which, if any, of the many conflicting views are true, and thus suspend their judgment on all things, Montaigne probes behind the multiplicity. He wants to know why there are so many different views of things, and why the same things are always being reexplained. The recurrence of certain questions and themes across cultures and across time suggests to Montaigne something important about the human condition. The multiplicity that the Pyrrhonists cite reflects an astonishing amount of overlap in human concerns. Montaigne focuses as much on the ques-tions—and on what they imply about the psychology of the questioners—as he does on determining scientifically exact answers to them. By learning about the human psyche, he implies, one can learn how to live.

In the end, Montaigne even questions whether one can live in accor-dance with Pyrrhonism, asserting that "it is almost incredible that it can be done" (II.29, 684 [533]). Montaigne's doubts are easy to understand. Pyrrhonists live their lives by following their internal, immediate impulses and by conforming to external pressures where necessary. They eat but they never judge that it is good to satisfy their hunger pangs. They just eat. Like commoners and the cannibals, they follow the local customs, and they do not judge the possible consequences of doing so. They merely obey. However, unlike commoners and the cannibals, Pyrrhonists are aware of the groundlessness of their actions and willfully and obediently accept them. But, one may wonder, what happens when impulse and custom conflict? Must not they *choose* between them? But how? Will they, just as Descartes purports to do, act as everyone else does? But is it not likely that different people will act differently? And why choose any one method over others? Can they not calculate at all? But how can they avoid it? Perhaps this explains why Montaigne calls Pyrrhonism an "amusing science" (II.29, 683 [533]) and summarizes its doctrine by calling it a *"fantasie"* (II.12, 485 [374]). What Montaigne finds absurd is the overapplication of this "science of ignorance" (II.29, 683 [533]). At one and the same time, the Pyrrhonist character is inflexible while its mode of argument is weak and spineless (II.12, 482-6 [372-4]). Pyrrhonists argue that true ignorance means *"une entière ignorance,"* including being ignorant of oneself (II.12, 482 [372]). This is too rigid, because Montaigne thinks that at least some self-knowl-edge is possible. Pyrrhonism is spineless, because it prevents its adherents from arguing truly and consistently based on what can be known. Moreover, the Pyrrhonist call to suspend one's judgment completely is antithetical to Montaigne's own self-critical approach: Montaigne strives for self-knowledge; it is the aim of his life's writing and thinking. The aim behind his *Essays* is to essay himself, to refine his judgment. He seeks to develop and refine his judgment, not to eliminate it. Montaigne is not a Pyrrhonist. This is important, because it shows that Montaigne is not a blanket skeptic. Unlike the Pyrrhonists, his skepticism stops short of nihilism. If some kinds of knowledge are possible and therefore can serve as the basis on which to make sane moral judgments, then there is a possible ground on which to build.

In the "Apology," Montaigne never thematically analyzes Academic skepticism, paradoxically I believe, because his entire book exemplifies this position.[106] He is an Academic skeptic—with his own unique twist. Academic skepticism, so called because it originally came out of Plato's Academy (second and third centuries B.C.), argues that no knowledge is possible. This assertion, traced back to Socrates' "I know that I know nothing," is paradoxical and problematic for a skeptic. Academic skeptics must paradoxically admit to knowing one thing, that human beings cannot possess knowledge. Although this may not seem like much, it is surprisingly troublesome for a skeptic: how does one know that one knows nothing? What kind of knowledge allows one to be certain of this? Unlike other types of knowledge, Montaigne considers some knowledge of the self both possible and worthwhile. But before we examine how Montaigne tries to obtain self-knowledge, let us examine why he thinks no other types of knowledge are possible.

Montaigne rejects the idea that transcendent knowledge is possible for human beings knowingly to possess. That is to say, he claims that knowledge of eternal, unchanging moral or physical principles is not available to human beings with certainty. Montaigne aims to make us all "wise at our own expense" and to show us why (II.12, 546 [423]). He does this by showing that human reason and the human senses, the only two means by which human beings can obtain knowledge, are pliable and therefore cannot serve as a foundation for knowledge. (He omits the possibility that such truths might be divinely revealed, because that possibility has been dispensed with.) If a firm foundation is lacking, he says, everything else falls flat. In making these arguments, Montaigne draws heavily on the Pyrrhonist arguments of Sextus Empiricus but with one crucial difference: unlike the Pyrrhonists, Montaigne is not unsure of his critique. He asserts limits based on truth claims about the self.[107] These truth claims about self-knowledge reveal the "Academic" nature of Montaigne's skepticism, and this knowledge of ignorance forms the foundations on which he builds his moral and political views.

Montaigne cites five factors that prevent human reason and judgment from being pure.[108] The first factor is the distortion that necessarily occurs in human sense perception. As proof that we do not perceive an object's essence, Montaigne notes how the same object is perceived differently by different people and even by the same person at different times. For example, Montaigne cites wine as affecting sick and healthy people differently, and he says that wood feels different to "normal" and chapped skin (II.12, 545 [422]). Human beings are aware both of changing perceptions and of the way their senses are influenced by their bodies.

Second, Montaigne argues that "it is certain" that our body affects our judgment and all the faculties of the soul (II.12, 547 [424]). Physical things, it seems, can be known. Some bodily movements, such as diseases, fever, or a cold, are noticeable, and we can try to compensate for the way we expect them to affect our judgment. But is it possible to determine exactly how much to compensate? Other imperceptible bodily movements also affect us and dislodge reason from its natural equilibrium. Insofar as these alterations are continual, can reason ever be in its natural home?

Third, our emotions affect our reason, even more so than the body does. This is apparent to everyone. We act, react, and think differently when we are angry, afraid, jealous, or in a tranquil state of mind. And "no eminent and lusty virtue is without some unruly agitation" (II.12, 550 [427]). If we always have an emotion, our reason is always disturbed. We should note, however, that both the effects of the body and the emotions are mitigated in proportion to the achievement of tranquility.

Montaigne raises two other factors that affect our reason and judgment: time and place (II.12, 559-60 [433-4]). The three factors discussed in the preceding paragraphs are caused by nature alone. Time and place, however, are caused by happenstance and human decisions. They are a testament to the power of custom more than to that of nature. Peoples and epochs have a character. They are more or less bellicose, just, temperate, and docile. Montaigne asserts that people, like animals and plants, grow differently in different physical locales and atmospheres. And because there have been so many different nations in so many different centuries, who is to say that this or that people—or all of them—were not mistaken?

Three internal, natural factors (perception, body, and emotion) and two outside factors (time and place) lead Montaigne to consider reason to be completely unreliable. "Reason," he says, is "that semblance of intellect that each man fabricates in himself" (II.12, 548 [425]). It is bendable, stretchable, pliable, and adaptable to all biases and all measures, easily justifying conflicting sides in any case. Ask any lawyer. "All that is needed is the ability to mold it" (II.12, 548 [425]).

Montaigne then proceeds to dash our last hope for knowledge by systematically criticizing the human senses (II.12, 571-86 [443-55]). He raises many problems. First, human beings may not have all the senses of nature. If we are lacking any senses, our reason and other senses cannot discover the lack. For all we know, all of mankind can be doing something very foolish for lack of some other sense. Our five senses form the limit to our faculties. Second, as we already said, our senses are inaccurate. At best, we sense partials and not essences. This is further confirmed by the many animals with particular senses that are keener than ours. Third, our mind also limits our sensory data. How often do we alter or completely miss something because our mind is occupied or looking elsewhere? Finally, different senses can give conflicting data. Something can look smooth but feel rough. To get an objective measure one would need an adjudicative instrument. To verify the instrument we would need a demonstration, but to verify the demonstration we would also need an instrument: there's the circle! Reason cannot judge because in and of itself it has no contact with outside objects. Even if our reason were completely unbiased, which it is not, the uncertainty of our senses makes everything they produce or that depends on them uncertain. Thus, no transcendent knowledge is possible.

Before concluding our analysis of Montaigne's skepticism, however, we must consider one other epistemological possibility: that Montaigne believes that knowledge is possible through scientific means. Schaefer has argued that Montaigne is the first scientist in the modern sense, that the "new conception of science," usually first associated with Descartes and Bacon, "was fully, not just partly, in accordance with Montaigne's teaching."[109] It might be argued that despite Montaigne's doubts about human reason and human senses *in themselves*, the problem of knowledge might be overcome through scientific methods. If Schaefer is correct, which I do not think he is, Montaigne would—despite his skeptical doubts—be thoroughly modern and not skeptical in the end at all.

Montaigne discusses science in the context of his discussion of the human and natural sphere, which begins by considering bodies, heavenly and human, and ends by considering procreation, but the bulk of which examines the soul. The placement of his discussion of the soul under the heading of "human and natural" things indicates that Montaigne does not consider the soul to be divine, and by putting science here Montaigne seems to indicate that only bodies are a potential object of science. Montaigne clearly rejects all of the so-called science of the past, simply treating it as just another example of dogmatic philosophizing. His entire discussion of science is framed by the idea that "philosophy is but sophisticated poetry" (II.12, 518 [401]). It "gives us," he says, "the best it has succeeded in inventing . . . for that matter, philosophy offers us not what is, or what it believes, but the most plausible and pleasant thing it forges" (II.12, 518 [401]).[110] Past efforts at science have achieved nothing. Philosophers disagree on how our body works, what the life force is, and how the body is attached to the soul. Philosophers have not agreed on where the soul is, let alone what it is. Nor can philosophers explain procreation, what the seed is, where it comes from, and where it goes. The problem with science as it was then practiced is that it did not probe deeply enough. Instead of questioning first principles and assumptions, it focuses on secondary and tertiary issues. Montaigne says that we ask what someone means, not whether he is correct or not. Montaigne most likely has Aristotle and the religious uses of Aristotle in mind as he makes this complaint. Several times in the remainder of the chapter, he mentions Aristotle as the contemporary authority or "the god of scholastic knowledge" (II.12, 521 [403]). The problem, as Montaigne sees it, is that "[w]hoever is believed in his presuppositions, he is our master and our God . . . he will be able to raise us, if he wants, up to the clouds" (II.12, 522 [404]).[111]

Running through the discussion of bodies, however, is a digression concerning three possible ways to remedy our ignorance: through the divinity, by recovering our natural simplicity, or by restructuring the scientific project. The first two ways, corresponding to religious simplicity and the simplicity of the animals or cannibals, have previously been raised in the first part of the "Apology."[112] The third, and newly suggested, way to overcome our ignorance is by perfecting science. In a passage emphasized by Schaefer, Montaigne tells us what such perfected knowledge would have to look like:

> They must not tell me: "It is true, for you see it and feel it so." They must tell me whether what I think I feel, I therefore actually do feel; and if I feel it, let them tell me why I feel it, and how, and what I feel. Let them tell me the name, the origin, the ins and outs of heat and cold, the qualities of him who acts and of him who suffers; (II.12, 523 [405])

Montaigne's conception of science is compelling, and Schaefer concludes that Montaigne is actually the first full scientist, deserving the title normally reserved for Bacon, Spinoza, or Descartes.[113] Schaefer, however, fails to cite the remainder of the paragraph:

> or let them abandon their profession, which is to accept or approve nothing
> except by the way of reason. That is their touchstone for every kind of
> experiment; but indeed it is a touchstone full of falsity, error, weakness, and
> impotence. (II.12, 523 [405])

Here Montaigne calls reason "full of falsity, error, weakness, and
impotence"; his systematic critique of reason was dedicated to proving why
this is so. While Montaigne might conceive of what a true science need look
like, he clearly does not believe human beings capable of possessing it.

It is true that since Montaigne's time science has been systematized and
successful beyond Montaigne's imagination. But to what extent does his
critique fail because of this? Even today, what do we know for sure? Does
science give certainty about the essence of things or merely the most
plausible "legitimate fiction"? Like scientists, Montaigne hopes for more
useful descriptions of things. Indeed, this is what he tries to do with his
essaying: "handling again and kneading this new material, stirring it and
heating it, I open up to whoever follows me some facility to enjoy it more
at his ease, and make it more supple and manageable for him" (II.12, 543
[421]). But can such a process ever lead to certainty? Scientists today would
not claim so. Theories are affirmed if results are reproducible and if they
explain all the observed phenomena as simply as possible, not based on
certainty. Science deals with relations and effects, not essences. While
Montaigne might have conceived the questions that science has to answer,
he did not believe that such questions would or could be definitively
answered. Schaefer is correct that Montaigne turns his emphasis away from
transcendent truth and toward experiential or phenomenological knowledge,
but Montaigne's aim in this is centered around the attainment of self-
knowledge, not the "conquest of nature."[114]

Given Montaigne's skeptical attacks on the status of reason, revelation,
science, and the senses, is there any criterion for judging how to live?
Rejecting the paean to obedience that he had sung on behalf of the unwise
earlier in the essay, and in contrast to the strand of his thought that
proclaims that it is simply necessary to obey the law (which we have seen
in several places throughout the "Apology," notably in his warning to the
princess (II.12, 540-42 [418-20]), and which appears in other essays as
well), Montaigne in the end refuses to have his "duty" determined by an
arbitrary standard such as custom, because "I cannot have my judgment so
flexible" (II.12, 563 [437]). Montaigne's calls to follow the law are in

tension with his claim that law, both legal and customary, is "filled and soaked with twaddle and lies" (II.12, 521 [403]). Why should one follow a falsehood? This tension is harmonized in the following way. Montaigne deems custom and habit necessary for the sake of a stable *political* order, but he considers following custom alone an unsatisfactory *moral* principle for reflective individuals. While stable politics might be a prerequisite for moral behavior, it is not itself a sufficient foundation of a moral system.

Following "experience" emerges as the alternative to uncritically following laws or reason. Of course, all critical activities use reason, and Montaigne does not want to abandon this tool altogether. And while he sometimes proclaims that "reason alone must guide our inclinations" (II.8, 366 [279])], he nonetheless takes great and repeated pains to moderate our attachment to our own reason by showing how unreliable it is. We need reason, but we need to use it to scrutinize its own shortcomings. Montaigne wants us to be aware of reason's tendency to run away with itself, to mislead human beings as much as it helps them. Reason needs to be grounded in something, and this something is not the conventional law. Law represents nothing but the "changes of passion" of the prince or people (II.12, 563 [437]). Montaigne turns to the self and its experiences, because it is the thing that we know best and to which we can have access. To paraphrase the old joke, wherever we go, there we are. We have direct, unmediated contact with ourselves at all times. (Unless, of course, learned opinions mediate ourselves to ourselves. But if this is so, Montaigne wants us to overcome it.) This is not to say that we have clarity or transparency about ourselves; far from it. Rather, we have the experience of changes, aches, pains, and pleasures that seem undeniable. We feel these phenomena within us, but from whence they came and what they mean are totally separate questions. Often, reason cannot explain these phenomena, but Montaigne would not therefore have us reject them. Every healthy person trusts his or her own faculties, feelings, and judgment more than anything else. As Montaigne says, referring to the tortured claim that snow is black (because it is made of water and when water is in a deep pool it looks dark), "We are nearer to ourselves than the whiteness of snow" (II.12, 544 [421]). We have experiences that can and must control and guide a self-aware reason and that together with reason, considering the alternatives, serves as the best guide to life.

Experiential "knowledge" is phenomenological, not transcendent. Montaigne gives up his search for universal truths that are always and everywhere true, and instead focuses on subjective appearance, the truth as it is perceived by a particular person at a particular moment in time. It is only by changing the definition of what constitutes knowledge that Montaigne is able to look for it at all. Thus, Montaigne asserts that "we see clearly enough" that human sense perception does not receive the forms of its objects (II.12, 545 [422]), that "it is certain" that our judgment is affected by our body (II.12, 547 [424]) and that "there is no doubt that judgment is biased" by emotions (II.12, 547 [424]). All of Montaigne's truth claims relate to phenomenological knowledge of the self. He shows his awareness of the subjectivity of these "facts" by quickly downgrading them from being "the truth of experience" to "the apparent facts of experience" and finally to the "more likely things" (II.12, 554-55 [430]). But he still says "I would rather follow facts than reason" (II.12, 554-55 [430]) because the alternatives to "experience" are worse.

Here lies Montaigne's explanation of his—and Academic skepticism's—paradoxical claim that he knows that he knows nothing. The two "knows" in this sentence refer to different types of knowledge. By phenomenologically knowing the inconstancy of his body and sense organs, he knows that he could never possess any transcendental truth. The statement that one knows that we can know nothing implies knowledge of the limits of human capabilities. Knowing nothing is a function of self-knowledge.

The nature of Montaigne's skepticism is thus clear: a wise individual will be fully aware of his ignorance of all transcendent matters (i.e., he will not be a fideist or a dogmatist) and understand what can be known (i.e., not a Pyrrhonist) while appreciating its merely phenomenological status. This interpretation of Montaigne as an Academic skeptic is supported by several comments Montaigne makes during his discussion of these various epistemological positions. Indeed, Montaigne begins the inquiry by approvingly citing the original Academic skeptic, Socrates: "The wisest man that ever was, when they asked him what he knew, answered that he knew this much, that he knew nothing" (II.12, 480-81 [370]). He was able to do this because he had some self-knowledge: "Ignorance that knows itself, that judges itself and condemns itself, is not complete ignorance: to be that it must be ignorant of itself [*s'ignore soy-mesme*]" (II.12, 482 [372]). Self-knowledge is the key. It is for this reason that Montaigne approves of the tale told of the Milesian "wench" who tripped the philosopher Thales who was spending all his time gazing upwards in contemplation of the heavens. "She gave him good counsel," says Montaigne, "to look rather to himself [*à soy*] than to the sky" (II.12, 519 [402]).[115] With this quotation, Montaigne echoes Cicero's famous praise of Socrates as the first to bring philosophy down from the heavens. Cicero knew that Socrates and

Plato were not dogmatists. For Montaigne, doubting is to "test [*essaye*] our common impressions," which reveals our "natural weakness" (II.12, 521 [403] and II.12, 486 [375]). What Montaigne praises in Socrates is equally true about himself: Socrates always brings everything back to the "conditions of his present and past life, which he examined and judged, considering any other learning subordinate to that and superfluous" (II.12, 488-89 [376-77]). Montaigne, like the Socrates he portrays, is an Academic skeptic. Montaigne's Academic skepticism, based on ignorance of transcendent truth and the search, not for a universal science, but for self-knowledge, serves as the positive pivot on which his moral and political views are based.

IV. Living with Skepticism

Neither God nor science, according to Montaigne, offers human beings sufficient answers to the most pressing human problems. Until now, the only guides for human life that have survived Montaigne's skeptical doubting are a recovery of natural simplicity, the path that follows from the early sections on the animals and simplicity, and blind obedience to conventional laws. However, based on his Academic skepticism, Montaigne articulates another possible guide for human life: a phenomenological knowledge of the subjective self. Just as the Indians of the New World are the icon for *habitude naturelle*, the iconic embodiment of this way of life is equally provocative: some unnamed "licentious" philosophers who find a natural way of living in a skeptical world.

Montaigne discusses this alternative mode of coping with skepticism in between his critique of reason and his critique of the human senses. The discussion comes unannounced, unfolds in a dialectical manner, and juggles all of the possible ways of living with skepticism that have survived his skeptical attack—blind obedience to law, following natural law (i.e., *habitude naturelle*), and following oneself. The discussion follows a definite pattern. It consists of two separate inquiries, both of which begin with anti-Pyrrhonian remark, then they attempt to imagine (but ultimately reject) some kind of natural law, and finally they conclude by showing the problems inherent in following the law unquestioningly. Every option is attacked except for following oneself. Out of this discussion emerges the icon for the life of Academic skepticism: the licentious philosophers.

The first inquiry, not as explicit as the second, begins with a swipe at Pyrrho for his excessive stubbornness. The context is Montaigne's vivid description of the effect his own ambition has on his judgment:

I would feel it come to life, grow, and increase in spite of my resistance, and finally seize me, alive and watching, and possess me, to such an extent that, as from drunkenness, the picture of things began to seem to me other than usual. I would see the advantages of the object of my desire visibly expanding and growing, and increasing and swelling from the breath of my imagination; the difficulties of my undertaking growing easy and smooth, my reason and my conscience withdrawing. (II.12, 552 [428])

Montaigne describes in equally vivid terms the vanishing of this fire. Afterwards, Montaigne asks, "Which of these states is the more truthful, Pyrrho does not know" (II.12, 552 [428]). But Montaigne does. It is clear from his description which is the norm and which the distortion caused by desire. Montaigne tells us that "from the knowledge of this mobility of mine I have accidentally engendered in myself a certain constancy of opinions" (II.12, 553 [428]). Montaigne is the accidental philosopher with accidental constancy.[116] Flux leads to constancy in the same paradoxical way that self-knowledge leads to ignorance. But what is his constancy? He tells us that he is not capable of choosing, so "I accept other people's choice and stay in the position where God put me. Otherwise I could not keep myself from rolling about incessantly" (II.12, 553 [428]). Again, this is the "obedience" solution to the skeptical problem that Montaigne first recommends in the "Apology" and in his warning to the Princess.

The idea of Montaigne passively accepting other people's choices is difficult to accept. Can constant accepting not lead to incessant switching in unstable times? Montaigne's times were more unstable than most, yet he never switched sides. He dealt with the heads of both factions of the religious wars, both of whom must have constantly been after him to change his actions, yet he maintained a steady course. Montaigne here attributes this to the luck of God, yet later, and more consistent with his overall outlook, he says, "I have never up to this moment followed any [judgment] but my own" (III.2, 792 [618]). It is not surprising that Montaigne concludes that we must be wary of following intellectual or any other kinds of trends. Otherwise, "all the common herd [*le vulgaire*]—and we are all of the common herd [*le vulgaire*]—would have its belief as easy to turn as a weathercock" (II.12, 554 [429]). But how does following trends differ from letting other people decide for one? If there is a distinction at all, it is a fine one. Judgment is always necessary.

Following "experience," one's own empirical observations, emerges as an alternative to following the law. Montaigne does this, oddly enough, by resurrecting Theophrastus (whom he has previously savaged) and defending him from someone who denied that the Greeks knew how to sail. Montaigne reports the following conversation:

> "What?" I said to him. "Then did those who navigated under the laws of Theophrastus go west when they headed east? Did they go sideways or backward?" "That was luck," he replied; "at all events they miscalculated." I then replied to him that *I would rather follow facts than reason.* (II.12, 554 [430]) [emphasis added]

He would rather follow facts than reason. But this calls into question the very standard for judging truth in that Theophrastus made no pretense to possessing first principles. His knowledge is admittedly partial, and Montaigne had vehemently attacked Theophrastus for this earlier. Yet, his view here has the advantage of liberating oneself from the tyranny of being subjected to the laws, customs, and fads that happen to surround one. Judging "facts" for oneself allows one to swim amidst the steady stream of opinions. By siding with experience and empiricism as opposed to logic and law, Montaigne is developing another guide for life. Montaigne wants what works. If it works, as William James and the pragmatists later argued, does it not have a claim to be knowledge? It would not be knowledge in the traditional sense (i.e., transcendent knowledge of essences), but a phenomenological knowledge good enough to help people navigate their way in this world. The key is utility. Montaigne also notes how limited experience is: a thousand years ago it would have been regarded as mad to suggest that there were other continents. Citing a number of eerie cross-cultural similarities, Montaigne briefly entertains the possibility that these might reflect some transcultural and transhistorical natural laws to which we should conform, but he concludes that if these similarities reveal some deep truth about the human condition, it is not some natural law, but that these seeming coincidences result from the fact that "the human mind is a great worker of miracles," i.e., it easily deludes itself into believing what it desires (II.12, 556-57 [431]).[117] Similar minds generate similar thoughts. Truth is reflected here, not of natural laws but of the human condition. Pyrrhonism, conventional law, and natural law are all rejected in favor of following experience.

The second discussion of the alternative ways of living with skepticism unfolds in exactly the same way as the first one. Montaigne criticizes the Pyrrhonists for being too rigid in their application of *ataraxy*, tranquility. He suggests, however, that they cannot help this. Reason is, by its nature, too rigid to maintain the flexible position to which Pyrrho originally aspired. Then, Montaigne's discussion of the rigidity of reason leads to his critique of the rigid dictates of reason: follow the law. Montaigne advocated this in his own name in his warning to the princess, but here ascribes the position to "philosophy" and "reason" and seems shocked by its consequences. Merely following the law puts one in the same morally questionable position that we have previously seen: if we simply follow the law, "our duty has no rule but an accidental one" (II.12, 562 [436]). Montaigne, it seems, only likes things to be accidental when he is in charge of them. He may be an accidental philosopher with an accidental constancy, as said earlier, but he cannot have his own obligations resting on such accidental foundations: "There is nothing subject to more continual agitation than the laws" (II.12, 563 [436]). It is unacceptable to be bound "to follow the laws of our country—that is to say, the undulating sea of the opinions of a people or a prince, which will paint me justice in as many colors, and refashion it into as many faces, as there are changes of passion in those men. I cannot have my judgment so flexible" (II.12, 563 [437]). Notwithstanding his abandonment of a quest for transcendent truth, he says, "Truth must have one face, the same and universal" (II.12 562 [436]). Natural law meets this latter criteria, but Montaigne rejects this as inapplicable to man as he is. To be natural, he says, a law must be "firm, perpetual, and immutable" (II.12, 563 [437]). The only test to see if a law is natural is "universality of approval," which we might assume is his criterion, because there is universal agreement about the need to eat, drink, and breathe (II.12, 564 [437]). Consent is the key issue, but there is no moral doctrine on which all human beings agree. "Let them show me just one law of that sort," Montaigne demands; "I'd like to see it" (II.12, 564 [437]). The possibility of universal consent is destroyed by "domineering and commanding, muddling and confusing" human reason (II.12, 564 [438]). Again, Pyrrhonism, conventional law, and natural law are rejected.

After twice criticizing Pyrrhonism, twice rejecting the idea of simply following conventional law, and twice rejecting the idea of following natural law, the dialectic focuses and presents the main thesis, which would not have been widely recognized as useful and necessary without the previous consideration and rejection of the other views. Ultimately, the "Apology" articulates a way of living with skepticism that follows from Montaigne's "Academic" views. After criticizing philosophy for teaching that one must always obey the law, Montaigne now notes that philosophers themselves often do not obey it: "Excessive license, remote from common usage, even the soundest philosophy allows" (II.12, 567 [440]). But whereas this contempt of law at first might have seemed to be a serious problem, Montaigne again reminds us of the limp foundations of law. "The laws take their authority from possession and usage; it is dangerous to trace them back to their birth. They swell and are ennobled as they roll, like our rivers: follow them uphill to their source, it is just a little trickle of water, barely recognizable, which thus grows proud and strong as it grows old" (II.12, 567 [440]). The laws which philosophers are so contemptuous of are founded on nothing but human custom and usage. Their basis is not transcendent but contingent upon human history. Philosophers refuse to conform, Montaigne says, because the foundations of law are

> so trivial and frail that it is no wonder that these *people who weigh everything* and refer it to *reason*, and who accept nothing by authority and on credit, have judgments often far removed from popular judgments. Since they are men who take as their pattern the *original image of nature*, it is no wonder if in most of their opinions they deviate from the common way. (II.12, 567 [440]) [emphasis added]

These philosophers' judgments are guided by two standards: "reason" and "their pattern of the original image of nature." Montaigne has already explored reason's limits and demonstrated that it is an unreliable judge when it lacks firm foundations. However, even if it is incapable of supplying transcendent truth, might it not, if employed properly by wise and prudent people who "weigh everything," still be a useful contingent guide? If coupled with a "pattern of the original image of nature"—that is to say a good foundation—reason might be useful, indeed. The pattern of nature seems to be a standard that Montaigne likes, being the same basis as his praise of the animals and the cannibals and his recurrent laments of humanity's loss of it. The fact that Montaigne here speaks of an "image" of nature might mean that the philosophers of whom he speaks possess but a mere verisimilitude of it. In any case, a life based on a pattern of nature would be very different from a life that simply followed the conventional laws or a crazy pattern produced by an unruly imagination. Following a pattern of nature, moreover, might be identical to following experience. After all, experience was the basis for the Greeks' understanding of sailing and the natural phenomena on which that art is based.

Montaigne considers the costs entailed in such an alternative. He describes philosophers who act according to reason and nature as often rejecting the most prevalent conventions of the West. In doing so, he tries to shock the readers by listing the behavior that nature and reason allow: free sex ("wives to be held in common and without obligation"), a rejection of property, no embarrassment by farting in public, and no shame if they are seen copulating (II.12, 567 [440]). "These philosophers set an extreme price on virtue and rejected all other studies but morals; yet," Montaigne tells us, they "ordered no other bridle on sensual pleasures than moderation and the preservation of the liberty of others" (II.12, 569 [441]). Insofar as this image of nature insults conventional and religious Western morality, Montaigne implies that the conventions have veered from a natural basis. If we have enough heart to accept these improprieties—these licentious vices "which are better hushed up than published to weak minds"—then Montaigne's alternative of these licentious philosophers might appeal to us (II.12, 567 [439]). But we must be clear about the conditions. Sensual indulgence is limited by two things: moderation and the preservation of the liberty of others. Insofar as this ideal underlies Montaigne's later philosophical and political recommendations, these conditions always apply. Montaigne never advocates immoderate, cruel, or zealous indulgence. Although Montaigne does not here explain why these two conditions must be respected, we can guess that moderation is required by the uncertainty of the philosophers' actions. Living a life based on reason and an image of nature might be the best of the available alternatives to guide human beings, but it provides no guarantee of truth or correctness. Thus, moderation to oneself and not hurting others are warranted.

This image of self-based but tolerant hedonism comes to characterize modernity in general and the morality of liberalism in particular. Insofar as this is a result of Montaigne's influence, we need note that Montaigne advances it not as his own invention but as a resurrection of an ancient pagan ideal. It is neither Christian as many commentators claim, nor is it new as others claim. Commentators, such as David Schaefer, shrewdly note Montaigne's important place in the origins of modern and liberal values, but Schaefer considers this to be a uniquely Montaignean invention. By contrast, Montaigne presents it as a hearkening back to an ancient vision, not that of Plato or Aristotle but nonetheless ancient. And Montaigne attaches clear limits to it. Like liberalism, Montaigne argues that such behavior must be consistent with the liberty of others. But unlike liberalism, Montaigne's "Apology" does not suggest liberty for everybody but only for philosophers, and only if pursued within the confines of nature, moderation, and experience-based reason.

Where does this leave us? If human beings know nothing, how should they live? There are only three paths left after Montaigne's skeptical attacks on transcendent reason and revelation. The first is simply to follow tyrannical, groundless custom, but Montaigne rejects this as fickle and arbitrary. This might be necessary to secure social and political order, but it has no claim as a moral guide for how an individual ought to live. The second possibility is to follow natural habits, such as embodied by the animals, commoners, and Brazilians. This option seems primitive, but it celebrates a simple, phenomenological mode of being-in-the-world and is left standing. Finally, one can follow one's own individually rooted judgments. For individuals whose minds are led astray by their unruly natural faculties, this option is disastrous both for themselves and for those who live around them. Law (i.e., option one) is needed to regulate their behavior. However, if the individual's judgments are based on an experiential-based reason and a pattern of nature, including a full awareness of all the things that they do not and cannot know, this option might produce shocking and licentious behavior, but it can be compatible with moderation and the liberty of others. This leaves us two desirable images, both of which are based on phenomenological perceptions of nature, and both epitomized by shocking icons: the cannibals and sensual philosophers. Which does Montaigne choose? Not only does he not tell us in the "Apology," but he goes so far as to tease us about his silence. The very next topic that he takes up is the difficulty of interpretation. In a long passage, Montaigne tells us that every reader finds what he wants (II.12, 570 [442]). Montaigne purposely does not resolve the problem, because his philosophy is centrally concerned with the intent that each reader resolve it as he or she sees fit. That the reader will then ascribe his or her own conclusion to Montaigne is an amusing and inevitable fact of human nature.

Montaigne wants it all. He wants the simplicity and innocence of nature, the freedom and self-awareness of philosophy, and the safety of laws. This book attempts to explain Montaigne's analyses of the advantages and disadvantages of these moral and political goods in his attempt to bring them together. The succeeding chapters systematically examine the fate of these disparate "visions" of living with skepticism. Chapter 2 examines the innocence and simplicity embodied in the cannibals. Chapter 3 examines the refined hedonism of the sensual philosophers. As different as these visions might seem, both embody images of nature known phenomeno-logically. And the same *moeurs*—free sex, lack of property, and a lack of shame concerning the body—characterize both. But because the behavior of the cannibals is based on natural habits, the cannibals represent a solution that is necessarily political and that can only be achieved *en masse*. By contrast, the solution personified by the philosophers is radically individual-istic and can be manifested only in one individual self at a time.

V. Conclusion: The Historical Importance of Montaigne's Skepticism

In "The Apology for Raymond Sebond," health and the other goods of the animals emerge as a good for human beings. Health is mental as well as physical; avoiding fear and anxiety is as important as avoiding pain and disease. Montaigne idealizes a sensual and robust tranquility, happily compatible with bodily pleasures, which more closely resembles the lusty, sensual tranquility recommended by Epicurus than the know-nothing tranquility of Pyrrho or the asceticism of saints. This combination of inner peace (*ataraxy*) and sensual satisfaction, free of the falsities produced by unruly minds, serves as a standard for human health throughout the *Essays*.

Montaigne's task will be to reconcile his desire for freedom with the need for stability. On the one hand, Montaigne wants to recover as much of mankind's natural condition as possible, and he seems to think that this will lead to better, more moderate, and more tolerant human behavior. Montaigne prepares the way for this moderation and toleration with his skeptical attack on human presumption. He hopes that if we accept his epistemological view that transcendent knowledge is impossible, we will moderate our zeal for any and every cause. Heartfelt convictions and our proudest deductions become mere opinion—and opinion is not worth dying for. People only die for ideas when they conceive them as part of their identity. On the other hand, Montaigne knows that not everyone will be convinced by him, so there might be a need for a strong authority to preserve law and order. He offers no hope of manufacturing perfect laws from scratch. One must, within limits that we shall explore, accept imperfect laws or the laws that are. He would like, however, for the laws to be as tolerant and unrestrictive as possible; after all, their epistemological groundlessness has been uncovered, too. In the following chapters we shall see that although Montaigne desires both the freedom to think and the freedom to act, he emphasizes freedom of thought. It is his judgment and conscience that he values most.

In conclusion, the doubting that Montaigne did came to characterize modern philosophy, which has been preoccupied with the search for foundations ever since. This search for foundations is a result of the crises of authority that Montaigne and others exacerbated, leading to questions of epistemology and logic dominating modern debates. Rather than having confidence in our natural abilities to know the world, epistemologists question it. Before we can make decisions or judgments about the world, they argue, we have to know what, in fact, we are capable of knowing. This concern gave rise to the great epistemological philosophies that characterize early modernity. For example, Descartes, Locke, Hume, and Kant all placed the epistemological question first. Descartes, often cited as the first "modern" philosopher, insisted on articulating a reliable method before allowing philosophy to turn to its traditional substantive questions. Indeed, he went into retreat until he could assure himself that his method was sound. Locke explains how he came to write his *Essay Concerning Human Understanding*:

> Five or six Friends meeting at my Chamber, and discoursing on a subject very remote from this, found themselves quickly at a stand, by the Difficulties that rose on every side. After we had a while puzzled our selves, without coming any nearer a Resolution of those Doubts which perplexed us, it came into my thoughts, that we took a wrong course; and that, before we set our selves upon Enquiries of that Nature, it was necessary to examine our own Abilities, and see, what Objects our Understandings were, or were not fitted to deal with. This I proposed to the Company, who all readily assented; and thereupon it was agreed, that this should be our first Enquiry.[118]

Similarly, Kant refuses to "rest satisfied with the mere appearance of knowledge."[119] His first task is to launch "a powerful appeal to reason to undertake anew the most difficult of its duties, namely, self-knowledge, and to institute a court of appeal which should protect the just rights of reason, but dismiss all groundless claims, and should do this not by irresponsible decrees, but according to the eternal and unalterable laws of reason. This court of appeal is no other than the *Critique of Pure Reason*."[120] However, over time, epistemology gave way to logic as the first concern of philosophical inquiry. In debating what can be known about the world, the epistemologists assumed that the languages used to articulate their thoughts were unproblematic. Gottlob Frege was the first to argue that the mode of thought and linguistic structures—the tools used in every inquiry—had to be explained before human beings could even ask what they can know.[121] This further step in the search for knowledge has characterized the philosophical debates, especially in Anglo-America, for the last century or so. Once the epistemological question came to dominate, it is almost inevitable that the debate proceeded to where it is today. Montaigne's skeptical epistemology predates all of these thinkers, including Descartes; and to the extent that a preoccupation with epistemology characterizes "modern" thought, Montaigne might indeed be numbered among the first moderns. Montaigne even anticipated the linguistic turn, raising questions about the nature and fundamental inadequacy of language.[122]

It was in large part through Montaigne that modern skepticism arose, and it was the influence of skepticism that helped cause epistemology to become the preoccupation of modern thought. By being the first writer in centuries to articulate so philosophically the problems and challenges of skepticism, Montaigne profoundly influenced the agenda of modern philosophical debate. As Popkin correctly says, Montaigne's *Essays* were "to be the womb of modern thought, in that it led to the attempt either to refute the new [skepticism], or to find a way of living with it."[123] Montaigne's importance to modern skepticism can be traced from Charron and the *libertine érudite* to Bayle, Voltaire, Hume, Emerson, and Nietzsche.[124] The call for special epistemological or scientific methods arose only after these crises of authority came to the fore. Montaigne, however, does not turn to science as the way to live. He does not embark on the project that Bacon and Descartes began nor imagine that technological advances will help solve the human problems. Rather, he focuses only on phenomenological self-knowledge. He encourages human beings to turn inwards to conquer themselves rather than to turn outward in a quest to conquer nature. Montaigne's skepticism takes him away from the Christian preoccupation with God and an afterlife and back to the self. It is a turn more reminiscent of Socrates and Hellenistic Academic skepticism than modernity's turn to unlimited acquisition. If one defines modern epistemology by its particular solutions, Montaigne would not be modern, because he is not "scientific"; if one defines modernity by the problems with which it wrestles, Montaigne would thoroughly be so. In either case, Montaigne is a key figure at the head of the turn and one from whom we have much to learn. For while modernity turned toward scientific solutions to the problems of skepticism, Montaigne did not. Insofar as he catalyzed the skeptical crises, Montaigne was important in the rise of modernity. But Montaigne rejects in advance the scientific enterprise as unable to solve the deepest moral and political problems. To the extent that modernity's various scientific projects might be felt as dead ends, Montaigne has a powerful alternative vision to offer.

Chapter Two

Cannibals in Utopia:
Habitude Naturelle and the Politics of Primitivism

As we have seen, Montaigne's skeptical doubting in the "Apology for Raymond Sebond" leads him to idealize a phenomenological relationship to life. We have also seen that he postulates two ways that a person might achieve a life of such a close, direct relation to nature: the way of *habitude naturelle* and the way of sensual philosophy. Each of these approaches to the world is extensively analyzed in subsequent essays: *habitude naturelle* in "Of Cannibals" and "Of Coaches," sensual philosophy throughout the *Essays*. The relevance for political theory of Montaigne's analysis of *habitude naturelle* is the focus of the present chapter; we will reserve our examination of the political and moral implications of sensual philosophy for chapter 3.

Montaigne's decision to write an extensive essay on "Cannibals" has more to do with political theory than many scholars of Montaigne have recognized. One strain of scholarship has considered his interest in Indians to be purely anthropological, and among this group, many have criticized the numerous inaccuracies in his portrayal.[1] Taking note of those very same inaccuracies, another group of scholars has argued that the purpose of the essay is not an accurate representation of America, but rather a compellingly scathing portrait of Europe. These scholars argue that Montaigne developed out of a web of facts, borrowings, and speculations about inhabitants of the New World a utopian fantasy whose ultimate purpose was to condemn the cruelty and corruption of "civilized Europe."[2] I agree with this latter position. However, because this debate has largely focused exclusively on "Of Cannibals" considered in isolation from the rest of Montaigne's work, the pivotal role of the essay in Montaigne's larger project has been largely ignored. Montaigne's corpus as a whole seeks to develop a coherent understanding of the moral and political factors most conducive to a good and just life, and "Of Cannibals" is an important component in this larger agenda, misunderstood if read in isolation. David Schaefer has gone a considerable distance in remedying this misunderstanding, examining as he does Montaigne's discussion of the Indians in the context of his political thought as a whole. He correctly, I believe, argues that the Indians are intended "only to indicate the direction" that Montaigne wants to take the modern world rather than serving for him as a comprehensive ideal for emulation. However, I hope to show in this chapter that even Schaefer has not fully understood the role this essay plays in Montaigne's political theory. Schaefer proposes that Montaigne advocates two goals in "Of Cannibals"—equality and the "satisfaction of animal wants"—and minimizes all other positive qualities that the cannibals reveal about nature.[3] While Montaigne does indeed affirm an equality of the human condition and the pleasures that would accompany an acceptance of the human body, his vision also reveals important ingredients about the standards to which the mind must be kept. Schaefer rightly notes that Montaigne finds an insufficient amount of "mind" in this vision, but there are more positives in it than Schaefer allows. It also indicates an essential ingredient of the mind—mental tranquility—that, outlasting the vision itself, becomes a key ingredient of Montaigne's conception of the good life and a necessary attribute of all further human development. Montaigne concludes, however, that though a purely "natural" way of life has much to recommend it, it must exist at the expense of reason, and it is therefore unstable and not productive of the best human life.

Montaigne's analysis of the Indians is a thought experiment, a hypothetical imagining of the risks and pleasures of a society governed by *habitude naturelle*. Ultimately, he rejects his own imaginings, and those readers who wish only to know Montaigne's "bottom line" should skip to the next chapter, where that is presented in full. However, the fact that he rejects his vision is no reason to skip the pages in which it is essayed. For without understanding Montaigne's analysis of *habitude naturelle*, no scholar will fully be able to appreciate the importance and relevance of his political theory. The powerful praise of simplicity that Montaigne articulates marks the beginnings of a peculiarly modern kind of romanticism, and it is exactly this romantic creation of his that he ultimately rejects. Romanticism, as exemplified in the Bible's account of the Garden of Eden and ancient Greek accounts of a mythical "golden age," has existed throughout Western history. However, Montaigne's mixing of the golden age with his praise of the inhabitants of the New World gives birth to a whole new phenomenon: the celebration of primitive peoples and the (misguided) desire to "go back" to some natural beginning, to humankind's origins and roots. Romanticism often praises human beings as naturally good, condemns the political and social world as an artificial corruption, and draws the political conclusion that only a minimal state, if that, is necessary. Beyond that, all political and social control is deemed excessive and evil. Montaigne imagines just such a vision: tranquil and contented people with a minimal state and maximal happiness—and he rejects it. Montaigne rejects this kind of romanticism on both theoretical and practical grounds, arguing that it is impossible in practice and theoretically unsatisfying.[4] Ironically, his thought experiment was so provocative that it motivated the kind of thought he rejects. It gave rise to a whole tradition, the romanticism of Rousseau and of the nineteenth century, that is inimical to his views. In the process, Montaigne inaugurated two major traditions in modern political theory: the idea of the noble savage and a tradition of identifying natural man based on his beginning, i.e., mankind's original pre-cultivated state, instead of judging human nature by its final developmental endpoint, as Aristotle did and as was done throughout medieval times. These concepts powerfully inform his vision of the good, and they dictate the kinds of political systems he believes are most likely to secure that good.

I. Context: Views of the Indians Before Montaigne

The vehicle for Montaigne's radical thought experiment is his representation of the Indians. Far from saying that the recently discovered Indians of the New World were inferior or underdeveloped, as just about every other European in his century did, Montaigne heralded them as morally superior to Europeans. Montaigne, virtually alone in his century, rejected the notion that modern European man was the epitome of humanity. He held up the Indians as a model of natural purity by which "civilized" man could judge his decline. Although Montaigne gave neither an anthropologically accurate account of the Indians nor unqualified praise of their condition, he was the first Western thinker to represent them in a significantly positive way. His provocative and influential association of humankind's natural state with its primitive origins was a major turning point in Western political philosophy.

Before Montaigne, few Europeans cared about the Indians or about "underdeveloped" peoples of any kind. Views such as those held by the Paduan Lazzaro Buonamico, who in 1539 called the discovery of the New World one of the two greatest revolutions of the modern era (the other was the invention of the printing press), which was amplified by the French historian Louis Le Roy in the 1570s, were shared by only a minority.[5] Contrary to the significance which we have in retrospect ascribed to Columbus' voyage, most people, even among the educated elites, were uninspired by the discovery of America. For example, leading intellectual figures of the sixteenth century, such as Machiavelli, Bodin, Hooker, and Jacques-Auguste de Thou, gave little thought to the New World. Hooker's *Chronicles* (2nd ed. 1586) attribute little significance to the New World and Thou's *Histoire de son Temps* (1604) allots only one paragraph to the voyages of Columbus and the Portuguese.[6] Machiavelli, preferring new modes and orders over the New World, barely discusses it,[7] and Jean Bodin, who compiled what is probably the most complete bibliography of history in the sixteenth century in the appendix to his *Methodus ad facilem historiarum cognitionem* of 1566, lists only three titles on the New World.[8]

There were many reasons for the lack of interest in and appreciation of the significance of the discovery of a wholly new people on a wholly new continent. First, there was confusion over what exactly had been discovered. Many of those who made the voyages thought they had gone someplace else. Throughout his life, Columbus maintained that America was Asia, as did Las Casas.[9] Second, while the information was confused, there was also a lack of it. The only complete and reliable accounts of the various voyages and explorations were kept in the Spanish archives, and few were published before 1550.[10] There was also a lag between their original publication in Spain and their translation into the other European languages. Some exceptions, such as Cortés' accounts of his exploits, were translated into the main languages of Europe within a few years of their original publication, but these were rare. Most of the accounts were not published for decades.[11] Third, there was a lack of interest in travel generally which can be attributed to serious turmoil in Europe, such as the religious wars. Interest in events outside of one's national territory was not as widespread as concern over religious fervor, popular science and medicine, or abuses of temporal power.[12] Fourth, those interested in exploration were more concerned with other places. Throughout the sixteenth century, twice as many books were published on the Turks as on North America, South America, and the West Indies combined. Three times as many were published on the East Indies.[13] The Turks represented a threat, and China was considered both more exotic and a source of wealth. The implications of the discovery of a new people on a new continent were slow to be comprehended. Finally, there were reasonable grounds for the tales about America to be disbelieved. Aside from the unbelievable technical feats involved in getting to America, myths of magical and exotic islands had been published throughout the Middle Ages. There had also been a number of fictitious travel journals, such as those by Mandeville and (later) by Swift.

While most people in Europe were indifferent to the discovery of the New World, Montaigne was one of the few thinkers who sought out information on the New World. Montaigne employed a man who had been to America and had him bring his friends and other travelers to his estate. Montaigne interviewed them and collected artifacts from the New World. He critically evaluated what and who could be believed. Montaigne also made great effort to meet and speak with some Indians who were brought to France.[14] If Montaigne's interest in the Indians was unusual among scholars, his views of them were even more so.

Of those before Montaigne who dealt with the Indians, three views dominated their thinking—one of which saw the Indians as full human beings worthy of dignity and respect.[15] The first view barely recognized the Indians' humanity. As illustrated in the actions of the Spanish discoverers and conquerors—and in their own writings—murder and exploitation of the Indians posed not even a shred of a moral conundrum. Columbus, for example, somewhat inconsistently sees the Indians both as potential converts and as potential slaves.[16] But mostly Columbus is indifferent to the people whom he meets. He takes care to describe the flora and fauna of the New World and maps its coastlines with care, but he shows little interest in the customs and *moeurs* of its people. It never occurs to him that he might have anything to learn from them. While this also applies for the other early explorers, some of them, such as Cortés, do inquire about the Indians' beliefs—not out of detached interest in their views but only to learn how to manipulate them. While Cortés and Bernal Diaz express wonder at some of the beautiful craft work and magnificent cities that they find, more often they express a simple revulsion at the Aztecs' human sacrifices and brutality. But while doing this, they seem not to notice the barbarism and cruelty that they themselves inflict almost everywhere they go. They kill and maim not only as means of conquest but also for sport, sharpening their swords by running people through. They plunder villages and murder the inhabitants without remorse or guilt, indeed without a second thought. Their juxtapositions of their clean-conscience, guiltless murders with their Christian beliefs and their professions of piety indicate a radical "othering" in their thinking about the Indians' natures.[17] A similar inability to "see" the Indians is evident when the conquistadors rape women and then mock their unwilling victims as whores.[18] It is thanks to this concept that the *encomienda*, the brutal colonial system of forced labor, could institutionalize the horrid treatment of the Indians. In short, the Spanish in the New World gave the Indians so little regard as fellow human beings that they could systematically massacre them in a manner consistent with their Christian consciences.

One peculiar factor preventing some explorers from seeing the Indians for what they were was the array of mythical accounts of bizarre peoples that had been passed down from antiquity and believed throughout medieval times. Originating with Herodotus and passed to Christendom largely through Pliny the Elder, these stories were grossly elaborated by Pomponius Mela, Solinus, Isidore of Seville, Vincent of Beauvais, Bartholomew, Sir John Mandeville, and others. Accounts of wild men varied; but tales of cannibalism, nakedness, and the monstrously deformed, including giants, the completely hairy, and the dog-headed, had so much credence during the Middle Ages that mapmakers often put them on islands at the edge of the known world.[19] These myths both reflect and dictate European attitudes toward the "other," and Columbus, in his *Travel Journal* and in the famous "First Letter" he wrote immediately upon returning to Europe, reveals just how compelling and influential they were. Immediately after noting how good-looking and happy the Indians appeared, he records that he has located the cannibals and giants of the tradition. Even though he admits that he could not speak the language of his interlocutors, he nonetheless believes that they told him that there were cannibals (Carribs?), giants, dog-faced peoples, and other monstrosities on nearby islands.[20] Obviously, such monstrosities did not exist, and it is hard to imagine the Indians' happening to raise the subject of monsters, the specter of which existed only in the European imagination. Rather, it is more probable that, believing the long history of myths about wild men, Columbus allowed myths to shape his interpretation of events. Obviously, Columbus, like many of the early travelers, was looking for and finding what he expected to locate in America, not what was actually there.[21] America was being constructed in addition to being discovered. Nor did this constructing end with Columbus. As late as the nineteenth century, explorers claimed to have found the legendary Patagonian giants.

The second and third views of the Indians before Montaigne were more thoughtful than the views of the explorers. These views were articulated by political theorists in response to the moral questions raised by the discovery of the New World. Spain's original claim to the New World was based on Pope Alexander VI's papal bulls of donation of 1493, but these bulls stipulated that the Indians must be well treated and encouraged to convert to Christianity.[22] Queen Isabella took this charge seriously and wanted the

Indians to be treated like all other citizens of Spain. However, these stipulations got in the way of Spanish earthly aims, especially in the way of the colonists who brutally mistreated the Indians in their search for quick gold. The settlers did what they wanted until Dominican priests began to arrive in 1510. In 1511, one such priest named Montesinos gave his famous sermon condemning the Spanish settlers and withheld their communion. "Are the Indians not Men?" he asked. "Do they not have rational souls? With what right do you keep them in this servitude? With what authority have you waged these detestable wars against these peoples who lived peacefully in their own lands?"[23] Controversy raged. King Ferdinand set up courts of inquiry to review colonial policy and to determine what to do with and how to treat the Indians. What to do with the Indians, however, depended on what they were. The debates over the nature of the Indians were learned and scholarly and greatly influenced by the full weight of Christian scholarship, in particular by Aquinas and Aristotle. In these debates, the Indians were considered barbaric for two distinct reasons: they lacked Christianity and they lacked civilization. They were both infidels and brutes.[24]

In the century between Columbus' voyage and Montaigne's writing, two positions dominated Spanish, indeed European, thinking. The first position argued that the Indians were semihuman *natural* slaves. Since the papal bulls did not justify the forced labor of the *encomienda* system, new grounds of sovereignty and subjugation were needed. These grounds were supplied by the Scottish theologian and historian John Mair, professor in the Collège de Montaigu at Paris. Mair argued that the Indian was the concrete embodiment of Aristotle's natural slave, a category, according to Mair, that Aristotle in his genius had merely hypothesized without ever having seen any such slaves in the flesh.[25] The Spanish, he argued, had now found them. This idea was embraced by Juan de Sepúlveda, a theorist of the Spanish crown. Spain's right of sovereignty, Sepúlveda argued, was not based on the juridical claims of the conqueror, i.e., on the papal bulls, but on the *nature* of the people being conquered.[26] It is easy to see the appeal of this idea. Everyone agreed that the Indians were in some sense barbaric. It was only a small step to say that the reason for this was because the Indians had inferior minds, i.e., they were unable to live rationally.[27] This use of Aristotle's theory allowed the Spaniards to incorporate the Indians into the Christian-Aristotelian world view. The Indians now had a place in the larger cosmology. They were not slaves by human will or human law; they were slaves by nature. Freedom was unnatural and harmful to them. Subjugation brought them to their natural, God-given place. The Spanish, it was argued, were acting justly in their conquest and benefitting all involved.

The second theoretical view that dominated the debates about the Indians before Montaigne arose out of the problems of the first one. How could a perfect God create defective beings? If the Indians were not complete human beings by nature, it would be God's fault, and this could not be. These problems were raised by another person educated in Paris (at the Collège Saint-Jacques), the Dominican Francisco de Vitoria (1492-1546). Vitoria was the chief figure of the Spanish Renaissance and the head of what came to be known as the Salamanca school.[28] Vitoria argued that the Indians were fully human. They obviously possessed rational minds, as witnessed by several key criteria: their language, their knowledge of arts and economics (household management), and their complex political systems. These criteria were taken as the main signs of mature human development, since they are the stages of human maturation according to Aristotle's account of the natural development of the city.[29] Nonetheless, he saw some serious deficiencies in Indian life. For example, they were reputedly cannibals and lacked a written language and the true religion.[30] Vitoria argued, what was to become the dominant view of the sixteenth century (and perhaps even until recently), that the Indians' defects could not be attributed to some lack in their natural essence[31] but to the fact that they were underdeveloped. Their lack of growth was due to their environment, not in the sense of climate but in the more encompassing sense of Aristotle's habituation. They had no training and no examples to imitate. Like children and the illiterate peasants of Europe, what they needed was education.[32] Vitoria took the Indians out of the Aristotelian category of natural slave and invoked another Aristotelian idea. He said their souls were *in potentia*.[33] They needed to be actualized—that was the Spanish mission. Vitoria counted the Indians as men and admitted them into society, although on its lowest level. Nonetheless, they had to be governed by consent, but because they were underdeveloped, not by their actual, formal consent, but according to what would be agreed to based on natural law (which, he argued, the Spanish possessed).

Not even Bartolomé de Las Casas (1474-1566), the most tireless and dedicated defender of the Indians of the sixteenth century, was able to think beyond these categories. Las Casas is famous for his unqualified statement that "all the races of the world are men," but he also admitted that the Indians were underdeveloped.[34] Indeed, he only claimed to have proved empirically what Vitoria proved through logic. Borrowing heavily from Cicero, he put human development on a chart of historical development to argue that progress was due to the inventions of great or wise men, allowing a people to evolve out of a primitive horde into a social body, and eventually develop religion. Since the Indians had developed a culture, the next step, he said, was to bring them religion. Like Acosta after him, he believed that just as the Roman empire preceded the coming of Christ, so too the Mexican and Incan empires presaged the coming of the Spanish.[35] This argument, consistent with both ancient and Christian historiography, explained the cultural distance between the Indians and the Europeans and provided a justification for the missionary zeal. Unlike the other missionaries or Vitoria, Las Casas demanded that proselytization and conversion occur with the Indians' explicit, formal consent. This was humane, but he nonetheless deemed the Indians' lack of Christianity a serious problem, indeed.

In sum, before Montaigne there were three main views of the Indians. The first view "othered" the Indians and led to no moral scruples in their being murdered on a massive scale. The second view condemned the Indians as merely semihuman beings and justified a policy of war, conquest, and exploitation. The third, more liberal, view admitted that the Indians were full, rational human beings, but humans whose development had been retarded. This led to a policy of paternalism and conversion. All of these views assumed that European man represented the epitome of humanity, his superiority determined by two components, Christianity and civilization. If the Europeans were confident in themselves, the Indians had to be the aberration. The idea that Christian European categories could be too narrow or wrong was heresy. Giordano Bruno, for example, challenged those categories by suggesting that the American discoveries were irreconcilable with Biblical chronology, postulates of a universal flood, and a unique creation.[36] By challenging some aspect of the medieval cosmology, Bruno threatened all of it. In 1600, eight years after Montaigne's death, Bruno was convicted of heresy and burnt at the stake.[37]

Rather than articulate a paternalistic attitude toward the Indians as almost everyone in his century did,[38] Montaigne used the existence of the Indians as a point of departure to question European beliefs and to reflect on the possibility of objective standards to critique both the Indians' culture and his own. As we saw in the "Apology," Montaigne praises the animals, a plowman, and the native Brazilians of the New World for living a life based on a simple, direct relation to nature. These three praiseworthy examples are remarkable for their lack of civilization and refinement, and it is exactly this quality that Montaigne wants to highlight. He engages himself and his readers in a thought experiment in which he explores the virtues and limitations of the phenomenologically simple life, arguing that those commonly dismissed as brutish, underdeveloped, or inadequate by thinkers such as Vitoria live happier, more contented lives than the sophisticates of Europe. Montaigne agrees with Vitoria's linkage of the Indians to peasants, but he makes the opposite appraisal of them. The best life, he argues here, is the simple life. This is a strand of his thought that radically reverses the normal moral valuations and makes Montaigne, two centuries before Rousseau, the first modern critic of culture and the first great critic of modern civilization.[39]

Not content to declare a universal equality of cultures, Montaigne explicitly sided with the Indians. A careful reading of Montaigne's praise of the Indians shows both that he knew it was an inaccurate description and that he sees problems with it even as a theoretical ideal. But rather than give an accurate or mixed judgment of them, the rhetoric of Montaigne's presentation is one of lavish praise. Whereas the most enlightened men of Montaigne's times defended the Indians as human beings, they nonetheless saw them as inferior ones. The closest Montaigne comes to adopting such a paternalistic attitude toward the Indians is when he wishes that they had been discovered by the ancient Greeks or Romans, who "would have strengthened and fostered the good seeds that nature had produced in them."[40] But Montaigne unpatronizingly also asserts that such an interchange also would have benefitted "our side of the ocean" (III.6, 888 [694]). Montaigne thus praises both the virtues of the ancient pagan and newly discovered pagan worlds—but not the Christian Europe of his own times. Such conceptions were insupposable to the Christian cosmologists, not only to Mair and Sepúlveda but also to Vitoria and Las Casas. Even though Montaigne in the end backs away from his unqualified praise of living such a simple, phenomenological life, his presentation both redefined natural man and the criterion used to judge him, thus marking an important turn in the history of political philosophy.

II. *Habitude Naturelle* as Humanity's Natural State

Montaigne's skepticism truly enabled a radical break with medieval religious cosmology and allowed him to consider "natural man" in a fresh and powerful way. To explore the possibility of a "normal" course for nature that can serve as a norm for all human behavior, Montaigne stakes out a unique vision of natural man. He attempts to define the natural not by looking at the most developed human beings and the most developed human societies as Aristotle did, but by looking to an image of human beings before they have been altered by the artifice of social and political life.

However, unlike Hobbes (whose *Leviathan* was published seventy-one years after Montaigne's *Essays*), Locke, Rousseau, and the numerous other later contract theorists who followed Montaigne in this way of redefining nature, Montaigne's account does not portray human beings in a totally prepolitical or presocial state. Montaigne's ideal of natural man is a balance between nature and civilization that I call *habitude naturelle*.

As we saw in chapter 1, *habitude naturelle* is a phrase that Montaigne uses—and which I connect to his account of natural man—to explain how human beings can deviate from nature but still be in accordance with it (II.12, 470 [362]).[41] Usually he speaks of nature and habit as opposing sources of impulse, movement, or action, but this is only because most customs deviate from nature most of the time. However, such deviation is neither necessary nor inevitable. Sometimes habits can reinforce the dictates of nature, which is a much happier situation for an individual to be in than to be tugged in different directions by different forces. *Habitude naturelle* is Montaigne's ideal of natural simplicity, because its customs (and the corresponding manner in which it cultivates human beings) and the pure dictates of nature are one and the same—or as close as is humanly possible. By describing this combination of nature and customs as his ideal of tranquil simplicity, Montaigne implies that human beings do not have the choice between living in an unadulterated pure form of nature or living according to custom; they are always born into a particular culture and thus raised in a particular way with particular habits. The only thing one can hope for is to be born into a society that has habits which deviate least from the laws of nature.

The harmonious balance of nature and civilization that makes up Montaigne's ideal of simple phenomenological nature is readily apparent in his description of the native inhabitants of the New World. In describing the Indians' way of life, Montaigne first emphasizes its "naturalness," then praises its beautiful arts. He says the Indians are savage ("*sauvage*")—if one understands the word properly. "Those people are wild [*sauvage*], just as we call wild the fruits that Nature has produced by herself and in her normal course" (I.31, 203 [152]). Savagery or wildness is redefined as the natural. The Indians "are still very close to their original naturalness" and live in "a state of purity" according to "*les loix naturelles*," which, he says, "still rule them" (I.31, 204 [153]).[42] Their condition is characterized by a "naturalness so pure and simple," because their society has "been fashioned very little by the human mind" (I.31, 204 [153]). They have been "very little corrupted" by artificial development. Montaigne contrasts the naturalness of the Indians to Europeans, who "have changed artificially and [gone] astray from the common order," saying that it is those who deviate from Nature "that we should rather call wild" (I.31, 203 [152]). The Indians live in accordance with nature; the Europeans live against it. "The former retain alive and vigorous their genuine, their most useful and natural, virtues and properties, which we have debased in the latter in adapting them to gratify our corrupted taste" (I.31, 204 [153]). It is precisely on the basis of their naturalness that Montaigne advances the Indians as an ideal.

In defining simple "naturalness" as good and "civilization" as a corrupt deviation from the laws of nature, Montaigne defines human nature by its origins, not its end. Following a well-worn path in the history of political thought, Montaigne implies that the way to know what a thing *is*, and therefore to know what it *ought* to do, is to know its nature. However, the method Montaigne uses here to determine a thing's nature is radically new. The way to know a thing's nature, he says, is not by seeking its end in Aristotle's teleological sense of the word but to see it in its precultivated state, according to its "original naturalness" (I.31, 204 [153]).[43] Echoing the arguments in the first half of his "Apology," Montaigne emphasizes the limits and perversity of human creations and praises an image of original nature as better for man than civilization, culture, and art, which are portrayed as negative and corrupting:

> It is not reasonable that art should win the place of honor over our great and powerful mother Nature. We have so overloaded the beauty and richness of her works by our inventions that we have quite smothered her. Yet wherever her purity shines forth, she wonderfully puts to shame our vain and frivolous attempts. (I.31, 203 [152])

In arguing that nature is purer, more powerful, and more beautiful than any human creation, Montaigne closely parallels the arguments that he makes for a simple phenomenological conception of nature in the "Apology." Even some of the examples he uses are the same. In both places he mentions the nest of a bird and the web of a spider as creations unparalleled by mankind.[44] But just as in the "Apology" he ultimately concedes that human capabilities (due to reason) transcend the animals' nature, so too does he ultimately defend natural man as more than "simply" living on instinct.

Whereas Montaigne first defends the Indians as simply natural, in the latter part of the essay he emphasizes the opposite, that the Indians are more than dumb beasts acting by instinct alone. Montaigne gives two examples of the Indians' creations: a war song and a love song. Both are poetic and celebrate the most praiseworthy aspect of their character, their tremendous courage and valor in war, and the central role of easy living in their culture. About their steadfast character he says, "Truly here are real savages by our standards; for either they must be thoroughly so, or we must be" (I.31, 211 [158]). He means the latter. About their poetry, he says it possesses "nothing barbaric," and in fact he compares it to the style of Anacreon, one of the stylists most celebrated in the sixteenth century (I.31, 212 [158]).[45] He also praises their language, comparing its lyrical endings to ancient Greek. Montaigne here argues the opposite of what he did at the beginning of the essay, where barbarism was shed of its negative connotations, and savagery, understood as the complete conformity to nature, was praised as the highest possible ideal. Montaigne does this to show that the Indians are human; they do not act on "a simple and servile bondage to usage and through the pressure of the authority of their ancient customs, without reasoning or judgment, and because their minds are so stupid that they cannot take any other course" (I.31, 212 [158]). They are more than dumb beasts; the Indians have minds and arts and customs of their own. While their arts seem to be based on the works of the other animals, and thus might be called as simple and natural as artificial creation can be, they are nonetheless arts. Montaigne abandons the supposed dignity of acting by nature alone and instead praises actions based on human will. Thus, if simply acting like the animals is desirable, the Indians are not ideal. If, on the other hand, the Indians represent the ideal, acting like the animals seems neither desirable nor possible.

So where does this leave us? Montaigne first praises the Indians as natural, then he denies it. This apparent difference is mitigated, however, when one realizes that Montaigne uses the terms in both their conventional and unconventional senses. His statements are opposed only because he uses the same words in opposite ways. When he calls the Indians "natural," "savage," and "barbaric," it is only because he is praising these concepts or has denuded the terms of their negative connotations. When he praises the Indians for their arts, he has restored to the ideas of "nature," "savagery," and "barbarism" their more conventional negative, brutish connotations.[46] The two perspectives balance and correct each other. The first argues that nature is good and deviation from it is bad. The second adds that an unthinking obedience to anything is unsuitable for a human being. Reflection and choice are also good for human beings. The two can be combined to recommend a policy of limited art, art limited by natural ends and natural means. Indeed, this is exactly what the Indians—and *habitude naturelle*—represent.

Because of this balance between nature and simple habits, Montaigne's account of nature might be positioned between Aristotle's and that of the later social-contract theorists. Like Aristotle, Montaigne seems to deem human beings to be social creatures that can exist only in communities from the very beginning (even though the human faculties are much less developed in Montaigne's vision of *habitude naturelle* than in Aristotle's account of the *polis*). Montaigne thus rejects the radically unsituated individualism of Hobbes and later liberalism. But unlike Aristotle, and like the later social contract theorists who follow Montaigne in this respect, Montaigne judges nature not by the teleological endpoint of human development but by its origins in a precultivated, barely developed, "natural" society. Montaigne conceives of natural man as possessing reason, but he deems it only partially developed. Unlike Hobbes and Locke, Montaigne does not imagine natural man as possessing fully formed reason capable of understanding the rational laws of nature; unlike Rousseau he does not imagine natural man as having no reason. Reason is developed only enough to foster the simplest and most natural customs.

III. Cannibals in Utopia

What would a society that embodies *habitude naturelle*, Montaigne's vision of natural simplicity, look like? This section examines the benefits of a life lived according to *habitude naturelle*, and these are legion. One of its main benefits is that it offers an antidote to skeptical angst, though if truth be told, it does not do so in a sufficient way. Montaigne's musings here do not rise to the level of philosophical profundity that the rest of his inquiry does. But if these imaginings do not give philosophical answers with certitude, they do highlight the problems and solve in a quotidian way moral problems raised by skeptical doubt.

Montaigne's thought experiment about what a society based on *habitude naturelle* would look like is designed, right from the start, to challenge his readers by creating a kind of dissonance. Montaigne does not approve of cannibalism, yet the essay in which he most fully describes a society based on *habitude naturelle* is titled "Of Cannibals." To give his vision a positive connotation, Montaigne could have called the essay "Of Natural Habits (*Habitude Naturelle*)." Or he could have called it "Of the Brazilians," "Of the Indians," or "Of Natural Man," which are neutral descriptions, or even "Of Savages" or "Of Barbarians," which have negative connotations but which are not as frightful as "Of Cannibals." Montaigne refers to his subjects in all of these terms, so it seems reasonable to assume that he purposefully chose to jolt his readers by giving his topic the most extreme initial formulation possible. Savages and barbarians are not necessarily cannibals, but cannibals are by definition, it would seem, barbaric and savage. Despite this, Montaigne has barely a harsh word to say about the Indians in the entire essay. Every reader, except those who mistake the irony of the closing remark about wearing pants,[47] senses Montaigne's sympathy for the cannibals and the high esteem in which he holds them. The dissonance between his mostly praiseworthy account of the Indians and the shocking label that he applies to them—cannibals—is meant to jar the reader into self-questioning.[48]

The issue that Montaigne forces the reader to confront is the issue that bedevils every skeptic: is there any universal standard of moral behavior, or must everything be accepted, including cannibalism? Montaigne highlights cannibalism to provoke the question of whether or not there is a morality that transcends cultural relativism. Cannibalism crosses what seems to be the most obvious "natural" limit of human behavior and takes savagery and barbarism to what seems to Westerners a most revolting extreme, the eating of human flesh. If there is one thing that we think we know, it is that we should not eat our own kind—but why not? Vitoria and another prominent sixteenth-century thinker, Girolamo Cardano, consider cannibalism a barbaric mistaking of categories, caused both by a lack of intelligence and a lack of self-control, but Aquinas offers some circumstances under which it might be justifiable.[49] If abhorrence of cannibalism is not a universal impulse like breathing, what prevents us from saying that it is simply conventional? What standard condemns this practice, and what defines the group that we will not touch? Normally, we think of this prohibition as based on species, but as we saw in the previous chapter, Montaigne sometimes argues that we have obligations to the other animals.[50] Conversely, why do we have an obligation to respect *every* individual being of our own species? We justify killing human beings under several circumstances, and draw drastic distinctions between citizens of different nations, practitioners of different religions, and those in different economic and social classes. Why should we not eat these "others"? These are the questions that are opened by Montaigne's decision to raise the issue of cannibalism without immediately dismissing those who practice it. Cannibalism is Montaigne's stark wedge issue to raise the more general question of natural standards for human behavior.[51]

Having raised the question of whether there are natural grounds upon which the immorality of cannibalism can be asserted, Montaigne does not exactly seek an answer. Such a quest would require of him a definition of natural justice and of the good by nature, and for some reason (perhaps deeming this task impossible), he does not attempt it. What he does instead, however, is assert the middle ground position that I am calling *habitude naturelle*. In exploring the morality of cannibalism, Montaigne juggles three different standards for deciding: nature, reason, and that of "civilized" Europe. When Montaigne writes that "we may well call these people [cannibals] barbarians, in respect to the rules of reason, but not in respect to ourselves, who surpass them in every kind of barbarity" (I.31, 208 [156]), he indicates that there *are* "rules of reason," and distinguishes between these rules and European ones.[52] Europe has developed humanity's rational capabilities more fully than the Indians, and Europe has reasoned out the immorality of cannibalism, but Montaigne presents the Europeans as falling short of the Indians with respect to natural morality—after all, that is the whole point of comparing them. Cannibalism, Montaigne implies, violates the rules of reason, though it may not violate the laws of nature. Therefore, skeptical doubting as to the morality of cannibalism cannot find any natural ground that would necessitate the universal wrongness of cannibalism.

However, Montaigne suggests, there is a middle ground that we can call *habitude naturelle*: while cannibalism *in general* violates reason, this is not *always* the case. Montaigne cites three kinds of philosophical and medical authorities that accept cannibalism under certain circumstances of natural emergency, so reason must be tempered by nature.[53] Similarly, nature must be tempered by reason. As we saw in chapter 1, the only passage cited twice in Montaigne's "Apology for Raymond Sebond" is Epicurus' claim that without law human beings would eat each other. Such a claim indicates that cannibalism may well be "natural," though it violates "common sense" norms of reason. In fact, what was perceived as a natural tendency toward eating our own kind gave rise to a tradition of natural law that developed from antiquity through the seventeenth century. Puffendorf and Grotius, for example, argued that "if there were not any justice, each of us would eat one another."[54] Nature can violate reason-based conceptions of justice just as reason-based conceptions can stray from nature. In avowing that cannibalism violates the rules of reason, Montaigne is asserting the need for positive law. But in pointing out the equally barbarous nature of "civilized" citizens governed by misguided, denatured reason, Montaigne is insisting that the justice system be flexible and tempered by natural needs and circumstances, not inflexibly bound either to purely natural or purely customary claims. The endpoint of Montaigne's skeptical meditation upon the possible naturalness of cannibalism is an affirmation of *habitude naturelle*: a norm for behavior that follows from simple, phenomenological man but reconciles the dictates of nature with those of reason.

Accordingly, Montaigne describes the Indians' form of warfare as a worthy exemplar of *habitude naturelle*. Although some readers of the *Essays* might expect Montaigne to condemn war *a priori* as a deviance from nature, Montaigne does not do this. Instead, he describes the Indians' form of warfare as "wholly noble" ("*toute noble*") and "as excusable and beautiful as this human disease can be" (I.31, 208 [156]). By calling war a human "disease" Montaigne is clearly expressing dislike and disapproval of it. One might say that parallel to Montaigne's analysis of cannibalism, war is against the rules of reason. But by including—and praising—it in this ideal state of simplicity to begin with, which he did not have to do (Rousseau, Voltaire, and Diderot describe war as a consequence of social and political corruption), Montaigne seems to be indicating that it is unavoidable.[55] Some sort of aggression seems inevitable to him; the only question is how it will manifest itself. In this respect, the Indians' culture of war is an ideal embodiment of *habitude naturelle*; Montaigne admires both why and how the cannibals fight. Unlike Hobbes, Montaigne does not describe the natural state as one of horrible and continual war of all against all. Unlike Europeans, who murder under the guise of religion or commit massacres to expand their "traffic in pearls and pepper" (III.6, 889 [695]), the cannibals do not fight for land, piety, or material gain. Rather, Montaigne describes the Indians as channeling the aggressive aspects of human nature into a noble form of personal challenge. They fight to determine and prove their worth, to test themselves by testing their abilities. Although he does not use the word "essay," he makes fighting seem to be their way of testing, or essaying, themselves.[56] Fighting enables each cannibal to discover and push his limits. And even though they fight their neighbors, their own society is factionless, exhibiting no signs of domestic discord. They fight, he says, as nobly as the greatest Spartan generals did in their greatest battles. The fact of physical captivity or the threat of death means nothing to them; conquest to them is not physical but psychological. Montaigne tells the story of an Indian prisoner whose captors taunted him by threatening to eat him. Rather than begging for his life, he proudly retorts that when they eat him they will be eating their ancestors, implying that in the past his village has won many victories over theirs. Montaigne admires this kind of Stoic character and defiance. If they do not give in to their captors, they are not beaten, because inner freedom is all that matters. They can be killed but not conquered. They may be beaten but not by their enemies, only by fortune.[57] "The worth and value of a man is in his heart and his will; there lies his real honor," Montaigne says; "Valor is the strength, not of legs and arms, but of heart and soul" (I.31, 210 [157]). They fully participate in the horrors of war, but unlike the hypocritical crusaders in Europe or the greedy and rapacious conquistadors in the New World, they do it for the most excusable reasons. They are thus portrayed as the embodiment of a natural society and as a living critique of European corruption and artifice. They are noble savages.

As good as their style of warfare is, in condemning the Indians' cannibalism and warfare as less than perfect embodiments of reason, Montaigne more fiercely condemns Europe's self-proclaimed "civilization" on the same grounds. Montaigne treats the issue of cannibalism not as one of food alone, but also as an issue of punishing one's enemies. Montaigne condemns the Indians' eating of their dead prisoners as barbaric and as "extreme revenge," but he decries the torture and ignoble warfare practiced by Europe as the equivalent of eating people alive, proclaiming:

> I am not sorry that we notice the barbarous horror of such acts, but I am heartily sorry that, judging their faults rightly, we should be so blind to our own. I think there is more barbarity in eating a man alive than in eating him dead; and in tearing by tortures and the rack a body still full of feeling, in roasting a man bit by bit, in having him bitten and mangled by dogs and swine (as we have not only read but seen within fresh memory, not among ancient enemies, but among neighbors and fellow citizens, and what is worse, on the pretext of piety and religion), than in roasting and eating him after he is dead. (I.31, 207-8 [155])

Montaigne's criticisms of torture and punishment in Europe are unconditional and never qualified in any way. The fact that it is done under the "pretext of piety" makes it even more revolting. He considers torture when rationalized by appeals to piety to be inexcusable, especially as was occurring in the religious wars that were tearing France apart, in the brutal slaughter of the New World Indians by the Spanish, and in the Inquisition in which several of his relatives were burned at the stake. Every society would be found lacking if compared to the "rules of reason" in the abstract, but the society of *habitude naturelle* proves less cruel and less barbaric than Europe.

Just as the cannibals' manner of warfare proves to be almost as good as possible, so too does their domestic tranquility. The cannibals' domestic life is described as tranquility and bliss. Their lifestyle is joyous, playful, and based on a kind of phenomenological simplicity. The cannibals' "sole concern [is] with passing life happily and pleasantly" (III.6, 889 [695]). They possess "that great thing, the knowledge of how to enjoy their condition happily and be content with it" (I.31, 209 [156]). They have no occupation but leisure and spend the whole day dancing, although young men also hunt animals with bows.[58] Moderation, simplicity, and equality rule almost every feature of their lives. Their homes are communal and Spartan, which means they have no private property and "no riches or poverty" (I.31, 204 [153]). Their diet is limited. Religiously, they believe in the immortality of the soul and that good and bad souls go to different places, but there is no established religion or special religious training. Political and economic ambition is nonexistent, so lying, trickery, and coercion are unnecessary. Montaigne contrasts the Indians' harmony with European disorder: "There never was any opinion so disordered as to excuse treachery, disloyalty, tyranny, and cruelty, which are our ordinary vices" (I.31, 208 [156]). In short, the cannibals embody the ideal of the first part of the "Apology," where Montaigne praised the Brazilians as having "tranquility and serenity of their souls, unburdened with any tense or unpleasant passion or thought or occupation" (II.12, 471 [362]). In contrast to European corruption, *habitude naturelle* is the calm enjoyment of life within simple and natural limits.

In addition to his general praise of this simple, natural society, Montaigne alludes to three specific ways in which it is superior to the domestic practices of Europe. In tropes of criticism which were to become the standard criticisms that eighteenth-century *philosophes* put into the mouths of natural man, Montaigne, at the end of his essay, describes some Indians who came to France and criticized three aspects of French society (although he claims only to remember two). The two explicit charges against France are on political and economic grounds. They find it absurd that the ruler could be a child, a criticism of hereditary monarchy, and that some people were "gorged with all sorts of good things" while others were "emaciated with hunger and poverty" (I.31, 212-13 [159]). Rousseau, in the concluding sentence of his *Second Discourse*, similarly equates "civilization" with three gross violations of natural law: "for a child to command an old man, for an imbecile to lead a wise man, and for a handful of people to gorge themselves on superfluities while the starving multitude lacks necessities."[59] Rousseau's first and third criticisms are identical to Montaigne's. Rousseau's second criticism is vaguer, but insofar as it has to do with the realm of the understanding, it might be a criticism of religion. Could this be the criticism that Montaigne has "forgotten"? Indeed, together with Montaigne and Rousseau's other two, criticism of religion is the third main strand of Voltaire and Diderot's attack on "civilization." This might be confirmed for Montaigne by reflecting on his discussion of the Indians' religious practices. They have a "sort of priests and prophets," Montaigne says, but to discourage them from making trouble or creating fear—and in what might humorously be seen as Montaigne's solution to the religious wars of his own day—false prophets, after making just one wrong prediction, are "cut into a thousand pieces" (I.31, 206 [154]). The Indians' natural society, even with its cannibalism, is politically, socially, economically, and religiously superior to Europe's unnatural and corrupt ways. It is the purest embodiment of the virtues of health, justice, and equity.

The virtues of the cannibals' simple society lead Montaigne to go so far as to make the highly dubious claim that this ideal of simplicity transcends the ideals of the golden age of all past poets and philosophers. "What we actually see in these nations surpasses not only all the pictures in which poets have idealized the golden age and all their inventions in imagining a happy state of man," he says, "but also the conceptions and the very desire of philosophy" (I.31, 204 [153]). Surely this claim is hyperbolic to Montaigne as well as to us. It is highly doubtful whether this society meets, let alone surpasses, the desires of Montaigne himself, let alone all of the ancient poets and philosophers. For Montaigne's claim to be true, all past philosophers would have had to desire tranquility and simplicity above all else, which Montaigne sometimes asserts to be the case.[60] All of the main schools of philosophy in the Hellenistic era did value mental tranquility (*ataraxy*), but they did not value it to the exclusion of everything else. In fact, as much as Montaigne praises the virtue of mental tranquility, he seems almost incapable of imagining the substance of a simple way of life devoted almost exclusively to it. Just as in the "Apology" Montaigne presents his ideal of simplicity largely in terms of what it is not—"life in admirable simplicity and ignorance, without letters, without law, without king, without religion of any kind" (II.12, 471 [362])—so too does he portray the cannibals' society largely in terms of its absences:

> There is no sort of traffic, no knowledge of letters, no science of numbers, no name for a magistrate or for political superiority, no custom of servitude, no riches or poverty, no contracts, no successions, no partitions, no occupations but leisure ones, no care for any but common kinship, no clothes, no agriculture, no metal, no use of wine or wheat. The very words that signify lying, treachery, dissimulation, avarice, envy, belittling, pardon—unheard of. (I.31, 204 [153])[61]

Whereas Karl Marx describes his vision of life after the communist revolution as the absence of that which he despises—private property, religion, the state, nations, the family—it is unlikely that Montaigne himself similarly despises all the negated aspects in the cannibals' society. Indeed, Montaigne, in numerous places throughout his work, praises several of the missing ingredients of this society. Montaigne praises "knowledge of letters and numbers" when understood properly. To abandon them entirely just because they are often misunderstood or abused would be to throw the baby out with the bath water. Similarly, he condemns people who know "no pardon"; toleration and clemency are among his chief recommendations for the frailty and foibles of the human condition.[62] These absences indicate that this society, as good as it is, does not surpass Montaigne's imaginings about a golden age. The main reason, however, that one doubts that the primitive nature of this society excels the expectations of all past philosophers is because it clearly omits the kind of development of the human soul that was advocated, for example, by Plato and Aristotle. Although Socrates in Book II of the *Republic* calls just such a simple city "healthy," any society based on "no knowledge of letters, no science of numbers" and the complete absence of philosophy marks it as far from his ideal.[63] Even the sober Hobbes, who has never been accused of being too idealistic, decries the lack of arts, letters, science, agriculture, industry, and trade—all absent from the cannibals' society according to Montaigne—as among the most incommodious and nasty aspects of the state of nature.[64] But despite these indications that there is something wrong, there is a consistency to this strand of simplicity in Montaigne's thought. Elsewhere, Montaigne praises the "cannibals, who enjoy the happiness of a long, tranquil, and peaceable life without" being corrupted by "the precepts of Aristotle" or "the name of physics" (II.12, 523 [404]). Knowledge which is not based on direct perception is clearly not part of Montaigne's natural man or natural society.

While the simplicity of the cannibals' society does not exceed the dreams of all past philosophers, a society based on *habitude naturelle* does allow it to avoid one of the worst calamities of more complicated, civilized life—competing and conflicting authorities. The conflict among public institutions and between them and private citizens is a chief source of human unhappiness. These conflicts can be caused by problems either in the institutions or in the individual. The cannibals' society avoids both of these problems. It avoids the craziness of reason and of the human imagination, which Montaigne blames as the cause of a great number of human ills, such as anxiety, ambition, and fear. With the exception of their military combat, they never flee themselves in the search for unreal or illusory goods, such as honors, wealth, and external recognition. To this extent, the cannibals' domestic society does embody a positive quality of natural health that Montaigne values dearly. And because the cannibals control themselves, they do not need overbearing, Leviathan-like political institutions. Institutions are created to keep people in line, but institutions, just as the individuals who compose them, often go astray. Institutional oppression or misguided institutions that force sane people to do crazy things or pit them against other institutions, such as conflicting requirements between political and religious authorities, are another great source of human misery. Being so close to their original naturalness, the cannibals barely need human laws to rule themselves and barely develop their political or religious institutions. Politically, they have "no name for a magistrate or political superiority" (I.31, 204 [153]). There is no hierarchy, and they all have equal rights. They have a nominal ruler, but he is entitled to only two things: having the paths cleared of underbrush when he visits his villages and marching first into battle. With privileges such as these, no wonder there is no temptation to political ambition. The cannibals can live without these things because the material goods they need to survive are all at hand. Nature, as Montaigne describes it, is abundant and plentiful. More importantly, however, they have what they need, because they limit their needs to what is natural. By European standards, they live in poverty, but the cannibals do not experience scarcity because they control both sources of artificial desires: their minds and their habits. Their desires are simple and natural, and their customs reinforce this pure path.

In sum, the greatest benefit of a society based on *habitude naturelle* is that its simplicity allows individuals' roles and souls to be the same, thereby embodying the only authentic harmony of public and private. Nature and the cannibals' artificial conventions are largely in accord. The public accommodates itself to the private; that is to say it demands no more (or barely more) from individuals than nature itself. They have this harmony for both psychological and institutional reasons. Their purely natural desires, unencumbered by any public prohibitions or demands, enable them to possess simple and tranquil souls and noble and steadfast characters. Because their desires are so pure, their society can be maintained with "little artifice and human solder" (I.31, 204 [153]). Regulated passions and a minimal state are the keys to the cannibals' happiness. They desire only as much as their natural needs demand; everything else they reject as superfluous. Institutions are needed only to temper vice, and vice is vice only when there are institutions to label it as such—if cannibalism is not vice, nothing is. Thus, a minimal state lessens the chances of conflict between their private and public selves, freeing them from the unhappiness that results from the conflict between one's natural desires and the demands of one's society. When these conflicting demands are internalized, it leads to psychic stress, internal disharmony, and to the self being divided against itself, such that no matter what it does it cannot satisfy all its masters and be content. When the conflicting demands are between an individual and the powers that be in his society, the individual must negate or efface himself or risk externally induced punishment. The cannibals' simplicity avoids all of these potential human pitfalls. Consequently, their duties are few but practicable and healthy. The citizens get happiness, the society stability.

IV. The Downfall of the Ideal of Simplicity

One might suppose that Montaigne would back away from this vision of *habitude naturelle* because the Indians fight wars and eat their prisoners, but this is not the case. Montaigne condemns cannibalism, but he rejects *habitude naturelle* for a deeper reason: it lacks reflective self-awareness. Montaigne conceives a society that embodies simplicity as necessarily lacking in the cultivation of reason, and he illustrates this fault with comparisons to ancient Rome and to Socrates and himself, concluding that a purely phenomenological existence is neither entirely practical nor entirely desirable. It is not desirable, because the Indians, peasants, and all such simple people, lack something—the self-awareness that is necessary to have an individuated authenticity—that Montaigne highly values. And while such a simple society might be internally stable, when confronted with another society, it lacks the tools—flexibility of mind and the ability to deal with new things and diversity—to enable it to hold its own. Montaigne, however, does not entirely discard the ideal of phenomenological simplicity but looks to supplement it in order to correct its problems.

The happy state of the cannibals, and the reconciliation of public and private that they represent, is possible only because the cannibals barely develop their rational capacity. As if to emphasize the point, Montaigne uncharacteristically repeats himself to tell us that their "whole ethical science" consists of only two articles, valor versus the enemy and affection toward their wives (I.31, 206 [154]). Note two things about their moral doctrine. First, the men need reminders concerning both their foreign and domestic affairs. They need to be reminded to be tough toward the enemy but kind toward their wives. Uniform behavior in either direction would lead to disaster, the unnecessary subjugation of the entire population (failing to defeat the enemy) or of half of it (treating their women like enemies or slaves). These are the first distinctions that any society has to make and reveal the bare minimum moral code for every society, cannibal, European, or other. The fact that the cannibals need reminding of these principles shows their closeness to nature and lack of development. Second, and more revealing, the cannibals' moral universe values only what Plato calls *thumos* and *eros* but not reason. These categories correspond to two of the three parts of the soul that Plato identifies in the *Republic*, a work referred to earlier in the essay. By repeating that their "*whole* ethical science" concerns only these two things, Montaigne highlights the obvious: the cannibals barely develop their rational capacity. Montaigne further links only these two qualities to his conception of natural law. In general, Montaigne dismisses the idea that there is a natural law for all human beings, but in one of his few speculations on what such a natural law would be, if it existed, Montaigne states that "any instinct that is seen universally and permanently imprinted in both the animals and ourselves (which is not beyond dispute)" would include two things. First and foremost, Montaigne puts "[t]he care every animal has for its own preservation and the avoidance of what is harmful, the affection that the begetter has for his begotten ranks second" (II.8, 365 [279]). So we see that the two qualities that Montaigne chooses to put in the cannibals' character are those he considers most permanent and universal. But this leaves out their rational development. Their lack of reason conduces to their contentment in that if they were more sophisticated or more shrewd, Montaigne seems to think that their imaginations would necessarily carry them away from their natural tranquility, and they would need institutions to keep them in check. Indeed, this is exactly what happens in the drama of Plato's *Republic*. The first city of necessity is rejected by the ambitious Glaucon who wants "relishes," i.e., luxuries. Once the mind detaches itself from simple necessities, excessive desires are similarly awakened. In their natural state, the cannibals can rely on character alone.

Because the cannibals barely develop their rational faculties, their society proves untenable on both theoretical and practical grounds. It lacks key aspects of a fully developed human and politically viable way of life. *Habitude naturelle* as illustrated by the cannibals is vulnerable to outside influence. Montaigne describes the cannibals as isolated, and such a simple society can in fact survive only in isolation. But since they are human with the attendant curiosity and imagination, they are bound to undermine the grounds upon which their society rests. At the end of "Of Cannibals," Montaigne mentions three cannibals who, seeking knowledge of the outside world and "tricked by the desire for new things," venture out from the serenity of their own sky only to discover the sickness of others (I.31, 212 [158-59]). Such an innocent and simple people are helpless when confronted with cynical and corrupt people like Europeans. Thus, they are doomed to ruin. These people are vulnerable because they are too simple. Their knowledge is natural and habitual, not based on reason or self-understanding. They know how to live, but due to a lack of reflection, they do not know that they know this. Without the self-consciousness that comes with the mature development of reason, they are vulnerable to change—and to fall. Deeper knowledge is the only thing that can protect them from outside influence and it is exactly the thing that they cannot possess.[65] This might explain why Montaigne does not call the military self-testing in which the cannibals engage "essaying." Essaying, as Montaigne understands it, requires self-consciousness.

The need for deeper understanding is further developed in Montaigne's other systematic discussion of the Indians in "Of Coaches" (III.6). Montaigne offers the same kind of praise of the Indians there that he does in "Of Cannibals," and close examination reveals the same problems. The central comparison in "Of Coaches" shows the inadequacy of both Europe and the Indians.[66] It contrasts the viciousness of Europe as embodied in the brutality and greed of the Conquistadors[67] with the inadequate development of the Indians. Though the Indian cultures he describes—those of Peru and Mexico—are composed of the most advanced peoples America has to offer, he says even these cultures lack maturity and development, referring to their "infant world" and calling their knowledge "so new and so infantile" (III.6, 886-87 [693]). Moreover he laments that they were not conquered by the ancient Greeks and Romans, who "would have gently polished and cleared away whatever was barbarous in them, and would have strengthened and fostered the good seeds that nature had produced in them" (III.6, 888 [694]). To be able to educate and refine the Indians, the ancients would have had to possess some quality that the Indians do not. Indeed, this is exactly the case. The comparisons that Montaigne asks us to make reveal the key weakness of the natural life: its lack of sophistication, by which I mean its lack of mature judgment that results from critical and philosophical self-awareness.

The Indians' problems result from a lack of judgment. Montaigne reveals their fault when discussing their fearlessness. Montaigne favorably compares the courage of the Indians to that of the ancients: "As for boldness and courage, as for firmness, constancy, resoluteness against pains and hunger and death, I would not fear to oppose the examples I could find among them to the most famous ancient examples" (III.6, 887 [694]). The Indians, he says, possess an "indomitable ardor" and a "noble, stubborn readiness to suffer all extremities and hardships, even death," which led thousands of men, women, and children to hurl themselves into danger to defend their gods and their liberty, rather than succumb to the domination of the Spanish (III.6, 888 [694]). But if the Indians were so courageous and the Spanish so base, the Indians so many and the Spanish so few, why were the Indians defeated? Many scholars say it was due to the Spaniards' superior technology,[68] which Montaigne considers a partial, but not the most important, ingredient of the Indians' defeat. Rather, his answer to this question is contained in the seemingly innocuous introduction to "Of Coaches," where he asserts that "fear sometimes arises from want of judgment as well as from want of courage" (III.6, 877 [685-86]). The implication for the Indians, and for the natural life itself, is that courage is not enough to live successfully. A successful life also requires good judgment. Just as those in "Of Cannibals" had to live in isolation, and the unfortunate three who wander abroad are easily corrupted, so advanced Indians who stay at home are easily conquered when newcomers arrive. Montaigne explains it in one very long sentence:

> take away the ruses and tricks that they used to deceive them, and the people's *natural astonishment* at seeing the *unexpected* arrival of bearded men, different in language, religion, shape, and countenance, from a part of the world so remote, where they had *never imagined* there was any sort of human habitation, mounted on great *unknown* monsters, opposed to men who had *never seen* not only a horse, but any sort of animal trained to carry and endure a man or any other burden; men equipped with a hard and shiny skin and a sharp and glittering weapon, against men who, for the *miracle* of a mirror or a knife, would exchange a great treasure in gold and pearls, and who had *neither the knowledge nor the material* by which, even in full leisure, they could pierce our steel; add to this the lightning and thunder of our cannon and harquebuses—capable of disturbing Caesar himself, if he had been *surprised* by them with as *little experience* and in his time—against people who were naked (except in some regions where the invention of some cotton fabric had reached them), without other arms at the most than bows, stones, sticks, and wooden bucklers; people *taken by surprise*, under color of friendship and good faith, by *curiosity to see strange and unknown things*: eliminate this disparity, I say, and you take from the conquerors *the whole basis of so many victories*. (III.6, 887-88 [694], emphasis added)

This passage underlies the key weakness of pure reliance on *habitude naturelle* as a mode of living: its inability to anticipate or prepare for the unexpected.[69]

The Indians' incapacity when confronted with something new is mirrored in Montaigne's comparisons between the Indians and ancient Romans.[70] Montaigne describes the Indians as having beautiful and functional objects and noble characters. For example, he describes their coaches (the subject which gives the title to the essay) as made of gold and carried by self-sacrificing porters. In describing the coachmen, Montaigne creates a picture of reverence for the king, nobility and sacrifice in serving him, and an empathy, on the part of the reader, for the king's impending doom. In contrast to the Indians' courage, which could not prevent their imminent destruction, Montaigne juxtaposes Rome's brutality and extravagance but discusses the coaches Rome used in its *victory* parades. Whereas the Indians honored dedication, the Romans honored innovation. Victorious Roman generals, Mark Antony and Firmus, for example, used lions and ostriches, respectively, to pull their coaches (III.6, 879 [687]). While this is extravagant, it exposed Roman citizens to new sights; unlike the Indians, they would not be astonished to see new beasts. Similarly, Montaigne praises a road in Peru: "straight, even, twenty-five paces wide, paved, lined on both sides with fine high walls" (III.6, 893 [698]) and Montezuma's garden, which had a gold replica of "all the living creatures native to his country and its waters" (III.6, 887 [693]). These accomplishments are impressive but sterile and lifeless. By contrast, Roman amphitheaters were filled with living creatures, not only from their own country but from all over the world; in fact, the amphitheater sometimes was flooded to show sea life. Such spectacles were for the entire citizenry, not just the ruler. Indian life (and relying on custom generally) was like their road—straight and walled in. They were not prepared for the new; Rome flourished on the new. Perhaps Rome's craving for the new bordered on the perverse, which is why Montaigne's praise of Rome is qualified, but this is why Rome could conquer the world and why the Indians were doomed to be conquered. Montaigne praises "the inventiveness and the novelty" of Rome's spectacles, because they provided "amazement," which is the beginning of inquiry and philosophy (III.6, 885 [692]). To the extent that the pleasure of Rome was to seek "an infinite capacity to produce innumerable forms" (III.6, 886 [692]), Montaigne sees benefit in its lavishness. The flexibility in encountering the new is not only pertinent to warfare and spectacles, but to thinking. Montaigne discusses the myths of the Indians as simpleminded: "to what notions will the laxness of human credulity not submit!" (III.6, 893 [698]). By contrast, Montaigne cites two contradictory quotations from Lucretius stating that the world is both old and young as a sign of the philosophical mind's ability to grasp both sides of an issue, which is an essential ingredient for success in a varied world. The benefits of this kind of training parallel the benefits gained by the exposure to novelty and diversity that the Roman spectacles and coaches provided. The Roman world trained its citizens for all possible occurrences; the Indians' did not. The lack of development of the Indians' mental faculties mitigates the benefits of their tremendous characters. They are easily stunned and shocked, which is not a reflection of their courage but of their limited ability to judge.[71] Rome was superior in cultivating prudential judgment.

The remedy for the problem of oversimplicity is not to imitate Rome (with its attendant cruelties) but to develop human judgment in a more tranquil manner, to be more like Montaigne himself and Socrates. In the introduction to "Of Coaches," Montaigne writes of himself that "all the dangers I have seen, I have seen with open eyes, with my sight free, sound, and entire" (III.6, 877 [686]). As a philosopher who tries to make sense of every situation, he acts "without terror and without dismay [*estonnement*]"; he can be excited but not dazed or distracted. Similarly, Montaigne explains how Socrates' "presence of mind and resolution" "considering and judging what was going on around him" actually deterred attack; potential enemies prefer to attack the frightened or astonished (III.6, 877 [686]).[72] Montaigne admires the tranquility and contentedness that a simple, phenomenological life avails, but the best human life will combine mental tranquility with the kind of self-conscious judgment that the Indians lack.

V. Conclusion: The Legacy of Montaigne's "Natural Man"

Montaigne's skepticism freed him to engage in a radical thought experiment regarding the concept and consequences of "natural man." He praises the mental tranquility of the Indians of the New World who represent the embodiment of his conception, momentarily calling them the best society that ever existed or was ever imagined. But like monarchy in Book III of Aristotle's *Politics*, Montaigne's "best" regime undermines itself. Its very "perfection" is its weakness. It only can exist if reason is not developed, but it cannot survive or thrive without it. This does not really matter, because, politically, there is no way to move a complex modern society to the society of the Indians. There is no going back. Montaigne does, however, indicate that such a move is not only possible but can be improved upon on the individual level. Montaigne wants to combine the simplicity of the Indians with the self-awareness of a philosopher, to achieve a self-conscious, i.e., sophisticated, simplicity, which is illustrated throughout the *Essays* and is the subject of the next chapter.[73]

But if Montaigne ultimately rejects the way of life of the Indians and the natural man that they represent, why does he let such praise of them—that they exceed even the golden age imaginings of all past philosophers and poets—remain in his text? One possibility is that he never bothered to reread his essays or change anything. Scholars, however, have revealed that Montaigne continually inserted passages into his text, and that despite his written claim that he never made deletions, he did in fact change passages and delete text.[74] Perhaps Montaigne intended to change these passages and forgot; but after several publications and years of editing, this too seems unlikely. The answer, I believe, is eloquently stated in the very first words of "Of Coaches":

> It is very easy to demonstrate that great authors, when they write about causes, adduce not only those they think are true but also those they do not believe in, provided they have some originality and beauty. They speak truly and usefully enough if they speak ingeniously. (III.6, 876 [685])[75]

Consistent with Montaigne's claim that all philosophers invent fictions to be useful (discussed in chapter 1), his Indian studies are fictions intended to explore underlying philosophical truths about natural man. Montaigne attributes his vision to "cannibals" in order to shock his readers out of lazy torpor. Just as the Indians' astonishment led to their downfall, so Montaigne employs shock in order to undermine the unnatural, unreasonable, and cruel customs thoughtlessly accepted by his contemporaries.

Like Montesquieu with the English, Montaigne chooses the Indians as the closest existing approximation of his own vision,[76] but he makes it clear, however, that the picture he presents in "Of Cannibals" is not the whole story. While the Indians are consistently praised in "Of Cannibals," the essay immediately preceding it, "Of Moderation," concludes with a lengthy description of the Indians' "horrible cruelty," including their mortal sacrifices of living human beings for religious purposes, which rivals any of the horrors committed by Europeans (I.30, 199 [149]).[77] Did Montaigne put down his pen and forget the excesses he vividly describes in one essay before writing the next? No, rather Montaigne places the two accounts together to portray a complete vision, but separates them in order to conduct his philosophical meditation upon the virtues and detriments of *habitude naturelle* without it being undermined by inconvenient historical facts. As a stratagem of making his criticisms inexplicitly or so as to go unnoticed, this clearly worked. Most scholars and university courses that treat Montaigne's views of the Indians deal only with "Of Cannibals" and ignore the corrective passage that immediately precedes it, perhaps because it is inconveniently located at the end of a completely different discussion under a different chapter heading. Both by omission and creation, Montaigne is the first to arrange his account to give the Indians good press, and if one is going to be misrepresented—we saw how Mair, Sepúlveda, and Vitoria represented them—better this way than the opposite.

Although Montaigne himself backs away from his counterideal of the noble savage, he wittingly sets in motion a process of cultural criticism that has had profound markings on Western civilization.[78] Everything about the structure of his presentation, from the shocking title to the implied criticisms, from his encouraging of comparisons to the separation of some horrible truths, seems calculated to raise questions about real problems in Europe. Just as important as his critique of European civilization is his thought experiment about the nature of natural man. The Indians represent a "moment" in Montaigne's thinking, the epitome of a recurring strand of thought in which he tries to imagine a simple life of tranquility of mind. Ironically, Montaigne's vision was so powerful and provocative that it set in motion a whole movement of back-to-nature romanticism that Montaigne himself rejected. Most powerfully in Rousseau, whose first and second discourses are greatly indebted to Montaigne, the praise of natural simplicity emerged as a powerful tool of Western cultural and political criticism. From Voltaire's Hurons and Diderot's Tahitians to Thoreau's Walden, the nineteenth-century Luddites, and 1960s hippy-style naturalism, the conception of a simpler, preartificial notion of natural purity has been used as a billy club to bash the political, economic, and social institutions of the modern world.[79] This strand of criticism comes out of Montaigne's cannibals.

It is impossible to say whether Montaigne could have imagined how influential his thought experiment was to become. Before Montaigne, the Indians were rejected as the nonhuman or semihuman embodiment of Aristotle's natural slave. They were deemed imperfect creatures who needed the benefits of European civilization. After Montaigne, the debate about the Indians completely changes. No longer does any major political theorist question their humanity, but the opposite. The Indians and other primitive peoples from all over the world are identified as natural man *par excellence*; their way of life comes to characterize the state of nature itself, and Montaigne's idea of judging man by his original state rather than his end becomes philosophically established, conceptualized in thinkers such as Hobbes, Locke, Rousseau, Voltaire, and Diderot. While ending one debate, Montaigne begins another. No longer does anyone doubt the naturalness of the Indians; everyone comes to agree with Locke's famous assertion that "in the beginning all the World was America."[80] The question shifts to whether nature is a brutish state to be overcome or an innocence to recapture. Montaigne's thought experiment about natural man forever changed not only how the Indians of the New World were viewed by the Old, but the very course of political philosophy itself.

Chapter Three

Sophisticated Simplicity:
The Reflective Self and the Good Life

Since Montaigne concludes that a simple, pure relation to nature as epitomized by the cannibals' is both practically and theoretically unsatisfactory, we must examine the other model of the good life that he promotes: the sensual philosopher. This way of philosophical and sensual self-seeking does in fact emerge as Montaigne's ideal life in the remainder of the *Essays*. Montaigne does not completely discard the standard of mental health that the cannibals suggest; rather, he more fully elaborates it to meet the demands of self-consciousness. According to Montaigne, a true solution to the human problem must combine the simplicity and mental tranquility of the cannibals with the self-reflection of a philosopher.[1] This "sophisticated simplicity," as I call it, is exactly what Montaigne sets out to attain for himself and represents his vision of the ideal human life.

Although Montaigne prods all of his readers toward this ideal form of self-reflection—which the *Essays* both advocates and exemplifies—he does not expect that everyone will be introspective or think that introspection is necessary for most people's happiness. According to him, most people do not have the interest or ability to examine themselves thoroughly; they do not combat, but live according to, habit. In his embrace of all humanity, Montaigne in a certain sense accepts the diversity of ways of life that accompanies the array of human customs and thus does not mind pious or passive believers who cause no trouble, because even if not living authentically, they do no harm. On another level, however, since all followers of custom are still mere followers, they are in some sense not unique individuals. This is a problem for Montaigne insofar as he values freedom and genuine authenticity.

An even greater problem, however—especially for a skeptic—is articulating a standard by which the authentic can be delineated and judged. Montaigne uses nature as his standard, but he never says exactly what nature is, because he feels unable to define it precisely. But this does not paralyze his inquiries, because he thinks that he knows enough.[2]

The challenge for Montaigne is to describe a normative notion of nature and still be able to explain the deviations from it. Thus, he speaks of nature in two different senses: descriptive and normative. It is in the normative sense that he refers to nature's "constant and universal countenance" (III.12, 1026-7 [803]), tells us that nature can help us live and die if we follow her rules, and says that "I have very simply and crudely adopted for my own sake this ancient precept: that we cannot go wrong by following Nature, that the sovereign precept is to conform to her" (III.12, 1036-7 [811]). In short, he indicates that if we follow nature, we can be happy and content "at home" within ourselves. However, in his descriptions of the world as it is, Montaigne also says that natural human faculties—reason, judgment, and the imagination—and natural human tendencies—such as presumption, vanity, and anxiety—cause mankind's disordered and disturbed state. Unhappy paradoxes abound: the psyche is described as orderly and disorderly at the same time. By nature the soul can be tranquil and harmonious, but by nature imagination and reason often make men flee this natural harmony. Nature is both the goal and part of the problem.

It is because of this paradoxical tendency of human nature that the life of sophisticated simplicity is, according to Montaigne, the ideal life for man. The solution for our confusion is self-exploration—to essay oneself. Human beings can cultivate and maintain a natural order in the self by combating its natural tendencies to flee itself. Indeed, for "sophisticated" human beings like ourselves who are not born into a world characterized by a simple, direct harmony with nature, as represented by the cannibals' for example, self-exploration is the only way that peace of mind can genuinely be achieved. We must come to know and fight against our natural tendencies to flee from ourselves. We must scrutinize the internal fantasies that the imagination projects. And because self-consciousness itself and the customs according to which we are educated and reared are responsible for our deviance from nature's simple directives, we must work hard both to attain and to maintain a natural connection to ourselves. We must work hard, because we must untangle our own inner impulses and the tendencies propagated by outside cultural forces which have been internalized within ourselves. Thus, it is clear that not every desire, thought, or action felt by an individual is considered authentic by Montaigne; he considers many to be "diseased" and "monstrous"—the product of ignorance of the human condition, inauthentic thoughts, and unnatural concerns. Unlike some existentialist and postmodern thinkers, then, Montaigne does not support individuality based on any and all wills, whims, or other *unreflective* forces. For Montaigne, an individual can truly be authentic only after having undergone a rigorous process of self-exploration.[3]

Montaigne's ideal of sophisticated simplicity both draws on key concepts of ancient philosophy and inaugurates a new strand of modern thought. Like the ancients, Montaigne preserves a conception of nature as a normative guide for human behavior. However, like the moderns, he does not specify substantive goods rooted in nature by which every human being can be judged or insist on criteria (aside from essaying oneself) that must be affirmatively performed if an individual is to be judged happy and good. He does not call for a life to be regulated by an ancient conception of an all-knowing reason, a medieval conception of an all-knowing God, a Rousseauian general will, or a Kantian categorical imperative. Rather, the conditions that he thinks must govern a life if it is to be healthy and happy involve respecting humanity's *natural limits*. He focuses on the negative aspects of the human condition, how nature sets barriers to what human beings can know and which therefore circumscribe legitimate human claims. Within these limits, he wants individuals to explore and to celebrate the unique phenomena, mental and physical, that constitute themselves. Self-exploration involves phenomenologically knowing oneself as well as savoring the pleasures that the self affords.

Montaigne's celebration of the body and individual subjectivity came to characterize a huge strand of modern thought, culminating in Nietzsche's diagnosis of nihilism and his recommendation for unlimitedly willing one's will; but because Montaigne sees natural limits and conditions that govern the processes of self-exploration and human subjectivity that he otherwise celebrates, he himself has ground on which to stand to avoid falling into the nihilistic abyss of complete subjectivity. This chapter analyzes what Montaigne considers to be the limits to human subjectivity, including accepting a world with no metaphysical guarantees, confronting and accepting death, and recognizing and accepting mankind's ignorance about transcendent matters. This chapter also explores his views on how properly guided and properly limited subjectivity should be explored. Montaigne's emphasis on human subjectivity paves a path for the modern celebration of individual freedom, while his insistence on limits serves as the ultimate and necessary basis of his call for toleration and prevents his moral skepticism from degenerating into nihilism.[4]

I. Montaigne's Conception of the Self in Context

Montaigne's *Essays* has been proclaimed the first book of its kind both for its stylistic and its substantive emphasis on the self. This self-indulgence, as it was considered, was criticized at the time (and into the eighteenth century) as ill-mannered and vain by those unaccustomed to the public display of self-discussion and self-analysis.[5] Twentieth-century scholars, however, saw Montaigne's emphasis on the self as nothing short of revolutionary. Leading Montaigne scholar Hugo Friedrich calls the *Essays* "the most personal book that had appeared to date in world literature."[6] Leading intellectual historian Karl Weintraub considers it "a pivotal document in the gradually growing consciousness of man's individuality."[7] Leading political theorist Charles Taylor says that "Montaigne inaugurates one of the recurring themes of modern culture" by being "at the point of origin of [a] kind of modern individualism, that of self-discovery" which he characterizes as nothing less than "a turning point."[8] Montaigne himself was well aware of the uniqueness of his undertaking. He writes, "finding myself entirely destitute and void of any other matter, I presented myself to myself for argument and subject. It is the only book in the world of its kind" (II.8, 364 [278]).

Reflections on the self have been a part of Western civilization since at least as long ago as the famous Delphic injunction to "know thyself." According to the ancient Greeks, Heraclitus was the first to make the self a focal point of philosophical inquiry. His idea was that self-knowledge had to precede all other knowledge because the self projected itself into its interpretation of all things.[9] Socrates acknowledged the prevalence and power of this human tendency, but he held out the possibility of some universal knowledge outside the subjective inquirer. While both Heraclitus and Socrates give theoretical statements about the importance of self-knowledge, they give but little presentation of how they themselves strive to attain it. Plutarch and Seneca similarly talk about the importance of self-knowledge, but their writings are not significantly more personal than Heraclitus' writings or the Socrates that has been bequeathed to us by Plato or Xenophon.[10] St. Augustine in his *Confessions* is the first really to describe himself in writing, but he does so not for the sake of self-knowledge itself but to show his sins and the need for God to complete the lives of all wretched sinners. "What I do know of myself," Augustine declares, "I know by Thy shining upon me." The point of his description of himself is not to turn his readers to themselves, but to turn them away from themselves and toward God: "Thou Thyself art all my good." Mere human knowledge is nothing. God alone, he argues, can "perfect [our] imperfections," and this theocentric perspective characterizes all medieval Christian discussions of the self.[11] The worldly self reemerged in the Renaissance in a largely autobiographical fashion. The writings of Petrarch and of Montaigne's contemporaries Cellini and Cardano are often cited as the first secular autobiographical writings in Western history, and Cardano and especially Cellini discuss at length the minutiae of their lives and the injustices that they suffer.[12]

Montaigne's self-description is quite different from that of his predecessors. In contrast to the ancients, Montaigne is much more personal; his inquiries are not solely theoretical but involve many quirky revelations about his own self. In contrast to Augustine, Montaigne does not explore himself to turn to God but rather the opposite; to the extent that he explores God, it is to turn to himself. In contrast to other Renaissance figures, Montaigne uses himself as a model to explore universal phenomena with which every human being must wrestle and rarely discusses his individual accomplishments. For example, there is little mention of his service as mayor, the political and military negotiations that he conducted, whom he slept with, who slighted him, or his financial successes. He alludes to these but does not give details. Clearly, then, his book is neither a "kiss and tell" nor an autobiography in the usual sense, if indeed it is an autobiography at all. Nonetheless, insofar as Montaigne reveals quirks of and medical problems afflicting his body; explores the paradoxes, vanities, and inanities of his mind; and reflects on, in a first person voice, the most important moral and political questions of human life, the commentators are right that the *Essays* was the most personal book that had yet appeared in Western literature. Indeed, Montaigne inaugurated the essay genre of writing which was to become the style of choice for most later self-explorations that appear in print.[13]

However, despite scholarly agreement that what Montaigne is doing is new, there is less agreement on why he does it. A common view is that Montaigne is simply expressing his unique individuality without intending to create a model to be imitated or a moral to be learned. A representative expression of this view is Malcolm Smith's notion of an essay as "a personal intellectual exercise with no claim to instruct others."[14] Yet for the scholars who maintain this position, there is an ambiguity which is ill-resolved. They all recognize that while Montaigne clearly speaks of himself, the *Essays* is not autobiography in the usual sense. If he is simply describing himself so his friends and family may remember him, as he claims in his introductory note ("To The Reader," 9 [2]), why bother to publish at all, let alone publish aggressively, as Montaigne did, five publications during the last twelve years of his life? Wondering about the same thing, in 1674 the French philosopher Malebranche asked, "If this was true [that he was writing only for his family and friends], why did he publish [several] editions? One alone wouldn't be sufficient for his parents and friends?"[15] The fact of publication raises an important consideration about motive. Publication can bring Montaigne fame, which is a motive that Montaigne disclaims and few others suspect.[16] Publication might also incite imitation, but imitation would be precisely the opposite of the individuality that these scholars rightly say Montaigne seeks to celebrate.

The questions on this issue might be cleared up by considering that Montaigne's self-description has a pedagogical intention. By describing himself, he teaches others about themselves. In thinking original thoughts and questioning, probing, and examining himself right before the reader's mind's eye, Montaigne hopes to incite the reader to a similar originality and individuality. Montaigne's style of writing exemplifies how he explores and cultivates himself; he desires that his readers explore themselves as he does, for it is only from self-knowledge that reflective individuals can achieve happiness and tranquility, he believes.[17]

Montaigne illustrates the nature of individuality at the same time that he calls attention to the universal human attributes—the framework—that underlie it, enabling him to search for a middle ground description of self-development—between a domineering, categorical universalism on the one hand and complete subjectivity on the other. The very notion that he has something to teach his readers, even about individuality, implies something common between Montaigne's self and his readers: it implies the desire or need for individuality which concerns all reflective selves. Thus, at the same time that he promotes individuality, Montaigne also reveals the structural features—which are universal—that both underlie the need to live autonomously and that hinder its realization. The scholars who see Montaigne's thought as a key step along the modern journey toward individualism are right, although in emphasizing what is new in Montaigne, they tend not to describe the whole picture. When it comes to Montaigne's analysis of the self, there is a tendency to emphasize his innovations and pay less attention to the more universalistic, i.e., traditional or "ancient," aspects of his thought. While this is understandable, it loses sight of the mean that Montaigne strives for and lets the creative tension in his thought escape from view.

Only by recognizing both the subjective and universalistic aspects of Montaigne's thought can one reconcile what otherwise would appear to be contradictory claims: that "I am myself the matter of my book" ("To The Reader," 9 [2]) and that he aims to describe man as such: "the study I am making, the subject of which is man" (II.17, 617 [481]). Montaigne aims to prod his readers toward what they most lack but most need—"knowledge of themselves and their own state, which is ever present before their eyes, which is in them" (II.17, 617-8 [481])[18]—by showing how he gains knowledge of his own self. Friedrich, Weintraub, and Taylor are right to emphasize Montaigne's innovations, but this cannot be done at the expense of the other elements that balance his thought; it is the tension between these aspects that gives his thought its depth. Only by acknowledging that Montaigne recognizes some shared universality between all the radically different selves can one avoid describing Montaigne as fatally contradictory—and as plunging headlong into total relativism.

The combination of the universal and the personal that Montaigne strives for, animated and held together by a conception of human health, is a balance worth trying to (re)capture, because his balanced conception celebrates what is best about modern conceptions of the self—individual freedom—while simultaneously anchoring the view in a conception of nature that prevents it from degenerating into total relativism and nihilism. If the universal aspects of Montaigne's thought are not fully recognized, one misses the glue that binds Montaigne to his readers. In describing his own subjective self-explorations, he—for the first time in print—models the process in which every self must engage.

II. Diversity and Unity

Nowhere is the balance between the universal and the particular more evident in Montaigne's thought than in his fascination with the differences and similarities that exist among human beings. Montaigne's emphasis on both the similarities and differences among human beings marks the essence of his conception of the self and shows the manner in which he bridges the divide between the ancient and modern worlds. One useful way of categorizing the difference between the ancient and modern ways of looking at the world is to note whether they see it as homogenous or heterogenous. Believing that fundamentally different kinds of things exist by nature, the ancients might be described as having a heterogenous view. By contrast, modern scientists, by considering all things to be but different arrangements of the same material, and giving little or no natural weight to form, have a homogenous view of what *is*. Bacon's statement— "forms are figments of the human mind, unless you call those laws of action forms"—characterizes the modern view.[19] Unlike Bacon, Descartes, and the other modern scientists, Montaigne does not try to reduce every-thing—including human phenomena—to one simple substance. Nor does he use the ancients' notion of form to dictate one single "best" way of life. Rather, he does something in between: he conceives of nature as creating limits within which each individual is free to explore and to be what he or she is—but only within these limits. Thus, Montaigne seeks simultaneously to celebrate the unique differences of all human beings and to identify their fundamental similarities.

It was a lifelong source of wonder to Montaigne how both differences and similarities could coexist among human beings. His preoccupation with this theme is readily notable in the very first and last passages of his original work. The first essay's title is "By Diverse Means We Arrive at the Same End" and the last essay of his original publication concludes that the "most universal quality is diversity" (II.37, 766 [598]).[20] Both portray the relation of unity and diversity, but their emphases are different. The first essay indicates how diverse policies can lead to the same results; the last emphasizes the eternal existence of difference. Diversity and unity can lead to one another, but neither can be overcome or destroyed.[21] Indeed, Montaigne emphasizes difference throughout his work, writing, "I believe in and conceive a thousand contrary ways of life; and in contrast with the common run of men, I more easily admit difference than resemblance between us" (I.37, 225 [169]). While *différence* became a popular concept in the last half of the twentieth century, Montaigne's ideas on it are unfashionable today.[22] He argues that there are "many degrees in minds," in fact an "innumerable" variety (I.42, 251 [189]), and that no two opinions are exactly alike, "not only in different men, but in the same man at different times" (III.13, 1044 [817]). He goes so far as to assert that there can be more difference between two given men than between a given man and a given animal (I.42, 250 [189]). However ironic Montaigne might be in this last claim, if difference is not based on species, it certainly is not based on the contemporary view that race, ethnicity, and gender are the key dividers. For Montaigne, biological or any group identification leads to conformity. Real differences, to him, exist on a level deeper than socially constructed roles (which the poststructuralists deny exists), are based on universally available attributes, and have their locus in the individual.

Montaigne thus makes seemingly contradictory celebrations of both the universality of and differences among human beings. On the one hand, he celebrates diversity and can truly declare that everyone has "in himself a pattern all his own, a ruling pattern" (III.2, 789 [615]).[23] On the other hand, he truly believes in the universality of, to use the phrase he coined, the "human condition:"[24] "Each man bears the entire form of man's estate" (III.2, 782 [611]). This fundamental similarity enables communication and identification between people. For Montaigne every human being is different, but the differences between individuals consist of different quantitative and qualitative arrangements of the same universal phenomena. Depending on the arrangements, sometimes the similarities, sometimes the differences, are more apparent. These differences exist to some extent by nature but are greatly exacerbated by culture, convention, and belief.

Individuals are not so different, however, that they cannot be compared and assessed. Montaigne frequently judges noteworthy individuals, considers the actions and character of some men—Caesar, Alexander, and Epaminondas, among others—as far above his own, and recognizes that he could not do what they have done. Nonetheless, he does not hesitate to "judge the powers that raise them so high, of which I perceive in some degree the seeds in me" (II.32, 703 [548]). Just as Montaigne recognizes superiors, he recognizes inferiors and finds some degree of the baseness of the worst characters in himself (II.32, 703 [548]). Montaigne is sensitive to human differences, because he can either find or imagine those different qualities in himself. The universality of the human condition enables Montaigne to judge whole epochs in a similar manner. For instance, on several occasions he cites the uncommon, almost incredible, deeds of the ancient Spartans; but Montaigne, unlike small-minded historians who debunk all greatness, does not dismiss them simply because his contemporaries are incapable of doing the same (II.32, 702 [547]). He is perfectly content to say that he lives in a corrupt age without virtue and heroism.[25] Just as individuals differ, so do historical epochs and cultures.

The theme of diversity and unity also works its way into Montaigne's normative recommendations, for in evaluating differences, Montaigne implies the existence of criteria by which to judge. Individuals and epochs alike are judged by the extent to which they secure human goods, such as tranquility of mind and health. On several occasions Montaigne states that he is jealous of nothing so much as his freedom[26]—a very modern concern for individuality—but he makes it clear that for a human being to be happy, freedom must be restrained in accordance with the human condition. "Since philosophy has not been able to find a way to tranquility that is suitable to all," Montaigne writes, "let everyone seek it individually" (II.16, 605-6 [471]). He wants everyone to find tranquility according to his own light, but like the Hellenistic skeptics, he is convinced that the good for man is tranquility—not any random, subjective choice of the good. Montaigne does not posit tranquility as a good *a priori*, but rather he conceives it to be the good result—the phenomenological result—of purging the mind of all the ambitions, false hopes, and dreaded fears that take it away from itself. We thus see two kinds of cultures that Montaigne is unwilling to celebrate without qualification. The cannibals have not enough reason, but possess the tranquility that comes with "the seed of universal reason that is implanted in every man who is not denatured" (III.12, 1037 [811]). By contrast, "civilized" societies let reason and imagination carry them astray. Such "denatured" and corrupt cultures reject nature's guidelines. Thus, the fact that many human beings do not consider tranquility and health (as Montaigne expansively understands them) to be key human goods is, according to Montaigne, a failure of judgment due to their denatured state. Unlike total relativists, he is unwilling to validate every way of life or every culture as equally sound. Montaigne does not celebrate all "differences."

The intensive labor required for a reflective individual to fight through artificial human creations to secure health and tranquility requires the cultivation of judgment,[27] and it is exactly here where one sees the need for sophisticated simplicity. Simplicity represents a direct, phenomenological way of relating to the world, but since we do not possess such a relation as manifested in natural habits, man must work hard to attain it. Thus, Montaigne calls on his readers to "enlighten our judgment by reflecting upon this continual variation of human things" (I.49, 285 [216]) and asserts that "[j]udgment is a tool to use on all subjects, and comes in everywhere" (I.50, 289 [219]). Montaigne himself declares that "I essay my judgment," "in the tests [*essais*] that I make of it here" (I.50, 289 [219]). His writing is an attempt to use his universally available capability to try to understand, explore, *essay*[28] himself and the world. Montaigne's judgment must be contrasted to the so-called dogmatists' emphasis on reason. Dogmatists claim that reason is able to know *what is* fully and truly, that the cosmos is intelligible by reason. By contrast, Montaigne's emphasis on judgment (as opposed to knowledge) does not offer certainties; judgment is more tentative and qualified than an outright truth statement.[29]

Self-aware judgment teaches about the uncertainty of human abilities, which is one of the universal constraints that Montaigne wants to guide human action. He does not tell his readers specifically how to live, only how to enlighten their judgments. He offers a middle ground between the alleged certainties of dogmatism and the total ignorance claimed by Pyrrhonism. For Montaigne, few certainties can be stated, but he neither despairs of the chase nor of the possibility of making provisional judgments of better and worse. He continually seeks and encourages his readers to seek the certain from the supposed, the true from the false, the universal and necessary from the accidental and indifferent. Final conclusions might not be reached, for human beings live in the realm of opinion. Final answers might not be available to human beings (except perhaps for knowing this), but life must still be lived. Ignorance of transcendent truth must be accepted if a reflective soul is to live a healthy life.[30] In a world in which we cannot have knowledge, human beings must nonetheless make choices, choices that matter. Better choices are distinctly possible for human beings if they try to understand the nature of things and act accordingly. Good judgment never definitively discovers some "truth" and then stops thinking, but good judgment forms the most reliable basis on which to act. The possession and employment of this well-cultivated judgment is what I am calling sophisticated simplicity.

The normative conclusion that follows from this analysis of Montaigne is that reflective human beings should not be forced to live according to any one single conception of the good but should be left to live according to their own particular natures within the general structural constraints imposed by the human condition. This interpretation of Montaigne has two interlocking parts: 1) allowing individual self-development but 2) only within a framework limited by nature. Montaigne's emphasis on individuality is apparent: "I have a singular desire that we should each be judged in ourselves apart, and that I may not be measured in conformity with the common [i.e., conventional] patterns" (I.37, 225 [169]). Yet, he also writes that for a reflective individual to be happy, he must accept his "universal and common" and "natural and original condition" (III.9, 950 [743] and I.42, 253 [191], respectively). This begins to hint at what Montaigne's answer might be to Nietzsche and those others who Montaigne thinks flee from themselves. His problem with their behavior is based less on moral grounds than on what he deems a misunderstanding of self-interest. To buck human nature is a recipe for personal unhappiness. And they buck nature, he would argue, in two ways. First, by trying to inflict their wills on the world without taking into account the nature of things that exist outside their subjective wills, they misrepresent and disrespect what exists outside their wills. Second, and more importantly, they ignore their own natural limits. Instead of simply surrendering to a strong impulse, passion, or will and trying to impose it on the world, Montaigne wants each individual first to essay his or her will. An honest essayer, Montaigne thinks, will discover the murky presuppositions that underlie the will, leading to a reconsideration of it on prudential grounds, if nothing else. Essaying reveals the limits beyond which one cannot go. But within these limits, within the confines of the essaying process, each person is encouraged to explore, locate, and create his own particularity. Montaigne thus concludes with Cicero, "'We must so act as not to oppose the universal laws of nature; but, these being safeguarded, let us follow our own nature'" (III.9, 967 [756]).[31] Montaigne's aim is to recognize the universal and accept it while preserving and cultivating each individual's unique qualities within that sphere. Montaigne thinks that the process of self-discovery and self-creation within the essaying framework will provide an immense and never-ending source of wonder, more than enough to keep an individual happy and whole "at home."

Given Montaigne's conception of the independence of each self, telling someone how to live is nonsensical and counterproductive. It cannot achieve the desired result, because if the listener (or reader) follows an author's advice, he is living the author's life, not his own. It is in this sense that Montaigne decries systematic philosophy and refuses to write treatises. Insofar as Montaigne explores himself in writing to spur his readers to similar self-explorations, he desires that his readers come to conclusions on their own based on their own judgment. Therefore, he does not give "answers." Instead, he writes in such a way as to force his readers to essay his essays, to engage in that activity of self-exploration along with him, so that their conclusions, although guided by him, will be their own. To understand Montaigne, the reader must mentally perform the substantive activity he recommends. This is the organic relation between Montaigne's message and his style, and the reason why he never explicitly asserts limits to be obeyed.

At the risk of denaturing Montaigne's effort by practicing the kind of merely "learned" scholarship he despises—and thus perhaps allowing the reader to learn by rote without performing the introspective essaying that Montaigne wants to produce in his readers—one can specify (based on careful study of the themes that Montaigne himself emphasizes) the structural features of human life that must be accepted in order to achieve the healthy life that Montaigne seeks.[32] The remainder of this chapter examines these universal constraints, put largely in terms of negatives by Montaigne—avoiding metaphysics, overcoming the fear of death, and accepting our fundamental ignorance—and then examines what Montaigne deems the sphere of freedom, the legitimate sphere for subjectivity and self-creation, that exists within these constraints.[33]

III. Overcoming the Metaphysical Impulse

The first structural limit of the human condition that must be accepted if one is to achieve sophisticated simplicity requires abandoning "metaphysics" as a guide for human life. Montaigne deems this necessary for an individual to live a healthy and tranquil life, because he considers metaphysical questing often to be a symptom of a common kind of human dissatisfaction with the world as it is, which leads people to inflict horrible cruelties to "remedy" the situation. Rather than flee to some imaginary ideal, Montaigne, like Nietzsche, wants people to accept the world.

Montaigne's skepticism indicates how and why metaphysics should be dismissed. Believing that human beings cannot know anything about other-worldly reality, Montaigne wants to eradicate metaphysical posturing from life.[34] Montaigne praises those philosophers who bring philosophy down from the heavens, and this attitude is notable in his writing; it is striking how few of his more than 850 pages worry about metaphysical truth.[35] Aside from deciding that nothing useful for human life can be known about any metaphysical question and recommending pleasant and useful (but not necessarily true) ways for mankind to think about cosmic questions,[36] Montaigne does not pursue, concern himself, or recommend that his readers concern themselves with otherworldly issues. Unlike the writings of Augustine, Calvin, and Luther, Montaigne's text has no anxious speculation about Hell, sin, or Judgment Day.

Montaigne wants human beings to live in and for this world. He accepts the world's ever-changing nature, describing it as flux and flow: "The world is but a perennial movement. All things in it are in constant motion. . . . Stability itself is nothing but a more languid motion" (III.2, 782 [610]). Human beings have no knowledge of a creator who bestows dignity or meaning on their lives. Their coming into the world, as Montaigne describes it, resembles Heidegger's notion of "thrownness." Life is assigned to human beings without prior consent, and living well remains their job until death, the fundamental fact of life. According to Montaigne, an awareness of ignorance often creates a frantic anxiety in human beings. But as his depiction of the cannibals illustrates (in contrast to Heidegger's view), Montaigne does not deem anxiety to be part of mankind's natural condition. Rather, Montaigne thinks that anxiety results from a vain concern with our transcendent emptiness that causes us to flee from ourselves.

Montaigne's *Essays* as a whole (and his "Apology" in particular) aims to expose and explain the psychological foundations of human metaphysical and spiritual questing so that human beings will both accept and be comfortable in a world without metaphysical foundations. The metaphysical search for dignity and meaning may be a perennial human activity according to Montaigne, and he approves of this kind of searching, but he thinks that wise people will discover the psychological drives underlying their vain desires, not answers that satisfy their vanity. Each person's imagination runs away with itself and away from its possessor. Rather than accepting metaphysical emptiness, the mind produces answers it would like to be true: "our fancy does whatever it pleases with itself and with us" (II.29, 689 [537]). "People easily fool themselves," Montaigne says, "about what they desire," and Montaigne thinks this is especially so with respect to the supernatural (II.37, 756 [590]).[37] Rejecting as fallacious and as the epitome of wishful thinking reasonings such as Descartes' (perhaps ironic) later "proof" that God must exist because otherwise man would not be able to imagine such a perfect being, Montaigne argues that awareness of one's problems merely suggests to one's imagination a remedy, and thereby a notion of perfection, which is no more than a state where those very problems do not exist. As Heraclitus asserted before him and Nietzsche afterwards, Montaigne proposes that each vision is nothing but the confession of its author, intimately linked to his or her problems, needs, and desires. As we have seen, Montaigne says that if animals make gods, "they certainly make them like themselves, and glorify themselves as we do" (II.12, 514 [397]). Humans crave a *raison d'être* and create gods and *weltanschauungen* to support this desire. Montaigne believes that a self-conscious knowledge of the existence of these desires within oneself is crucial to living a contented life in the world as it truly is, because otherwise one's imagination and impulses are much more likely to run away with oneself. Awareness of self does not make one's unruly impulses disappear, but such an awareness allows one to approach the impulses more directly and gives the individual a certain healthy detachment from them.

Mankind's metaphysical delusions originate from a natural faculty: the imagination. It is the imagination that finds the answers we so seek and which is thus responsible for many metaphysical claims. In an essay entitled "Of the Power of the Imagination" (I.21), Montaigne cites numerous "miracles." However, he does not point to miracles in which he believes but to the true (and unflattering) miracle—the facility of human gullibility and self-deception.[38] On the one hand, Montaigne writes, "It is probable that the principal credit of miracles, visions, enchantments, and such extraordinary occurrences comes from the power of the imagination, acting principally upon the minds of the common people, which are softer. Their belief has been so strongly seized that they think they see what they do not see" (I.21,

97 [70]). Ordinary humans feel weaknesses and deficiencies, and they imagine remedies for them. We have fears which are so powerful that they become self-fulfilling, and hopes so strong that we swear that they are realized. But these phenomena do not "seize" only the ignorant masses; they seize educated people as well. Montaigne tells the story of an easily duped count who, fearing that he had been hexed and would be unable to "perform" on his wedding night, sought Montaigne's aid. Knowing that such fears are often self-fulfilling, Montaigne decided to bestow upon him a "miracle, which was in my power," telling him a bunch of nonsense, such as that before going to bed, "he should withdraw to pass water, say certain prayers three times and go through certain motions." The miracle cure worked, Montaigne tells us, because the count "had his soul and his ears so battered that he did not find himself fettered by the trouble of his imagination" (I.21, 98-9 [71]). "These monkey tricks," he concludes, "are the main part of the business, our mind being unable to get free of the idea that such strange means must come from some abstruse science. Their inanity gives them weight and reverence" (I.21, 99 [71]). According to Montaigne, religion is the sphere of "monkey tricks" and "abstruse science" *par excellence*; it is not for nothing that he commanded the count to say a prayer or that he gives the moral of another such ridiculous tale as: "As usual in matters of fancy, she referred him to religion" (I.21, 99 [71]). These "miracles" are, of course, all false, but they reveal an important psychological truth about human beings: we are easily deceived when we want to be. It is laughably miraculous how humanity allows itself to believe that it discovers what it seeks. Montaigne does in fact learn something important from the claims of so-called miracles, but not what the claimants want to teach: "in the study that I am making of our behavior and motives, fabulous testimonies, provided they are possible, serve like true ones. Whether they have happened or no, in Paris or Rome, to John or Peter, they exemplify, at all events, some human potentiality, and thus their telling imparts useful information to me" (I.21, 104 [75]). Montaigne singles out the seats of political and religious authority and the names of saints in his debunking. The "useful information" that he learns is unfortunately known by demagogues and charlatans all too well: desires render human beings weak and easily manipulable.

The point of explaining the human origins of man's metaphysics and so-called miracles is twofold. The first reason is political. Montaigne wants to combat the insupportable and iniquitous actions of fanatical believers. Montaigne worked his "miracle" in useful play, but he fears that those who most aggressively promote metaphysics and miracles, whether sincerely or not, are the most ambitious troublemakers. He describes those who desperately or fanatically seek to overcome man's metaphysical void as dangerous: "They want to get out of themselves and escape from the man. That is madness: instead of changing into angels, they change into beasts; instead of raising themselves, they lower themselves" (III.13, 1096 [856]). Sincerely believing falsehoods, fanatical believers not only live their lives on a false basis, but they also force others to do so. To realize their conception of some divine good, they take hellish actions. And, for Montaigne, this link between horrifying actions and improper appreciation of the human condition is direct: "these are two things that I have always observed to be in singular accord: supercelestial thoughts and subterranean conduct" (III.13, 1095 [856]). "Supercelestial thoughts," which might serve as shorthand for any utopian ideology, endanger human tranquility and safety. Pursuit of imaginary ideals leads to the death and destruction of real people. If only to control the threats that fanatical believers pose to others, their enthusiasm must be tamed.

Montaigne's second reason for insisting on the removal of metaphysics from life is more profound and personal. Metaphysics must be overcome so that human beings may be content with their true situation. Those who live and judge by otherworldly standards tend to reject and to despise the world that we have and the beings that we are. This leads to what Montaigne detests most: self-hatred and self-cruelty. Montaigne continually returns to the theme of self-hatred: "the most barbarous of our maladies is to despise our being" (III.13, 1091 [852]); "We are ingenious only in maltreating ourselves; that is the true quarry of the power of our mind—a dangerous tool when out of control" (III.5, 857 [670]); "As for the opinion that disdains our life, it is ridiculous. For after all, life is our being, it is our all . . . it is against nature that we despise ourselves and care nothing about ourselves. It is a malady peculiar to man . . . to hate and disdain himself" (II.3, 334 [254]). Montaigne condemns and rejects human self-hatred in the strongest possible terms, because he thinks that the human condition is hard enough to bear as it is. The self-loathing commonly enshrined in religious and philosophical doctrines, such as the idea of original sin, represents this world as worse than it is, especially in comparison to some imagined utopia. Rather than making the world a better and happier place, Montaigne fears that such self-loathing causes misery and self-laceration.

Despite his condemnation of self-hatred, Montaigne pokes fun at the human species—but he condemns it only for lacking modesty and good sense. Montaigne does not, as do the metaphysicians, decry the essential emptiness of man; for him, it is the truth of the human condition and must be recognized and accepted—we can only be what we are. Montaigne condemns only the insecure vanity that does not allow human beings to accept their limitations, but he does not describe mankind's incessant inability to embrace its condition as tragic; to do that would be to take human existence too seriously. Rather, preferring to ridicule man's puffed-up pretensions, he describes the human condition as comical. In an essay entitled "Of Democritus and Heraclitus" (I.50), Montaigne mulls over Democritus' "mocking and laughing" attitude toward humanity and Heraclitus' "face perpetually sad with tears." Montaigne considers it harsher to describe human existence as comedy, because it expects less. Pretending that human beings have any greater dignity, even from which they have fallen, would be to accord them too high a value. The world is a comedy, and human beings are the fools of the farce. Though Montaigne consciously chooses to describe the affairs of human life as light and whimsical, he is not always able to do this. Sometimes an exasperated tone creeps into his voice: "We are not so full of evil as of inanity; we are not as wretched as we are worthless" (I.50, 291 [221]). Nonetheless, Montaigne generally laughs at those who make man out to be something important and rejects all attempts to glorify the human situation.[39]

According to Montaigne, there is no discernible cosmic purpose in life. As far as we know, there is nothing that expects anything of man, and no demands are made on him. Metaphysical speculations are unverifiable or untrue and are inevitably doomed to condemn man-as-he-is in the here-and-now. Yet, Montaigne generally argues that there is no reason to fear or despair. Life is sweet. "Nature has put us into the world free and unfettered" (III.9, 950 [743]); all we have to do is be. But human beings cannot leave well enough alone. Rather than accepting the limits of the human condition, we torture ourselves. As a first step toward ending this self-torture, we must reject conceptions of man based on metaphysical speculation.

IV. Accepting Death

A second structural feature of the human condition that human beings must accept in order to be happy, according to Montaigne, is the need to face and accept the fundamental limit of life: death. Just as he thinks that fear about our place in the cosmos leads human beings to invent soothing metaphysics, so too does he think that mankind's fear over its mortality leads to hypotheses of an afterlife. Both of these, he argues, tend to lead to more, not less, fear. Not only must human beings fully confront and accept death so as to avoid these errors, but Montaigne thinks that doing so can be profoundly liberating in this world.

Montaigne exemplifies what he preaches: he says that he feels death continually gripping him by the throat,[40] and, indeed, death appears throughout the *Essays*. Montaigne writes that the *Essays* was conceived in part to fill the void created by the death of his great friend La Boétie (I.8, 34 [21]), and the *Essays* ends with speculations about his own oncoming death. Several essays, such as "That Our Happiness Must Not Be Judged Until After Our Death" (I.19); "That To Philosophize Is To Learn To Die" (I.20); and "Of Judging The Death Of Others" (II.13) are dominated by the subject of death, and death is prominent in many others: Montaigne judges the legitimacy of suicide and burial customs, and he recounts at length his own near brushes with death.[41]

But Montaigne is not obsessed with death. He seeks the middle ground between being cowardly overwhelmed by the fear of death and a stoical indifference to it. On several occasions he notes what he deems to have been the prudent actions he has taken to avoid the risk of dying (III.1, 769-70 [601]). Montaigne neither recommends a morbid preoccupation with death, nor a silly seeking of it, nor a cowardly refusal to consider it. He wants the reader to think through the possibility of death, understand the limits of our abilities to deal with it, and face the difficulty of anticipating its moment of arrival. He sensibly prefers a known good (life) to a total unknown (what is after life). He wants us to essay death insofar as is possible and consistent with a healthy life and to be prepared for its inevitability in a reflective manner without foolishly hastening its occurrence.

Death must be accepted, according to Montaigne, because fear of death cramps and corrupts life. Because death is so strange and alien to human beings, who know that it is inevitable yet do not have a clue as to what it is, they fear it. This fear, according to Montaigne, leads to torments and feverishness: "consequently, if it frightens us, it is a continual source of torment which cannot be alleviated at all" (I.20, 81 [57]); "If it frightens us, how is it possible to go a step forward without feverishness?" (I.20, 82 [57]). To appreciate how horrible Montaigne deems such "torment" and "feverishness," one need only recall his definition of human happiness as tranquility. Human beings who are aware of death cannot simply ignore it or choose not to think about it; this would not satisfy their curiosity and would leave them, when dying, unprepared, frightened, and shocked.[42] But thinking about death tends to create fear, and, according to Montaigne, it is this fear above all that leads to human anxiety. To allay their fear, humans invent gods and create religious institutions on Earth, but Montaigne fears that all too often, terrors, both physical and psychological, are increased—not lessened—by this process. Thus, fear of death brings about the same earthly problems as the preoccupation with metaphysics and for the same reasons: they attempt to alleviate human anxiety about the unknown and unknowable with fixed answers but often aggravate the problems that they intend to remedy.

Montaigne wants to divorce mankind's attitude toward death from concern for an afterlife. He himself neither seriously speculates on an afterlife nor recommends others to do so. Nor does he alter his life due to concern about an afterlife or recommend that others do so. Rather, Montaigne considers death to be an organic part of life. Of course, it is not a part of life like any other, for human beings do not have life with which to judge death fully. But Montaigne wants to treat death, the inevitable end of life, like any other life experience. In order both to lessen our fear of it and to know it as well as mortal creatures can, Montaigne recommends consciously confronting death. Declaring that "in truth, in order to get used to the idea of death, I find there is nothing like coming close to it" (II.6, 357 [272]), he recommends exploring the sensations of death within oneself if one happens to be wounded or seriously ill.[43] Montaigne does not advocate risky experimentation with it—that would be foolhardy—but he writes, "let us learn to meet it steadfastly and to combat it. And to begin to strip it of its greatest advantage against us," which is lack of knowledge (I.20, 85 [60]). This does not mean launching oneself into suicide or others into a fire; a natural death, like everything in life, has its rhyme and rhythm.[44] Montaigne merely recommends the essaying of death just as he wants us to essay all of life's other experiences. He wants us to know it insofar as we are able through its phenomenological manifestations and by studying the deaths of others, observing their actions and reactions.[45] This will not answer any of the cosmic questions that Montaigne deems unanswerable by human beings, but he thinks it will lessen the barrier that separates death from all the other activities of life. If death is accepted and experienced as part of life, even as a part that generally ought to be postponed, it will remove, according to Montaigne, the fear which all too often distorts both death and life.

Death must be accepted not only for the negative reason that failure to do so often leads to fears and distortions, but also according to Montaigne, for positive reasons. Death is a moment of truth. We can go through life pretending and masquerading and fooling everyone including ourselves, but dying is a solitary, lonely act. No one can help us and we cannot fool ourselves. There is no future to be drawn into; there is only the here and now.

As Montaigne eloquently states, dying is for someone

> to play the last act of his comedy, and beyond doubt the hardest. In everything else there may be sham: the fine reasonings of philosophy may be a mere pose in us; or else our trials, by not testing us to the quick, give us a chance to keep our face always composed. But in the last scene, between death and ourselves, there is no more pretending; we must talk plain French, we must show what there is that is good and clean at the bottom of the pot. (I.19, 78 [55])

It is for this reason that Montaigne (contrary to the religious customs of his time) encouraged people to seek solitude when dying (III.9, 961 [752]): "Dying is not a role for society; it is an act for one single character" (III.9, 957 [748]). We might hypothesize that this is why Montaigne did not send for a priest when he himself lay dying.[46] More importantly, Montaigne believes that despite even the best efforts of philosophy or the most strenuous trials, dying can reveal important truths about oneself to onself. In this sense, death and truth are allies.[47] Of course, those interested in deceiving the rest of the world can playact in death, too; Montaigne acknowledges some of the "most execrable" people he has known had deaths that were "ordered" and "composed to perfection" (I.19, 79 [55]), so one's death does not necessarily reveal anything about one's character to someone else. But for those interested in knowing themselves, death can be a supreme moment of authenticity.[48]

By liberating us from the fear of death, Montaigne hopes to liberate us to live. As Jean Starobinski writes, "death unmasked becomes death the unmasker."[49] Once we are not afraid of dying, we are not afraid of living. Sometimes Montaigne wants us to accept uncertainty about the possibility of life after death, other times he wants us to accept without fear that we are finite and that there is nothing after death, that "once out of being, we have no communication with what is" (I.3, 20 [10]). In either case, he always says that by accepting death as our end (not as a final cause but as a limit), death frees us to live. When Montaigne writes, "Premeditation of death is premeditation of freedom" (I.20, 85 [60]), he is not echoing the Christian teaching that one should look forward to death because after dying one will be free of bodily and earthly constraints. Rather, Montaigne, like the twentieth-century existentialists, means the opposite, that by accepting death one is free to live and act courageously—without fear—in this life. Montaigne writes, "He who has learned how to die has unlearned how to be a slave. Knowing how to die frees us from all subjection and constraint.

There is nothing evil in life for the man who has thoroughly grasped the fact that to be deprived of life is not an evil" (I.20, 85 [60]).[50] Accepting the fact of death and keeping it in full consciousness at all times is both a kind of psychological break with life and an enhancement of it. But this should not be overstated—Montaigne loves life. He does not want to relinquish life easily, but reducing one's fear of death reduces the threats that can be used against an individual, thus enabling a fuller, freer, and happier life. By making us aware of the possibility of life ending at any moment, Montaigne hopes that it makes us enjoy life more; every moment and every flavor can be savored as if it were the last. Paradoxically, it is by giving up one's tenacious clinging to life that one is liberated to enjoy it more. Consciousness of the possibility of not living liberates one to revel in life most freely and fully—which does not mean that life under many circumstances is not worth fighting for—Montaigne fights against his kidney stones with tenacity, for example. But the fight for life should be done without the fears that cripple life.

One might ask Montaigne why he thinks heightened consciousness of death leads to tranquility and not to fear. Might not the prospects of losing everything lead to a Hobbesian-like clutching to life? Montaigne's answer seems to be based on his ontology. Any fair appraisal of the human situation, according to Montaigne, reveals the same thing: that we are empty and void and really have little to lose. If we have little to lose, we have little cause to fear losing it. Moreover, if we act in the opposite way, we become completely enslaved to our desires and to those who have power to control our satisfaction of them. In arguing for this attitude toward death, Montaigne is echoing the attitude of the ancient practitioners of both the *vita contemplativa* and the *vita activa*, foreshadowing the centrality of death and heroism in existentialism, and rejecting the "life at all costs" philosophy, which shortly after Montaigne becomes the bedrock of liberalism through Hobbes. Montaigne knows that what he is teaching may be beyond the comprehension of most and beyond the power of others to enact. Indeed, it can simply be rejected as insane. Nonetheless, in what might be considered his *a priori* judgment of liberalism as it was to develop, he insists that all persons of understanding will come to the same conclusions. Wisdom about death and life is essential to dying well and to living well—and is thus a key universal which must frame what he would consider any healthy and sound experiment in individuality.

V. Ignorance and Self-Knowledge

Montaigne's knowledge of human ignorance is more than simply an acknowledgment of human limits; it is also an exploration of the human essence. It is exactly here that Montaigne's doubting ends and his positing of man begins. Like the Academic skeptics and unlike the Pyrrhonists, when discussing human ignorance, Montaigne asserts a knowledge of it: "There is a certain strong and generous ignorance that concedes nothing to knowledge in honor and courage, an ignorance that requires no less knowledge to conceive it than does knowledge" (III.11, 1008 [788]).[51] According to Montaigne, to recognize one's ignorance, i.e. humanity's inability to know what it craves to know, requires both courage and knowledge, knowledge of human limits and the courage not to delude oneself about them. To be aware and accepting of human ignorance is, according to Montaigne, an honorable way to live and the only way of life that is not based on a false presupposition. It is an ignorance that requires knowledge of the limits of the human condition, and as such reveals something important about man's essential nature. If these epistemological limits are correctly stated, man would be the animal of opinion, as opposed to knowers (gods) and non-askers (animals), and this uncertainty would be a fundamental and inescapable characteristic of human life.

The kind of knowledge upon which ignorance is based results from humanity's grasping its limits. Montaigne's account of the nature of these limits is discussed above in chapter 1 but should be briefly recapitulated here. Montaigne argues that the two ways that human beings can acquire knowledge, through their senses or reason, are both faulty. (Montaigne entertains revelation as another possible means of knowledge, but unless God reveals His word directly to someone, that person is dependent on the accounts and claims of other human beings.) Thus Montaigne urges all people to fall back on their own faculties and judgment and pay special attention to the things in and closest to them—movement in their bodies and minds, feelings of pleasure and pain, and so on. These cannot definitively tell human beings anything transcendently "true" about the objective essence of the world; they only give them phenomenological, subjective impressions of it. This, according to Montaigne, is all human beings can know. Here lies the explanation of Montaigne's paradoxical claim that he knows he knows nothing. The two "knows" in this sentence refer to different types of knowledge. By phenomenologically knowing the inconstancy of his reason, body, and sense organs, he knows that he could never consciously be sure to possess any transcendental truth about the essence of things. The statement that one knows that one knows nothing implies knowledge of the limits of human capabilities. Knowing nothing is a function of self-knowledge.

The Academic-like self-knowledge that underlies both a deeper ignorance and the conception of human nature that Montaigne extols is illustrated by his own self-presentation. Montaigne attempts to set the example for his readers, to concretely demonstrate what he advocates—both about what he does not know and about what he does. He says: "I speak ignorance pompously and opulently, and speak knowledge meagerly and piteously, the latter secondarily and accidentally, the former expressly and principally. And there is nothing I treat specifically except nothing, and no knowledge except that of the lack of knowledge" (III.12, 1034 [809]); that "in truth I understand nothing" about education, even though that is what he seeks and does (I.26, 147 [109]); that "there is virtually nothing that I know I know" (II.17, 617 [480]); that "I consider myself one of the common sort, except in that I consider myself so" (II.17, 618 [481]); and that "I value myself only for knowing my value" (II.17, 618 [481]). But despite these denials of possessing truth, and despite the claims that he knows nothing, Montaigne says that he knows himself as well as anyone has ever known anything: "no man ever treated a subject he knew and understood better than I . . . and that in this I am the most learned man alive" (III.2, 783 [611]). These statements of ignorance and self-knowledge are not contradictory. Rather, they exemplify the essence of Montaigne's teaching about what can be known by man: nothing—except how the phenomena of his own self operate in himself.

We have now arrived at the essence of Montaignian wisdom: as opposed to all the self-certain dogmatists of the world, Montaigne extols primarily only negative wisdom—knowledge of what is *not* true and what we should *not* fear—except for matters of the self. Montaigne does make affirmative truth claims about how a human being should live his or her life, and in this way his views resemble what Isaiah Berlin calls positive liberty. However, Montaigne avoids many of the negative or totalitarian tendencies that Berlin associates with positive liberty, because almost all of his truth claims refer to negatives. The human inabilities to know metaphysical truth about life or afterlife are but two cases of a more general ignorance that he thinks characterizes the human condition in its entirety. "Many abuses are engendered in the world, or, to put it more boldly," he says, "all the abuses in the world are engendered, by our being taught to be afraid of professing our ignorance and our being bound to accept everything that we cannot refute" (III.11, 1007 [788]). The human uneasiness with ignorance is a problem that must be overcome. Montaigne's insistence on and acceptance of ignorance places him in the finest philosophical traditions, those of Socrates and of the Academic and Pyrrhonist skeptics (and it resembles the Christian and Epicurean evaluations of the natural human condition— without offering their escapes: God or science).

To use twentieth-century terminology, Montaigne is clearly a non-foundationalist thinker. That is to say, upon critical reflection, he does not think that there is any self-consciously knowable truth that is sufficient for human beings to use in ordering our moral world. He argues that human beings cannot obtain transcendent truth and that ignorance is "the most certain fact in the school of the world" (III.13, 1053 [824]). "We are born to quest after truth," Montaigne says, but "to possess it belongs to a greater power. . . . The world is but a school of inquiry. The question is not who will hit the ring, but who will make the best runs at it" (III.8, 906 [708]). He further argues: "Anyone who wants to be cured of ignorance must confess it. . . . Wonder is the foundation of all philosophy, inquiry its progress, ignorance its end" (III.11, 1007-8 [788]). Human beings can inquire if they are moved to do so, but if they inquire, ignorance is the only conclusion that can legitimately be reached. Man, according to Montaigne, can make descriptions, take runs at the truth, or—to use the contemporary language of Richard Rorty—tell stories, and while some of these will be more accurate than others, we can never know that we have reached truth itself (other than knowing this). This knowledge of ignorance is the essence of his Academic skepticism.

Rather than creating new myths to ease human anxiety, which Montaigne says all past philosophers have done,[52] he wants reflective individuals to be comfortable with what he considers to be man's foundationless existence. To be comfortable with the lack of foundations, however, Montaigne, unlike the unbounded optimists of the Enlightenment, soberly argues that man must be taught to accept his limits with modesty. This is, as we have seen, the point behind his skeptical arguments in the "Apology," and it is also why Montaigne praises cautious scholarly phrases, such as "perhaps," "to some extent," "some," "they say," "I think," and the like, which "soften and moderate the rashness of our propositions" (III.11, 1007 [788]). He wants children to inquire into problems but not to pronounce answers. He would be happy if their mouths were full of the following utterances: "'What does that mean? I do not understand it. That might be. Is it true?'" (III.11, 1007 [788]). In short, Montaigne encourages "an honest curiosity to inquire into all things," but he wants an inquirer to "choose if he can; if not . . . remain in doubt. Only the fools are certain and assured" (I.26, 155 [115] & 150 [111]). Human ignorance, where it exists, should be built into every aspect of education and life. Montaigne understands that custom and myth have roles in human life, but he deems it essential that those in power understand the contingent nature of these practices. The alternative, as Montaigne discusses with respect to various personal experiences with purported witches, so-called miracles, and civil courts, is unconscious ignorance; and "it is putting a very high price on one's conjectures to have a man roasted alive because of them" (III.11, 1010 [790]). In short, Montaigne urges reflective individuals consciously to recognize their limits and lacks.

In finding his own limits, Montaigne claims to have stumbled across the universal limits for the species as a whole. Montaigne's truths pertain to negative abilities, to limits on what can be attained by human beings. While he acquires this knowledge through subjective, phenomenological means, his self-portrait is nothing short of a call for his readers to make the same self-experiments, to verify his truths in themselves. And Montaigne was manifestly successful in evoking this response from his readers. Pascal testifies most eloquently on this point when he says, *"Ce n'est pas dans Montaigne, mais dans moi, que je trouve tout ce que j'y vois."*[53] Voltaire expresses the same thought more bluntly by saying of Montaigne that *"il a peint la nature humaine."*[54] Montaigne's concomitant calls for human beings to recognize their ignorance while pursuing self-knowledge embody the essence of his human wisdom.

VI. Montaigne's Socrates

To specify precisely the moral implications of Montaigne's conception of the self, Montaigne's views must be compared to and distinguished from those of Socrates. Montaigne's ideal of ignorance and self-knowledge notably echoes the ideas of Socrates, the first philosopher who, like Montaigne, brought philosophy down from the heavens. Being the chief figure in the writings of Plato, the founder of Academic skepticism, it is not surprising that Socrates emerges as a great hero in the *Essays*, epitomizing Montaigne's human ideal (as we have described it so far). Yet, Montaigne does not simply imitate Socrates or uncritically accept his views. Montaigne reinterprets the Socratic quest for self-knowledge in bold and morally significant ways which are key to understanding Montaigne's moral vision and his arguments for toleration. By systematically examining Montaigne's similarities to and differences from Socrates, we shall achieve two important results. Historically speaking, by establishing what is Socratic and ancient in Montaigne's thought and specifying Montaigne's own innovations, we shall see both the origins of some of the most significant characteristics of modernity and Montaigne's unique blend of ancient and modern thought. From a philosophical perspective, pinpointing Montaigne's differences from the "traditional" Socrates enables us precisely to identify the moral and political significance of Montaigne's ontological innovations, which prove pivotal to his justification for toleration.

Montaigne bestows tremendous praise on Socrates, the (reputed) founder of the moral universalism he is supposed to reject. Indeed, Socrates emerges from the third and final book of the *Essays*, with Montaigne himself, as a model human being.[55] As we saw in our examination of the Indians in "Of Coaches," Montaigne's criticism of natural simplicity is contrasted with praise of two people: Montaigne himself and Socrates. But this is not the only praise that Socrates receives from Montaigne's pen. Montaigne calls Socrates "the first of all human souls in reformation" (III.5, 870 [680]), "a perfect model in all great qualities" (III.12, 1034 [809]), "a saintly model of human nature" (III.12, 1031 [807]), and "the master of masters" (III.13, 1053 [824]), and he calls Socrates' soul "the most perfect that has come to my knowledge" (II.11, 402 [308]). Montaigne says that Socrates is "the man most worthy to be known" (III.12, 1014 [793]), because he knew and accepted what he was: "Socrates was a man, and wanted neither to be nor to seem anything else" (III.5, 870 [681]). Calling Socrates a man in this context is the equivalent of calling him a true man, the highest praise that Montaigne can bestow. In a world where almost everyone either is or pretends to be something else, true men are rare. Montaigne admires authenticity above everything else, but Montaigne praises Socrates not merely for authentically being himself; Montaigne praises him as authentically human. (In Montaigne's understanding, however, these two claims are integrally related.) Socrates reveals human capabilities in their essence. Consistent with his understanding of human limits, Montaigne says that Socrates reveals the human soul as "neither elevated nor rich," and—echoing his praise of human psychological health as the ultimate good (as we saw in chapters 1 and 2)—Montaigne says that Socrates excels in what a human being can be: "he shows [the soul] only as healthy, but assuredly with a very blithe and clear health" (III.12, 1014 [793]). The health that Socrates embodies is, for Montaigne, a shining example of the human form at the peak of perfection. Montaigne says it is easier to talk like Aristotle and live like Caesar or Alexander than either to talk or to live like Socrates. Socrates' life, Montaigne concludes, represents "the extreme degree of perfection and difficulty" (III.12, 1032-33 [808]).

Socrates embodies Montaigne's model of human perfection, because he is nature incarnated, pure and healthy. Socrates lives properly. Montaigne imagines how Socrates would answer the question of what he knows how to do: "he will say, 'Lead the life of man in conformity with its natural condition'" (III.2, 787 [614]), and then Montaigne praises this answer that he put into Socrates' mouth as displaying "a knowledge much more general, more weighty, and more legitimate" than anything else (III.2, 787 [614]).[56] According to Montaigne, Socrates dies properly, too. Montaigne praises Socrates' manner of dying as essaying death, achieving everything Montaigne can imagine: "It belongs to the one and only Socrates to become acquainted with death with an ordinary countenance, to become familiar with it and play with it. . . . [D]ying seems to him a natural and indifferent incident" (III.4, 810 [632]). Indeed, Montaigne's reaction to Socrates' speech at his own trial for a capital offense bursts with admiring emotion: "Is that [Socrates' speech] not a sober, sane plea, but at the same time natural and lowly, inconceivably lofty, truthful, frank, and just beyond all example—and employed in what a critical need!" (III.12, 1031 [806-7]). Montaigne says other speeches have been prettier and more artful, but it is Socrates' directness and simplicity that he praises most. One may doubt that Socrates' "Apology" really reflects "an unstudied and artless boldness" and "*simplicité*" (III.12, 1032 [807]); indeed, Montaigne should remember his own ideal of artless art or the art of seeming natural (see, for example, I.26, 171[127]).[57] In any case, Montaigne's core praise of Socrates' speech directly reflects what we have been saying about Montaigne's own views on ignorance. Montaigne says Socrates' speech "represents the pure and primary impression and ignorance of Nature" (III.12, 1032 [807]). This statement reveals Montaigne's praise of Socrates (and his own striving) in both key senses: Socrates at one and the same time has both a "primary impression" and an "ignorance" of nature. That is to say, he both understands his condition (through a phenomenological "impression," not via reason) and knows what he does not know. It is by virtue of this that Socrates provides the most powerful model both of what can be known and done by a human being with his own unaided powers and of what cannot be. In sum, Montaigne says that Socrates "did a great favor to human nature by showing how much it can do by itself"—which also reveals what it cannot do (III.12, 1015 [794]). Man can explore and control himself on Earth. He cannot definitively know whether death is good or bad or what comes after death. Socrates takes human abilities to the very edge and does not pretend to go beyond.

Even though Montaigne praises Socrates as the greatest man that ever was, he is not entirely satisfied with Plato's Socrates as the model of human perfection. The relationship of Socrates to those who wrote words in his name is a complicated subject that is beyond our present scope. Montaigne was familiar with the writings of those who most famously put words into Socrates' mouth, Plato and Xenophon, and has indeed been called the sixteenth century's greatest interpreter of Plato.[58] Montaigne puts many things in many people's mouths, including Socrates', but in his own book, he chooses to use himself as his main character, not someone else. This is a difference between Montaigne and Plato that is worth exploring, but the aim here is not to compare their methodologies or to define definitively who Socrates was and what he believed. Rather, our aim is to examine Montaigne's account of Socrates and to see where—in Montaigne's eyes—Socrates falls short. By pinpointing Montaigne's differences from the "traditional" Socrates, we can most clearly see the moral and political significance of Montaigne's ontological innovations.

Montaigne dismisses two differences between himself and the traditional Socrates as only rhetorical and, therefore, minor. First, Montaigne discounts Socrates' talk of the supernatural and nonobservable. He dislikes Socrates' speaking of his "daemon" and doubts that Ideas exist independently of man (III.13, 1096 [856] and II.12, 491-92 [379]). In general, Montaigne rejects the supernatural aspects of Socrates' presentation and reject Plato's epithet of "divine" for what he considers to be the nobler label, "human" (III.13, 1096 [856]). Montaigne downplays this difference between Plato's Socrates and himself, however, because he does not think that either Socrates or Plato takes the Ideas seriously. Indeed, in chapter 1 we saw Montaigne explicitly reject such claims, saying that he cannot believe that Plato presents them "as good coin of the realm" (II.12, 491 [379]). Montaigne dismisses the metaphysical language in Plato's vocabulary by arguing that philosophers tailor both the substance and presentation of their ideas to the existing beliefs of their times, framing and diluting them in order to make them digestible and useful. To the extent that otherworldliness appears in Plato's Socrates, Montaigne ascribes it to a desire to be politically useful and to rhetorical need, not belief. Montaigne's Socrates is the human Socrates, and Montaigne himself strives to be Socrates without the otherworldly rhetoric.[59]

A second rhetorical difference between Montaigne and Socrates concerns Montaigne's accounts of their personal demeanors. Montaigne often claims that he has an easygoing, gentle disposition and that he lets himself go; "I let myself go as I have come" (III.12, 1037 [811]). He often backhandedly praises his careless and carefree qualities as testaments to his easy and spontaneous nature. For example, in contrast to his condemnations of many philosophers' self-imposed rigors and self-disciplining, Montaigne advances himself as an accidental philosopher with an accidental constancy: "What rule my life belonged to, I did not learn until after it was completed and spent. A new figure: an unpremeditated and accidental philosopher!" (II.12, 528 [409]).[60] Similarly, he claims, "My virtue is a virtue, or I should say innocence, that is accidental and fortuitous" (II.11, 406 [311]). While Montaigne often praises Socrates for having a similarly free nature, sometimes he seems to lump him with the other philosophers, noting that Socrates had "corrected [his] natural disposition by force of reason" and "corrected it by discipline" (III.12, 1037 [811] and II.11, 408 [313]). This is an indication that Socrates is perhaps insufficiently natural. However, this account of Socrates parallels Montaigne's discussion of the unnamed licentious philosophers in the "Apology," whom Montaigne praises for following both nature and reason. If the outside force to which Socrates regulates himself is based on reason grounded in reality, and not in a reason run amuck, and Socrates really does have the power to alter his actions and disposition accordingly, then Montaigne would approve of it. Indeed, this is the only way to reconcile Montaigne's praise of Socrates' naturalness with Montaigne's praise of Socrates' reliance on reason (II.11, 402 [308]). In any case, we also know that despite Montaigne's claim of possessing a contingent and provisional nature and to presenting himself as he simply and directly is, Montaigne really presents himself in a careful and highly artful manner.[61] Socrates and Montaigne must both have been blessed with extraordinary natural talents and been largely self-created as well; they both work hard to achieve their natural states. Montaigne does not often level this charge of lack of spontaneity at Socrates, and it likely follows from the particular rhetoric that Montaigne builds around himself. Thus, this criticism does not amount to much.

Montaigne does, however, differ from Socrates in two major substantive ways that reveal the most original aspects of Montaigne's conception of the self. First, Montaigne and Socrates differ on the role of subjectivity in human life. Montaigne gives subjectivity much greater scope and credit than does Socrates, constantly focusing on the haphazard stirrings of his body and mind, which he asserts to be characteristic of life itself. If in interpreting Socrates one takes the various "doctrines" that Socrates presents as sincere truth claims (and thus finds a dogmatic Socrates who emphasizes "transcendent" truth), Socrates will be radically different from Montaigne. On the other hand, if one, like Montaigne, downplays these aspects of Socrates' presentation (and thus finds a Socrates who knows that he knows nothing), Socrates will be much closer to Montaigne. Whichever interpretation one prefers, Socrates talks little about the stirrings of his body and mind (if Plato's and Xenophon's dialogues are any indication). Socrates, like Montaigne, searches for universally valid, rationally knowable, moral truths, but Montaigne more explicitly doubts that these can be known by human beings. Whatever Socrates thinks about the substance or even the existence of such truths, he continually pursues them throughout his life. Being more explicitly skeptical about reason's ability to possess such truths, Montaigne falls back onto a kind of experiential knowledge as all that is attainable by human beings. Socrates says various things in various places about the value of experiential knowledge; Montaigne clearly describes it as worth attaining. As a result, Montaigne pursues the Delphic injunction to "know thyself" in a much more subjective and phenomeno-logical way.

In addition and related to their difference on the role of subjectivity in human life, Montaigne also differs from Socrates in his evaluation of the body. Socrates barely discusses the body or bodily pleasure and to the extent that he does, he does not hold a high opinion of either. In the *Republic*, the pursuit of pleasure is first associated with the city of pigs and those who indulge in it are later banished to the just city's lowest class. In the *Symposium*, he refers to the body as "of no account."[62] And even if these statements do not represent his final judgment, Socrates does condemn the body as belonging to the lowest, most animalistic side of man, and his ideal philosopher, who takes pleasure only in philosophy, is almost entirely immune to the body's charms. By contrast, as one might expect based on his praise of the animals and cannibals, Montaigne does not consider man's physical nature to be undignified; rather, he celebrates it as an integral part of man's being. As the rest of this chapter reveals, these two central features of Montaigne thought—the celebration of the body and the exploration of the subjective self—distinguish him from Socrates and form central compo-nents of his vision of the good, and therefore of his political philosophy.

VII. Self-Exploration as Going "Home"

Montaigne's glorification of sensual self-seeking is the "carrot" that his philosophy dangles. If the "stick" in his thought is his skepticism—his warnings about what human beings cannot know and should not do—his voluptuous conception of the self aims to give people quite enough to do to keep them happy and whole "at home." He revels and luxuriates in his self-explorations, because he considers this process the most pleasant and energizing, and far from leading to atomism, he considers self-exploration to be the ground for the greatest social goods: philosophic discussion and friendship. Moreover, while he argues for self-exploration only for people's own self-interest, since the good is found "at home," self-aware people will have no interest in forcing anything on anyone else. Others are accepted not because they have "rights," but as a consequence of Montaigne's conception of self-interest.

Montaigne's ontological innovations come together in his call for human beings to go "home" (*"chez soi"*). Just as he warns his readers against being taken outside of themselves by concerns for metaphysics or fear of death, so he harkens his readers to return to themselves. The "home" analogy is central to Montaigne's conception of the self. A normative notion of "home" allows him to reconcile the existing reality, "We are never at home, we are always beyond" (I.3, 18 [8]), with the moral injunction, "You have quite enough to do at home; don't go away" (III.10, 981 [767]). Montaigne judges harshly those who flee themselves rather than staying home. To him, self-abandonment is responsible for most of the man-made ills. It is on this basis that he pleads for man to "break free from the violent clutches that engage us elsewhere and draw us away from ourselves" (I.39, 236 [178]) and condemns those who wander into other things as seeking "business only for busyness" (III.10, 981 [767]).

Yet, in his descriptive accounts of the world, Montaigne knows that human beings are usually not at home: "Every man rushes elsewhere and into the future, because no man has arrived at himself" (III.12 1022 [799]). "We shall never heap enough insults," he says, "on the unruliness of our mind" (I.4, 27 [15]). The ordinary psychic disorder of the soul causes human beings to lash out in every direction and flee themselves, for "it seems that the soul, once stirred and set in motion, is lost" (I.4, 25 [14]). Disorder, inconstancy, and irresolution characterize the normal state of the human psyche—and, unlike the ancient philosophers, Montaigne seems to think that this disorder is existentially part of the human condition. He refers to mankind's "natural instability"(II.1, 315 [239]); says "It may be questioned, given the soul's natural condition, whether it can ever be [orderly]" (II.2, 328 [249]); argues "In all antiquity it is hard to pick out a dozen men who set their lives to a certain and constant course" (II.1, 316 [240]); and claims that "Out of a thousand souls, there is not one that is straight and composed for a single moment in a lifetime" (II.2, 328 [249]).

Montaigne's fascination with "order" does not make him advocate strict discipline, for the soul rebels against that; Montaigne aims to bring merely a semblance of order to our psychic chaos by proposing that people's minds have a subject to occupy them: "Unless you keep them busy with some definite subject that will bridle and control them, they throw themselves in disorder hither and yon in the vague field of imagination" (I.8, 33 [21]); "The soul that has no fixed goal loses itself" (I.8, 34 [21]); "We must always give it an object to aim at and act on" (I.4, 25 [14]). Although people commonly use external concerns such as metaphysics, moneymaking, religion, etc. to help them order their soul's energy, Montaigne dismisses these objects of self-order as merely being what Pascal was later to name *divertissement*.[63] Diversions away from oneself might lead people to act orderly for a while, but since the underlying cause of disorder is in the mind, people who occupy themselves with objects outside themselves for which they do not have any intimate care, are likely to grow bored, or switch the objects of their attachments. To the extent that people occupy themselves with things that cause no trouble to anyone else, Montaigne does not have a problem with it, but neither does he see it as a long-term solution to the problem of internal disorder. Since the source of the disorder comes from within, Montaigne argues, order can only truly come about by looking inward and sorting through the threads of one's own disordered self.

Montaigne proposes self-exploration as the particular subject around which human beings should order themselves, because only such self-essaying gets at the root of the problem.[64] And besides, what is more appealing to people than themselves? Montaigne signals the difference between those who live in themselves and those who live outside themselves by distinguishing the different directions their movements take: the former go inward or in any case always come back to themselves, even if by a circular or circuitous route; the latter take straight lines away from themselves. The difference between the two groups is clear in the following quotation: "The world always looks straight ahead; as for me, I turn my gaze inward, I fix it there and keep it busy. Everyone looks in front of him; as for me, I look inside of me; I have no business but with myself" (II.17, 641 [499]). Thus, Montaigne tells us that his own mind's "principal and most laborious study is studying itself" (III.3, 797 [621]), and that "my professed principle . . . is to be wholly contained and established within myself" (III.2, 793 [618]). To know oneself and accept oneself is the source of tranquility of soul and human happiness. "The greatest thing in the world," Montaigne says, "is to know how to belong to oneself" (I.39, 236 [178]). He tells us that the "counsel of true and natural philosophy" is "to be content with yourself, to borrow nothing except from yourself" (I.39, 242 [183]), that "[t]rue freedom is to have power over oneself for everything" (III.12, 1022 [800]) and approvingly quotes Seneca: "He is most powerful who has power over himself" (III.12, 1022 [800]). Similarly, Montaigne also thinks "The worst condition of man is when he loses knowledge and control of himself" (II.2, 322 [245]). The process of exploring oneself, of essaying oneself, is sophisticated simplicity.

Montaigne's essays have everything to do with going home: they capture both his own direct and indirect attempts to "go home," and they are written in a manner to bring others home, too. They are direct attempts for self-knowledge if his topic is himself, indirect if he discovers himself in the course of another inquiry. For not only can he study any topic and learn about himself—"Every movement reveals us" (I.50, 290 [219])—but he thinks it imperative to explore the world, for human beings need to know the range of possibilities in the world and measure and compare themselves to these possibilities as part of their essaying process. Indeed, given the complexities of human nature, it is sometimes even easier to learn by chance, since the difficulty of doing something often increases in proportion to one's desire to do it.[65] That is to say, it is sometimes easier to do things inadvertently or accidentally rather than intentionally. "I do not find myself in the place where I look; and I find myself more by chance encounter than by searching my judgment" (I.10, 41-2 [26-7]); "what he did naturally and by chance, he will not do as exactly by design" (II.17, 634 [493]). It is in this sense, I think, that Montaigne calls himself an accidental philosopher.

Although he considers himself to be an accidental philosopher, his intention in describing himself is carefully thought through. Montaigne's aim in writing his book is not only to tell people that they should engage in more self-reflection, but to illustrate how to do it by showing how the process works in himself. He is the exemplar *par excellence* of essaying oneself. His book is simultaneously his method, teaching, and proof. Thus, he declares "whatever I make myself known to be, provided I make myself known as I am, I am carrying out my plan" (II.17, 636 [495]). When he finds himself, he finds man: "the study I am making, the subject of which is man" aims to make men see what they refuse to pursue: "knowledge of themselves and their own state, which is ever present before their eyes, which is in them" (II.17, 617-18 [481]). Just as Montaigne discovers himself, others should discover themselves by going through the self-exploratory process that he illustrates.

And what does Montaigne find at the core of the self? Montaigne finds paradox there. He finds everything and he finds nothing. Sometimes, for example, he asserts that we are "entirely destitute and void" (II.8, 364 [278]) or "null" [*neant*] (II.2, 328 [249])—and this is true about transcendent things. More commonly, however, Montaigne finds many things. He stresses that he does not find a single "will" or "essence" at the core of the self, but instead finds a hodgepodge of all sorts of different wills, impulses, and tendencies: "Man, in all things and throughout, is but patchwork and motley" (II.20, 656 [511]); "Life is an uneven, irregular, and multiform movement" (III.3, 796 [621]); "We are all patchwork, and so shapeless and diverse in composition that each bit, each moment, plays its own game" (II.1, 321 [244]). "What I chiefly portray," he says, "is my cogitations, a shapeless subject" (II.6, 359 [274]). Because much of the self is unformed, unarticulated, or patchwork, Montaigne finds "natural weakness" (II.12, 486 [375]), i.e., unlike Nietzsche, he does not find a strong will that must be willed. This is crucial, because if self-knowledge led to the discovery of a titanic will, Montaigne would have no grounds to condemn the willing of it, even if it meant others were hurt in the process. Nonetheless, Montaigne does find things in himself that horrify him: "the more I frequent myself and know myself, the more my deformity astonishes me, and the less I understand myself" (III.11, 1006 [787]). He finds that all his so-called virtues are tinctured with vice, that he is self-interested and prone to want to break many moral strictures, and is eminently aware of his own tendencies to unruliness. In one sense, the lack that Montaigne finds "at home" is disappointing. But it is disappointing only if one expects cosmic answers.

If one is less demanding, more realistic in one's expectations, one can find oneself full of never-ending delights—for so much is there, waiting to be found, explored, and shaped. Montaigne regards the process of self-exploration, of essaying *chez soi*, as extremely pleasurable. Wherever he looks and everything that he thinks, feels, or believes serve as raw material for his self-questing: "being consists in movement and action. Wherefore each man in some sort exists in his work" (II.8, 366 [279]). He finds beautiful, moving, and noble wills and desires in himself, too. In fact, it is precisely the juxtaposition and entanglement between the good and the bad, the beautiful and the ugly, and the noble and the base that make human beings so fascinating. And there is no better place to find them than in oneself, because each of us has more access to his or her own feelings, wills, and desires, than he or she does to those in other people. For although we mask ourselves to ourselves, others mask themselves to us much more. In short, Montaigne constantly discusses the wonders of self-exploration and attempts to make the reader feel the joy of the activity by writing down his own self-explorations. Many scholars have tried to explain the joys and horrors that Montaigne finds in himself,[66] but a good part of the thrill concerns Montaigne's attentiveness to minute details and subtle shifts in himself. Any scholarly attempt to recapture it necessarily falls flat.

If self-exploration is done for the pleasure of it, it also makes people as authentic as they can be. Self-exploration is based on movement between the passive and active aspects of each individual. On the one hand, we simply are. On the other hand, we are active and critical, aware of, yet distanced from things, including ourselves. In the former case, our body, impulses, thoughts and habits are beyond our control. They are flux and movement caused by nature or a fixed pattern caused by habit. In the latter case, we perceive and have a probing judgment that engages and affects its objects.[67] Only when the active self engages the passive self and comes to know how phenomena work in itself can a human being begin to have any knowledge at all. Our only choice is whether we should consciously affirm how nature and habit work in us or whether we should fight those unchosen tendencies. In either case, through reflection we make ourselves and the world more our own than do unreflective people, such as the cannibals. We are freer than they because our actions are self-consciously accepted and affirmed. Like Montaigne, we must make ourselves the subject of our work and reflection. If we do business or something else outside of our self, with which we have no intimate care, we take our self out of itself.

Self-exploration also helps people regulate their unruly impulses. Our active and passive natures lead Montaigne to hypothesize a double self. He says, "We are . . . double within ourselves, with the result that we do not believe what we believe, and we cannot rid ourselves of what we condemn" (II.16, 603 [469]). This doubleness goes a long way toward explaining the unruliness of the human mind and the unhappiness that plagues the species. Man's critical faculties can lead an individual away from himself, as can the natural impulses and anxieties of his disposition. The fact that there is no necessary relation between the dictates of one's critical faculties and the desires of one's disposition, however, opens each individual to conflict between one's passive, habitual self and one's evaluation of it. This gap can result in self-hatred and can be widened through the internalization of external views, such as religious, metaphysical, or political doctrines. Montaigne hopes to minimize this divide by encouraging human beings to essay both parts of themselves. To restore the tranquility of soul that Montaigne believes either does or can exist by nature, one must probe the various particulars of one's own passive, habitual disposition—fears, anxieties, desires, hopes, inclinations—and subject one's critical faculties to their own scrutiny. It is only by engaging in these forms of self-seeking that one can begin to peel away the things that one *thinks* are driving one's actions and move toward the things that really *are*. We might not be able to fully comprehend what truly moves us or fully eliminate our unruly impulses or internal gaps, but by being aware of them, one is able both more directly to confront the actual source of one's difficulties and gain a distance from them, which prevents these problems or impulses from totally possessing one.[68] It is because of this psychological astuteness that Jacques Lacan called Montaigne the first psychoanalyst.[69]

The tools available to human beings are inadequate for possessing essential knowledge of oneself. In addition to the problems with reason and the sense organs that we discussed in chapter 1, the process of describing oneself in language, according to Montaigne, necessarily distorts the phenomena one wants to describe. Language, "this airy medium of words" (II.6, 359 [274]), represents but a clumsy attempt at self-articulation. It is neither subtle nor flexible enough to capture human thoughts and feelings. Not only is it overly rigid and insufficiently penetrating in its descriptions, but it imprisons the self in the terms and analysis it uses and invents. Human beings use language to reveal, but it creates and conceals at the same time.

Feeling emerges for Montaigne as a less articulate but more reliable guide than language. Because human beings live in a phenomenological world, feeling serves as a conduit to life: "I shall know it well enough when I feel it" (III.13, 1050 [821]); "I judge myself only by actual sensation, not by reasoning" (III.13, 1074 [840]). Feeling oneself, and feeling for oneself, are both active and passive. Montaigne wants the individual to focus attention on his natural movements, literally to 'get in touch with oneself.' It is not surprising therefore that Montaigne uses numerous reflexive verbs with corporeal connotations: *se sonder* [to sound oneself], *se gouter* [to taste oneself], *se regarder* [to look for oneself], and the like. He uses verbs that echo all of the five senses; for example, in this one line he refers to himself through three senses and knits them together with a childlike sense of play: "I continually observe myself, I take stock of myself, I taste myself. Others always go elsewhere . . . as for me, I roll about in myself" (II.17, 641 [499]). This fully echoes Montaigne's desire to "judge by experience" that we saw in the "Apology." If human beings cannot know essences, they can feel phenomena. If they cannot know truth in the abstract, they do have the power to know truths about themselves.

Not only can we have experiential knowledge of ourselves, but to a limited extent we can also *create* ourselves. The process of exploring oneself leads not only to the uncovering of a preexisting self, but to the creation of oneself. Montaigne speaks of his *Essays* as "a book consubstantial with its author;" each makes the other: "I have no more made my book than my book made me" (II.18, 648 [504]). "I have had to fashion and compose myself so often to bring myself out, that the model itself has to some extent grown firm and taken shape. Painting myself for others, I have painted my inward self with colors clearer than my original ones" (II.18, 647-8 [504]). Self-exploration not only locates and amplifies a preexisting self, but the process changes the self that is being sought. Unlike Nietzsche, however, Montaigne does not conceive self-creation to be a violent process in which suffering is integral. His is gentle. By actively examining (and thereby affecting) the passive tendencies that determine one's character, one can gain some formative control over one's otherwise preexisting habits, but there are limits to this, because we cannot simply will ourselves to be more fully or other than what we are. Changing the self comes about, paradoxically, by accepting the self and its elusiveness.[70]

Going "home," however, is not radically atomistic, as Montaigne conceives it. Rather, for Montaigne, self-awareness is the necessary condition for the world's most sublime social goods: philosophical discussion and friendship. If self-exploration is the greatest individual good, then "[t]he most fruitful and natural exercise of our mind, in my opinion," Montaigne writes, "is discussion. I find it sweeter than any other action of our life" (III.8, 900 [704]). Unlike Mill, Montaigne does not argue that free and unfettered discussion will necessarily advance the cause of truth or lead to social progress as a result of the innovations and discoveries of geniuses. Discussion affords the opportunity to test oneself, but instead of being merely an internal dialogue, it is an essaying of oneself through others. Montaigne does not deem any and every exchange of words to be discussion; flattery or sycophantic speech do not provide a true test of reality or any real resistance. They do nothing but uncritically reinforce one's existing opinions, and this provides no benefit at all. Therefore, one's interlocutors must be strong and independent. Montaigne seeks his verbal sparring partners from among "those who are called talented gentlemen . . . the rarest type among us, and a type that is chiefly due to nature" (III.3, 802 [625]).[71] He describes these discussions as both playful and serious. On the one hand, he emphasizes their cheerful qualities: good spirits, "joking wittily," and sees them as "an exercise" for his "natural gaiety."[72] And in this vein, he emphasizes that the point of such noble discussions is solely the process itself: "The object of this association," he says, "is simply intimacy, fellowship, and conversation: exercise of minds, without any other fruit" (III.3, 802 [625]). But on the other hand, he suggests that not any frivolous topic of conversation will do. They are serious: as "in quest of that which is" (III.8, 904 [706]), "for the needs of life" (III.8, 904 [707]), and pursuing "the cause of truth" (III.8, 902 [705]). If no definitive truth is reached, discussions are not a waste of time, both because there is always pleasure in the chase and because the intimacy and exercise of such intense striving is beautiful and moving in itself. Discussion leads to intimacy—with oneself and others.

Properly speaking, discussion can also serve as an outlet for the natural aggression in mankind; Montaigne wants to replace the physical warfare in which the cannibals and princes engage with this kind of mental exercise, jousting, and mutual essaying. Thus, when Montaigne describes his ideal of conversation, he often uses military analogies: "If I discuss with a strong mind and a stiff jouster, he presses on my flanks, prods me right and left" (III.8, 900 [704]). He also compares his ideal of discussion to fencing (III.8, 905 [707]), sword fighting (III.8, 914 [715]), altercations (III.9, 934 [730]), and a military campaign (III.8, 917-18 [717]). Moreover, he says discussion requires contestation: "I like a strong, manly fellowship and familiarity, a friendship that delights in the sharpness and vigor of its intercourse, as does love in bites and scratches that draw blood. It is not vigorous and generous enough if it is not quarrelsome . . . if it fears knocks and moves with constraint" (III.8, 902 [705]). But Montaigne does not consider any verbal form of contestation to be discussion, nor does he praise every form of verbal exchange. Just as he praises the cannibals' noble manner of combat, so he seeks a similar nobility in these verbal tests. His aim is not to win an argument by any means but actually to improve himself: "I feel much prouder of the victory I win over myself when, in the very heat of battle, I make myself bow beneath the force of my adversary's reason, than I feel gratified by the victory I win over him through his weakness" (III.8, 903 [706]). Like war, such noble discussions push people beyond their ordinary limits and ideas: "his ideas launch mine. Rivalry, glory, competition, push me and lift me above myself" (III.8, 900 [704]). But unlike in war, one's success in discussion is compatible with one's jouster's; both can be stimulated and learn. The qualities tested and the potential growth are greater in philosophical than in physical sparring, too. Remembering that Montaigne never refers to the cannibals' physical struggles as "essaying," we can see that this kind of redirection of energy represents, for Montaigne, the wisdom and maturation of man. Self-development benefits from, may even require, tolerating and challenging differences.

Self-knowledge is not only a prerequisite for noble discussion, it is a prerequisite for the most sublime connection available to human beings: friendship. True friendship, which he says occurs extremely infrequently but claims to have had himself, is a "complete fusion of . . . wills and a "truly perfect" union, so much so that it is a "relationship being that of one soul in two bodies" (I.28, 189 [141]). He describes it as so intimate that friends can neither lend nor give anything to each other, because everything of each properly belongs to the other already (I.28, 189 [141]). He describes friendship in a very physical, visceral manner, echoing the importance of phenomenological knowledge that he has emphasized, even when describing the mingling of souls: "our souls mingle and blend with each other so completely that they efface the seam that joined them and cannot find it again. If you press me to tell why I loved him, I feel that this cannot be expressed, except by answering: Because it was he, because it was I" (I.28, 187 [139]). He similarly describes the mingling of wills in a physical, homoerotic language: friendship "having seized my whole will, led it to plunge and lose itself in his; which, having seized his whole will, led it to plunge and lose itself in mine, with equal hunger, equal rivalry" (I.28, 187 [139]). Finally, he describes friendship as two people being "fused into one" and as an "insatiable hunger for bodily presence" (III.9, 955 [747]). This kind of beautiful bond must be, according to Montaigne, grounded in self-knowledge and an attachment to the goods of the human condition. Without these, human beings would run amuck, and "[i]f their actions went astray," he says, "they were by my measure neither friends to each other, nor friend to themselves" (I.28, 188 [140]).

In conclusion, sensual self-seeking is the basis for all of mankind's greatest goods, individual and social. Without self-exploration one can be neither a friend to oneself nor a friend to others. For all healthy associations depend on healthy people, and one cannot be authentically healthy if one is dominated by the unruly aspects of one's self. Thus, each individual must take care of himself or herself: "He who would do his job would see that his first lesson is to know what he is and what is proper for him. And he who knows himself no longer takes extraneous business for his own; he loves and cultivates himself before anything else; he refuses superfluous occupations and useless thoughts and projects" (I.3, 18 [9]). "Life," he says, "should be an aim unto itself, a purpose unto itself; its rightful study is to regulate, conduct, and suffer itself" (III.12 1028-9 [805]). "The main responsibility of each of us is his own conduct; and that is what we are here for" (III.10, 984 [769-70]). A human being cannot know abstract truths, but he can gain knowledge of himself by studying and exploring his movements and actions, including thoughts. This is nothing to glory in, but it can and should be a never-ending source of wonder and delight.

VIII. The Body and Pleasure Properly Pursued

Montaigne does not just seek the cultivation of the mental self, but he wants to celebrate and cultivate the body, too. He conceives the self as an integral unity of body and soul: "there is nothing in us . . . that is purely either corporeal or spiritual"; everything is both in a "close and brotherly correspondence" (III.5, 871 [681] & III.13, 1094 [855]). To sequester the body and soul, as both Socrates and Christians do, he says, is "to tear apart a living man" (III.5, 871 [681]). Body and soul communicate with each other, and in a well-ordered person, they harmonize and complement each other. There is but a "narrow seam" between them, "through which the experience of the one is communicated to the other" (I.21, 103 [74]). They need "mutuality and reciprocity" (III.5, 872 [682]). Given the dual but closely interconnected natures of a human being, it is no wonder that Montaigne represents the good life as including the pleasures of both soul and body and that he warns against the extremes of neglecting either. Not only does Montaigne praise both sources of pleasure, but he maintains that each partakes of the other, according to "the general human law" (which, as he describes it, is very un-Christian and un-Socratic) that all pleasure is "intellectually sensual, sensually intellectual" (III.13, 1087 [850]). Hence, Montaigne's celebration of the sensual philosopher is a celebration of both parts of a human being, body and soul.

Given the dominance of Christianity (and its extreme denunciations of the body) in his times, Montaigne's desire to recognize and accept the body in a healthy manner sometimes seems to take excessive forms. For example, he once makes a plea to "hatch" and "foment" bodily pleasure (III.5, 871 [681]). Another time, he calls for the soul to share its own pleasures with the body and "to inspire and infuse into the body all the feeling their nature allows" (III.5, 871 [681]). The question is what nature allows, and according to Montaigne, nature seems to allow for a great deal of pleasure. Montaigne asserts that "All the opinions in the world agree on this—that pleasure is our goal—though they choose different means to it. Otherwise they would be thrown out right away; for who would listen to a man who would set up our pain and discomfort as his goal?" (I.20, 80 [56]). Of course, no one sets pain as his goal, but many goals, enterprises, and relationships that Montaigne recognizes as legitimate involve enduring pain. Montaigne would have to argue that such pains are borne in the pursuit of a deeper pleasure, even if based on a kind of voluptuous psychological satisfaction. "Whatever they say," he concludes of many advocates of a particular view of the good life, even "in virtue itself the ultimate goal we aim at is voluptuousness" (I.20, 80 [56]).

Not only does Montaigne praise the sensual philosopher, but he delights in acting the part. Just as the "Apology" praises unnamed licentious philosophers for their free and unembarrassed attitude toward bodily activities such as sexual intercourse and flatulence, so Montaigne makes it a part of his rhetoric to talk plainly and unapologetically about his body and bodily functions. Already by page eleven he tells the reader he is shy about going to the bathroom and other acts that "our custom orders us to cover up" (I.3, 22 [11]). Nonetheless, in the course of the book, he discusses wet dreams (I.21, 96 [69]) and sexual impotency (I.21, 97-8 [70], I.21, 100 [72], III.5, 865-6 [677]), confesses to two bouts of venereal disease (III.3, 804 [627]), tells us he achieves orgasms quickly (III.5, 859 [671]), and makes a mock-defense speech for his "member" in a court of law in a suit brought by the other body parts which are jealous of the one part's prestige (I.21, 100-1 [72-3]). There is also an entire essay dedicated to examining the various psychological and physical aspects of love (III.5, "On Some Verses Of Virgil"), numerous discussions of his passing painful kidney stones, and discussions of vomiting blood (II.6, 353 [269]), toilet behavior (I.49, 286-7 [217]), and a mystical medicine that relies on ingredients such as "urine of a lizard" and "pulverized rat turds" (II.37, 749 [584]). Indeed, Montaigne describes his very thoughts as "excrements of an aged mind, now hard, now loose, and always undigested" (III.9, 923 [721]). And this is but a brief listing of Montaigne's playfully shocking revelations about what were taboo subjects.

Contrary to the impression that this concentrated list of references might give, however, Montaigne is neither lewd nor excessive in presenting these personal details as was, say, Rabelais, the famous French writer of the first half of the sixteenth century. Montaigne habitually presents his discussion of his body in a natural, unforced, and charming way. Indeed, this was Rousseau's complaint against Montaigne, that he confesses only to "lovable" vices.[73] Montaigne's point is to make the body lovable and thereby ease the reader's attitude toward natural bodily phenomena. It is the repressive and embarrassed conventional attitude toward the body which Montaigne condemns and combats by mentioning his body in his writing (II.17, 615 [479]). Montaigne's aim is not only to condemn the contradictions and paradoxes of "civilized" behavior but also to loosen up polite society's squeamish hypocrisy toward these subjects. Is it civilized, he asks, to consider the species' most necessary activity "shameless and indecent" (III.5, 856 [669])? "Are we not brutes to call brutish the operation that makes us?" (III.5, 856 [669]). Is it not strange that "[e]veryone shuns to see a man born, [but] everyone runs to see him die" (III.5, 856 [669])? That we blush and hide to make a man but that it is a source of glory and many virtues to unmake one? But this does not mean that Montaigne thinks that everything should be said or revealed. He implies affairs but never says with whom. He tells tales of his friends' naiveté but never mentions names.[74] Nor does he revel in titillating gossip. Montaigne is a man with tact and taste; he thinks "he who says everything satiates and disgusts us" (III.5, 858 [671]). He does not want everything to be discussed without prudence or judgment, but rather judges that it would be prudent for human happiness to relax the prudish obsessions with our essential bodily nature. According to Montaigne we have enough problems by nature. It does not make sense to be ashamed of our very selves or be burdened by wholesome pleasure. The point here is to accept the body as part of the person, to make one's notion of happiness conform to *what is* rather than to twist or contort oneself to some idea or the product of someone's imagination.[75]

With the aim of liberating the body from its conventional restrictions and oppressions, Montaigne criticizes numerous customs and views—including some of the most widely practiced and deeply entrenched practices of Western civilization—as overly restrictive or misguided. Throughout his work, he rejects conceptions of the world that seem to him inhuman, that despise mankind's corporal character in the name of a more "divine" vision. In urging that unnecessary moral rules be relaxed, Montaigne rejects many Western traditions as overly restrictive of human nature and too severe. Virtue, like everything else, Montaigne argues, must be pursued in moderation, in proper *human* proportion and *human* scale. Otherwise it can become monstrous and denaturing. In essays such as "To Flee From Sensual Pleasures At The Price Of Life" (I.33), "Of Virtue" (II.29, which is about fanatics and details cruel and horrible deeds committed in the name of purity), "The Story Of Spurina" (II.33, which is about all sorts of excesses committed in the name of virtue), and "Of Drunkenness" (II.2, which compares reputedly heroic deeds to drunken madness), Montaigne rejects many acts of "heroism" and "virtue" including murder, suicide, and self-maiming as twisted tributes to a human nature gone awry. In doing so, he implicitly and explicitly attacks many of the most heralded notions of pagan manliness, the medieval knight, and Christian piety. For example, Montaigne dryly decries St. Hilary of Poitiers, the first bishop of France, who prayed for the death of his only child and encouraged his wife's suicide so they might more quickly enjoy the blissful companionship of God. (He did not choose to employ such drastic actions on his own behalf.[76]) Montaigne rejects these extreme actions in many ways. Sometimes he directly and explicitly rejects these "extreme virtues" as nothing but "*fureur*," "*manie*," "*folie*" (II.2, 328-330 [251]), as "fantastic and irrational humors" (II.3, 335 [255]), as "enemies to my rules" (II.33, 712 [555]), and as "against himself and against . . . nature" (II.33, 712 [555]). Sometimes Montaigne uses irony to make his criticisms, as when he describes St. Hilary as acting "with Christian moderation" (I.33, 216 [162]). Sometimes he dismisses such actions with understatement, such as describing self-mutilators as "to my mind, a little lacking in wisdom" (II.33, 712 [555]). However he dismisses these acts, Montaigne always rejects contempt for the body and the religious or philosophical ideas which drive it.

Montaigne's condemnations extend not only to those who mutilate the body but also to those who simply deny it. For example, even in the earliest publication of his *Essays*, Montaigne rejects asceticism and "Stoical harshness" (I.33, 216 [162]). He considers their rejections of pleasure and their denials of pain to be too rigorous and stiff. He would rather have the one and avoid the other, but he insists that purposefully to avoid pleasure or to pretend one does not feel pain when one obviously does is to deny reality in both cases. He considers such self-delusion to be the height of philosophical stupidity. Montaigne is rejecting these kind of vain denials when he says, "I am no philosopher. Evils crush me according to their weight" (III.9, 927 [725]).[77] One must strive for pleasure and tranquility, but one must recognize the truth of one's situation. Montaigne wants one to control pain and not let it dominate or destroy one's character, but one need not pretend there is no pain. Pain is to be avoided, but if it cannot be, one must dominate it, not vice versa. Just as he praises the courage of the cannibals regardless of whether they win or lose their battles, so he asserts that in man's struggle with pain, it is the personal struggle for self-mastery that counts—not the appearance of it; Montaigne decries as "formalistic" any philosophy which counsels otherwise (II.37, 739 [576]). "Let her," he says of philosophy, "boldly grant to pain this cowardice in the voice, provided it is neither in the heart nor in the stomach . . . let her be content! What matter if we twist our arms, provided we do not twist our thoughts? Philosophy trains us for ourselves, not for others; for being, not for seeming" (II.37, 739 [576-7]).[78]

In short, Montaigne rejects outright ascetic sects that deny the corporeal parts of life or that try to twist human nature according to some idea. As far as human corporeal existence is concerned, Montaigne wants mankind to recognize what is. He wants us to accept and enhance the pleasure of which human beings are capable and to limit and avoid pain—but within the confines of moderation and nature. He wants to celebrate the whole human being, every part of the human body, including its sexual and sensual aspects. This fully rejoins Montaigne's praise in the "Apology" of the sensual philosopher.

IX. Conclusion: The Historical Importance of Montaigne's Conception of the Self

Montaigne can best be described as a transitional figure in the evolution from ancient and medieval to modern thought. Montaigne preserves the ancient and medieval concern for a substantive universal morality but bases it on the phenomenal subject—not on a transcendent dictate of either reason or God. Like the ancients, he speaks of a good that is best for human beings, even if only formally and even if all are not capable of achieving it. Like the moderns after him, he tries to ground it, not on a self that is capable of knowing transcendent truth through reason, but on a subjective self that can only know its limits and phenomena. But unlike Kant, Montaigne does not distinguish the phenomenal realm from a supposed, more dignified noumenal realm. For Montaigne, the phenomenal world is all human beings know, and Montaigne does not lament but celebrates this world. It represents the human condition and is the world in which we dwell. He thus allows more and puts more emphasis on personal freedom and self-creation than either Kant or the ancient political philosophers. It is by making this key substitution that Montaigne can be counted as one of the inaugurators of modern individualism. He thus opens the door to the radical subjectivism which comes to characterize modern and postmodern thought while possessing a limit that prevents him from going that far and from avoiding relativism and nihilism.

Montaigne's ideal life of sensual self-seeking set the tone for liberalism. As Nannerl Keohane says, "More than any other writer, Montaigne succeeded in making such a self-centered life attractive."[79] By doing this, he helped create the *weltanschauung* of liberalism, the cultural intuition of why an individual's private life should be protected from governmental interference. Individuals should be free to pursue pleasure and to cultivate their inner self. Both the hedonistic and philosophic aspects of his ideal influenced the course of Western moral and philosophical development.

Montaigne's conception of the good life as sensual self-seeking contributed to two trends important in the evolution of the modern self. First, he contributed to the revaluation of pleasure and of the body. While several humanists of the fifteenth and sixteenth centuries also praised bodily pleasure, what was perhaps unique about Montaigne was that because he rejected metaphysics, he celebrated the body in clear conscience. He restored man in his full earthly dimensions by giving the body its place without shame or embarrassment of any kind. Most humanists, Petrarch, Mirandola, Ficino, Tasso, and Marguerite de Navarre included, interpreted pleasure and the body in a Christian context and thus had some nagging doubts about it. At the same time, Montaigne avoided the humorous but gross vulgarities of Rabelais' account of the body. Rabelais breaks free of Christian constraints, but in doing so he lunges to the opposite extreme. By stripping metaphysical morality of a legitimate role in human life, Montaigne gave a theoretical justification for worldly living which was perhaps without precedent in the modern era. This freeing of the body and the self from ideological constraints while embracing it as a normal, sensual part of human life compatible with a healthy and tranquil soul are among Montaigne's most important contributions to the self's redefinition and liberation.

The profundity and organic wholeness of Montaigne's conception of the self is both healthier and more compelling than most of the conceptions of the self that later became enshrined in liberalism. Liberal accounts of the self typically do not have the same handle on dissonant feelings and movements caused by the imagination, fear, and anxiety. The simple pleasure-pain calculations of Hobbes and Bentham seem simplistic in comparison to Montaigne. The scientific accounts of the soul proffered by Descartes' *Treatise on the Passions*, Locke's *Essay Concerning Human Understanding*, and Hume's *Treatise of Human Nature* seem overly analytical and flat compared to that offered in Montaigne's *Essays*. In striving for scientific precision, these thinkers often omit the joys, inanities, and richness of the human condition. Some of liberalism's more recent critics, Nietzsche, Freud, and Foucault, explore these paradoxes in fascinating ways, but Montaigne more than holds his own against them in terms of understanding the body and its movements. Montaigne's description of the self is powerful, and, as we shall see in the next chapter, it serves as a basis for toleration and thus proves useful to political theory.

Montaigne's main ontological innovation was his emphasis on individuality and subjectivity. Montaigne's conception of knowledge only as subjective and phenomenological marks him as a key originator of modern subjectivity and the subjective self. Descartes, for example, follows Montaigne in accepting these essential limits within which knowledge could take place.[80] Descartes is more celebrated for having made this move than

Montaigne is, however, because Descartes claims to use subjectivity as a building block for an objective science. For better or worse, Montaigne rejects the possibility of building a science based on the subjective self. He calls on individuals to explore and essay their particular subjectivity—not to abstract from it. Unlike today's nonfoundationalist thinkers (who share with Montaigne this difference from Descartes), Montaigne's conception of the subjective self is rooted in a nature with a universal good—health understood as self-aware and sensual tranquility. According to Montaigne, if a self is to be truly free and truly its own, it cannot follow any will, whim, or desire without first subjecting itself to intense scrutiny and self-exploration. It must be "at home," that is to say within the healthy limits established by our natural condition.

The important political consequences of Montaigne's view of the self derive from its radically private nature. To secure his private life of self-seeking, Montaigne advocates toleration as a political principle and calls for the creation of a private sphere of free conscience and free political judgment. But in debunking all religious and metaphysical restraints external to individuals and in letting loose the desire for physical pleasure and material goods, how can Montaigne also insist on toleration? Why should a hedonistic individual who lives in Montaigne's world not maximize his pleasure even at the expense of others? In opening the door to the radical subjectivism which comes to characterize modern and postmodern thought, how can Montaigne possess a limit that prevents him from going that far and from avoiding relativism and nihilism? It is to an analysis of these questions that we now turn.

Chapter Four

Montaigne's Politics of the Good Life: Toleration and the Private Sphere

The previous chapter examined Montaigne's conception of the good life; this chapter explains and assesses the political vision that stems from it. Since Montaigne conceives the best human life as a radically private one, he calls for the toleration of individuals so that a space may be created in which individuals may pursue the good as he sees it, including both parts of the life of sensual philosophy: the cultivation of physical pleasure and the essaying of oneself. Montaigne seeks to embody this toleration politically by creating and institutionalizing a separation between the public and private spheres. While this separation is so common today as to be almost taken for granted, Montaigne's call for a private realm free from public coercion was, after a thousand years of the Christian domination of Europe, extremely radical.

From the perspective of twenty-first-century liberalism, Montaigne's political recommendations have two main limitations. First, he considers the private sphere of freedom of conscience to be so important that in order to secure it, he yields great control over actions to the state. In relinquishing a principled claim to public action, Montaigne might be seen both as securing too narrow a private sphere and as promoting quietism, the complete acceptance of the status quo, without allowing any avenues for political or social change. Second, while arguing for the creation of a private sphere, he does not advocate any particular political structures as necessary or more likely to secure it. For example, he does not demand a written constitution, the separation of powers, checks and balances, intermediate bodies, or even direct elections. Since all government was ruled by human beings, he thought all was prone to the same vices.

However, even though Montaigne does not call for as large a private sphere as we today might deem necessary and does not provide institutional guarantees to secure it, his political thought is much richer and more useful than it might seem. He creates the space for freedom of thought, which necessarily precedes the demands for freedom to act on it in public. Moreover, although he cedes the freedom of action to state regulation *in principle*, he seeks to expand private freedoms *in practice*. Montaigne knows that thinking often leads to the demand to act, and he wants to maximize freedom without causing anarchy. The reason he distinguishes between principle and practice concerns the most prudent way to bring about change. To a certain extent, the requirement for public conformity is not a bad thing. Too much change too fast leads to revolutions, which often spin out of control into bloodshed and anarchy. By contrast, conformity fosters stability, which creates the conditions for a dialogue between public and private—the precursor to healthy change. Change that results from such a dialogue is likely to be more long-lasting and to protect life and limb along the way. It is a slow process, perhaps, but that is how stable change occurs on this earth. Moreover, where to draw the line between private and public, he thinks, is a prudential judgment that will vary from age to age and will be considerably different in a time of civil wars (such as his) and a relatively stable era (such as ours). Montaigne's indifference to particular political institutions disqualifies him from being called a liberal, but his desire to promote all the freedom possible without jeopardizing the political stability that serves as its base clearly situates him as a protoliberal.

Although Montaigne's particular institutional recommendations (or lack thereof) might have been superseded, the manner in which he argues is powerful and worth recovering, because it gives a ground for toleration that does not appeal to metaphysics, religion, or custom. Montaigne argues for toleration only by appealing to the self and self-interest. Instead of speaking about the "rights" of potential victims, he speaks to rulers and would-be rulers, arguing why it is in their self-interest not to abuse others. More importantly, his arguments speak to philosophers today who wrestle with the question: "why tolerate?" We have democratic instincts, but the traditional philosophic grounds for toleration have been argued away. Montaigne offers a ground for toleration that avoids these problems.

I. Montaigne's Call for Toleration and a Private Sphere

The boldest expression of Montaigne's desire for toleration is found in an essay entitled "Of Freedom of Conscience." Scholars have called attention to the importance of this topic by noting both that "Of Freedom of

Conscience" (II.19) is the central essay in the central book of Montaigne's publication,[1] and that Montaigne himself emphasizes the importance of this placement with a remark that precedes the central essay of his first book: "As I was considering the way a painter I employ went about his work, I had a mind to imitate him," Montaigne says, "He chooses the best spot, the middle of each wall, to put a picture labored over with all his skill, and the empty space all around it he fills with grotesques" (I.28, 181 [135]). Montaigne refers to his work as his paintings,[2] so one may assume that the center space is reserved for an important message, and the three essays which constitute the center of the *Essays'* three books bear out this hunch. The relation of "the center" to Montaigne's political teaching is emphasized by Montaigne's statements about his original plan for the center of Book I: he there intended to publish his dear friend Etienne de La Boétie's *La Servitude Volontaire*, which Montaigne describes as an "essay . . . in honor of liberty against tyrants" (I.28, 182 [135]).[3] And given Montaigne's assertion that he and La Boétie agreed on everything, Montaigne, too, must be strongly in favor of freedom against tyranny. Similarly, the center of Book III is "Of the Disadvantages of Greatness" (III.7), which is one of Montaigne's most eloquent denunciations of extreme political power (and which is discussed in the next chapter). Montaigne's most important arguments for freedom seem to be structurally located in the center of his work, and study of "Of Freedom of Conscience" supports this conclusion.

"Of Freedom of Conscience" is a clarion call for toleration. In it (and in the passage which immediately precedes it),[4] Montaigne favorably compares pagan toleration to Christian intolerance. The intolerant actions of Christians are widespread, but to illustrate his point Montaigne here cites only two examples of them, one modern and one ancient—and his examples detail Christian attacks on exactly the two "ideals" that we identified in chapters 2 and 3 above. No commentator has noted the full significance of these examples, and Montaigne's choice of these examples both buttresses the importance of the visions of a good life discussed above and highlights the hideous nature of Christian barbarism. His modern example lambastes the "monstrous and unheard-of" slaughter by Christians in the New World which destroyed even the Indians' "names, which are no more" (II.18, 650 [505-6]). His ancient example decries the "zeal" of the early Christians who tried to eradicate all of ancient wisdom by burning "every sort of pagan books, thus causing men of letters to suffer an extraordinary loss. I consider that this excess did more harm to letters than all the bonfires of the barbarians" (II.19, 651 [506]). In both instances, Montaigne portrays Christians as attempting to eradicate those who differ from them—down to their books, their histories, and even their very names. Montaigne highlights the fanatically destructive behavior of the early Christians by citing the case of Tacitus, the great Roman historian who wrote a celebrated history of pagan Rome. Montaigne notes that since Tacitus was the relative of an emperor, his work had been distributed to all the libraries of the ancient world. But, Montaigne writes, because of "five or six insignificant sentences contrary to our belief," not one complete copy of his work has come down from antiquity (II.19, 651 [506-7]).[5] And if not a single complete copy of such a widely distributed book survived the book burnings of early Christianity, Montaigne wants us to imagine how much else has been destroyed. Just as Christians wiped out the identity of whole Indian peoples that they did not respect, how many books of their ancient pagan enemies—including their philosophies and their histories of heroes, deeds, and whole peoples—were similarly destroyed so that their "names . . . are no more"?

In contrast to his condemnation of Christian intolerance, Montaigne wistfully praises pagan tolerance, strongly conveying a sense of his political desires—and their limits. He lauds what he calls the "novel and strange" policy of pagan antiquity, according to which individuals, even emperors such as Caesar and Julian the Apostate, could be insulted "without having a quarrel over it" (II.18, 650 [506]). Since Montaigne claims that such tolerance was widespread in pagan Rome, it is "novel and strange," therefore, only in the Christian era.[6] Montaigne longs for the toleration of differences that seemed to him to be routine in the ancient world. In particular, he is amazed at the freedom of their speech: "we see how free are the invectives they use against each other . . . where words are avenged merely by words, and do not lead to other consequences" (II.19, 651 [506]). This difference between speech and deed is what Montaigne wants to bring back into political practice. He does not seek toleration of actions nearly as much as he wants there to be a private sphere of free conscience and free judgment: a sphere in which individuals are *free to* think what they want, *free from* state control.

"Of Freedom of Conscience" celebrates the political life of Julian the Apostate, an early exponent of toleration. Julian was a *bête noire* of the Christian world because as emperor, he renounced his Christian faith, which had been made the state religion by Constantine, and converted back to the traditional paganism of ancient Rome. Montaigne praises Julian for many reasons, including his justice, chastity, sobriety, vigilance, and military ability. He lauds him in terms parallel to the criteria articulated in chapter 3, comparing Julian's death to the death of Epaminondas, one of the people

Montaigne admires most,[7] and lauds his life for its philosophic nature, describing him as "a very great and rare man, being one whose soul was deeply dyed with the arguments of philosophy" (II.19, 651 [507]). The quality that Montaigne praises above all others, however, is Julian's tolerance. Even as an all-powerful emperor, Julian demonstrated "philosophic patience" by not persecuting his personal and political critics (II.19, 652 [507]). It is Julian's tolerant attitude toward matters of conscience, however, that is Montaigne's primary concern. Montaigne argues that Julian was improperly surnamed "the apostate" because he probably never truly believed in Christianity. It is more likely, Montaigne thinks, that "out of obedience to the laws, he had dissembled until he held the Empire in his hand" (II.19, 653 [508]) and that "because all his army was composed of Christians, he dared not reveal it" (II.19, 654 [509]). As an ancient historian whom Montaigne identifies as his source wrote, "Experience had taught [Julian] that no beasts were more dangerous to man than a Christian was to his co-religionist."[8] It was only after Julian was sufficiently strong that he revealed his true pagan beliefs and reopened the ancient pagan temples. But Julian did not force others to convert back to paganism. Rather, he instituted what Montaigne admiringly calls "complete freedom" and "freedom of conscience," allowing every citizen to believe what he or she willed (II.19, 654 [509]). In an irony that would not have escaped Montaigne and which further illustrates his laments about Christian behavior, the *Essays'* praise of Julian was one of the main reasons it was condemned by the Church's censors in Rome.[9]

Montaigne indicates that Julian's practice of toleration is both desirable and feasible. In a short essay entitled "Of A Monstrous Child" (II.30), Montaigne recounts how he saw a newborn infant with one head and two bodies. From this, Montaigne concludes: "This double body and these several limbs, connected with a single head, might well furnish a favorable prognostic to the king that he will maintain under the union of his laws these various parts and factions of our state" (II.30, 691 [539]). Montaigne sees his France and Julian's Rome as identical to the newborn: two religious bodies under the guidance of one sovereign ruler. The "head" cannot be of either body alone but must be able to guide each. It must be a political head ruling with equanimity over the warring religious groups. Contrary to the prevailing political philosophy of his day, which was summarized with the slogan "*un roi, un loi, un foi*" ["one king, one law, one faith"], Montaigne does not consider the institution of a private sphere to be "monstrous," unthinkable, or a freak of nature. Rather, he agrees with the *politiques*, those thinkers who argued that to secure peace the state should abandon its control of religion, that there is nothing unnatural about the existence of a private sphere of free conscience within a political sphere marked by obedience. Montaigne concludes his discussion of the "monstrous child" by arguing: "We call contrary to nature what happens contrary to custom; nothing is anything but according to nature, whatever it may be" (II.30, 691 [539]). Montaigne is again playing with the descriptive and normative usages of the concept of nature. While one might hesitate to celebrate a deformed baby as being equally as natural as a "normal" one, there is no such reason to hesitate accepting a different custom—all customs are artificial.[10] Some customs are more conducive to human goods than others, and Montaigne accordingly urges careful analysis of the idea of a private sphere. Echoing his analysis of the Indians' ruin, Montaigne cautions against rejecting this institution just because it is new and different: "Let this universal and natural reason drive out of us the error and astonishment[11] that novelty brings us" (II.30, 691 [539]). The Indians of the New World, Montaigne argued, were defeated because they were astonished by so many new things that they could not adopt; Montaigne wants his Europe not to suffer from the same faults. He calls for flexible adaptation of a new political order. Religious toleration and the peaceful coexistence of different religious "bodies" or peoples in one sovereign state are living—and desirable—political possibilities.

Montaigne is not quite a modern-day Julian. Although both objected to the zealousness of Christian dogmatism and both were condemned by the Church after their deaths, Montaigne was not a direct political participant on the scale of Julian. Montaigne was a mayor, advised kings and would-be kings, and conducted secret negotiations between the warring factions in France's civil wars, but he never attempted to revolutionize political institutions through direct political action.[12] Both Montaigne and Julian submitted to the authorities, traditions, and beliefs of their times, while simultaneously struggling for a realm of free conscience so that those authorities would tolerate other views. Yet, Montaigne never dared seize power to institute his vision as Julian did. While their different stations in life (emperor versus mere aristocrat) undoubtedly had something to do with this, there is a theoretical reason, too. As odd as it may seem for someone who is preoccupied with individual freedom and with overcoming the un- chosen tendencies instilled and internalized through habit and convention, there is a whole other strand of Montaigne's thought that is extremely deferential to existing authority. To grasp fully Montaigne's political recommendations, we must understand this strand of his thought.

II. The Nature and Extent of Political Obligation

Based on Montaigne's evaluation of and yearning for the private life, and given his tremendous concern for individual freedom, one might conclude that Montaigne—as in his praise for the cannibals' society—favors a political sphere that is as narrow and as limited as possible. While this might be his ultimate aim, he does not advocate it in a simple sense or without qualification. He wants the political sphere to protect certain private activities, but to do this he argues both that the state must be strong enough to squelch threats to the activities protected in the private sphere and that private activities may have to be sharply curtailed in order to ensure public stability and tranquility. This sharp separation of public and private is one of the most characteristic elements of Montaigne's political thought.

Montaigne delineates what he considers to be the legitimate boundary between the public and private spheres in a stark manner: "All deference and submission is due to [the political authorities]," he says, "except that of our understanding. My reason is not trained to bend and bow, it is my knees" (III.8, 913 [714]). In stating this formula, Montaigne, echoing the distinction that he so praised about pagan antiquity, separates the sphere of action—his "knees"—from the sphere of thought—his "reason." This sharp distinction, and the amount of liberty it cedes to the state, is unlikely to seem satisfactory to people accustomed to liberal political traditions; instituting Montaigne's line today, for example, would involve relinquishing freedoms that have been built up over the centuries, such as the freedoms of speech, press, assembly, and all the other guaranteed *actions* secured in modern constitutions.

Montaigne legitimizes a broad sphere of control for the state, because, paradoxically, he has grave doubts about what political institutions can consciously achieve. Fearing the potentially disastrous outcomes of trying to do too much, he doubts that political institutions can consciously do more than maintain stability. To grasp Montaigne's skeptical view of political institutions, we must examine his conception of the political: its origins, nature, and necessities.

When discussing politics, Montaigne presents himself as a hard-headed, anti-utopian, realist. For him, politics is not about achieving virtue, piety, or any other thing that claims to uplift the soul or ennoble the spirit. He rejects all such idealistic schemes as unsuitable to politics and the human condition. Making a criticism very much like those of Machiavelli, Hobbes, and other modern theorists, Montaigne declares:

all those imaginary, artificial descriptions of a government prove ridiculous and unfit to put into practice. These great, lengthy altercations about the best form of society and the rules most suitable to bind us, are altercations fit only for the exercise of our minds; as in the liberal arts there are several subjects whose essence is controversy and dispute, and which have no life apart from that. Such a description of a government would be applicable in a new world, but we take men already bound and formed to certain customs; we do not create them. (III.9, 934 [730])

Like Hobbes and Machiavelli, he wants to keep "imaginary" philosophical speculations out of politics—and for the same reason: politics is the sphere of the practical and the real; it must be concerned with governing human beings as they are.[13]

However, in contrast to Machiavelli and Hobbes, who trumpet the originality and newness of their political proposals, and in contrast to his own advocacy of the "novel and strange" policy of toleration and a private sphere, Montaigne often presents himself as an unshakable political conservative.[14] While this conservatism clearly is not the whole of his political thinking, it does represent a deeply ingrained strand of it. Deeming "humility, fear, obedience, and amenability" as "the principal qualities for the preservation of human society" (II.12, 477 [368]), he accordingly calls for obedience to existing laws, customs, and norms. Similarly, he fears political change: "In all things except those that are simply bad, change is to be feared" (I.43, 261 [198]). While this basically conservative statement implies that some things might be "simply bad" and therefore necessitate change, he argues that this qualification rarely, if ever, applies to politics: "In public affairs," he says, "there is no course so bad, provided it is old and stable, that it is not better than change and commotion" (II.17, 639 [497]). Old and stable institutions are institutions that are working and that must be enjoying widespread consent, even if only tacitly or grudgingly. Montaigne fears change not because he thinks that every society that exists is just, but because he is skeptical of the human ability to rectify injustice without causing all sorts of other unforeseen problems. The criticism that this induces him to level against political revolutionaries might equally apply to the political revolutionaries of the twentieth century:

to undertake to recast so great a mass [as the state], to change the foundations of so great a structure, that is the job for those who wipe out a picture in order to clean it, who want to reform defects of detail by universal confusion and cure illnesses by death, 'who desire not so much to change as to overthrow everything' [Cicero]. The world is ill fitted to cure itself;

it is so impatient of its affliction that it aims only at getting rid of it, without considering the cost. We see by a thousand examples that it usually cures itself to its own disadvantage. Riddance from a present evil is not cure, unless there is an all-around improvement in condition.

The surgeon's aim is not to kill the diseased flesh; that is only the road to his cure. He looks beyond, to make the natural flesh grow again, and restore the part to its proper condition. Whoever proposes merely to remove what is biting him falls short, for good does not necessarily succeed evil; another evil may succeed it, and a worse one, as happened to Caesar's slayers, who cast the Republic into such a state that they had reason to repent of having meddled with it. To many others since, right down to our own times, the same thing has happened. The French, my contemporaries, could tell you a thing or two about it. All great changes shake the state and overthrow it into disorder. (III.9, 935-36 [731-32])

It is precisely to warn against radical experimentations on human beings and on human societies—such as employed by the revolutionary regimes of Jacobin France, Nazi Germany, and Soviet, Maoist, and Khmer communism, which resorted to murder and torture to institute arguably noble and lofty visions of a "new man" and "new politics"—that Montaigne declares, "Nothing presses a state hard except innovation; change alone lends shape to injustice and tyranny" (III.9, 935 [731]). Montaigne has no illusion that what is perceived to be just is universally perceived as such, he merely thinks that "the oldest and best-known evil is always more bearable than an evil that is new and untried" (III.9, 936 [732]). There may very well be portions of every society which unfairly suffer, but Montaigne fears that in trying to end that suffering, revolutions make everyone suffer more. He doubts mankind's ability to bring about the desired changes through *political struggle*: "By whatever means we may have power to correct and reform [polities], we can hardly twist them out of their accustomed bent without breaking up everything" (III.9, 934 [730]). Since everything is interlocked, revolution is to be avoided at all costs.

Montaigne's fear of change leads some to condemn him as a political quietist, and the most obnoxious aspect of this quietism, as it strikes the modern reader, is its complete indifference to the form of government or regime type.[15] Indeed, Montaigne often avows the necessity of obeying the existing authorities, whoever they may be: "We may wish for different magistrates, but we must nevertheless obey those that are here. . . . As long as the image of the ancient and accepted laws of this monarchy shines in some corner, there will I be planted" (III.9, 972 [760]). Although Montaigne himself once calls democracy probably "the most natural and equitable"

form of government, he also says that he is "almost ready to vow irreconcilable hatred" against it for its harsh treatment of exceptional men (I.3, 23
[12]).[16] Thus, in contrast to the twenty-first-century Western view, he
categorically refuses to define legitimate government based on access to
voting, representative assemblies, or any other institutional features. In fact,
Montaigne does not take into account the form of political institutions or
regime type at all when evaluating the best governments. Instead, he usually
appeals only to the *existing* institutions:

> Not in theory, but in truth, the best and most excellent government for each
> nation is the one under which it has preserved its existence. . . . We are
> prone to be discontented with the present state of things. But I maintain,
> nevertheless, that to wish for the government of a few in a democratic state,
> or another type of government in a monarchy, is foolish and wrong. (III.9,
> 934 [731])

The Western, liberal, democratic contempt for such indifference to the form
of government might be dismissed by Montaigne as parochial: "Nations
brought up to liberty and to ruling themselves consider any other form of
government monstrous and contrary to nature" (I.23, 114 [83]). However,
Montaigne, against the partisans of liberty, also asserts, "Those who are
accustomed to monarchy do the same [i.e., condemn other regimes]. And
whatever easy chance fortune offers them to change, even when with great
difficulties they have rid themselves of the importunity of one master, they
run to supplant him with another . . . because they cannot make up their
minds to hate domination itself" (I.23, 114-15 [83-4]).[17] While Montaigne's
point is to show how custom colors all citizens' views equally, he interestingly uses two pejoratives to describe monarchic rule; the monarch himself
is described as a "master" [*maistre*] and his rule as "domination" [*la
maistrise*]. At other times, however, he refers to democracy in the same
way, labeling it "*domination populaire*" (I.3, 23 [12]). Montaigne does not
deem any form of government inherently better than any other and thus
repeatedly warns that changing the form of government is not worth risking
the stability that government offers.

Unlike Burke, de Maistre, or other reactionaries against the French
Revolution—and as his description of monarchy as domination suggests—Montaigne's political conservatism is not due to a romantic or
nostalgic attachment to a glorious past. This is clear when we consider the
grounds on which Montaigne thinks the state merits obedience. He never
argues for the virtues of one specific *ancien régime*. Rather, he wants

everyone in every regime to obey the law. Moreover, he continuously debunks and demystifies the grounds of all authority, including monarchy, the traditional government of his day.[18] Similarly, he never praises national traditions or law, as do romantic conservatives, because of some alleged past glory. Nor does he argue, as do nationalistic or religious conservatives, that tradition and law should be obeyed because they embody the essence of truth or of some ethnic, cultural, or religious community. He deems all such views to be but nostalgic myths. Underlying Montaigne's political conservatism is only one legitimate reason to obey the law: the need for stability. Montaigne's main purpose in discussing politics and law is to debunk any other claims to political authority and any other grounds for obedience.

Like Plato, and unlike the later Enlightenment philosophers, however, Montaigne is the kind of disillusioned conservative who thinks it necessary, inevitable, and good that laws be shrouded in mystical authority for most of the citizens. Like religious conservatives, he says, "no laws are held in their honor except those to which God has given some ancient duration," but he argues this for the most irreligious of reasons: "so that no one knows their origin or that they were ever different" (I.43, 261 [198]). Montaigne is merely making a psychological point about the conditions under which laws are honored or venerated by most people.[19] Montaigne thinks it important that for them the origins of the law be obscure, because he considers the origins of almost all laws to be ignoble. He thinks it important that laws be old, because it is only with time that laws acquire veneration and power. He compares the power of authority to a river: it can be powerful and mighty at its end, but if one traces it back to its source, one finds a mere trickle. Exceptions to this are those few occasions when wise men, such as Solon, are recruited to draw up a code of laws, but even then, as Montaigne cites Solon as saying, such laws are not simply good but merely the best that will be accepted by the people for whom they are designed (III.9, 934 [730]). The apparent contradiction between stating the need for mystical authority while unmasking its legitimacy is no mystery. Like Plato, he tells the rational truth about irrational phenomena.

Accordingly, Montaigne attaches little dignity or concern to the origins of a state or to political participation. Unlike the contract theorists, he offers no account of the legitimate origins of law, because he thinks that political legitimacy is not to be judged based on its procedural origins. Sometimes Montaigne describes the creation of the state as happening in a ridiculous and haphazard manner, "just as ill-matched objects, put in a bag without order, find of themselves a way to unite and fall into place together" (III.9,

933 [730]). Other times, he describes law as resulting from chance and necessity: "Necessity reconciles men and brings them together. This accidental link afterward takes the form of laws" (III.9, 934 [730]). This haphazardness is not condemned by Montaigne, because he has little confidence in man's ability consciously to create something better. "Chance," he says, often leads men to arrange themselves "better than they could have been arranged by art" (III.9, 933 [730]). But if Montaigne shares the view with Hobbes and Locke that the state is an artificial creation, he seems to agree with Aristotle that the creation of some kind of political body is inevitable among human beings: "Whatever position you set men in, they pile up and arrange themselves by moving and crowding together" (III.9, 933 [730]). Human beings are to this extent "political animals," but Montaigne considers them so without endowing any of the nobility that Aristotle attaches to the claim. Montaigne differs with Aristotle both on the extent to which human beings are perfected through their participation in politics and on the extent to which reason is manifested in the state-building process. Aristotle thinks not only that human beings can set up reasonable institutions, but that reason itself only fully comes into being with this very process, the distinguishing of the good from the bad, the just from the unjust.[20] Conversely, Montaigne believes that laws are generally made by ideologues and manipulators and thus has little hope that political institutions or laws will be made in a rational manner or achieve a rational end. He does not imagine the lawmaking process to resemble the sincere inquiries associated with what he might consider genuine "essaying." Participating in such a process, then, does not ennoble or perfect the individual either—and so Montaigne does not demand political participation as a right.

Montaigne fears that political institutions will never be reasonable, because of two mutually reinforcing impediments: custom and human nature. Montaigne conceives that custom determines most of man's political institutions and moral values, not vice versa. Custom, he says, makes men "fix their aim and limit by the ways to which they were born" (I.49, 284-85 [215]). Like Plato, Montaigne argues that "the custom and practice of ordinary life bears us along" in such a manner as to render profound choice and robust consent but hollow political concepts: "Long sufferance begets custom, custom consent and imitation" (III.12, 1019 [797]); "like those who by artificial light extinguish the light of day, we have extinguished our own means by borrowed means. And it is easy to see that it is custom that makes impossible for us what is not impossible in itself" (I.36, 222 [167]). Nor does Montaigne think this limit to reasonable creation affects only the uneducated. "Most of my actions," he says, "are conducted by example, not by choice" (III.5, 830 [648]), and he says following custom "is a common vice, not of the vulgar only but of almost all men" (I.49, 284 [215]).[21] It is a vice, he indicates, because custom is often based on "twaddle and lies," made up, consciously or unconsciously, by cynics or fools (II.12, 521 [403]).

Law, then, is usually the result of custom and human frailty: ignorant men create ignorant laws which then create similarly ignorant men. Law has its origins in a series of haphazard events, both comic and sad. Laws are made primarily by fools, frauds, and the greedy, who seek to institute personal advantage. In any case, they are always made by "men, vain and irresolute authors" (III.13, 1049 [821]).[22] Just as Montaigne describes human nature as a "hodgepodge" and "patchwork," so he deems all the political systems that human beings create. What men "call 'justice,'" he says, is "the hodgepodge of the first laws that fall into our hands" (II.37, 744 [580]). And since virtue and vice are inextricably intertwined in every human being, they are similarly intertwined in every human creation: "Our structure, both public and private, is full of imperfection" (III.1, 767 [599]). Indeed, he cites mankind's various conceptions of justice as "a singular testimony of human infirmity" (III.12, 1026 [803]). Anticipating Montesquieu, Montaigne concludes, "The private error first creates the public error, and afterward in turn the public error creates the private error" (III.11, 1005 [786]).

If the substance of law is notoriously unreasonable, there is one thing that a reasonable person will take into account when making laws: in relations with other individuals and with the state, each individual is fundamentally self-interested. As much as Montaigne advocates his conception of self-interest as essaying oneself "at home," he has no illusions that everybody, or even most people, will act accordingly, so it would not be prudent for a state to assume such enlightenment on the part of its citizens. Moreover, he argues that no one is purely moral; people always seek profit at the expense of others. If one would "sound himself within," i.e., essay oneself, he says, "he will find that our private wishes are for the most part born and nourished at the expense of others" (I.22, 106 [77]). As far as politics is concerned, Montaigne agrees with this dictum of Livy: "'We feel public calamities only so far as they concern our private affairs'" (III.12, 1023 [801]). Montaigne finds this self-interest everywhere: "When I confess myself religiously to myself," he says, "I find that the best goodness I have has some tincture of vice" (II.20, 656 [511]). This "tincture of vice" is thus a fundamental aspect of human nature which cannot, according to Montaigne, be changed: "Whoever should remove the seeds of these qualities [vices] from man would destroy the fundamental conditions of our life" (III.1, 768 [600]). Given the narrowly understood self-interestedness of most human beings, Montaigne does not imprudently want to undermine the external constraints that keep men in check. This is why he supports existing institutions—something is better than nothing. As we saw in chapter 1, he agrees with Epicurus and anticipates Hobbes in thinking that, without law, human beings would devour each other (II.12, 541 [419]).[23] He agrees with the statement that he attributes to Plato (again anticipating Hobbes) that without laws men would live like "brutish animals" (II.12, 541 [419]). Law is necessary for order and protection.[24]

The problem with relying on law to control human behavior, however, is that the means available to control human behavior all suffer from having been invented by the same imperfect beings they are meant to control. Montaigne agrees with Cicero: "'We have no solid and exact image of true law and genuine justice; we use the shadow and reflections of it'" (III.1, 773 [604]). Trying to remove injustice from law would be like trying to cut off Hydra's head (II.20, 657 [511]). He says similar things about public morality: "The virtue assigned to the affairs of the world is a virtue with many bends, angles, and elbows, so as to join and adapt itself to human weakness; mixed and artificial, not straight, clean, constant, or purely innocent" (III.9, 970 [758]). "Innocence itself," he says, "could neither negotiate among us without dissimulation nor bargain without lying" (III.1, 772 [603]). Montaigne says that he "once tried" to act in politics using rules that were as virtuous as he could discover, but:

> I found them inept and dangerous for such matters. He who walks in the crowd must step aside, keep his elbows in, step back or advance, even leave the straight way, according to what he encounters. He must live not so much according to himself as according to others, not according to what he proposes to himself but according to what others propose to him, according to the time, according to the men, according to the business. (III.9, 970 [758])

Mankind's public and private imperfections are less a lament of Montaigne's than a recognition of a fundamental truth about the human condition. Based on this insight, he wants his readers to recognize the unflattering truth about the nature of politics. Political "justice" is not entirely just and never will be: "The very laws of justice cannot subsist without some mixture of injustice" (II.20, 656 [511]).[25]

One of Montaigne's aims in revealing the true nature of the political is to set obedience on a proper, and he therefore hopes firmer, footing. By stripping away the hypocritical rhetoric that surrounds politics, Montaigne hopes to introduce realistic expectations and moderate demands into the political sphere. Citizens should obey the laws but not, according to him, for any grandiose or noble reason. "There is nothing so grossly and widely and ordinarily faulty as the laws," he says, so: "Whoever obeys them because they are just, does not obey them for just the reason he should" (III.13, 1049 [821]). Indeed, he criticizes the lofty self-sacrificing idea that "we are not born for our private selves, but for the public" as a "fine statement under which ambition and avarice take cover" (I.39, 232 [174]). Montaigne is neither a communitarian nor an advocate of civic or republican virtue. He recognizes that laws and policies are driven by "private interest and passion," "treacherous and malicious conduct," and a "propensity to malignity and violence" (III.1, 771 [602]), but by uncovering this he wants to strip the false labels—"zeal," "courage," and "duty"—from political deliberations and motivations (III.1, 771, [602]). By exposing the illusions that fuel fanaticism in the political sphere, Montaigne hopes to extract fanaticism from, and bring calm and moderation into, it. Montaigne wants his readers to be open-eyed and clear-sighted. Thoughtful citizens are less likely to become disillusioned with the laws if they entertain no illusions to begin with. And they are less likely to prosecute the laws to an extreme degree if they do not fanatically believe the highfalutin theoretical justifications that are offered for them. Thoughtful citizens are left with a sufficient—and moderate—ground for political obedience. Montaigne illustrates just such a moderate sense of obedience in himself, saying he obeys "simply with a loyal and civic affection" and that he is "attached to the general and just cause only with moderation and without feverishness" (III.1, 769 [601]). In short, Montaigne gives the factual and what he hopes, at least among the educated, will be the only normative reason for obedience: "laws remain in credit not because they are just, but because they are laws. That is the mystical foundation of their authority; they have no other" (III.13, 1049 [821]).

This *realpolitik* view of politics leads to a powerful argument for political moderation and toleration. Since Montaigne considers human nature and the political world to be necessarily impure, he cautions do-gooders who seek to improve the world with their innovations to temper their actions. Montaigne rejects utopian, theoretically based schemes for human organization as unrealistic; political engineering, he says, is a feat that transcends the bounds of human abilities: "Government is like a structure of different parts joined together in such a relation," he says, "that it is impossible to budge one without the whole body feeling it" (I.23, 118 [86]). Montaigne concludes that "to speak frankly . . . it takes a lot of self-love and presumption to have such esteem for one's own opinions that to establish them one must overthrow the public peace and introduce so many inevitable evils, and such a horrible corruption of morals, as civil wars and political changes bring with them" (I.23, 119 [87]).[26] Thoroughly disgusted with the innovators of his own time whose good intentions "accidentally produced" political catastrophes, Montaigne hopes that if people heed his wisdom and "would reflect on it before taking any action," i.e., essay themselves and their motives, they might "cool off about setting [their] hand to it" (I.23, 118 [86] and III.9, 936 [732]).

In conclusion, Montaigne considers it "the rule of rules, and the universal law of laws, that each man should observe those of the place he is in" (I.23, 117 [86]). This applies to travelers—and to each person in the place where he happens to be born. This deep strand of conservatism in Montaigne's political thought results from his deep disillusionment with human beings and his skepticism about institutions created by such faulty creatures. There is no "ideal" public morality, and no individual has a claim to rule based on wisdom or any other virtue: "private reason has only a private jurisdiction" (I.23, 120 [88]). Since private affairs require stability and order, public rules have to be made to enable private persons to go about their business. Rather than risk anarchy or public conflict, Montaigne, like Hobbes, is happy to let someone's private reason be the public voice. It matters little to him whether it is the voice of one person, few, or many; whoever is currently filling the role is acceptable, indeed preferable—as long as he or she is tolerant with respect to private conscience. The fact that there be a voice is much more important to him than whose it is. And if it is not the current ruler's, there will be endless arguing—and perhaps civil war—to decide upon a replacement. Montaigne's conservative political tendencies do not give an ideal, or even the only conceivable, solution to the political problem. It gives *a* solution, which he hopes will achieve the *minimal* acceptable goal: stability. That is enough for Montaigne: the perfect is the enemy of the good, so the minimal is the maximal at which he aims. Montaigne's openness to tolerating an array of different institutions in different places is possible because, according to him, all the best things in life are not primarily political, but primarily private.

III. Role Playing and the Limit between the Public and Private Spheres

While the distinction between thought and deed seems clear, it is difficult to know the exact extent of the "sphere of reason," the sphere that Montaigne says is not owed to the state. Since the political exists to secure and promote the private, it is not surprising that the principle that Montaigne ultimately ends up with seems to be: secure stability with as much freedom as is possible. However, the question remains: how much is "possible"? The answer, for Montaigne, depends on the times, circumstances, etc.—and can only be determined by prudence. The worst-case scenario for Montaigne is to strive for too much and ruin everything. This does not mean that he is indifferent to principled action, just that it must be prudently limited.

Giving up the right to act on one's beliefs generally seems to Montaigne a worthwhile price to pay for being able to safeguard them. While the freedom to act based on one's beliefs has been demanded by every liberal from Mill to Rawls,[27] Montaigne, like Hobbes, does not demand it. Sacrificing the right to act might seem a high price to pay for freedom of conscience, but Montaigne deems thought more fundamental. To grasp his reasoning, consider how his principle might apply to a situation like the Inquisition. It would mean that even if one could not act based on one's beliefs, one would be neither subjected to inquisitors' demands about matters of faith nor tortured into confessions. Montaigne's principle eliminates all such inquisitions from the world, and as such it must be seen as major progress in the struggle for freedom; indeed, Mill recognizes freedom of conscience as the first and most basic freedom. Montaigne downplays the costs of his principle, asserting that the inanities of law "do not deter a man of understanding from following the common style. . . . [T]he wise man should withdraw his soul within, out of the crowd, and keep it in freedom and power to judge things freely; but as for externals, he should wholly follow the accepted fashions and forms" (I.23, 117 [86]). "Will and desires are a law unto themselves," he says, but "actions must receive their law from public regulation" (III.1, 772 [603]). If he cannot maintain control of his actions, Montaigne considers it a major accomplishment to be able to control and regulate his judgment; at least he can keep "this sovereign part free from corruption" (I.37, 225 [169]).

Montaigne thus seems content to keep a "corner in my soul" (II.15, 601 [467]) free from outside influence. He calls on the reader to create an *arrière boutique*, "a back shop all our own, entirely free, in which to establish our real liberty and our principal retreat and solitude. Here our ordinary conversation must be between us and ourselves, and so private that no outside association or communication can find a place" (I.39, 235 [177]). This essaying process of self-exploration "between us and ourselves" is Montaigne's ultimate court of appeal, and he does not care if he must seem to be something else to others: "I have my own laws and court to judge me, and I address myself to them more than anywhere else" (III.2, 785 [613]). Montaigne is content if an individual is free to probe his conscience and exercise his judgment without government interference. Indeed, he writes: "Princes give me much if they take nothing from me, and do me enough good when they do me no harm; that is all I ask of them" (III.9, 945-46 [739]).

Ironically, however, Montaigne's sharp separation of the public from private, advocated to promote a sphere of authenticity, forces individuals to play roles.[28] The stark separation between thoughts and deeds would be unproblematic only for hermits, because they take no social actions, but few people live this way and Montaigne does not recommend it. "We are born to act," he says, and he wants people to be in the world, because experiences are necessary to and excellent opportunities for essaying oneself. Accordingly, he describes the world as his book—"everything that comes to our eyes is book enough"; says that "For this reason, mixing with men is wonderfully useful"; and recommends foreign travel in order "to bring back knowledge of the characters and ways of those nations, and to rub and polish our brains by contact with those of others" (I.26, 151-52 [112]).[29] But if one is to be in the world and to act—not according to one's conscience but—according to the dictates of the existing authorities, one will be forced to act prescribed parts, to play roles. Montaigne thus argues that role playing is both inevitable, because people must be in the world, and desirable, because of the insulation it affords to the self. By viewing the world as a stage, and oneself as an actor, one gains a healthy detachment from and skepticism toward one's roles. In this sense the postmodern theorists have embraced Montaigne: both seek detachment from and an irony toward social roles. For example, Derrida approvingly places Montaigne's line that "[w]e need to interpret interpretations more than to interpret things" at the head of one of his essays.[30] Montaigne's embrace of role playing also parallels to a certain extent Judith Butler's theories of performativity.[31] Similarly, the following line from Montaigne, quoting from the tradition of Latin poetry and showing his influence on Shakespeare, could have been written by Lacan or Derrida: "Most of our occupations are low comedy. 'The whole world plays a part' [Petronius]. We must play our part duly, but as the part of a borrowed character. Of the mask and appearance we must not make a real essence" (III.10, 989 [773]).

However, there is a moral problem with role playing that Montaigne addresses in a way that postmodern thinkers do not and cannot. If all there is in human life is role playing, as deconstructionists and contemporary sociologists claim, then there is no basis to criticize the all-too-human excuse for bad behavior: "I was only following orders," i.e., fulfilling one's role. Role playing cannot be compellingly critiqued from the point of view of role playing alone.[32] In order to critique behavior, one must have some other criterion by which to judge. Deconstructionists do not recognize the existence of such a criterion, either in Montaigne or in the world.[33] In fact, they deny that there is any stable ground from which criticism can be made. For Foucault, Butler, and a host of other followers of Nietzsche, individuals can only resist power complexes or sociolinguistic discourses; there is no ground from which oppressive institutions can be evaluated as better or worse. Derrida claims that "There is no nature, only the effects of nature."[34] Similarly, Butler argues that human beings are identical to their scripts, that there is no self underneath the script.[35] However, Montaigne has a criterion to guide and to judge role playing: his conception of the self that we analyzed in chapter 3. Thus, while Montaigne, like the poststructuralists, says that we must not mistake masks and appearances for essences, he also says we should not make the opposite mistake—treating the universal aspects of the human condition (our mortality, inability to know transcendent truths, general ignorance, horror of pain, joy in sensual pleasure, and delight in essaying ourselves) merely as social conventions, as do the postmoderns.

Unlike the deconstructionists, Montaigne offers more than merely social roles for human beings: "whatever role man undertakes to play, he always plays his own at the same time" (I.20, 80 [56]). Montaigne employs numerous metaphors to drive home his insistence on the existence of a human condition that underlies the dominant discourses, including his laments over those who cannot distinguish "the skin from the shirt." And "it is enough," he also says, "to make up our face, without making up our heart" (III.10, 989 [773]). In short, by distinguishing "what is foreign" from "what is our very own" (III.10, 989 [773]), Montaigne wants us to keep our eyes on the prize: the universal human condition that manifests itself as the unique phenomena that make up each of our own particular beings. A self-knowing self, according to Montaigne, focuses on its main role, which is not social, linguistic, economic, political, or religious but human: "there is nothing so beautiful and legitimate as to play the man well and properly, no knowledge so hard to acquire as the knowledge of how to live this life well and naturally" (III.13, 1091, [852]). By contrast, Foucault asserts that "Nothing in man—not even his body—is sufficiently stable to serve as the basis for self-recognition or for understanding other men."[36] This is nihilism.

According to Montaigne, the underlying human condition is what we can begin to known through the essaying process. While Montaigne makes but modest claims about what he finds, it is enough to avoid total relativism. Postmoderns have gravitated to Montaigne, because like them, he emphasizes ignorance about transcendent things, the power of custom, and all the lacks of the human condition. However, unlike them, Montaigne does not begin with the assumption that all claims about a self deeper than its socially constructed parts are purely fictional. Indeed, he rejects this claim as philosophical Pyrrhonism. If not everything that we seek to know is available to us, we can know more than nothing—we can phenomenologically know the structural aspects of ourselves which prevent us from knowing transcendent truths. Thus, while Montaigne agrees with post modern thinkers about the numerous difficulties and obstacles in the way of self-knowledge, he nonetheless keeps trying to attain it. Even if Montaigne is incorrect, which I do not think he is, his view has an advantage over the postmoderns' Pyrrhonistic conception of the self—he gives reasons to keep thoughtful people happy and content at "home" in a way that postmodern thinkers cannot. Postmoderns do not promote cruelty, but based on their thought, there is no reason why one should prefer self-exploration and self-cultivation to moving, in Foucault's phrase, "from domination to domination."[37] If there truly is nothing to strive for and no criteria by which to judge, then there is no principled objection to the Nietzschean-Foucauldian power struggle with no other end than to will one's will or to seek "the reversal of a relationship of forces, the usurpation of power,"[38] even if doing so inflicts cruelty and suffering on others. Montaigne's conception of the self serves as a *principled* means for restraining human actions, for rejecting cruel and intolerant behavior, in a way that the postmodern conception cannot.

By prioritizing an internal human role over one's social roles, Montaigne hopes not only to enable individuals to keep an inner peace regardless of what happens, but to set role playing on a foundation that will lead to humane actions in the world. Playing roles should always be moderate, balanced, and guided by one's underlying sense of the human condition. Thus, Montaigne avoids the extremes of both overly enthusiastic attachments to roles and total disregard for them—either of which could lead to the victimization of or indifference to others. He wants every individual to play his parts wisely and humanely, and not be detached to the point of boredom. For example, in roles regarding love, he says, one should not just be "like actors, to play the standard role of our age and customs and put into it nothing of our own but the words" (III.3, 803 [626]). Learning which roles to embrace and which not is the essence of wisdom. Since everyone inherits numerous roles in the normal course of life, he thinks it is better to play those well rather than running around in a frenzy simply to play "newer" and "other" roles, since a self-knowing person would be aware of their contingent nature, too.

In short, Montaigne's notion of a self at home does something that the deconstructionist understanding of the self cannot do: it creates a standard separate from one's role that can be used to critique it. Only by having such a standard, which in Montaigne's case is based on knowing the fundamental weaknesses and lacks in human beings, can one criticize those who claim that they were only following orders, i.e., fulfilling their roles—or simply, perhaps violently—reacting against them. Montaigne's understanding of the self, especially in political actors, greatly promotes decent and moderate politics. Cultivation of oneself and one's conscience leads to limits on what one would do for the state or against one's fellow man.

Montaigne knows, however, that role playing, when sufficiently understood by the actor as role playing, might require wisdom, strength, and a sense of playfulness that exceed the capacity of many or most individuals. A true role player must be wise because he must see the world as it is and understand the necessity of playing roles. He must understand why roles exist, why they must be upheld, and the demands of his particular role. He must be strong because it is difficult to live such a complicated, multilayered life and strive for excellence in something that one knows to be artificial. He must be playful, because he must enjoy his roles. Role playing should not be prosaic and boring like the life of a bureaucrat. Montaigne wants us to delight in our roles and be creative; this requires lightheartedness. While the role playing demanded by a complex society can be compatible with tranquility of mind in strong, playful individuals, one wonders whether unsophisticated people can act successfully; taking one's roles too seriously might lead to the anxiety that role playing was set up to avoid. Failure seems inevitable for many people. Montaigne's solution is aristocratic. It can be achieved only by the most self-knowing people. Montaigne accepts that most people will believe the customs into which they are born. He is addressing, rather, the more reflective people who understand the contingent nature of mores and beliefs. Nonetheless, distinguishing what are merely social roles from an underlying universal humanity is the first step in freeing those who are burdened by their societies with loathsome social roles.

In any case, Montaigne purposely renders his theory of political obligation tenuous. The boundary he draws between a free private *judgment* and restricted public *actions*—which could be bridged by mindless role playing—has a more demanding legitimate reconciliation. Montaigne clearly encourages us to judge everything: "My freedom being so very free" (I.21, 105 [76]), he reserves for himself "an unusual freedom" (III.3, 801 [625]), where his main aim is to keep his judgment free (I.37, 225 [169], II.17, 638 [496], II.17, 641 [499]).[39] And political judgment is no exception: "we should conform to the best rules, but not enslave ourselves to them" (III.13, 1063 [831]). But if we are to judge and withhold ourselves from the best laws, what more should we do with poor ones? Confronted everywhere with oppressive governments and oppressive customs, does Montaigne want us simply to conform? No, based on his conceptions of the human condition and the good life, Montaigne articulates different scenarios when it would be legitimate and good to criticize, resist, or change oppressive power structures.

Criticism is allowed by Montaigne insofar as it is prudent. Only prudence can dictate what to say and when and where to say it. While the realm of unuttered thought is surely protected by Montaigne's private sphere, the public expression of ideas is a speech-act that illustrates the problematic nature of the line between word and deed. On the one hand, the expression of an idea is just talk; but on the other hand, speaking is among the most powerful and persuasive *actions* available to human beings. To what extent does Montaigne's principle allow an individual rightfully to share his criticisms and convictions, privately with friends and family, or to announce them publicly to other citizens? If one has to bow before the king, can one tell him he is pretentious or wrong, or must one pretend that the king is sacred? For Montaigne, this is not merely a theoretical question: his book is replete with criticism of every authority of his era, but his principle does not categorically protect his right to publish. Montaigne refuses to sanction such a right in principle, but he continually pushes for more and more free speech, even praising his "indiscreet freedom in saying, right or wrong, whatever comes into my head" (III.12, 1040 [814]). Montaigne defends his boldness not on principled but on strategic grounds. By speaking frankly to the powerful, he says, they can feel assured that he will not say or do worse behind their back. The success of such a policy, however, depends on how one's speech is perceived by the powerful. This requires one to have and to exercise good judgment, hence Montaigne's primary concern with it. But Montaigne's character seems bridled by his principle: "I am so jealous of the liberty of my judgment that I can hardly give it up for any passion whatsoever" (II.17, 642 [500]). He does not want to relinquish his freedom under any circumstances, if he can help it: "We must husband the freedom of our soul and mortgage it only on the right occasions; which are in very small number, if we judge sanely" (III.10, 981 [767]). Montaigne desires as much free speech as possible, but rather than enshrine his desire as a right, he makes it contingent on the need for stability.

Montaigne also argues that it is legitimate, even necessary, sometimes to break laws: "it is lawful for a man of honor," he says, "to refuse to do shameful deeds" (III.1, 774 [605]). "I would much rather break the imprisonment of a wall and of the laws," he says, "than that of my word" (III.9, 944 [738]), and he calls on all men to swear to themselves "that they would not deviate from their conscience for any command" (III.1, 775 [605]). And although he once, like Hobbes, asserts that a promise made under fear is still binding,[40] he dissolves this obligation under one condition: "if we have promised something wicked and unjust in itself; for the rights of virtue must prevail over the rights of our obligation" (III.1, 779 [608]).

Montaigne does not, however, specify the precise nature of the dishonorable actions that obviate political obligation; yet, in his typical fashion, some guidelines are clear. Montaigne is willing to obey the state except when compelled, by action or omission, to break a higher bond—not to his intellectual opinions, but to friends, family, or himself. For example, Montaigne praises Epaminondas, the great Theban general, for his faithful allegiance to exactly these human ties. Amidst furious battle and to the anger of his fellow countrymen, Epaminondas refused to violate the guest-host relationship and remained extremely loyal to his family and friends.[41] As we saw in chapter 3, these private bonds are legitimate because they are intimate; they (potentially) reach the core of the self and form the core of its private world. They involve a visceral and/or emotional attachment to particular souls and particular bodies. While one literally has a bodily relation to one's family, through genes or through shared physical habitation and shared activities, it is a kind of intimacy to oneself that Montaigne praises in friendship. All such bonds of affection and love are deeply rooted in the human condition. These greatest joys that human beings can experience, alone or with one another, Montaigne suggests, transcend all other obligations, political or otherwise.[42] Montaigne's beautiful description of friendship sheds light on the limits of political obligation: "A single dominant friendship," he says, "dissolves all other obligations" (I.28, 190 [142]).

Because of the sanctity of these private concerns, Montaigne concludes that it is necessary to limit what can be demanded by the political sphere. "[T]he common interest," he says, "must not require all things of all men against the private interest. . . . [N]ot all things are permissible for an honorable man in the service of his king, or of the common cause, or of the laws" (III.1, 780 [609]). Montaigne's book is full of stories of tyrants who were brought down because they pushed people too far. Indeed, he says, "only the violence of tyrants and the cowardice of the common people are hostile" to the deepest, most intimate private connections (I.28, 186 [139]). Montaigne is proud of his "limits": "a slave I must be only to reason, and even that I can scarcely manage" (III.1, 772 [603]).

Montaigne hopes to persuade the authorities, political and other, that it is their own selfish interest to yield an appropriately encompassing private sphere. He ventures to explain how rulers who relinquish or ease control over what is properly private will, paradoxically, strengthen themselves. First, he argues that by abdicating control over personal and indifferent things, it will be easier for rulers to command obedience about the necessary things:

> For there is danger that we dream up new duties to excuse our negligence toward our natural duties and mix them up. As proof of this: we see that in places where faults are crimes, crimes are only faults; that in nations where the laws of propriety are rarer and looser, the primitive and common laws are better observed; for the innumerable multitude of so many duties smothers, weakens, and dissipates our concerns. (III.5, 866 [677])

Second, Montaigne warns the authorities that citizens rebel when their most intimate private activities are violated. Montaigne gives several examples of such behavior throughout his book, especially in the essay "Of Friendship" (I.28). He does not demand the political acceptance of personal liberties as a "right" that people have, but rather tries to persuade the authorities, based on their interests, against unnecessary intrusions into the private sphere. Montaigne counts himself among those who might resist unreasonable regulations. For example, he writes:

> I am so sick for freedom, that if anyone should forbid me access to some corner of the Indies, I should live distinctly less comfortably. . . . [H]ow ill

could I endure the condition in which I see so many people, nailed down to one section of this kingdom, deprived of the right to enter the principal towns and the courts and to use the public roads, for having quarreled with our laws! (III.13, 1049 [820-21])

The limited access to cities, courts, and roads that Montaigne describes may refer to a policy that was instituted in France during the religious wars. The Catholic crown "tolerated" Protestants only on conditional and harsh terms: in limited places with limited civic and political rights, especially on the rights of the Protestants to assemble together for prayer and comfort. Thus, Montaigne obliquely relates his theoretical arguments to the most pressing public problems of his age.

Insofar as Montaigne might consider the banning of the Protestants' peaceful pursuit of public prayer to have been unnecessary and imprudent, he expands his conception of the private sphere to include all of the three criteria for complete freedom that Mill was later to advocate. The first freedom that Mill identifies as necessary if a society is to be called completely free is freedom of conscience, and we have seen that Montaigne clearly advocates this. But this quotation shows Montaigne advocating, insofar as prudent, Mill's other two criteria as well. The freedom to pursue one's conception of the good wherever one wants, even in "some corner of the Indies," echoes Mill's second kind of freedom, "the liberty of tastes and pursuits; of framing the plan of our life to suit our own character." And Montaigne's laments about people's inability to meet and associate echoes Mill's third criterion for freedom, the freedom "of combination among individuals; freedom to unite, for any purpose not involving harm to others."[43] Insofar as the crackdown on the Protestants led to horren-dous—Montaigne thinks intolerable—political persecution, he sends a warning to the authorities: "If those that I serve threatened even the tip of my finger, I should instantly go and find others, wherever it might be" (III.13, 1049 [821]). He does not here say what he would do to carry out this threat, whether he would quit France or start an insurrection. But his visceral reaction to such unnecessary restrictions is clear.

Montaigne also argues that if rulers demand obedience only to more essential laws, citizens would be psychologically more supportive of the state. Compulsion alone is not the best basis on which to build a state: "I am lax in following duties to which I should be dragged if I did not go to them" (III.9, 944 [738-9]). Nor is it a noble one: "If the action does not have something of the splendor of freedom, it has neither grace nor honor" (III.9, 944 [739]). The state—and therefore the rulers—gains more control over the public when it relinquishes its claims to the private.[44] In making this argument, Montaigne agrees with Bodin, L'Hôpital, and the other *politiques* that by shrinking the scope of its claim to power, the state can establish its control more effectively.[45]

Montaigne further argues that a broad private sphere would make the state, not less, but more secure by sowing factions and divisions among the citizenry. Montaigne argues that a private sphere makes the populace less likely to revolt from the state authority for two complementary reasons, both of which ring true in the American political experience: "It may be said, on the one hand, that to give factions a loose rein to entertain their own opinions is to scatter and sow division; it is almost lending a hand to augment it, there being no barrier or coercion of the laws to check or hinder its course" (II.19, 654 [509]). In his analysis of Julian the Apostate, Montaigne argues that this kind of "complete freedom," "freedom of conscience," leads to a multiplicity of sects that divide and factionalize the population, making an organized revolt from below more difficult. To some extent, but with a different focus, this anticipates *Federalist* 10. It may be objected, as it was at the time, that such factions would turn violent and lead to civil disorder, but Montaigne is not worried. Instead, making an argument that anticipates Tocqueville's description of the effects of freedom of religion in America, he asserts "that to give factions a loose rein to entertain their own opinions is to soften and relax them through facility and ease, and to dull the point, which is sharpened by rarity, novelty, and difficulty" (II.19, 654 [509]). Toleration is originally needed because of animosity, and it mitigates the causes of animosity at the same time that it controls its effects.

Indeed, according to Montaigne, almost everyone benefits from the creation of a private sphere of free conscience. The biggest winners are those who take advantage of the opportunity it affords for self-exploration and the cultivation of a robust private life. A private sphere also benefits the masses, because public stability enables them to live more tranquil lives. Montaigne thinks that they will probably not use toleration to pursue the eccentricities of an inner private life, because the inner life on the order of which he speaks is not the kind of thing that every individual pursues. It has to be chosen and willed, and while Montaigne undoubtedly thinks that everyone pursues it to some extent, he does not think that most people do it to a significant degree. But those who eschew self-essaying gain peace with the removal of contentious issues from the public arena. Agitators may still sway particular individuals or groups, but they will be less likely to kill each other over issues of conscience. More optimistically, Montaigne imagines that the multiplicity of arguments might degenerate into increasingly academic debates between intellectuals, leaving the mass of people untouched and unscathed.

The only real losers in the creation of a private sphere are the rambunctious intellectuals and religious zealots who, convinced of the correctness of their opinions, want to institute them and force them on everybody. These people get the right to maintain their own personal beliefs, and perhaps babble on about them, but not to institute them. The best way to neutralize unruly intellectuals, Montaigne says, is to tolerate them. By not persecuting them, Montaigne thinks that the rulers can drive a wedge between them and the people, for the sympathy and admiration that are aroused by suffering for one's beliefs greatly outweigh the proselytizing force of the views themselves. Montaigne's skepticism aims to change the unruly, presumptuous intellectuals into more reflective, humble people. He gives them reasons of self-interest to moderate and change themselves, but if they do not, they must be tamed and controlled. This is the price Montaigne is happily willing to pay for the creation of a private sphere.

Montaigne thinks that those who call for revolution must essay themselves to clarify their true motives to make sure they advocate their extreme measures for the right reasons and only as a last resort. Montaigne's robust conception of the good life as private and his view of the inherent groundlessness of politics make him reluctant to sacrifice too much for the state or to risk too much to fight against it. If Montaigne sees danger, he tries to avoid it: "In truth, and I am not afraid to confess it, I would easily carry, in case of need, one candle to Saint Michel and one to the dragon, according to the old woman's plan. I will follow the good side right to the fire, but not into it if I can help it" (III.1, 769-70 [601]). Montaigne does not advocate political fence-sitting as a general policy, but his skeptical detachment allows him to do it under certain circumstances. When a state suffers a crisis of authority, when the laws and sovereign contradict each other, or when the difference between the warring factions is "dubious and difficult to choose between," Montaigne, parallel to Socrates' description of the actions of a just philosopher in an unjust city, says that he would "steal away and escape that tempest" (III.9, 972-73 [760]).[46] He also says he would "follow with the wind, which I consider permissible when reason no longer guides" (III.9, 972-73 [760]). This detachment applies to political involvement, too. "The mayor and Montaigne are always two," he proclaims (III.10, 989 [774]). Ruling, and the exercise of all authority, is role playing and nothing grander. It is not and should not be considered part of one's core identity nor a goal of one's puffed-up vanity. This leads to an easygoingness and moderation in the execution of policy. A sense of humanity trumps vanity.

Montaigne's attitude toward state authority is as Nannerl Keohane says, "the reverse of that of the child in the fable of the emperor's new clothes; he noticed that there was no real emperor inside the handsome uniform, but continued to act as if there were."[47] Montaigne is willing to act, even act the fool, because he is confident in himself. He can separate himself from his roles. He is not, however, willing to do real damage to himself or others. Montaigne is willing to obey the state except when compelled to break a higher bond: to friend, family, or himself. The modern insistence on equal public recognition and the right to be heard publicly on every issue would, I think, strike Montaigne as vanity. If one truly knows oneself, one does not need to prove one's cleverness, seek external recognition, or worry about humbling oneself in obedience to established customs. One can be silent, one can play roles—as long as one can "*be*."

Montaigne practices what he preaches. He favors as much freedom as possible consistent with maintaining stability, so even as he articulates a stark separation of public and private *in principle*, he pushes for the expansion of the private sphere as a matter of prudent *action*. He advocates change not through the sword but through the pen, and he publicly and aggressively tries to change the attitudes and culture of his times through his writing. In his own times, he primarily emphasized freedom of conscience, because even that was not secure. In a culture in which freedom of conscience was firmly established, his arguments indicate that he would advocate other freedoms to promote his vision of the good as sophisticated simplicity. Montaigne provides a vision of the good and the idea of a politics tolerant of a private sphere in order to secure it, but he does not advocate any more specific political institutions, nor can he articulate a precise political principle on where to draw the line between the public and private. Ventures at changing the culture or changing the law are left to individual prudence. We struggle with this still.

IV. Montaigne's Justification for Toleration in Historical Context

While toleration and a private sphere might seem prosaic today, Montaigne's arguments were so radical at the time that he feared they would be rejected as a "monstrous child." No philosopher before him argued for toleration on the scale or on the grounds that he did. For

Montaigne, toleration follows from his conception of the self. Montaigne debunks the metaphysical reasons for intolerance and argues that the self properly understood is compatible with toleration. Since the good life is the pleasure and delight associated with self-seeking "at home," the self has no interest in going outside itself and victimizing others. And because the self is fundamentally patchwork and void, it has nothing to force.

To appreciate the radical nature of Montaigne's arguments for toleration, it is important to realize that before the sixteenth century, no major philosopher argued for toleration as a political principle. Philosophers in ancient Greece or Rome possessed both a genuine openness toward other philosophers on the one hand, while at the same time denying that such openness was a sound basis on which to build a polity. These thinkers wanted to prove their views to each other, thrived on argumentation, and never persecuted those of differing opinions; but they debated which concrete view society should adopt, not that a good state should tolerate all views. They practiced toleration while denying it theoretical justification.

Plato never advocates toleration as a political principle, although there are aspects of his writing that seem to imply toleration. For example, Socrates' famous dictum that the unexamined life is not worth living seems to imply that each person should be free to examine himself as he sees fit, free from the interference of others. Thus, it is striking that such freedom exists for no one in the "just city" of the *Republic*, except for the philosophers who reluctantly rule it. Accordingly, Socrates scorns the idea of free speech. In the *Republic*, he recommends tight state control of writers, artists, and musicians, and he does not celebrate democracy, but rather mocks its unruliness.[48] Of course, it can be well argued that Plato and Socrates would be happiest living in the freedom provided by a democracy, because only under that regime can philosophy flourish (and without the burden of ruling).[49] Nonetheless, it is notable that this is not the regime that Plato's Socrates recommends. The closest Plato, indeed any ancient, comes to advocating institutionalized free expression is the Nocturnal Council in Plato's *Laws*, where selected citizens are encouraged to state and debate their real opinions on many subjects for which the state has official, legislated answers. However, not only does this Council meet secretly at night, but its very existence is a state secret, unknown to the other citizens.[50] This limited, secret freedom is hardly an argument for toleration; it means that diversity will not be tolerated in public. Plato does not advocate toleration simply, because the same freedom that enables good people to flourish enables bad ones to become worse. Justice, he seems to argue, demands not freedom but a noble lie.

Aristotle does not explicitly praise—nor even list—toleration as one of the virtues. As with Plato, however, there are aspects of his thought that seem conducive to toleration. Rather than asserting a single, universally valid definition of political justice, Aristotle says it is relative to the regime, implying a tolerance of different views. Moreover, his dialectical method of weighing and considering a whole array of others' opinions is the epitome of a tolerant attitude, except that he proceeds to refute (at least partially) all other views. In the *Nichomachean Ethics*, Aristotle speaks of friendship and goodwill toward others, even strangers, but he is always careful to specify that these are only to be practiced in the right way, at the right time, as the man of practical wisdom would do it.[51] Aristotle is at pains to show the merits in many different kinds of lives, but perhaps he never explicitly argues for toleration in the *Ethics*, because he seeks more. He wants an individual to strive for virtue, not merely for the freedom to do whatever he or she wants as long as it does not hurt others.

While not advocated by the philosophers of antiquity, toleration of different religious views was a long-standing practice in ancient Rome. Conquered peoples were allowed to keep their gods and religious practices as long as they also accepted Rome's. This is how the pantheon grew and why Jews and Christians who refused the condition of toleration were persecuted. As we have seen, this tolerant policy helped shape Montaigne's thoughts on the subject. As far as I know, however, no Roman philosopher advocated such a policy as part of his description of the best state. Cicero, for example, does not advocate toleration in either his *Republic* or *Laws*. And Marcus Aurelius, widely regarded as one of the most enlightened men of Roman times, actually persecuted Christians.

Before Montaigne, certain Christian arguments were made for a limited toleration on religious grounds. Early Christians such as Tertullian and Lactantius argued for the separation of church and state and freedom of conscience on the basis of particular New Testament declarations such as "Render . . . unto Caesar the things which are Caesar's; and unto God the things that are God's."[52] But while separate from the state, the realm of conscience was to be ruled by the Church, not left to each individual's conscience. The parable of the tares, which cautions against pulling weeds lest some of the crop be plucked,[53] led to an argument for toleration based on human fallibility, and (following Saint Paul) was advanced by Origen and St. Cyprian. God alone, it was argued, knew what was truly in someone's heart, and He would judge on Judgment Day. Due to their fallibility, human beings should not judge, let alone punish, each other on earth for matters of faith. A third Christian argument for toleration had to do with the nature of belief itself. Forced belief was considered to be worthless, because faith had to be embraced freely and be held sincerely for salvation to be achieved. Finally, it was argued that Christian love and charity, not violence, should be directed toward the unenlightened, weak, or misguided. Coming from St. Paul, this was deemed the proper attitude toward unbelievers.[54] Montaigne uses various restatements of these Christian arguments, especially emphasizing human fallibility, but in doing so, he makes his appeals based on human weaknesses without appealing to God.

But for each of these Christian arguments, there were Christian counter-arguments that carried the day. While arguing that faith cannot be forced, St. Augustine still asked "what death is worse for the soul than the freedom to err?"[55] Unfortunately, Augustine's less tolerant remark was the more influential. Throughout medieval times—as the Arianists, Donatists, Catharists, Albigenists, Manicheans, and Hussites not to mention pagans, Jews, and Muslims discovered—toleration was extremely limited, and Augustine was the fountainhead of arguments both for and against it. St. Aquinas agreed with Augustine that *if* bad "tares" could be known, they could be pulled, although it should be noted that he was much harsher on heretics than on those outside the faith. "To accept the faith," he argued, "is a matter of free will, but to hold it once it has been accepted, is a matter of necessity."[56] Thus, he concluded that heretics "must be compelled, even bodily, to fulfil what they have promised, and to maintain what they have once accepted."[57] And since Aquinas saw heresy as contagious, he said that a twice-repentant heretic was too inconstant in faith and should be killed.[58]

The Christian humanists of the fifteenth century were the first to extend significantly the sphere of toleration beyond Christians, but they saw toleration as a means toward achieving doctrinal unity. The most prominent Christian humanists, Nicholas of Cusa, Marsilio Ficino, and Pico della Mirandola, argued for toleration on the grounds that all the world's religions and great philosophies led to the same truth—a Christian one. Arguing that each culture had something to contribute to our knowledge of truth, they each or separately were willing to tolerate Catholics, Greek Orthodox, Hussites, and even Jews, Muslims, Turks, Persians, Tartars, Hindus, and Platonists. (Erasmus used the same argument to preach reconciliation with the Protestants.) But their limit for toleration was stated by Ficino; he rejected atheism because "nothing displeases God so much as being scorned."[59] These Christian humanists were open to a wide array of cultures and ways of thought because the key premise of their arguments for toleration is an optimism that all cultures lead to the same truth, which is a toleration of differences as only a temporary measure.[60]

Much of the toleration controversy that raged throughout the sixteenth century had a fundamentally religious character—and the same limits. One of the best known sixteenth-century defenders of toleration is the French humanist, Sebastian Castellio, whom Montaigne described as "most outstanding in learning" (I.35, 220 [165]). Castellio made direct ethical and emotional appeals for toleration by doubting the morality of persecution: "To kill a man is not to defend a doctrine. It is to kill a man," but Castellio ultimately grounds his appeal for toleration on a religious principle: "I must be saved by my own faith and not by that of another."[61] His religiosity leads his tolerance to be less than Montaigne desires. For example, he would not tolerate atheists—explicitly excluding Rabelais for example—and because he shares the Christian contempt for the body, he thought "to force conscience is worse than to cruelly kill a man," whereas Montaigne had no problem with people pretending or playing roles about matters of conscience and considers cruelty to the body to be the worst fate a human being can suffer. While Castellio and other sixteenth-century figures such as Jacobus Acontius, Martin Bucer, Jacob Sturm, Faustus Socinus, Sebastian Franck, Caspar Schwenckfeld, and Michel Servetus are important figures in the history of toleration, their arguments are fundamentally religious, not based on skepticism or a conception of a secular, humanistic self.

In short, because of their attachments to a notion of fixed truth, whether found in nature or revealed religion, ancient and medieval philosophers did not advocate toleration as a major political principle. It was only when the crisis of authority became so acute in the sixteenth century that skepticism arose as a leading philosophical stance and toleration emerged as a desirable political idea. The political, economic, social, religious, and philosophical crises of the sixteenth century led to a widespread and profound breakdown of authority that could not be remedied with the traditional medieval appeals to religion nor by the innovative religious arguments of the Christian Humanists, not even by Erasmus.[62]

The French *politiques*, so called because of their placing the interests of the state above the interests of religion, tried to fill this gap by being the first to make primarily secular arguments for toleration. Such leading figures as Jean Bodin and Michel de L'Hôpital, both of whom were political acquaintances of Montaigne's, preferred that a state have only one religion. But given the realities of France's wars of religion in which there were two powerfully established religions, neither of which could eradicate the other at an acceptable price, they sought ways to allow the different religions to coexist by subordinating religious differences to the power of a central political authority. Undoubtedly some *politiques* saw this only as a temporary expedient until the Catholic powers could reorganize, while others saw it as a way to undermine the power of religion in general. Either way, however, it became the basis of a purely secular argument for state power that was to reach its fullest fruition in the later arguments of Hobbes' *Leviathan* and Locke's little-read *First Treatise of Government* and their attempts to subordinate—and tolerate—religious differences under one overriding sovereign political power.

Montaigne argues for toleration on grounds to which no theorists had ever before appealed and on a scale that exploded all previous, let alone sixteenth-century, confines. Montaigne was greatly influenced by the tolerant practices of pagan Rome, and he shared the stability-based arguments for toleration that the Romans and *politiques* recommended, but he does not rely on these arguments alone. Rather, his conception of the self is pivotal to his justification for toleration. Since he seeks toleration and a private sphere as means to secure and promote his ideal of self-exploration, he, unlike the previous advocates of toleration, has no problem tolerating—even celebrating—atheists, skeptics, ancient pagans, and "heathen" Indians. The *politiques* were willing for strategic reasons to tolerate powerful minorities; Montaigne was willing to tolerate every law-abiding individual.[63] Having suffered through ideologically driven war in a way that the ancient philosophers had never imagined, or at least never suffered, he advocates expanding the individual freedom that they practiced into a political principle. Montaigne wants to make the good of philosophy, reinterpreted in his more subjective manner, available for everyone who can or desires to pursue it.

Some of Montaigne's arguments for toleration parallel those made from within Christianity, but he consistently gives his borrowings a jarring twist. Like Tertullian and Lactantius,[64] Montaigne thinks that a conscience is sacrosanct, but he says it should be respected not because it is divine, but because it is characteristically human. Similarly, Montaigne argues for human fallibility without recourse to divine judgment. Montaigne shares the Christian fear that self-love and pride lead to an overconfidence which incites intolerance, and he wants to combat these vices, but he does not want to do so in the name of restoring Christian humility. Rather, considering Christianity itself to be a hubristic doctrine which encourages pride and false views about human beings, Montaigne describes the humility of frail and vulnerable creatures who must find and create their own way in the world. The Christian Humanists argued that all the world's religions and philosophies possessed some truth, but they thought Christianity was its purest expression; Montaigne was wary of organized religion, Christianity no less so. It is with respect to these innovations that Montaigne is a spiritual father to the atheistic arguments for toleration in the Enlightenment.[65]

Consistent with his own skeptical views—and thus particularly useful in a skeptical age such as our own—Montaigne's arguments for toleration all proceed from his rich conception of the self and its self-interest. No one before Montaigne argued for toleration on the grounds of self-development and self-exploration. Even Montaigne's contemporaries, such as Castellio, who are most celebrated for their tolerant arguments sought the metaphorical crucifixion of the self, not its worldly development. Suffice it to say that Montaigne's arguments for toleration exploded like a bomb into the intellectual milieu of his time. And as we shall see in the next chapter, they still prove powerful today.

Chapter Five

The Possibility of Skeptical Toleration: Essaying Montaigne's Arguments

We have seen—and dealt with—the metaphysical truth-based claims to intolerance; Montaigne debunks such claims as unknowable and urges human beings not to live their lives on such a basis but rather to return "home" to themselves. But insofar as Montaigne plays an important role in the turn to modernity and in the origins of liberalism—as I have argued—what, if anything, is there in his thought that allows it to avoid the problems with modernity and liberalism as they were to unfold? Indeed, many of the main scholars or critics of modernity and liberalism, from Marx and Nietzsche to Karl Löwith, Leo Strauss, Eric Voegelin, Alasdair MacIntyre, and Charles Taylor, have argued that once the first skeptical turn toward modernity is made, the problems of nihilism, materialism, and excessive individualism are inevitable.[1] How, if at all, does Montaigne avoid these problems?

By justifying toleration on a skeptical basis that appeals only to self-interest, Montaigne exposes his arguments to numerous problems that could lead to intolerance. This chapter analyzes Montaigne's arguments for toleration in light of the worldly dangers they might risk. It does not deal with every criticism that has been, or could be, leveled at liberalism, nor does it consider every aspect of the various charges that it does raise. Rather, it focuses on possible threats to toleration once metaphysical restrictions are removed from individuals and replaced by a self-interested, worldly calculus on how to live. Satisfactory answers to these problems require stating some limits to skepticism, because a skepticism without limits cannot justify anything, let alone toleration or moral behavior, and Montaigne does limit his skepticism. He limits it not by appealing to metaphysics, politics, custom, or anything else that exists outside the subjective self; his limit appeals only to his understanding of the self. But self-interest needs to be limited too, and Montaigne accomplishes this by appealing to his sense of self-interest properly understood (based on the limits inherent in the self's natural condition). If Montaigne's conception of the self were rejected, his ground for decent behavior would also be rejected. But if accepted, Montaigne's ground for toleration is able to do things that other theories are not, and for the following reason: unlike the narrower passion-based visions of the self that underlie liberalism, or the Christian and Kantian conceptions—all of which see worldly self-interest and toleration as being in tension—Montaigne's understanding of self-interest as self-exploration and self-cultivation leads him to devalue the goods the pursuit of which lead to intolerance and cruelty. It also leads him to the creation of a mindset in which toleration is not the goal but an organic consequence.

To nail down more precisely how Montaigne's conception of the self grounds toleration, and what the benefits and limits of his approach are, this chapter marshals objections to skeptically based and self-interest-based philosophies and examines and assesses Montaigne's thought in light of each charge. It also examines and assesses Montaigne's responses to the charges, for Montaigne anticipated many of these objections and addressed them in the *Essays*. The first section of this chapter deals with one challenge posed by the problem of nihilism. It compares and contrasts Montaigne's thought to Nietzsche's to see how Montaigne avoids the moral problems which plague Nietzsche's skeptical vision. If all metaphysical restraints are lifted and self-interest is lauded, as they are by Montaigne, what limit, if any, can be articulated to prevent one from inflicting the will-to-power-inspired cruelties at which someone like Nietzsche does not blink? The second section of this chapter gives Montaigne's critiques of the main worldly temptations to intolerance—wealth, power, and glory. It explores how Montaigne might defend his views from the charges often leveled at passion-driven liberalism: that its individualism is excessive, thus risking the harms not only of base materialism but also of the exploitation brought about by cold capitalism and associated with economic greed. And what self-interest-based reasons exist, according to Montaigne, to prevent one from seeking to be a tyrant, wiping out one's enemies or whole peoples or groups of peoples along the way? In short, in the absence of a higher truth, why should people not sate themselves silly, even if they need to hurt others to do so? The third section of the chapter takes a different tack and asks what, if any, affirmative obligations to help others are entailed in Montaigne's worldview. For if one is not affirmatively required to help others, it might mean tolerating all sorts of injustices that are part of the existing social, economic, or political order. Do Montaigne's arguments for toleration tolerate this? Is there any basis in a skeptical, self-interested world for civic-mindedness or the promotion of social justice? Finally, the chapter concludes by comparing Montaigne's arguments to the most commonly advocated justifications for toleration. Fully aware of the limits of and difficulties caused for his proposals by his rejection of metaphysics, Montaigne nonetheless avoids many serious problems associated with the grounds of justification offered today.

I. Cruelty, Pity, and Nietzsche's Challenge

Nietzsche's Challenge

Montaigne's similarities to Nietzsche—his skepticism about moral standards existing outside the subjective self and his emphasis on self-interest—it could be argued, might justify a kind of Nietzschean or fascistic will-to-power philosophy that would be indifferent to suffering in or the infliction of cruelty on others. This fear is reinforced by the fact that Nietzsche writes highly of Montaigne and lists him as one of only eight people to whom he must answer.[2] Fears about Montaigne's philosophy legitimizing cruelty to others are, however, without foundation.

The key difference between Montaigne and Nietzsche concerns what they find at the core of the self. As is always the case with skeptical thinkers, it is not their skepticism *per se* that colors their moral thought; it is what survives their skeptical doubting that matters. When Nietzsche explores himself and strips away the layers of culture and convention, he finds a will-to-power. While most people's wills, he says, are weak, and hence pose little danger to others, a few are strong. Since he says that the strong are responsible for all the greatness and creativity of the human species—and thus hold the key to the species' future—he argues that their wills must be pursued regardless of any cruelty or suffering inflicted on others. Both for the sake of their own health and to help the species overcome the abyss of nihilism, he says, the strong must overcome slave morality and will their wills—if anyone gets hurt along the way, so be it. Cruelty and suffering do not make him blink. But where Nietzsche finds strength and power at the core of the self, Montaigne does not. For him, there is no ineluctable will. Where Nietzsche considers the self to be nothing but will which can barely be consciously controlled, Montaigne argues that "there is nothing really in our power but will [*la volonté*]" (I.7,

32 [20]). Montaigne finds the self to be layer upon fascinating layer, with each moment playing its own delightful or odd game. But these unruly phenomena in oneself are not, he says, "will." Upon essaying himself, Montaigne finds a tendency for the self to be distracted and diverted from itself. Ordinary fears and anxieties and the desires for material goods, power, and glory lead people away from what is truly good for themselves —self-exploration—and lead them to flee into a socially constructed world in which appearance and acceptance from others is all that matters. Moreover, the unlimited nature of the imagination and the unlimited wishes of human vanity, he warns, together lead the self to construct and to pursue visions of the world and the good that have no basis in reality other than being in an individual's mind. Whereas Nietzsche celebrates these impulses as authentic and thus encourages the will to forge its own unity and to act on it—even if it means hurting others—Montaigne considers such forging to be forgery. Although Montaigne favors the kind of self-creation that results from self-exploration, he thinks that strong assertions of one impulse cut a self off from its natural multiplicity. Such a move, therefore, leads not to authenticity but to a distancing from oneself. To surrender to the strong impulses that underlie such assertions leads to an internal imbalance. And since Montaigne doubts our ability to understand what these impulses mean and from whence they came—he suspects that they are but the manifestations of other things—he argues for moderation in exercising them and does not think they ever justify inflicting cruelty on others.

Indeed, for Montaigne, it is precisely the will which can be used to regulate oneself against these impulses. He thinks that the inner impulses that make people flee from themselves, to go outward into the world, are not at the core of the self, but rather one of the self's worst features. For it is precisely this tendency, according to Montaigne, that covers deeper, more primordial aspects of the self and prevents their discovery. Therefore, Montaigne warns against following these impulses outward and calls those who surrender to them insufficiently reflective, avaricious, and overly ambitious. He wants people to restrain themselves:

> The range of our desires should be circumscribed and restrained to a narrow limit of the nearest and most contiguous good things; and moreover their course should be directed not in a straight line that ends up elsewhere, but in a circle whose two extremities by a short sweep meet and terminate in ourselves. Actions that are performed without this reflexive movement, I mean a searching and genuine reflexive movement—the actions, for example, of the avaricious, the ambitious, and so many others who run in

a straight line, whose course carries them ever forward—are erroneous and diseased actions. (III.10, 988-89 [773])[3]

Montaigne rejects actions, such as Nietzsche advocates with his conception of the will-to-power, that take an individual away from himself. Montaigne wants people's action to come back to themselves. He would find Nietzsche's valorization of a strong will that needs to be expressed outwardly, physically into the world, to be a profound—and potentially disastrous—mistaking of the human condition. Unlike Nietzsche, Montaigne does not deem will to be "the essence of life."[4] To him, the attempt to impose oneself on the world is often not self-realization but self-abandonment. Such external actions prevent people from pursuing their more authentic selves, and he blames these kinds of external actions for most of the man-made ills. Thus, he judges harshly those who flee themselves rather than staying at home, within themselves.

Montaigne does, however, recognize the noble possibilities for "will" in human beings. Montaigne admires the warlike spirit of the cannibals, Alexander the Great, Caesar, and numerous other conquerors who could, in some sense, be seen as Nietzschean heroes. All of these types embody, for Montaigne, a kind of aristocratic honor that was highly valued in Montaigne's age, and which he admires in its noblest form. Indeed, aside from Socrates, Epaminondas, Homer, and some other philosophers, these world conquerors and heroic strugglers are praised more than any other people in the *Essays*. And they are praised in terms that Nietzsche would recognize. Paralleling Nietzsche's praise of Napoleon, for example, Montaigne calls Alexander "superhuman" and says his injustices cannot be judged by ordinary standards, because "such men require to be judged in gross, by the master purpose of their actions" (II.36, 732-33 [571]).[5] Moreover, in contrast to the liberal and Christian emphases on peace, he praises such heroes both for the ways in which they risk danger—"this prince is the supreme model of hazardous acts" and the "most daring commander that ever was" (I.24, 128 [94] & II.9, 384 [294])—and on aesthetic grounds, for the beauty and nobility of their actions—these "masters of the world, did not forget beauty in carrying out their affairs" (III.12, 1035 [810]). This parallels his praise of the cannibals' warfare as "*toute noble*." Montaigne recognizes a kind of good that accrues to the self based on the trials and tribulations that such heroes endure. These epic struggles, he acknowledges, reveal one's inner strength and will, test one's ability to marshal all one's forces for a goal, and offer one the opportunity to find characteristics and abilities in oneself that might otherwise never have been discovered (or about which one could delude oneself: "I could have conquered the world if I wanted, I just chose not to"). In short, it is easy to see why Nietzsche found in Montaigne a fellow traveler.

Montaigne's ultimate rejection of these figures as the embodiment of the good life is not based on moralistic finger wagging, on violating others *per se* (as is the Christian and liberal response), although he does express reservation about this; rather, he rejects will-based activities, because of *the kind* of struggles in which they engage. Since both see struggle as inevitable and good,[6] Montaigne's reservation with Nietzsche's position would not concern struggling for mastery in itself; it has to do with what one is struggling *for*. According to Montaigne, to struggle for mastery over others is not as noble or satisfying as to struggle for mastery over oneself. It is not too great an exaggeration to say that one of Montaigne's main aims is to replace the military, chivalric, and aristocratic-honor kinds of struggles with his conception of sophisticated simplicity, the attempt to struggle with oneself. It is Montaigne's insistence on self-struggle that leads him to rank Alexander's life as inferior to the life of Socrates: "If you ask the former what he knows how to do, he will answer, 'Subdue the world'; if you ask the latter, he will say, 'Lead the life of man in conformity with its natural condition'; a knowledge much more general, more weighty, and more legitimate" (III.2, 787 [614]). In political and military struggles, the stakes might be as high as everything in the external world. But in the struggle of self-exploration, the stakes are even higher: oneself.

Postmodern and liberal interpreters of Nietzsche, who want to use his skeptical thought as the basis for a private sphere in which self-fashioning is the goal, would be much better served to turn to Montaigne. These interpreters of Nietzsche say that his goal is in fact nothing but the struggle for self-mastery, self-creation, or self-fashioning that I am attributing to Montaigne, and I agree that this is a large part of what Nietzsche seeks.[7] However, since these thinkers want to argue that everyone should be allowed to pursue his or her own self-fashioning free from being physically violated by others, they must explain why *every* individual should be respected. To do this, they must supplement Nietzsche's moral skepticism with some other—anti-Nietzschean!—argument. The problem with Nietzsche's reasoning is that it allows physically violent expressions of the will-to-power. Indeed, Nietzsche speaks of the will-to-power as having three possible manifestations. The first is merely destructive (not creative), and is embodied by conquerors who "go back to the innocent conscience of the beast of prey, as triumphant monsters who perhaps emerge from a disgusting procession of murder, arson, rape, and torture, exhilarated and undisturbed of soul, as if it were no more than a students' prank, convinced they have provided the poets with a lot more material for song and praise."[8] The second manifestation of the will-to-power is constructive in the world, such as is expressed by the makers of states: "Their work is an instinctive creation and imposition of forms; they are the most involuntary, unconscious artists there are—wherever they appear something new soon arises, a ruling structure that *lives*, in which parts and functions are delimited and co-ordinated, in which nothing whatever finds a place that has not first been assigned a 'meaning' in relation to the whole."[9] Sometimes Nietzsche also refers to these creators as creators of worlds, in the way, for example, that Homer's writing created the ancient Greek world.[10] Finally, the third manifestation Nietzsche speaks of is the will-to-power over oneself, "this artists' cruelty, this delight in imposing a form upon oneself."[11] For Nietzsche, all of these manifestations involve the imposition of cruelty, just for different ends: the joy of inflicting it in itself on others—"To see others suffer does one good, to make others suffer even more"—which he calls "a genuine seduction *to* life"; to build something in the world, fully realizing, "If a temple is to be erected *a temple must be destroyed*: that is the law"; and, to attain mastery over oneself, which involves an imposition of cruelty on oneself.[12] Of these three, a good case can be made that Nietzsche most admires the constructive manifestations of the will-to-power, those that the liberal and postmodern Nietzscheans celebrate; and insofar as these creations are of new horizons alone, physical violence on others is not necessarily entailed. Indeed, Nietzsche himself tried to conquer the world not physically, but through the power of his words.[13] Nonetheless, Nietzsche articulates a vision that *in principle* refuses to condemn the imposition of cruelty on others. This is the greatest moral weakness of his theory, and it is where all liberal and postmodern attempts to use Nietzsche to support a tolerant conception of self-fashioning collapse. Nietzsche offers no limits, based on nature, self-interest, or anything else, that can restrain an individual's pursuit of power. Indeed, he delights in demolishing all such limits. If toleration is to exist in a skeptical world, some limits on the expression of violence that might follow from strong wills or strong desires must be imported from elsewhere. Montaigne's conception of the self supplies just such limits.

Cruelty

Montaigne's conception of the self gives a ground for condemning cruelty and enables us to reject Nietzsche's indifference to the cruel manifestations of the will-to-power. Like Nietzsche, Montaigne celebrates strength as strength, but he also condemns the infliction of cruelty, which by definition is the excessive infliction of pain. For example, he condemns Alexander for sometimes exhibiting "no pity," as evidenced by his actions against some towns that had resisted him: "the length of a day was not enough to satiate Alexander's revenge" (I.1, 14 [5]). Similarly, he writes:

> There is no more extreme valor of its kind than Alexander's; but it is only of one kind, and not complete and universal enough. Incomparable though it is, it still has its blemishes; which is why we see him worry so frantically when he conceives the slightest suspicion that his men are plotting against his life, and why he behaves in such matters with such violent and indiscriminate injustice and with a fear that subverts his natural reason. Also superstition, with which he was so strongly tainted, bears some stamp of pusillanimity. And the excessiveness of the penance he did for the murder of Clytus is also evidence of the unevenness of his temper. (II.1, 320 [243])

Alexander—and all destructive manifestation of the will—illustrates the psychological imbalance at the core of cruelty. Unlike Nietzsche, Montaigne condemns cruelty, but he does so not by appealing to the victims' "rights"; rather, he appeals to the health of would-be victimizers. Someone who inflicts cruelty, Montaigne argues, must be unbalanced to the point of unhealthiness. Moreover, Montaigne seems to think such imbalances tend not to be limited to one aspect of the self; it is not an accident that Montaigne condemns Alexander's cruelty at the same time as condemning his fears, superstitions, violent temper, and pusillanimity. All of these character faults are signs that Alexander is out of balance and not "at home." In his own individual self-interest, he should remedy these imbalances. Although Montaigne offers opposite assessments of Alexander on some of these points in other parts of the *Essays*,[14] this composite illustrates how not being at home leads to suffering in others and in oneself. Here is the genius of Montaigne's argument: he urges his readers to fix themselves *for themselves*—in the process, others are spared.

Montaigne does not approach the topic of cruelty naively; he knows that the world is full of cruelty and *schadenfreude*, enjoyment of the trouble of others. His book is full of stories, ancient and modern, that describe people who not only do not feel pity at the sight of others' suffering, but who also enjoy watching cruelty and suffering—and of those who enjoy inflicting it. For example, Montaigne writes:

I could hardly be convinced, until I saw it, that there were souls so monstrous that they would commit murder for the mere pleasure of it; hack and cut off other men's limbs; sharpen their wits to invent unaccustomed torments and new forms of death, without enmity, without profit, and for the sole purpose of enjoying the pleasing spectacle of the pitiful gestures and movements, the lamentable groans and cries, of a man dying in anguish. For that is the uttermost point that cruelty can attain. 'That man should kill man not in anger, not in fear, but only to watch the sight' [Seneca]. (II.11, 411-12 [315-16])[15]

To a large extent, Montaigne thinks that cruelty results from cruel customs. He explains how the ancient Romans cultivated their taste for blood and became "accustomed" to it: "after they had been accustomed to the spectacle of the slaughter of animals, they proceeded to that of men and of gladiators" (II.11, 412 [316]). As we have seen, culture can denature individuals and pull them from their natural "home." But Montaigne thinks that aggression also exists in mankind by nature. We have seen him illustrate this behavior by having his cannibals, his "natural men," fight and eat their neighbors and by his repeated references to Epicurus' phrase that without law, human beings would eat each other. And like Lucretius, Montaigne detects that human beings feel within them a "bittersweet pricking of malicious pleasure in seeing others suffer; even children," he says, "feel it" (III.1, 768 [599]).[16] Playing on the difference between his descriptive and normative uses of the concept of nature, Montaigne also says: "Our being is cemented with sickly qualities: ambition, jealousy, envy, vengeance, superstition, despair, dwell in us with *a possession so natural* . . . indeed even cruelty, *so unnatural a vice*" (III.1, 767-68 [599], emphasis added). He thus concludes: "Nature herself, I fear, attaches to man some instinct for inhumanity" (II.11, 412 [316]). As we saw in chapter 4, Montaigne takes no chances: the natural occurrence of inhumanity underlies his insistence on having a strong state.

Montaigne thinks that human cruelty also—perhaps especially—results from human beings not knowing themselves, from being uncomfortable with their inner wills and impulses. This is suggested by the paradigmatic examples of cruelty: the cannibals and children. They are quintessentially natural in the sense of being barely socialized, but the fact that they are not fully developed human beings, that their self-conscious and critical faculties are underdeveloped, sheds light on the origins of cruelty. Cruelty may be natural in the descriptive sense of existing in nature, but it is not, for Montaigne, natural in a normative sense. Cruelty, according to Montaigne, results from a lack of self-awareness and a lack of self-understanding. Montaigne makes this abundantly clear in an essay entitled "Cowardice, Mother of Cruelty" (II.27), in which he notes that "I have found by experience that the bitterness and hardness of a malicious and inhuman heart are usually accompanied by feminine weakness. I have observed that some of the most cruel are subject to weeping easily and for frivolous reasons" (II.27, 671 [523)]). On some occasions, Montaigne praises his own feminine softness, so this is not always a pejorative.[17] What Montaigne is highlighting is how the emotions in cruel people, as in Alexander the Great, are prone to numerous extremes: "Could it be," he asks, "weakness of soul that made them so easily bent to every extreme?" (II.27, 671 [524]). Those with "weakness of soul" are more likely to be cruel in large measure because they do not understand or essay their emotions or impulses.[18]

Accordingly, Montaigne blames cruelty on a whole host of ignorant, or undigested, or unthought-through fears and impulses. Sometimes, he attributes it to an ignoble "pusillanimity," to cowards in battle trying to make up for their cowardice by wreaking "massacre and bloodshed" on those who are already defeated: "what causes so many unheard-of cruelties in wars in which the people take part is that that beastly rabble tries to be warlike and brave by ripping up a body at their feet and bloodying themselves up to their elbows, having no sense of any other kind of valor" (II.27, 672 [524]). This kind of cruelty results from improperly essaying fear (and might be exacerbated by resentment). The problem would be averted if these people had essayed themselves and come to terms with their fear of death, as Montaigne urges his readers to do. If they had done this, they would not have been cruel to compensate for cowardice, because they would not have acted cowardly in the first place. Montaigne extends this critique of cruelty to the so-called nobles of his age who cowardly dueled through seconds and thirds, and did so for the pettiest reasons. Cowardice and improperly digested fear of death lead to disproportionate and cruel responses. Amplifying his lament about the difference between his times and those of Julian the Apostate, Montaigne repeatedly points out that his countrymen do not know how to seek revenge proportionately, inflicting death for every slight whatsoever, due both to a lack of confidence in themselves and to a horrible fear that anything and everything will be revisited back upon them. And the cruel consequences of not being "at home" applies, metaphorically and literally, to whole nations, too: "Immoderate nation! We are not content with making our vices and follies known to the world by reputation, we go to foreign countries to display them in person" (II.27, 675 [526]). In short, according to Montaigne cruelty results from unessayed impulses.

Montaigne applies his critique of cruelty especially harshly to tyrants and would-be tyrants—and this gives his answer to a would-be Nietzschean superman: essay yourself. Examine the wills and fears underlying your drive into the world. Sometimes, Montaigne suggests that tyrants are cruel simply due to their *schadenfreude*: "The first cruelties are practiced for their own sake; thence arises the fear of just revenge, which afterwards produces a string of new cruelties, in order to stifle the first by the others" (II.27, 678 [528]). Other times, Montaigne says that tyrants are bloodthirsty due to their excessive fears: "their cowardly heart furnishes them with no other means of making themselves secure than by exterminating those who can injure them, even to the women, for fear of a scratch: 'He strikes all things because he fears all things' [Claudian]" (II.27, 677-78 [528]). In either case, their first failure to stay "at home" leads to an escalating chain reaction of cruelties. If they were not so ambitious that they felt they had to rule the whole world, security would probably not be an issue for them in the first place. But once they victimize others, their ambition is compounded by fear, the fear of just revenge against themselves. Montaigne also says that resistance to tyrants angers them, which further escalates the cycle, since they then seek not only security but horrible revenge to slake their anger. According to Montaigne, then, tyrants can never have peace of mind and thus can never have anything even approaching happiness. If the insecure, ambitious, and angry sought critically and self-reflexively to understand their desires and impulses, if they opened a dialogue with themselves instead of running away from their discomforts and expressing against the world what they have trouble acknowledging to themselves, then they would live more tranquil and contented lives—and to the benefit of the rest of the world, a large portion of the worst human cruelty would be avoided.

Pity

Unlike Alexander, who showed "no pity," Montaigne's conception of the self has a corollary attribute that leads to moral behavior based on a kind of pity that naturally arises in those who are truly at "home." Pity might reside in some commoners (and Montaigne even suggests that animals might sometimes feel and possess it), but as his graphic descriptions of *schadenfreude* amply demonstrate, Montaigne does not hypothesize that pity is universally found in every human being; diseased people who have fled from their "home" certainly do not feel it. To assume that pity is universally manifest would be silly and naive, and Montaigne thinks it would be silly and naive for politicians to assume its existence as the basis for social interaction. But Montaigne does seem to think that a powerful and proper kind of compassion will inevitably arise in those who are "at home" within themselves. Thus, not only does he show a reflective person how his or her self-interest is incompatible with inflicting cruelty, but he also endeavors to show that to persecute someone would actually cause pain in a self-aware person.

Montaigne thinks that people who are healthy and whole, aware of themselves and their natural condition, and content to stay "at home," feel a sympathy with all other sentient beings.[19] Man's body is his connection to nature. Nature manifests itself directly and spontaneously in every human being without the need for any technical interpretive discourse, unless—and this is a very big unless—its impulse is covered by convention, but if so, Montaigne wants this blockage to be removed. Others are to be tolerated instead of victimized not because they are the bearers of some abstract "right," but because awareness of one's own weakness and precariousness creates a bond, a sympathy through identification, with other selves. It is the feeling of one's own weaknesses and of one's own pain and suffering that makes one identify with and want to prevent it in others: "The sight of other people's anguish," he says, "causes very real anguish to me" (I.21, 95 [68]). It is because of this "natural compassion, which has an infinite power over me" that Montaigne says he is more likely to devote himself to the "little people" (III.13, 1079 [844]), that he "sympathize[s] very tenderly with the afflictions of others" (II.11, 409 [314]), that "the dead I hardly pity, and I should rather envy them; but I very greatly pity the dying" (II.11, 409 [314]), and why he does not mind the cannibalism of the dead so much as the torturing of the living (II.11, 409-10 [314] and I.31, 207-8 [155] and III.6, 889-90 [695]).[20]

To clarify Montaigne's understanding of pity—and to see its limits, so we do not overstate the claim—it is helpful to compare it to that of the so-called Common Sense philosophers and to Rousseau, who made pity a central phenomenon of their understandings of natural human morality. All of these thinkers, as well as Montaigne, wrestled with the problem of trying to explain compassion without resorting to Christianity. Such a defense was deemed necessary, these later philosophers thought, because they doubted that a purely self-interest-based argument, epitomized by Hobbes, would be able to explain how and why human beings come together to form human societies, let alone to serve as a sufficient injunction to moral behavior. Rousseau is famous for his claim that pity or compassion is a characteristic of human beings by nature. He claims that every human being is born with "a natural repugnance to seeing any sentient being, especially our fellow man, perish or suffer," and he attributes this to "the inner impulse of compassion."[21] Without this, he says, human beings would be fundamentally self-interested and indifferent to the suffering of others. Most of the major Common Sense philosophers—Shaftesbury, Hutcheson, Smith, and Hume—made similar arguments. In their desire to explain the whole array of human compassion, the Common Sense philosophers expanded the definition of sympathy to include much more than pity. For example, Adam Smith, whose *The Theory of Moral Sentiments* stresses the empathetic aspect of his twofold view of human nature (whereas *The Wealth of Nations* stresses self-interest), defines sympathy not as related to suffering in particular but "to denote our fellow-feeling with any passion whatever."[22] David Hume, in his *A Treatise of Human Nature*, goes further than Smith in attributing sympathy to a wide array of human interactions, claiming that it applies toward the entirety of others' "persons, [and] therefore, their interests, their passions, their pains and pleasure."[23] However, the Common Sense philosophers explain the origins of these attachments differently, but their views break down into two major camps.[24] The first explanation, argued by Shaftesbury and Hutcheson, is that shared emotions come from an innate and natural "moral sense," which they describe as operating like any of the other five senses. According to them, all human beings possess a sense of right and wrong by nature and the perceptions of natural emotions in others leads naturally to an identification with them, which in turn provokes those same emotions in the observer.[25] The second explanation, argued by Hume and Smith, is that sympathy results from an act of the imagination: "the imagination . . . makes us conceive a lively idea of the passion, or rather feel the passion itself in the same manner as if the person were really actuated by it."[26] Montaigne never explains pity as resulting from a moral sense or "inner impulse" that belongs universally to every human being, as Rousseau, Hutcheson, and Shaftesbury later suggested. Instead, he more closely agrees with Smith and Hume that it follows from an empathetic act of the imagination. Unlike Hume and Smith, however, Montaigne never tries to explain how the empathetic imagination works in anything approaching the scientific manner that they attempt, perhaps because he deems such a scientific and universalistic account of pity to be naive and impossible.[27] Nor does he deem all identification and social relations to be based on it. Pity and compassion do not, for Montaigne, underlie all human connections.

Sympathy as a *general* concept is problematic for Montaigne. While Smith and Hume scientize the emotions, explaining them down to the three properties of the human brain (Hume) or calculating the extent and degrees of emotional responses (Smith),[28] they do not even attempt to explore the numerous ways in which the imagination runs amuck, nor do they enter into a critique of imagination to see which sympathies should be accepted and which rejected. By contrast, Montaigne continually plays with these phenomena, and it is here that he shows himself to be a psychologist of empathy superior to the others where the imagination is concerned. For example, he writes, "I catch the disease that I study, and lodge it in me. I do not find it strange that imagination brings fevers and death to those who give it a free hand and encourage it" (I.21, 95 [68]). Similarly, he says that "there is nothing that tempts my tears but tears, not only real ones, but all sorts" (II.11, 409 [314]). These kinds of imagined connections seem to be excessive. Just as we have seen Montaigne lamenting intellectuals who suffer before the pain actually arrives, is it not a problem to feel symptoms that one reads in a book? Perhaps such feelings are appropriate if one is reading an account of horrific suffering (nonfiction or fiction), but such feelings seem inappropriate if one is reading a purely descriptive medical textbook. Similarly, are we to credit people who are moved by false tears? Perhaps under certain circumstances it would be humane to be so open to others' sufferings that one allows oneself to be tricked. But must one not harden oneself to being repeatedly manipulated by children or to the one who continually cries that the sky is falling? These are exactly the kind of "sympathies" and "feelings" that Montaigne continually essays and explores in a way that the Common Sense philosophers do not.

However, there is a particular case of sympathy which is not at all problematic for Montaigne: pity for those genuinely suffering cruelties. This case underlies Montaigne's negative argument for toleration, as emphasized by Judith Shklar and David Quint: "I cruelly hate cruelty, both by nature and by judgment, as the extreme of all vices" (II.11, 408 [313]); "The horror I feel for cruelty throws me back more deeply into clemency than any model of clemency could attract me to it" (III.8, 900 [703]). Montaigne's visceral reaction to the sight of cruelty makes him identify and empathize with the sufferer, the other. Their suffering makes him suffer, too. The visceral nature of Montaigne's sympathetic identifications with sufferers is emphasized by the fact that his compassion extends beyond the human sphere alone and encompasses all sentient beings. For example, Montaigne relays his squeamishness at seeing a chicken's neck wrung and seeing a hare in the teeth of a dog (II.11, 408 [313]). He also writes how he hates to see an animal hounded down in the hunt (II.11, 412 [316]) and condemns everything beyond plain death as "pure cruelty" (II.27, 679 [530]

& II.11, 410 [314]).[29] Cruelty is so bad, according to Montaigne, because it—by definition—excessively and needlessly inflicts bodily pain. Pain is bad because it is the most real, most certain horror of human existence. If the body does not lie—and Montaigne argues that it is much more reliable than the imagination—physical pain "is certain knowledge" and "is the worst accident of our being" (I.14, 55 [37] & 56 [38]).[30] Pain should be avoided if possible: "in all the world I am the man who bears it the most ill will and who flees it the most" (I.14, 56 [38]). Montaigne accepts pain as a part of life, and if it cannot be avoided, he wants to bear it courageously without denying its existence; but being aware of one's own vulnerability to pain, he suggests, makes one empathize with such pain in others. To suffer anguish oneself for frivolous identifications with other beings is foolish. But cruelly inflicted pain is in reality so bad that Montaigne seems to think that people are *properly* moved by it.

Two points may be drawn from this comparison of Montaigne's and the later thinkers' arguments for pity. First, historians of the history of secular accounts of compassion and pity, of which there are many, totally and unjustly omit Montaigne from their accounts.[31] In searching for the origins of this movement, scholars have focused either on the third Earl of Shaftesbury, a student of Locke's, or have seen these arguments emerge out of seventeenth-century latitudinarianism.[32] However, as we have seen, a century before the supposed origins of this movement, Montaigne said many of the same things. Indeed, despite their universalistic pretensions, the later thinkers acknowledge many of the limitations on sympathy that Montaigne articulates. For example, all recognized, like Montaigne, that such feelings can be eclipsed by habit.[33] Even Shaftesbury, who believed that a moral sense exists by nature, argues that "nothing beside contrary Habit or Custom (a second Nature) is able to displace" it, and by habit he, like Montaigne, includes customs, education, political institutions, and religion.[34] Like Montaigne, all of these thinkers considered denaturing habits to be among the greatest evil for humankind. (The British thinkers acknowledge this analytically; Rousseau, like Montaigne, also powerfully portrays it.) Moreover, some of the later thinkers accepted another key point of Montaigne's, that sentiments are only properly felt when an individual is centered in himself, "at home." For example, Smith argues that sympathy works only when feelings are "brought home to ourselves, when we have thus adopted and made them our own." Only in this case, he says, do "we then shudder at the thought of what he [the victim] feels."[35] In another passage, Smith describes his normative "natural and ordinary state of mankind" as including three things: health, lack of debt, and clear conscience.[36] The first and third are very characteristic of Montaigne; the second might be expected from the author of *The Wealth of Nations*.

Second, and more important for our purposes, Montaigne's arguments for pity are more philosophically compelling—and give us more to work with—than both of the extreme positions. On the one hand, the idea that pity is universally possessed by all human beings—which the Common Sense philosophers, Rousseau, and sentimental writers emphasize—seems psychologically naive and contradicted by fact. Although these later writers attempt to get around this by acknowledging many of the limits that Montaigne cites, their approach has distinct disadvantages compared to Montaigne's. Because they emphasize the universality of compassion *by nature*, these later thinkers either focus less on the affirmative conditions that must be cultivated in human beings to make compassion a living force—or they deny the need to consider such conditions at all. By contrast, in emphasizing that pity is the result of self-awareness, awareness of one's weaknesses that serves as the basis for the sympathetic connection, Montaigne makes less grandiose claims about the existence of compassion in the world, more realistically attributes it to fewer people, and—most importantly—more sharply focuses on the means of increasing it. On the other hand, Montaigne's thought survives Nietzsche's challenge: his conception of the self gives a way of limiting Nietzsche's indiscriminate will-to-power, which itself cannot *in principle* limit cruelty against anyone. Montaigne sees compassion not as a form of self-denial, as Nietzsche argued, but as a natural result of self-knowledge.

In conclusion, Montaigne's understanding of both cruelty and pity is rooted in his conception of a self-knowing self, aware of its weaknesses and vulnerabilities. Only by straying or abstracting from one's own condition, according to Montaigne, can one be insensitive to another's. One's inner feeling of weakness and vulnerability leads to empathy for one's fellows' self-essaying. A self-knowing person will feel horror at the thought of a self being dispossessed of itself. If one wants to fight against cruelty and to promote compassion, one ought to advocate the essaying process that Montaigne, in an unrivaled manner, advocates and embodies.

II. The Worldly Allures to Intolerance:
Wealth, Power, and Glory

Not only does Montaigne's positive vision of the self foster toleration by promoting compassion and condemning cruelty in a manner consistent with and demanded by self-interest, but Montaigne buttresses his call for toleration by compellingly evaluating the main worldly motivations that tempt people to violate others. Montaigne cautions that wealth, power, and glory should be pursued only in moderation, because to seek more would hurt oneself. As a result of this moderation, others are not harmed.

Montaigne's critique of these worldly allures is important for politics and political theorists because of where and how he focuses his attention. For Montaigne, the root cause of exploitation and suffering is not the economic class system, the political regime, nor any other economic, social, or political institution that exists *external* to individual human beings. For Montaigne, the primary problem comes from *within* human beings, from the mind gone astray, which he says then manifests its diseased nature in these socially constructed institutions. Consequently, Montaigne does not focus his energies on attacking these human institutions, but on what he considers to be the root of the problem: the mind run amuck. This is critical, because if Montaigne is correct, all attempts at institutional reform will but treat the symptoms without even attempting a cure. While Montaigne does not think that a permanent or final cure for the unruliness of the human mind is possible, he wants reflective people to focus their main reformist energies on reforming themselves. Thus, Montaigne attempts to undermine the main worldly temptations that lure the self out of itself: wealth, power, and glory. He examines the benefits and costs of each, concluding that there is something good, although only in a limited sense, in each of them—if pursued in moderation. However, he warns that there is something in the nature of these temptations that tends to insinuate itself into an individual's psyche in an unlimited way. Individuals who get swept away by their ambitions to the point that they do not care whether they harm others along the way are likely to squander their opportunities for real happiness and harm themselves. It is to his critiques of these particular temptations that we now turn.

Wealth

What is there, if anything, in Montaigne's thought that prevents his hedonism from degenerating into a base materialism? In the first place, Montaigne's emphasis on the body is limited by his equal emphasis on the mind; the good of sensual pleasure is limited by the good of mental tranquility. Thus, Montaigne repeatedly condemns all desires that seize the soul with any sort of feverishness or rapaciousness. In agreement with almost all ancient, Hellenistic, and medieval thinkers, Montaigne deplores feverish and rapacious desires that dominate one's soul. In such states, the desires control the man and not the other way around. "It is right that things should touch us," according to Montaigne, "provided they do not possess us" (III.10, 980 [766]). Therefore he would reject Machiavelli's postulate about the never-ending need for acquisition and Hobbes' notion that happiness is the continual satisfaction of desire after desire that ceases only in death.[37] Montaigne would concede that many people live as Hobbes describes, but he considers such a life a sign of a "sick and disordered grasp" (I.53, 297 [225]). He considers unlimited desires "irresolute and uncertain" and says such a person "does not know how to keep anything or enjoy anything in the right way" (I.53, 297 [225]).[38] Rather, we should be like the animals and the Cannibals, or more properly, like Aristotle and Lucretius, desiring in proportion to our nature, not what Hobbes dismisses as "the repose of a mind satisfied"—i.e., sated—but the tranquility of a mind without anxiety and fear.[39] Sensual pleasure and voluptuousness are good for man, but, as we saw in chapter 3, they must be circumscribed by one key limit: the need of the mind to be tranquil and calm. Pleasures consistent with that limit may be heartily pursued, but Montaigne rejects Hobbesian or bourgeois grasping.[40]

This moderate and balanced conception of the self leads to Montaigne's criticism of a crude capitalism, thus combating the kinds of commercial ambition that might lead to exploitation in the feverish pursuit of wealth. Individuals who get swept away by feverish desires might not care if they harm others in the pursuit of their goals. Montaigne does not argue against such pursuits because feverish people will hurt others. Rather, Montaigne attacks their goals, arguing that such people are likely to squander their own opportunities for real happiness and harm themselves.

Montaigne does not criticize wealth *per se*, provided that it is used wisely and does not consume its possessor. He praises moderate and regulated wealth and those who enjoy its benefits "moderately and liberally" as opposed to either ascetics, who enjoy it too little, and the avaricious, who desire it too much (I.39, 238 [179]).[41] But if wealth itself is neither simply good nor simply bad, "the danger," according to Montaigne, "lay in the fact that one cannot easily set fixed limits to this desire" for it (I.14, 65 [45]). Unlike those who argue that the acquisition of material goods (when one is able to acquire) should be pursued without limit,[42] Montaigne warns that the desire to obtain wealth can make one "a slave to [one's] affairs, or still worse, to those of others, as so many people are for the sake of money" (III.9, 931 [728]). Interestingly, Montaigne says that this is particularly true of the wealthy, for in his opinion it is harder to keep money than to make it. He laments the wealthy who "go on ever fattening this pile and increasing it with one sum after another, until we deprive ourselves sordidly of the enjoyment of our own possessions and place our only joy in keeping them and not using them. . . . Every rich man is avaricious, in my opinion" (I.14, 65-66 [45]).[43]

Montaigne does not advocate surrendering one's wealth but finding the proper conditions that make it useful and pleasant—which are limited. Wealth can take care of immediate bodily needs, but since the possession of it is so uncertain, Montaigne fears that concern for it can disturb one's mental tranquility—without which one cannot enjoy its benefits. Thus, rather than organizing one's life around the pursuit of material wealth, whether it be through commercial enterprise or political means, Montaigne thinks that one should organize oneself to make due with easily attained and moderate resources: "Happy the man who has regulated his needs in such just measure that his wealth can satisfy them without his care and trouble and without the spending or acquiring of it interrupting his pursuit of other occupations better suited to him, more tranquil, and more congenial" (I.14, 67 [46]). Detachment from wealth is necessary. If one uses it to serve one's own pleasures, it is fine. However, if concern for wealth dominates one's soul, one can hardly be said to be happy no matter how much or little one has. "Thus ease and indigence depend on each man's opinion. . . . Each man is as well or as badly off as he thinks he is. Not the man of whom it is thought, but the one who thinks it of himself, is happy. And by just this fact belief gains reality and truth" (I.14, 67 [46]). While possessing such an opinion about oneself might not ultimately be sufficient for happiness—it may not be for ideologues, the starving, or those being tortured on the rack—neither is it necessary to take on the burdens of an empire. To be enjoyed, wealth must be accompanied by self-knowledge and self-regulation, but since these activities enable one to be happy without wealth, why dedicate one's life to moneymaking?

Montaigne agrees with the often-made objection that one can never have too much wealth, but he turns this objection against the conclusion that is ordinarily drawn from it. For example, Machiavelli says that "it is a very natural and ordinary thing to desire to acquire, and always, when men do it who can, they will be praised or not blamed."[44] Not only does this reject the idea of "too much," but the further argument is made that one must continually acquire more or risk losing what one already has. Montaigne refuses to enter this line of thinking and being: "I have no sort of concern with acquiring" (III.12, 1021 [799]). While this might seem easy for an aristocrat to say, Montaigne's point is that human beings can be happy with middling wealth. "I live from day to day," he says, "and content myself with having enough to meet my present and ordinary needs; for the extraordinary, all the provision in the world could not suffice" (I.14, 66 [45]). Once one starts planning for every kind of dire emergency, one runs the risk of slipping into an unlimited feverishness. There is no need—and much harm—in living a life feverishly pursuing wealth. Thus, while Marx and other community-minded thinkers try to persuade people to alter their behavior regarding an excessive and individualistic attachment to wealth based on the harms done to others, Montaigne achieves the same end by emphasizing the harm done to oneself.

Power

Just as Montaigne's emphasis on self-interest might be thought to harm others by enticing individuals to the unlimited pursuit of lucre, so too might it be thought to harm others by enticing people toward the unlimited acquisition of power. Although Montaigne's most systematic critique of political power, "Of the Disadvantage of Greatness" (III.7), begins with a jest of envy—"Since we cannot attain it, let us take our revenge by speaking ill of it" (III.7, 894 [699])—Montaigne's criticisms of "greatness" amount to a deadly serious indictment of political ambition.

If Montaigne is to argue against the acquisition of power and stay true to his emphasis on self-interest, he needs to show that one is harmed by pursuing and possessing power. Possessing power is not always bad, according to Montaigne. Citizenship and proper political participation can be a wonderful thing according to the Montaigne who speaks of "the finest science there is, namely, the science of obeying and commanding" (I.25, 143 [105]), but this balanced type of citizenship is not what is desired by the politically ambitious. The ambitious are "eager to get out from under command, under some pretext, and to usurp mastery" (I.17, 73 [51]). Although Montaigne sometimes characterizes all human beings as ambitious, asserting that "each man" has some degree of it within himself (I.17, 73 [51]), he primarily condemns only the unruly few, such as the religious leaders of his own time, who act on it in a major way (II.12, 420 [323]). In either case, he clearly dislikes how ambition manifests itself in politics: "I have a distaste for mastery, both active and passive" (III.7, 896 [700]). Nonetheless, Montaigne shows sympathy for rulers. "The toughest and most difficult occupation in the world, in my opinion, is to play the part of a king worthily. I excuse more of their faults than people commonly do, in consideration of the dreadful weight of their burden, which dazes me. It is difficult for a power so immoderate to observe moderation" (III.7, 896 [700]). Montaigne also recognizes that there is a certain pleasure in ruling: "There is a certain satisfaction in being in command, were it only of a barn, and in being obeyed by one's people." However, he rejects it as "too monotonous and languid a pleasure. And then it is necessarily mingled with many bothersome thoughts" (III.9, 925 [723]). A formal restriction on the king's possessions has to do with the distinction between the man and the office: "to be precise about it," Montaigne writes, "a king has nothing that is properly his own" (III.6, 881 [688-89]). Such technical arguments, however, are unlikely to deter an ambitious person. After all, even if a king's possessions are not formally his own, he still gets to enjoy them. However, Montaigne also argues that kingship not only entails constant security risks (as we saw in our discussion of tyranny above), but, more importantly, that the price of ruling jeopardizes one's very self, because a ruler "owes his very self to others" (III.6, 881 [689]). To stay true to his emphasis on self-interest, Montaigne needs to show that the ambitious are harmed by realizing their political ambitions.

Accordingly, Montaigne argues that the benefits of ruling are outweighed by its costs. Power does have some real benefits, according to Montaigne: it can ease one's tasks in life, supply the means to satisfy one's desires, and offer a certain amount of freedom.[45] But when power is ambitiously pursued, Montaigne thinks it aggravates, instead of lessens, one's burdens. The price that is attached to its benefits is too high to bear. Power attracts an annoying crowd of flatterers who get in one's way wherever one turns. The tremendous psychological pressure ruling brings to bear on the prince is sure to disturb his tranquility. Deciding questions of war and peace, life and death, is weighty, indeed. And even with the strongest kingdom in the world, power can do little to alleviate life's annoyances. For example, it cannot cure a fever or a migraine or help one deal with jealousy, old age, or death.[46] Not only can power not assure health, tranquility, or happiness, but political ambition delays and possibly prevents their attainment. To illustrate this point, Montaigne tells of King Pyrrhus, who when asked while on a campaign in Italy what he would do after conquering the land, replied that he would then conquer Gaul and Spain and Africa. And when his "wise counselor, wanting to make him feel the vanity of his ambition," asked what he would do after having subdued the whole world, he replied: "I shall rest and live content and at my ease." To this the counselor retorts: "In God's name Sire, tell me what keeps you from being in that condition right now, if that is what you want. Why don't you settle down at this very moment in the state you say you aspire to, and spare yourself all the intervening toil and risks?" What was preventing the king from enjoying this repose on that very day, or before he set out on his campaign? Montaigne answers these questions with a quotation from Lucretius: "Because he does not know the bounds of gain/And where true pleasure stops, and starts to wane" (I.42, 259 [196]). It is for this reason that Montaigne concludes: "The advantages of princes are *quasi-imaginary advantages*"; "All the real advantages that princes have are shared by men of moderate fortune" (I.42, 257 [194] and 258 [195], emphasis added).

Moreover, Montaigne argues that there are other real goods that are necessarily denied to an all-powerful ruler. The ruler is "deprived of all mutual friendship and society, wherein consists the sweetest and most perfect fruit of human life," because friendship cannot form "where there is so little relation and correspondence" (I.42, 258 [195]). The very power and heights of ruling place the ruler "outside of human association: there is too much disparity and disproportion" (I.42, 258 [195]). People humor, flatter, and generally just follow all-powerful rulers; they dare not risk offending power, so they tell it whatever they think it wants to hear and allow kings to triumph in every trifle. It is because of this that Montaigne relates a philosopher's jest that kings learn only how to ride horses, because while human beings continually defer to a prince, a horse will just as soon throw the son of a king as the son of a footman.[47]

> It is a pity to have so much power that everything gives way to you. Your fortune repels society and companionship too far from you; it plants you too far apart. That ease and slack facility of making everything bow beneath you is the enemy of every kind of pleasure. That is sliding, not walking; sleeping, not living. Imagine man accompanied by omnipotence: he is sunk; he must ask you for hindrance and resistance, as an alms; his being and his welfare are in indigence.
>
> Their good qualities are dead and wasted, for these are felt only by comparison, and they are out of comparison. (III.7, 897-98 [701-2])

In short, Montaigne summarizes the plight of the ruler as follows: "There is perhaps nothing more pleasant in association with men than the trials [*essais*] of strength we have with one another, in rivalry of honor and worth, whether in exercises of the body or of the mind; and in these sovereigns have no real share" (III.7, 896-97 [701]); "Their royal status stifles and consumes their other real and essential qualities; these are sunk in royalty. . . . It takes so much to be a king that he exists only as such" (III.7, 898 [702]).

Glory

Glory, the illusive charm for which men risk so much, is the other major motive that drives human beings to violate others, and Montaigne offers a systematic critique of it, too. Montaigne says that it is the pursuit of glory, not wealth or power, that the ambitious primarily seek; if King Pyrrhus had answered his counselor truthfully, it is likely that he would have confessed this as his true motive. Montaigne sees the quest for glory as an omnipresent and powerful force in human affairs: "Of all the illusions in the world," he says, "the most universally received is the concern for reputation and glory" (I.41, 248 [187]); "it has such live roots in us that I do not know whether anyone yet has ever been able to get clean rid of it. . . . For as Cicero says, even those who combat it still want the books that they write about it to bear their name on the title page, and want to become glorious for having despised glory," a charge that could be leveled against Montaigne himself (I.41, 248-49 [187]). Despite the omnipresence of the desire for glory among men, Montaigne does not find it to be one of man's more glorious attributes.

Montaigne produces a withering attack on glory. Glory itself, he says, has no real advantages. He agrees with those philosophers who argued that "all the glory in the world did not deserve that a man of understanding should so much as stretch out his finger to acquire it" (II.16, 602 [469]). He admits that glory has some incidental advantages, such as gaining one goodwill, making one less exposed to insults, and the like (II.16, 602 [469]), but glory itself he considers to be worthless because it depends on fortune, not virtue. Montaigne's main weapon in undermining the attractiveness of glory is to undermine its allure. Although Montaigne once says that fortune is made by character (I.50, 290 [220]), this statement relates to one's self-control. Montaigne does not think that one can ever fully control the outcome of events, let alone great events like politics or war. Human beings do not have enough information or knowledge to control grand events fully. He makes this clear with respect to politics: "The preservation of states is a thing that probably surpasses our understanding" (III.9, 937 [732]). Similarly, with respect to war, he argues: "It is unwise to think that human wisdom can fill the role of Fortune. And vain is the undertaking of him who presumes to embrace both causes and consequences and to lead by the hand the progress of his affair—vain especially in the deliberations of war" (III.8, 912 [713]). The *Essays* is full of stories of defeated virtue and triumphant luck. For Montaigne there is an inner integrity, an inner self, and it is more important and satisfying to essay it than it is to achieve any particular external "victory." Montaigne is concerned less with winning or losing a fight than with how one fights. If someone is beaten by fraud, "he is beaten not by us, but by fortune; he is killed, not conquered" (I.31, 210 [157]). Properly speaking, Montaigne thinks that "only that man considers himself overcome who knows he was downed neither by trick nor by luck but by valiance, man to man, in a fair and just war" (I.5, 27 [16]). In general, Montaigne seems to share this sentiment with the Roman poet, Quintus Curtius: "I would rather be sorry for my fortune than ashamed of my victory" (I.6, 31 [19]). Montaigne uses some of Machiavelli's slogans—we should "know how to arm ourselves" and gain "some foothold against Fortune"—but he interprets them in radically different ways (III.12, 1022 [799] and 1024 [801]). In Montaigne's mouth, each of these phrases means acquiring self-knowledge and self-control to gain the inner strength and wisdom to avoid and withstand misfortune. This is the only real control one has, according to Montaigne. To attempt to gain glory is to throw oneself into the winds of fortune.[48]

Montaigne further attempts to undercut the allure of glory by emphasizing its dependence on chance. In an essay entitled "Of Glory" (II.16), he argues this in numerous, interlocking ways. First, glory depends on appearance. The deeds that are glorified are based on the perception of those deeds, not on the deeds themselves. The observer can never know the actor's true motives or state of mind. Thus, cowards can later claim or be described as having acted with courage. Second, the story that is told has to please a huge audience, which by its very nature is not a good judge. Thus, to achieve glory, one has to appeal to, and be lauded by, vulgar sentiments. The greatest deeds can go unheralded, while lesser deeds are trumpeted because they are comprehensible to many. Third, great individual actions happen every day, on every battlefield for example, and are never recognized. Montaigne wonders about the many valiant men who struggled and died in the 1500 years of French history. Not only are the names of leaders forgotten, but the names of whole battles and victories are lost. Fourth, great deeds require a great historian to record them in order to be remembered (and similarly great historians require great deeds about which to write). Even if one acts splendidly, the fate of one's glory is in someone else's hands. Fifth, just as glorious deeds are subject to being forgotten, if one's deeds are recorded, those writings are subject to the same whims of fortune as the original deeds. Montaigne argues that many books which achieve fame do so for trivial and accidental reasons, whereas many splendid commentaries are forgotten, lost, or destroyed. From ancient Greek and Roman times, with so many glorious deeds and so many outstanding writers to record them, how many have survived? Sixth, even if the glorious reputations which have survived the trials and fortunes of time are the best that the West has produced, most of the world, throughout most of human existence, has not recorded its great deeds. Surely, if we had knowledge of those events, the deeds of many famous people would pale by comparison, so glory is based on ignorance, too. Seventh, even if one was lucky enough to have a historian and have the historian's work meet with lasting approval, the fame brings one no benefit when one is dead. "Can it," Montaigne asks, "designate and benefit nothingness?" (II.16, 610 [475]). In short, glory depends as much, if not more, on fortune as on skill, and it brings one no real benefit whether living or dead.[49]

Moreover, Montaigne argues that in the pursuit of glory, just as in the pursuit of wealth and power, the ambitious often sacrifice and risk real, tangible goods. In pursuit of "this fanciful and imaginary life," he asks, "shall we go and lose our real and essential life" (II.16, 612 [476])? Echoing the praise of health that we saw in chapters 1 and 3, Montaigne states:

> Surely my heart is not so inflated or windy that I would choose to exchange a solid, meaty, and marrowy pleasure like health for an imaginary, immaterial, and airy pleasure. Glory, even that of the four sons of Aymon,[50] is bought too dear by a man of my humor if it costs him three good attacks of colic. Health, in God's name! (II.37, 766 [597])

Based on his conception of "our real and essential life," the deed most worthy of praise is living one's life well: "All the glory that I aspire to in my life is to have lived it tranquilly" (II.16, 605 [471]). Unfortunately, Montaigne laments, "Who does not willingly exchange health, rest, and life for reputation and glory, the most useless, worthless, and false coin that is current among us?" (I.39, 236 [178]).

In conclusion, one revealing passage summarizes the logic behind all of Montaigne's critiques of the worldly spurs to persecution: "it has never occurred to me," he says, "to wish for empire or royalty, or for the eminence of those high and commanding fortunes. I do not aim in that direction, I love myself too much" (III.7, 895 [699]). His critiques appeal to nothing other than his conception of self-interest properly understood. Rather than criticizing the pursuits of wealth, power, and glory on the grounds that they hurt others, he repeatedly explains how they jeopardize one's own tranquility and health and destroy the possibility of enjoying the greatest goods that can be gained from other human beings—friendship and discussion. Consistent with the analysis of Montaigne's conception of the self presented in chapter 3, Montaigne rejects "goods" outside of oneself in favor of self-cultivation: "To compose our character is our duty, not to compose books, and to win, not battles and provinces, but order and tranquility in our conduct. Our great and glorious masterpiece is to live appropriately. All other things, ruling, hoarding, building, are only little appendages and props, at most" (III.13, 1088 [850-51]). The so-called worldly goods are but external appendages at best, whereas "[g]reatness of soul," he says, "is not so much pressing upward and forward as knowing how to set oneself in order and circumscribe oneself" (III.13, 1090 [852]). Montaigne thus limits his ambition to what he variously describes as "a middle station" (III.7, 895 [700]), or as "in a lowly way. . . strictly for myself" (III.7, 895 [699]). In making his arguments against the ordinary and ubiquitous human ambitions, Montaigne does not appeal to altruism or virtue but to self-interest. If ambitious human beings better understood their desires, they might change their behavior: "Since we will not do so out of conscience, at least out of ambition let us reject ambition" (III.10, 1001 [783]). By rejecting excessive and misplaced ambitions, Montaigne destroys an individual's worldly motives to persecute and to oppress.

By arguing based solely on self-interest, Montaigne is able to avoid many justificatory problems entailed in views that proceed from a metaphysical basis or that conceive interest and duty as irreconcilable. But given his claim that one's duty is not to compose books, but one's character, why does he write? Either he does not practice what he preaches, i.e., seeks glory, or he thinks he has something to offer, i.e., cares about his fellow human beings. In the preceding paragraph, we saw Montaigne speak of a duty to oneself. Might he conceive of duties towards others? If so, how would these be balanced by his emphasis on self-interest? The next section explores Montaigne's conception of the nature and extent of one's obligations toward others.

III. The Limit of Montaigne's Morality: Self-Essaying and the Obligation to Others

So far we have examined Montaigne's critique of the motives that lead people to take *actions* that hurt others; the next question concerns inaction, which, it is often argued, also hurts others. In situations of persecution, there are not only persecutors and victims, there is also, as the great holocaust historian, Raul Hilberg, points out, another class of people: bystanders.[51] Might the inward orientation that Montaigne encourages prove callous and catastrophic in times of barbarism and cruelty? What, if anything, does Montaigne have to say about those who tolerate intolerance and cruelty? In addition to the self-interested imperative not to inflict cruelty, which we have seen, does Montaigne's understanding of the self demand any affirmative actions to relieve the suffering of others?[52] And if so, what exactly does it compel? And on what grounds does it do so? Must one speak out against cruelty, denouncing those who commit it? Or does one have an even stronger obligation to relieve the suffering of others, either through material aid or through direct personal or political intervention?

Montaigne sometimes speaks of human beings having affirmative obligations. For example, he occasionally speaks of "civic duty" [*obligation civile*] (III.3, 808 [630]), and he once says that man has "some mutual obligation" to all living things, asserting a "general duty of humanity, that attaches us not only to animals, who have life and feeling, but even to trees and plants," claiming that we owe "justice to men, and mercy and kindness to other creatures that may be capable of receiving it" (II.11, 414 [318]). He there implies that mercy and kindness differentiate human beings from the other animals. Those men who tear each other or animals apart, act in accordance with our bestial nature. Human beings, Montaigne there implies, are capable of more, and he wants us to live up to our capabilities. However this may be, he neither constructs whole systems of these obligations, nor does he explore the implications of his stated duties in a rigorous or comprehensive manner. In fact, instead of speaking the language of obligation in general, Montaigne more typically speaks of what is good and honorable for an individual. Even political involvement is presented this way: "I am of the opinion that the most honorable occupation is to serve the public and be useful to many. 'The fruits of genius, virtue, and all excellence are most rewarding when they benefit some neighbor' [Cicero]" (III.9, 929 [727]).

Montaigne rarely speaks of obligations, because he does not believe that universal duties can be specifically stated. He has a moral sensibility—the well educated student, he says, knows how to do everything but chooses only to do the good—but he believes that all obligations are contingent on prudence and judgment. Because the world is so diverse and moral situations so numerous, tricky, and subtly different from each other, Montaigne seeks to cultivate not moral rules but "character and understanding" (I.26, 149 [110]). The key to good character and understanding, as Montaigne presents them in "Of the Education of Children" is judgment: "His education, work, and study aim only at forming this" (I.26, 151 [111]).

He thinks that it is more important for people to be able to make good judgments in all the concrete situations with which they are faced than for them to have general rules to apply mechanically. Montaigne's judgments about obligation are thus limited by necessity and prudence. Animals do not warrant the same obligations as human beings; although he expresses a squeamishness in seeing animals slaughtered, he eats them. But killing them humanely for food is very different from killing them cruelly for sport, as was practiced in the hunt. With respect to obligations toward human beings, it would be derelict not to end gross suffering that is within one's authority to prevent. But Montaigne does not postulate, as nobody does, a moral duty actually to alleviate all the suffering in the world. Such a duty would require living one's whole life for the sake of others, not for oneself, and would have to be pursued with a single-mindedness and feverishness that would keep one outside oneself until death. And since Montaigne believes that suffering could never be totally eliminated, such a moral obligation would doom everyone to feelings of perpetual guilt. (Montaigne clearly rejects such feelings of guilt when he states that "[t]he surest sign of wisdom is constant cheerfulness" I.26, 160 [119].) This does not mean that nothing should be done, it just means that Montaigne is reluctant to state obligations categorically.

Insofar as Montaigne presents himself as a model for emulation, it is instructive to examine what Montaigne actually did to help others. In the first place, Montaigne did speak out about cruelty all over the world. His verbal—and published—condemnations of the horrors of his age are as forceful as those of anyone in his century. For example, his condemnation of the slaughter of the native inhabitants in the New World, all for "trade in pearls and pepper," is more forceful than anyone's except perhaps Las Casas'. His repeated denunciations of the horrors of the civil wars in France, condemning them as worse than cannibalism and as "eating a man alive," and his repeated denunciations of the moral corruption and cruelty of his epoch are also unrivaled. He condemned the Spanish Inquisition, and gives a horribly eloquent account of Portugese "inhumanity" toward the Jews, who were sold refuge by the King of Portugal, only to be "treated roughly and villainously," sailed around on boats until their food ran out so that they were forced to spend every cent they had on exorbitantly priced food, had "all the children under fourteen snatched from the hands of their fathers and mothers, and taken elsewhere to be brought up in our religion," and forced to convert or be enslaved (I.14, 53-54 [35-36]). He also condemned witch burnings and spoke out against the customs—the hunt and dueling—which, as with the amphitheaters in Rome, he deemed to nourish the cruelty of his age.

Not only did Montaigne speak out against these egregious examples of cruelty, but he also spoke out against its common, everyday embodiment: torture. Torture, the epitome of cruelty, is Montaigne's *bête noire*, and he sought to destroy the two main public defenses of torture: to gain a confession and to set an example. Since torture is sometimes done in the name of the civic good—a justification which might trump the rights of an individual—Montaigne, as we have repeatedly seen, does not want to appeal to moral outrage alone, so he emphasizes its inutility to the torturer. He argues that confessions under torture are meaningless:

> Tortures are a dangerous invention, and seem to be a test of endurance rather than of truth. Both the man who can endure them and the man who cannot endure them conceal the truth. For why shall pain rather make me confess what is, than force me to say what is not? And on the other hand, if the man who has not done what he is accused of is patient enough to endure these torments, why shall the man who has done it not be also, when so fair a reward as life is set before him? (II.5, 348-49 [266])

And unlike Machiavelli, who advocates a spectacular execution at least every ten years (of the guilty or innocent) in order to keep people in line and focused on their duties,[53] Montaigne condemns tortures done for the sake of public display, "to keep the people at their duty," as unnecessary. He thinks it serves as a sufficiently powerful deterrent to allow brutal public demonstrations against a corpse: "For to see them [corpses] deprived of burial, to see them boiled and quartered, would affect the common people just about as much as the punishments they make the living suffer, although in reality it is little or nothing" (II.11, 411[315]). Similarly, he tells how when a notorious criminal was strangled to death the crowd hardly showed any emotion, but when the body was then quartered, the people followed every blow "with a plaintive cry and exclamation, as if everyone had lent his feeling to that carcass" (II.11, 411 [315]). Thus, there is no good rationale for cruelties against the living, especially not for reasons of piety. Speaking out against them, even at the risk of angering the authorities—as Montaigne's condemnation of torture did the Papal Censors in Rome—is consistent with the compassion and humanity that he advocates.

In addition to condemning cruelty verbally, Montaigne makes clear general guidelines about what greater actions his thought requires. Obligations depend on a whole host of factors, such as who is suffering, how much, and on the risks involved in helping out. He clearly argues that compassion should be applied at home first. We have seen Montaigne urging people to be more compassionate toward themselves, to have a more relaxed attitude toward their own bodies and to accept and explore their quirks and idiosyncracies. Montaigne works from this core principle outward. A true friend, by Montaigne's definition, is like another self, so one would venture for him everything one would venture for oneself. Although Montaigne notes that family connections are much more liable to being counteracted by contrary passions and interests than are true friendships, he nonetheless recognizes a general tendency of family members, especially parents toward children, to help each other. Accordingly, if no one harmed others and everyone took care of his or her circle at home, much of the suffering in the world would be eliminated. Beyond the circle of those nearest and dearest, Montaigne feels more of an obligation to those with whom he feels particular bonds. For example, he wrote about a "great shame for our century, that under our very eyes two personages most outstanding in learning have died so poor that they had not enough to eat: Lilius Gregorius Giraldus in Italy and Sebastianus Castalio in Germany" (I.35, 220 [165]).[54] Montaigne does not feel as intense a bond to all the world's poor, nor does he speak of caring for such people as a moral obligation; to him it is a charitable burden that he is willing to assume. Also, everything else being equal, Montaigne seems to feel a greater obligation to his fellow citizens, who might more readily share similar likes and dislikes and whose fates are more intimately linked with his, than to people of another country or culture. Indeed, although Montaigne discusses cultures, politics, and suffering all over the globe and throughout recorded history, he often relates them back to the policies and practices of France.

Montaigne is sensible to the fact that all people everywhere are equally human and share the same human condition, but one's obligations depend on how viscerally one feels the suffering of others and the resources at one's disposal to eliminate it. Individuals are right, he thinks, to spend more resources to protect their friends and family than to protect a stranger on the other side of the world. This is the nature of human attachment and how compassion works. Not to take special care of one's own is inhuman. According to Montaigne, one's duties toward others also depends on the personal risks involved. What risks would one be obligated to assume to help those with whom one has no intimate connection? Losing a business opportunity is not the same as risking the wrath of a cruel tyrant. And while Montaigne thinks that all people "at home" will feel the need to act humanely, since different people have different dispositions, he thinks it right that they act differently. Some people can handle, indeed might thrive on, more risk. Others might collapse under the same strain. In the end, each individual must know himself or herself, have a sense of empathy with all other human beings based on an awareness of oneself, and act both properly and prudently.

We have seen Montaigne's condemnation of do-gooders who want to rearrange the world; instead, he advocates decent action that will bring about long-term change. Not to end a cruelty that is in one's legitimate authority to stop, such as the use of torture by judges seeking a confession, is condemnable (II.5, 348-49 [266]). Accordingly, Montaigne tells us that as a magistrate, he was often less harsh on criminals than the law allowed. But Montaigne's visceral horror at cruelty aside, his sense of obligation to others is also partially relative to the place and times. Montaigne writes that one must treat one's servants humanely, but he does not suggest that the class system that upholds his privileges should be overturned. It is good to help the cleaning woman in one's office in her time of distress; one need not solve the civil war from which her family took flight. Similarly, in the context of a discussion of lawyers and financiers, he states: "An honest man is not accountable for the vice and stupidity of his trade, and should not therefore refuse to practice it: it is the custom of his country, and there is profit in it. We must live in the world and make the most of it such as we find it" (III.10, 989 [774]). This is related to specific jobs, and does not imply that Montaigne thinks every custom must be accepted. Indeed, Montaigne says that "we must not ignore the knavery there is in such callings" (III.10, 989 [774]). Even a prince, who is justified in doing ugly deeds for the common good, should feel bad about doing them, according to Montaigne. So Montaigne's acquiescence to general cultural norms is balanced by a demand for people to recognize the injustice of the practices in which they partake. Montaigne's acceptance of social injustice is far from a revolutionary's demand to eliminate such practices immediately.

One encounters the limits of Montaigne's sense of obligation when one comes to the oppressed and downtrodden that exist in every society. Montaigne's emphasis on self-seeking without an affirmative program for political or social liberation might seem to cement them in their misery, and there is a certain amount of truth in this charge. Although, as we have seen, Montaigne expresses empathy for the "little people" (III.13, 1079 [844]), he is not particularly sensitive to the ordinary indignities that result from social or economic class. He considers them inevitable—and not alarming—evils. Everyone, even aristocrats such as himself, has to put up with social indignities and economic inconveniences, so he adopts a stoic attitude toward them, focusing only on rooting out specific egregious violations instead of working to overthrow the system that produced them. He deems these ordinary indignities and deprivations to be bearable and not worth risking the anarchy and horrors that accompany revolutions. He is fully aware, however, that his vision of sophisticated simplicity is insufficient for those in dire circumstances: the starving (as opposed to the ordinary poor), those on the rack, or those in slavery, for example. When the body continually suffers or is violated, one's tranquility is disturbed and one cannot rest at home. This is fully acknowledged in Montaigne's celebration of both the mental and corporeal aspects of human existence. By Montaigne's own criteria, revolt would seem to be justified under these circumstances. Unlike Marx, however, he does not explicitly advocate it. And unlike Locke, he does not even systematically articulate when revolution is justifiable.

Montaigne's silence on the question of legitimate revolutions admits of many possible interpretations. On the one hand, it could be said that his own class background makes him indifferent to a fate that he will not have to endure. A more poignant consequence of his class background and interests, however, is that he speak less to the unjustly oppressed than to the would-be oppressors, his peers. If this seems unfeeling, it is also what makes his thought so useful for us today who individually have all sorts of power (weapons, wealth, political rights, etc.) but who lack a theoretical justification as to why it should not be used for ill. On the other hand, it could be said that Montaigne does, if unsystematically, show the grounds on which revolution would be justifiable—the violation of oneself, family, or friends. Moreover, Montaigne was not unaware of legitimate grounds for revolution in his own times; as we have seen, he was going to put a radical call for political revolution, *La Servitude Volontaire*—which expresses exactly the kind of impatience with ordinary injustice that seems lacking in Montaigne—in the center of the first Book of his *Essays*. Since this was written by La Boétie, Montaigne must have shared its sentiments because he says all true friends, as he says he and La Boétie are, are of one mind. Montaigne wrote that he took it out of his book, because it had been published by people with "evil intent, by those who seek to disturb and change the state of our government without worrying whether they will improve it" (I.28, 193 [144]). So in the end we return to prudence. Montaigne's appreciation of the disastrous consequences of revolutions—through which he was living—tempered his call for, and blanketed his interest in, revolution. Thus, instead of appealing to the downtrodden masses, he appealed to the self-interest of the powerful, to take prudent actions that would bring them stability and power, while simultaneously relieving the burdens on everyone else.[55] Reform—individual, philosophical, and political—not revolution, is the prudent path. For Montaigne, having a dialogue within oneself leads to decent behavior, and it holds open the possibility of social reformation by carrying that dialogue into one's professional and other public roles. Such reformation based on the reflection of participants is, according to Montaigne, a more solid foundation for promoting change than is revolutionary upheaval.

In the end, Montaigne cannot establish any definitive list of moral obligations to others, but what moral system can? Even Christianity and Judaism, the Western moral systems that preach the most compassion, recognize that prudence must be factored into moral calculations, which is why they have traditions of unending commentary on their seemingly simple rules. This is required to make them applicable to the array of circumstances in human life. Nonetheless, Montaigne does not even begin with simple precepts, such as the Ten Commandments. In the absence of a God to which he can appeal to justify such moral obligations, Montaigne grounds a sense of duty in the essaying of oneself. Indeed, for Montaigne healthy participation in the world requires an individual to be healthy "at home," and he calls this achievement "the summit of human wisdom and of our happiness" (III.10, 984 [769]). "This man [someone at home]," he says, "knowing exactly what he owes to himself, finds it in his part that he is to apply to himself his experiences of other men and of the world, and, in order to do so, contribute to public society the duties and services within his province. He who lives not at all unto others, hardly lives unto himself. 'He who is a friend to himself, know that that man is a friend to all' [Seneca]" (III.10, 984 [769]). It is this rootedness in oneself that allows one, even impels one, to think of others. Readers might not be satisfied with Montaigne's lack of enumeration of social obligations—to the economic poor, to social inferiors, or to the politically disenfranchised—but two things must be noted. First, Montaigne spells out the ground on which all obligations rest: a healthy sense of the self. Indeed, a list of rules in the hands of those who are not at home within themselves is not only useless, but it can be dangerous; how much cruelty has resulted from the perverse application of humane "duties"? Second, instead of obligating people to all the duties that one could imagine, duties that would be tenuous at best, Montaigne's conception of the self obligates individuals against the most egregious horrors that human beings commit. But more importantly, Montaigne articulates a basis on which to ground decent human behavior without appealing to metaphysics or custom, which is much more than can be said for most of the theoretical visions advanced today.

IV. Conclusion: Montaigne's Arguments in
Contemporary Context

Not only was Montaigne's justification for toleration unique in the sixteenth century, but it has hardly been paralleled since. Arguing for toleration without a liberal tradition to which he could appeal, he offers a justification that is singularly insightful. Not only does Montaigne argue, as we saw in earlier chapters, against the *metaphysical* spurs to intolerance, but he also argues against its main *worldly* spurs. Taken together, these two complementary arguments undermine most of the motives to persecute others—and avoid many of the pitfalls of later justifications of toleration.

The most striking—and in my opinion the most valuable—feature of Montaigne's politics of the good life is that he argues for toleration and the creation of a private sphere by appealing only to self-interest (as he understands it, of course). Unlike Christian morality or the philosophic views of Kant, for example, which assume a conflict between interest and duty, Montaigne conceives a world in which toleration and properly understood worldly interests are not at odds with each other. Unlike the hard-headed liberals, Montaigne sees toleration as more than a necessary pragmatic tradeoff. Montaigne's vision unites toleration and self-interest in a strong and organic manner; based on his rich and appealing conception of the self, self-interest is not only compatible with toleration, self-interest demands it. Few other arguments for toleration—before or since Montaigne's times—have attempted to link toleration and self-interest so tightly or organically.

While each of the more familiar later arguments for toleration solves one sort of problem or another, Montaigne anticipated and incorporated aspects of all of them, combining them in a uniquely compelling manner around his skepticism and his conception of the self. While his views, of course, can always be rejected simply as false, they have many attractive attributes that avoid several of the pitfalls of today's justifications. The most celebrated argument for toleration is the traditional view, attributed to Locke and embodied in the United States' Declaration of Independence, that toleration is based on natural or divine rights, but today these rights are not self-evident to philosophers and proving their existence is problematic, to say the least. Montaigne rejects metaphysical accounts of rights as unknowable and unverifiable by human beings. In this way, he anticipates the historicist critiques of Hegel, Marx, Nietzsche, and their followers. But unlike the historicists, Montaigne finds it easy to imagine that such doctrines were not offered simply and naively as "true" by their proponents. He argues that most philosophers have proffered doctrines in which they did not believe as a means to secure stability and tranquility for their societies. Thus, unlike the historicists who smugly assume a position of intellectual superiority towards such accounts of morality, I think Montaigne would be loathe to dismiss these natural rights views simply because he deemed them untrue. Rather, since he, like Plato, believes that all societies have customs and need myths to knit them together, he would not crusade against the traditional natural rights justification but would try to uphold it if he thought it was beneficial in effect. Wise men support such doctrines, he argues, not because they are true, but because they are useful.

To the extent that any thinker rejects metaphysics, however, toleration and moral behavior can be philosophically justified by appealing only to worldly considerations, and here we see Montaigne's arguments shine when compared to the main theories proffered today. For example, Montaigne's arguments for toleration are broader and deeper than the "political" arguments of Rawl and Rorty. Like Montaigne, Rawls appeals to critical reflection and individual intuitions, but since his is "a moral conception worked out for a specific kind of subject [and] . . . is framed to apply to what I have called the 'basic structure' of a modern constitutional democracy,"[56] it only "is intended as a political conception of justice for a democratic society, it tries to draw solely upon basic intuitive ideas that are embedded in the political institutions of a constitutional democratic regime and the public traditions of their interpretation."[57] In other words, by appealing to the intuitions of late-twentieth-century liberal democrats, Rawls assumes the validity of the philosophical conceptions that they share. The prudential and pragmatic strand of Montaigne might be content with such a political project, but Montaigne also thinks it important to articulate and defend the underlying suppositions, at least for the intellectual elites. Because Rawls limits the scope of his inquiry so drastically, he has little to say to Nietzsche's profound challenge—or other challenges—to liberal democracy. In fairness to Rawls, this is not his project. He merely wants to help explain turn-of-the-century liberal democrats to themselves. But this means that Rawls offers little help in justifying the deeper ground of toleration. Rawls himself writes, "We collect such settled convictions as the belief in religious toleration and the rejection of slavery and try to organize the basic ideas and principles implicit in these convictions."[58] Far from justifying toleration and decent moral behavior in themselves, Rawls says that "We can regard these convictions as provisional fixed points."[59] Unlike Montaigne, Rawls does not appeal to people with radically illiberal views or attempt to ground Western moral impulses in anything outside of or beyond its tradition. Rawls' aim of pragmatically solving *political* conflict within our society is admirable, but his *philosophical* views are insufficient in taking up Nietzsche's challenge or in dealing with the crisis of authority that has been plaguing Western philosophy since the close of the nineteenth century.

Similarly, Rorty's pragmatism suffers when compared to Montaigne's. Although both of Rorty's criteria for judging institutions—his pragmatic conception of what "works" and the prevention of cruelty—echo (or are derived indirectly from)Montaigne,[60] these arguments alone are insufficient. Pragmatism must be aware and take heed of the ideas and customs that underlie the political institutions and philosophical ideas that it seeks to reform. To the extent that Rorty defends democracy (the political system of his time), Montaigne would approve; but to the extent that he so straightforwardly attacks the traditional grounds for it, Montaigne might disapprove. Montaigne himself attacks the traditional grounds of monarchy and religion, but not as utterly transparently as Rorty dismisses the idea of natural rights. Insofar as Montaigne shares Bunel's fears about the political consequences on the masses of Luther's innovations, he would deem the Deweyian belief in publicly acknowledged political and philosophical reconstruction as a slippery and naively dangerous slope. At the same time as offering the masses too much, Rorty offers the intellectual elite too little. In daring to undermine the traditional justifications of his own society, Montaigne thinks it critical to offer more reflective individuals another ground for tolerant behavior—and he does. By contrast, Rorty wants to dismiss all philosophical justifications for moral behavior, explicitly eliminating theories such as those based on Montaigne's conception of the self: "For purposes of social theory, we can put aside such topics as an ahistorical human nature, the nature of selfhood, the motive of moral behavior, and the meaning of life. We treat these as irrelevant to politics as Jefferson thought questions about the Trinity and about transubstantia-tion."[61] This is a political and philosophical mistake. Deeper philosophical justification, if only for elites, is needed. Montaigne supports institutions based on two kinds of arguments: his distrust of change and their ability to protect and promote a private sphere for self-cultivation. Montaigne's conservatism and his deeper ground, based on the self, however, would both be rejected by Rorty, who is no conservative and who wants to bracket off Montaigne's deeper justification for liberalism—the self—from political consideration. This might prove acceptable to Montaigne if Rorty had an alternative ground for his preference, but since he does not, and does not feel the need to offer one, Montaigne would, rightly I believe, reject this kind of argumentation as willfully ignorant. This kind of philosophical Pyrrhonism is overly and unnecessarily mute. More can be known—and needs to be articulated—than Rorty allows. Without it, nothing can be said to Nietzsche's challenge. Montaigne allows us to speak where Rorty does not.

Montaigne shares with several postmodern thinkers their seeming desire for toleration so that authentic self-fashioning might take place, but he defends this in a way that they do not and cannot. Montaigne agrees with their playful and profound concerns for the self, with their insights about the intractable difficulties of knowing oneself, that the self is not "one" in any simple sense, and with the postmodern claim that metaphysical visions tend to unnecessarily limit and cramp the self. This is why Montaigne has been so embraced by Lacan, Lyotard, and Derrida. However, the postmodern thinkers who argue this today cannot answer Nietzsche and Dostoyevsky's challenge; if nothing is true, why isn't everything permitted? Far from encouraging cruelty or the violation of others, postmodern thinkers condemn it—but they cannot ground this condemnation. Based on their own description of the world, this is but a preference and any and every other preference, will, or whim is equally valid; their own egalitarian moral preferences are left unjustified and unjustifiable in the face of a strong inegalitarian critique. Perhaps they consciously refuse to defend their moral sensibilities, believing that if nothing is true, egalitarianism is as justifiable as anything else, but this leaves them vulnerable in principle and without any articulable response to those who, on the same grounds, choose a path of inegalitarianism, intolerance, or cruelty. One suspects that they know that their moral views are indefensible or that they are based on a hidden morality (liberal, Kantian, or Christian) that colors their moral vision. Their moral preferences are not only unjustified by them, but they often stand in contradiction to their explicit hostility toward the very same philosophical and religious traditions that inform them. Montaigne self-consciously addresses this problem that today's postmodernists cannot. To him, a tolerant worldview would be unjustifiable if it was not grounded in his meticulously articulated conception of a knowing but incomplete self whose self-interest requires toleration as a constitutive part of itself.

Finally, we have seen that Montaigne agrees with the hardheaded contractarians that some of one's self-interest (as normally conceived) must be sacrificed to secure the rest. He is in deep and fundamental accord with this prudential calculation. However, his view offers something that Hobbes, Shklar, Berlin, and the others do not. Since the desire-dominated strand of modern thought is assumed by and at the basis of this prudential calculation, every citizen who accepts this worldview is left with an uneasy compromise. They agree to sacrifice some of their good for the sake of securing the rest of it, but it leaves everyone with the temptation—which is unaddressed by this view—that if in the pursuit of one's desires, one could break the law and get away with it, one should. There is nothing outside or inside of oneself to restrain a rapacious appetite, except the fear of getting caught. Montaigne considers this position inherently unstable, and his conception of the good as sophisticated simplicity (as opposed to a more unidimensional conception of it as nothing but the maximization of pleasure or power) removes the allure of such temptations to violate others. Montaigne would consider the more standard liberal accounts of the self to be fundamentally unrooted and unsatisfying to thinking individuals and, insofar as they encourage voracious behavior, a risky basis on which to build a polity. Political rulers should assume such behavior, but thoughtful individuals should be encouraged to seek greater goods.

In short, Montaigne's superiority to all of these views might be summarized as follows. His skepticism and his conception of the self together create a one-two punch for toleration, undermining both its metaphysical and worldly allures. On the one hand, Montaigne's skepticism undermines the convictions that lead to intolerance. He debunks and exposes all metaphysical claims as illusory, unverifiable, or unreal fantasies. They might at times be useful, but they are always human creations or based on human interpretations (unless God has spoken to one directly). Rather than simply attack the epistemological weaknesses of these claims themselves, Montaigne compellingly focuses on the all-too-human fears, anxieties, and cynicism that spur these visions as well as the natural human urges (to find larger meaning in our lives and purpose in the cosmos) that underlie them. It is the awareness of the very weakness of human opinion and the fragility of the human condition that Montaigne says should make us tolerant of the opinions of others: "At least our faulty condition should make us behave more moderately and restrainedly in our changes. We should remember, whatever we receive into our understanding, that we often receive false things there, and by these same tools that are often contradictory and deceived" (II.12, 546-47 [424]). Understanding mankind's so-called divine views as expressions of human need saps the fanaticism out of belief, rendering humility to believers. Montaigne's skepticism about otherworldly claims de-fanaticizes them, leading to more tolerance of different views.

At the same time, Montaigne's substantive view of the human good, which survives his skepticism, removes the worldly allures of exploitation. The good for man, he argues, is the inner calm and delight that results from self-absorbed self-seeking. The best and most pleasing activities concern the real phenomena that human beings have direct access to and which they can therefore best know: the pleasure of the body and the pleasures of knowing the stirrings of one's mind and body. Montaigne thinks these are all human beings can know, so he thinks these are what human beings should try to know. And, as it turns out, Montaigne also thinks that this self-seeking proves to be the most enjoyable and satisfying human activity. And since it can all be done at "home," *chez soi*, an individual has no interest in forcing himself or herself on another. Since the proof of his claims is in experiencing them in oneself, Montaigne writes in his essay style to induce the reader to essay himself. To explore Montaigne, one must simultaneously explore oneself.

Just as important as the wonder and delight that results from the process of self-seeking, is Montaigne's conception of what a genuine human being finds in himself. What a human being finds at the core of the self is everything and nothing—but not a single core or primordial "will." While this lack is, in a certain sense, disappointing, it is disappointing only if one expects cosmic answers. If one is less demanding, more realistic in one's expectations, one can find oneself full of never-ending delights. But the key political implication of this conception is that the self properly understood has no interest in forcing anything on another self—and it has nothing to force.

In short, Montaigne's justification for toleration requires neither metaphysical doctrines of rights nor a reliance on arbitrary traditions, customs, or subjective personal preference. Montaigne's skepticism does not require the self to defer to any factor outside itself, while his conception of the self establishes a self-interest in toleration that allows one to act without being arbitrary. Toleration is grounded not on self-denial but on self-knowledge. Tolerating others and self-interest are united.

As healthy, original, and powerful as it is—we saw numerous and diverse tributes to Montaigne in the Introduction—Montaigne's view of the self did not form the core of liberalism as it was to develop. Nor is it likely to do so in the future. The very genius of Montaigne's conception is its greatest weakness; it is only likely to appeal to the most self-aware of thinkers. Thus, it is unlikely ever to serve as the basis for a whole society. It is unsurprising that less complex visions of the self, the self as materially motivated and desire-driven, came to dominate liberalism; more people act that way and can understand the vision. Montaigne played an important historical role in making the life of the self attractive and thus helped lead the way toward liberalism. He aimed to loosen the human reins and might be disappointed in how his notion of essaying oneself and the world has given way to indiscriminate impulses, but he would have expected as much, at least on the mass scale. Insofar as Montaigne's intention was to tame and persuade that middle class of human beings, the "half breeds" who have seen through the customs of their times without yet discovering wisdom, his thought is particularly timely today. We are half breeds at best. Every society will always be full of zealots and cynics, and the academy is no exception. It is full of half-baked intellectuals who embrace every kind of cockamamie theory or scheme. But since the philosophers of modernity and postmodernity have torn asunder all ground on which to stand, some have been tranquilly floating along (as some always do), others have desperately been swimming for new shore. Montaigne's thought will never serve as a beachhead for a whole society, but it is a sane and tranquil island for those who can scramble up its humane slopes. The ground we seek will not come by throwing philosophy overboard, and Montaigne's sensual philosophy is a welcome harbor from the storm.

Endnotes

Introduction

1. For textual citations to Montaigne's *Essais* I give four numbers. The first Roman numeral joined by a period to an Arabic numeral refers to the book and essay number, respectively. (II.12 thus means book two, essay twelve.) The middle number is the page number in the French Pléiade edition, Montaigne, *Oeuvres complète*, Albert Thibaudet and Maurice Rat, eds., (Paris: Gallimard, 1962). The last number [in brackets] refers to the page number in Donald Frame's English translation, *The Complete Works of Montaigne* (Stanford: Stanford University Press, 1957).

2. Some scholars, such as Donald Frame, deny that Montaigne divides humanity into different types. Or more precisely, Frame argues that Montaigne subscribed to these categories early in his life but came to outgrow them. Frame bases his claim on Pierre Villey's meticulous chronicling of the *Essays*, which dates all of the writing in Montaigne's text. The "A" text was part of the original publication, written between 1572 and 1580. The "B" text includes the major addition from 1580-88. The "C" and final text, published in 1595, posthumously incorporates the changes and additions that Montaigne made in his copy of the *Essays* from 1588 until his death in 1592. Frame's argument in *Montaigne's Discovery of Man: The Humanization of a Humanist* (New York: Columbia University Press, 1955), 3-4 rests on his citation of a single addition to the "C" text that "we are all of the common herd [*le vulgaire*]" (II.12, 554 [429]). However, the passages cited here are from the later "C" and "B" texts, too. Frame, *Montaigne: A Biography* (Harcourt, Brace & World, 1965), 300-2, elaborates unconvincingly on this view, because throughout the years of Montaigne's writing there are both positive and negative remarks on commoners. For slightly different but related divisions of humanity into three kinds of people, see also II.17, 640-41 [498] &

II.10, 396-97 [303-4].

In making this threefold division of humanity, Montaigne echoes a tradition that has existed since antiquity of philosophers who divided the world into "the many" and "the few"; however, Montaigne innovates on this theme in several important ways. These three human types do not represent ineluctable natures for Montaigne, as they do, for example, in Plato's *Republic*. Rather, they represent tendencies or possibilities that are in every human being, even if unequally distributed. Thus, at one time or another, Montaigne puts himself in each of the categories. In the two passages quoted from above, Montaigne puts himself once with the rustics and once with the troublemakers, yet he clearly, as we shall see in chapter 3, sees himself as belonging to the third category. Montaigne is no simpleton despite claims of this plebeian stupidity of mine" (III.10, 997 [780]). Nor does he consider himself to be a troublemaker, except insofar as every human being is. But insofar as Montaigne knows this about himself, he wants to combat it, which is the beginning of wisdom and a sign that he is in the third category. Perhaps especially innovative is Montaigne's emphasis on the "in between nature" of troublemakers. However, Montaigne's greatest originality lies in the ideals that he conjures to represent the well-worn categories of the many and the few. In this book, I label these ideals *habitude naturelle* and sophisticated simplicity, which are the topics of chapters 2 and 3, respectively.

3. This quotation echoes Aristophanes' parody of Socrates in *The Clouds*.

4. Blaise Pascal, "Pensée number 64," in *Pensées de Pascal,* Léon Brunschvicg ed. (Paris: Éditions de Cluny, 1934); "Pensée number 689" (according to Pascal's own text), in *Oeuvres Complètes*, Louis Lafuma, ed. (Paris: Éditions de Seuil, 1963), 591.

5. Nannerl Keohane, *Philosophy and the State in France* (Princeton: Princeton University Press, 1980), 99.

6. Such was the political origin of toleration in the stalemated religious wars in France. See Joseph Lecler, *Toleration and the Reformation*, T. L. Westow, tr. (New York: Association Press, 1960), vol. II: bk. VI; and Henry Kamen, *The Rise of Toleration* (New York: McGraw-Hill, 1967), 129-45. Practitioners of toleration embrace something as their own and reject the thing they tolerate. This should not be confused with an openness that is alive to the possibility that the thing in question, whether it be an idea or practice, may represent some truth or good. Openness delights in different possibilities; toleration, in the strict sense, accepts them only begrudgingly. Intelligent discussions of the definition, grounds, and scope of toleration can be found in the two aforementioned books and in Alan Levine, ed., *Early Modern Skepticism and the Origins of Toleration* (Lanham, Md.: Lexington Books, 1999); René Pintard, *Le Libertinage Érudit* (Paris: Boivin, 1943); Preston King, *Toleration* (New York: St. Martin's, 1976); Susan Mendus, ed., *Justifying Toleration: Conceptual and Historical Perspectives* (Cambridge: Cambridge University Press, 1988), 1-19; and Susan Mendus, *Toleration and the Limits of Liberalism* (Atlantic Highlands, N.J.: Humanities Press International,

1989). Consider also the following recent works: David Heyd, ed., *Toleration: An Elusive Virtue* (Princeton: Princeton University Press, 1996); Michael Walzer, *On Toleration* (New Haven: Yale University Press, 1997); Cary Nederman and John Christian Laursen, eds., *Difference and Dissent: Theories of Tolerance in Medieval and Early Modern Europe* (Lanham, Md.: Rowman & Littlefield, 1997); Laursen and Nederman, eds., *Beyond the Persecuting Society: Religious Toleration Before the Enlightenment* (Philadelphia: University of Pennsylvania Press, 1998); Laursen, ed, *Religious Toleration: "The Variety of Rites" from Cyrus to Defoe* (New York: St. Martin's, 1999); and, Nederman, *Worlds of Difference: European Discourses of Toleration, 1100-1550*, (State College: Penn State University Press, 2000).

7. See Isaiah Berlin, "Two Concepts of Liberty," in his *Four Essays on Liberty* (Oxford: Oxford University Press, 1969).

8. Consider, for example, Carl Schmitt, *The Crisis of Parliamentary Democracy*, Ellen Kennedy, tr. (Cambridge: MIT, 1985), chs. 1 and 3, and Vladimir Il'ich Lenin's idea that the people can have their own good forced upon them.

9. Jean-Jacques Rousseau, "The Social Contract," in *The Basic Political Writings*, Donald A. Cress, tr. (Indianapolis: Hackett, 1987), bk. I, ch. VII, 150.

10. Suggested long ago by Glaucon in Plato's *Republic* (357a-362c), this argument has been made in modern times from Bodin in his *Six livres de la république* (Paris, 1576) onward, although most famously by Hobbes, *Leviathan* (London, 1651). For a different account of the importance of this distinction between moral and prudential arguments, see John Dunn, "The Claim to Freedom of Conscience," in *From Persecution to Toleration,* Ole Grell, Jonathan Israel, and Nicholas Tyacke, eds. (Oxford: Oxford University Press, 1991), 171-93. For a history of the *raison d'état* argument, see Richard Tuck, *Philosophy and Government, 1572-1651* (Cambridge: Cambridge University Press, 1993).

11. See Plato, *The Republic* (357a-362c).

12. John Rawls' and Richard Rorty's appeals to "political" justifications of liberalism are apparent even in their titles: "Justice as Fairness: Political not Metaphysical"; *Political Liberalism*; and, "The Priority of Democracy to Philosophy."

13. Rorty says that in our society "there is no place for the questions that Nietzsche or Loyola would raise" and advocates that contemporary liberals "simply *drop* questions." He approves of Rawls' stance of not philosophically justifying first principles and rejects as crazy those thinkers with radically different views: "They are crazy because the limits of sanity are set by what *we* can take seriously. This, in turn, is determined by our upbringing, our historical situation." Richard Rorty, "The Priority of Democracy to Philosophy," in *The Virginia Statute for Religious Freedom*, Merrill Peterson, ed. (Cambridge: Cambridge University Press, 1988), 266, 267, and 268. See also 271. Similarly, Rawls dismisses thinkers with radically different perspectives: "Although to subordinate all our aims to one end does not strictly speaking violate the principles of rational choice . . . it still strikes

us as irrational, or more likely as mad." John Rawls, *A Theory of Justice* (Cambridge: Harvard University Press, 1971), 553-54.

14. Nietzsche's emphasis on the subrational, psycho-physical, instinctive will-to-power is well known. For Michel Foucault, "it is always the body that is at issue." "The soul is the prison of the body" and "we are invited to free it" (*Discipline and Punish*, Alan Sheridan, tr. [New York: Vintage, 1979], 25 and 30, respectively). For Foucault's account of his own similarity to Nietzsche, see "Nietzsche, Genealogy, History," in *The Foucault Reader*, Paul Rabinow, ed. (New York: Pantheon, 1984), especially 83 and 87-90. However, I believe that Foucault misses the key difference between himself and Nietzsche. Foucault's attacks on all existing power/knowledge complexes and his calls for self-liberation parallel Nietzsche's account of the liberation of free spirits, but not the Nietzsche who longs for a new horizon or the coming of the *übermensch*.

15. For example, Richard Rorty in his *Contingency, Irony, and Solidarity* (Cambridge: Cambridge University Press, 1989), 65, argues that "The compromise advocated in this book amounts to saying: *Privatize* the Nietzschean-Sartrean-Foucauldian attempt at authenticity and purity, in order to prevent yourself from slipping into a political attitude which will lead you to think that there is some social goal more important than avoiding cruelty," where avoiding cruelty is Rorty's definition of a liberal. See also Mark Warren, *Nietzsche and Political Thought* (Cambridge: MIT Press, 1988). Rorty and Warren do not say that postmodern thinkers prefer liberalism, but that liberalism can be justified, perhaps even more consistently, on postmodern principles—regardless of the political preferences originally attached to them.

16. Fyodor Dostoyevsky, "The Grand Inquisitor," in *The Brothers Karamazov,* David McDuff, tr. (New York: Penguin, 1993). Dostoyevsky never uses this precise phrase, but the tradition of identifying it with him is strong. Stated by Friedrich Nietzsche, *On the Genealogy of Morals*, Walter Kaufmann, tr. (New York: Vintage, 1967), essay III, aphorism 24, 150, although he attributes this phrase to the Islamic Assassins.

17. Amy Gutmann, "Communitarian Critics of Liberalism," in *Philosophy and Public Affairs* 14 (summer 1985): 319. I cite Gutmann's critique without accepting her defense of liberalism as sufficient. As an example of care theory, see Nel Noddings, *Caring* (Berkeley: University of California Press, 1984); Rosemarie Tong, *Feminine and Feminist Ethics* (Belmont, Calif.: Wadsworth, 1993) explores ways that Noddings' argument is naive.

18. La Croix du Maine called Montaigne another Plutarch, Pasquier called him Seneca, and Justus Lipsius praised him as the French Thales. Lipsius also said that Montaigne was the only one in Europe who shared his ideas. See Donald Frame, *Montaigne's Essais: A Study* (Englewood, N.J.: Prentice Hall, 1969), 3; Alan Boase, *The Fortunes of Montaigne: A History of the Essays in France, 1580-1669* (New York: Octagon, 1970), 18-25; and Richard Tuck, "Skepticism and Toleration in the Seventeenth Century," in *Justifying Toleration: Conceptual and Historical*

Perspectives, Susan Mendus, ed. (Cambridge: Cambridge University Press, 1988), 23. For short selections of sixteenth-and-seventeenth century reactions to Montaigne, see Pierre Villey, ed., *Les Essais de Michel Montaigne* (Paris: Presses Universitaires de France, 1924), vol. III, appendice II: 1201-22.

19. Pierre Villey, "Montaigne et François Bacon," in *Revue de la Renaissance* 11 (July-September 1911): 122-58. Bacon was the first to use word "essay" as a noun in English (other than by Montaigne's translator, John Florio). Bacon even wrote a book called *Essays.* On Descartes' debt to Montaigne, see Léon Brunschvicg, *Descartes et Pascal: Lecteurs de Montaigne* (New York: Brentano's, 1944); Michael G. Paulson, *The Possible Influence of Montaigne's "Essais" on Descartes' "Treatise on the Passions"* (Lanham, Md.: University Press of America, 1988); and Boase, *The Fortunes of Montaigne,* ch. 16.

20. Pierre-François Tissot, *Leçons et Modèles de littérature française,* 2 vols. (Paris: 1835-36), vol. I: 117. Cited in Schaefer, 3.

21. Jacob Feis, *Shakespeare and Montaigne* (London: K. Paul, Trench, 1884); J. M. Robertson, *Montaigne and Shakespeare* (London: A. and C. Black, 1909 [original, 1897]); Elizabeth Robins Hooker, "The Relation of Shakespeare to Montaigne," in *Publications of the Modern Language Association of America,* vol. xvii (1902); A. H. Upham, *The French Influence in English Literature* (New York: Octagon Books, 1965 [original, 1911]); George Coffin Taylor, *Shakespeare's Debt to Montaigne* (New York: Phaeton Press, 1968); René Galland, "Montaigne et Shakespeare," in *Quatrième Centenaire de la Naissance de Montaigne, Conférences organisées par la ville de Bordeaux* (Geneva: Slatkine Reprints, 1969), 333-71; Arthur Kirsh, "Virtue, Vice, and Compassion in Montaigne and *The Tempest,*" in *SEL* 37 (1997): 337-52; Arthur Kirsh, *Shakespeare and the Experience of Love* (Cambridge: Cambridge University Press, 1981), 38-39, 121-27; Leo Salingar, *Dramatic Form in Shakespeare and the Jacobeans* (Cambridge: Harvard University Press, 1959), 249-53; Robert Ellrodt, "Self-Consciousness in Montaigne and Shakespeare," in *Shakespeare Studies* 28 (1975): 37-50; and Pierre Villey, "Montaigne and Shakespeare," in *A Book of Homage to Shakespeare* (Oxford: University Press, H. Milford, 1916), 417 ff., denies the links. For Frame's views, see his "What Next in Montaigne Studies?" in *The French Review* 36:6 (May 1963): 577-87, *Montaigne: A Biography,* and *Montaigne's Discovery of Man: The Humanization of a Humanist* (New York: Columbia University Press, 1955).

22. Bernard Croquette, *Pascal et Montaigne: Étude des réminiscences des Essais dans l'oeuvre de Pascal* (Geneva: Droz, 1974), gives an 80 page listing of Pascal's borrowings from Montaigne. Pascal's explicit confrontation with Montaigne is most readily notable in his *Entretien de M. de Sacy sur la lecture d'Epictète et Montaigne* in *Oeuvres Complètes,* Louis Lafuma, ed. (Paris: Éditions de Seuil, 1963). See also Léon Brunschvicg, *Descartes et Pascal: Lecteurs de Montaigne* (New York: Brentano's, 1944); Boase, *The Fortunes of Montaigne,* ch. 25; and, T. S. Eliot, "The '*Pensées*' of Pascal," in *Selected Essays* (New York:

Harcourt Brace, 1950), 355-68.

23. Pierre Villey, *L'influence de Montaigne sur les idées pédagogiques de Locke at de Rousseau* (Paris: Hachette, 1911); Blair Campbell, "Montaigne and Rousseau's First Discourse," in *Western Political Quarterly* 28 (1975): 7-31; Frank Lestringant, *Cannibals: The Discovery and Representation of the Cannibal from Columbus to Jules Verne*, Rosemary Morris, tr. (Berkeley: University of California Press, 1997), 187-88.

24. Voltaire cited in Judith Shklar, *Montesquieu* (Oxford: Oxford University Press, 1987), 114. Montesquieu also praises Montaigne as one of "the four great poets: Plato, Malebranche, Shaftesbury, Montaigne"; and echoing Montaigne's own self-understanding, Montesquieu writes: "In most authors, I see men who write, in Montaigne, the man who thinks"; "Mes Pensées," no. 887, in *Oeuvres Complètes*, Daniel Oster, ed. (Paris: Éditions du Seuil, 1964), 977. Also on the connection between Montaigne and Montesquieu, see John Bomer, *The Presence of Montaigne in the Lettres Persanes* (Birmingham, Ala.: Summa Publications, 1988) and Émile Moussat, "De Montaigne à Montesquieu" in *Bulletin de la société des amis de Montaigne* 5:12 (1974): 2-4.

25. Voltaire praises Montaigne "because he paints human nature." He further describes him as "a wiseman in a century of ignorance, a philosopher among fanatics, and [one] who paints under his name our weaknesses and our follies, [he] is a man who always will be liked"; "Remarques sur les Pensées de M. Pascal" in *Oeurves Complètes de Voltaire* (Paris: Garnier Frères, 1879[1728]), vol. 22: 27-64. Alexandre Vinet, *Histoire de la littérature française au dix-huitième siècle* (Lausanne: Payot, 1960[1854]), compares Voltaire to Montaigne. He also "blames" the Enlightenment on the influence of Montaigne and Charron.

26. On Hume's debt to Montaigne, see Norman Kemp Smith, *The Philosophy of David Hume: A Critical Study of Its Origins and Central Doctrines* (London: Macmillan, 1960), 82 and 325. See also chapter 5, section on "pity," below.

27. Friedrich Nietzsche, *Assorted Opinions and Maxims*, aphorism 408, praises Montaigne as one of only eight figures that he will accept judgment from and with whom he has to come to terms. Nietzsche also favorably compares Montaigne to Socrates (*The Wanderer and His Shadow*, aph. 86), Schopenhaur (*Schopenhaur as Educator,* aph. 2), and Shakespeare (*Human, All Too Human*, aph. 176). As late as *Ecce Homo*, Nietzsche still mentions Montaigne favorably ("Why I Am So Clever," aph. 3). See also Brendan Donnellan, *Nietzsche and the French Moralists* (Bonn: Bouvier, 1982) and Dudley Marchi, *Montaigne Among the Moderns* (Providence, R.I.: Berghahn, 1994), ch. 2, "Emerson and Nietzsche: Between Tradition and Innovation."

28. Emerson lists Montaigne as one of his six great men. See Ralph Waldo Emerson, "Montaigne; Or, The Skeptic," in *Representative Men* (Boston: Houghton Mifflen, 1930[1849-1850]). Marchi, *Montaigne Among the Moderns*, ch. 2, is the most insightful on this connection. See also Charles Lowell Young, *Emerson's Montaigne* (New York: Macmillan, 1941).

29. See notes 24, 27, and 28 above.

30. Jean-François Lyotard, "Answering the Question: What Is Postmodern?" Régis Durand, tr. in Jean-François Lyotard, *The Postmodern Condition: A Report on Knowledge,* Geoff Bennington and Brian Massumi, trs. (Minneapolis: University of Minnesota Press, 1984), 81. Derrida's most political writing not only uses Montaigne but borrows its very title from him: Jacques Derrida, "Force de Loi: Le 'Fondement Mystique de l'Autorité'" ["The Force of Law: 'The Mystical Foundations of Authority'"] found in French and English in *Cardozo Law Review*: 11 (5-6) (July-Aug. 1990): 919-1045. See also Jacques Lacan, "Propos sur la causalité psychique," in *Écrits* (Paris: Le Seuil, 1966), 179; Hélène Cixous, *Three Steps on the Ladder of Writing*, Sarah Cornell and Susan Sellers, trs. (New York: Columbia University Press, 1993); and Derrida, *Politics of Friendship,* George Collins, tr. (London: Verso, 1997). For a postmodern overview of the postmodern interpretations of Montaigne, see Richard Regosin, "Recent Trends in Montaigne Scholarship: A Post-Structuralist Perspective," *Renaissance Quarterly* 37 (1984): 37-54. For a nice overview of various postmodern uses of Montaigne, see Marchi, *Montaigne Among the Moderns*, ch. 4.

31. Montaigne is not mentioned in Leo Strauss and Joseph Cropsey, eds., *History of Political Philosophy* (Chicago: University of Chicago Press, 1987) and barely mentioned in Bertrand Russell's *A History of Western Philosophy* (New York: Simon & Shuster, 1945) and Frederick Copleston's ten-volume *A History of Philosophy* (Garden City, NJ: Image Books, 1964). Copleston discusses Montaigne the most but places him "in the field of literature" (vol. IV: 19). He does play a small but important role in Robert Solomon and Kathleen Higgins, *A Short History of Philosophy* (Oxford: Oxford University Press, 1996), 178-81, 183, and 188.

32. David Lewis Schaefer, *The Political Philosophy of Montaigne* (Ithaca: Cornell University Press, 1990). A second, quite interesting, recent book on Montaigne's moral thought, although not by a political theorist, is David Quint's *Montaigne and the Quality of Mercy: Ethical and Political Themes in the Essais* (Princeton: Princeton University Press, 1998). Like me, Quint argues that Montaigne's thought is essentially a "taming" process, but whereas I see it as an attempt to tame the unruliness of the human mind, and therefore see it as of universal importance, Quint sees it only as an attempt at "taming an early modern aristocratic culture of violence and cruelty" (ix). I agree with Quint that this is *part* of Montaigne's most immediate historical aims, but I disagree that this is *all* that Montaigne intends.

33. The rise and consequences of the modern "disciplines" are elegantly recounted in Marc Fumaroli, *L'Age de l'éloquence* (Geneva: Droz, 1980), intro.

34. See Judith Shklar, *Ordinary Vices* (Cambridge: Harvard University Press, 1984); Charles Taylor, *Sources of the Self: The Making of the Modern Identity* (Cambridge: Harvard University Press, 1989); Quentin Skinner, *The Foundations of Modern Political Thought* (Cambridge: Cambridge University Press, 1978);

Tuck, *Philosophy and Government, 1572-1651*; Richard Flathman, *Reflections of a Would-be Anarchist* (Minneapolis: University of Minnesota Press, 1999); and John Christian Laursen, *The Politics of Skepticism in the Ancients, Montaigne, Hume, and Kant* (Leiden: Brill, 1992). Consider also Stephen Toulmin, *Cosmopolis: The Hidden Agenda of Modernity* (New York: The Free Press, 1990), ch.1 especially. Montaigne also indirectly finds his way via Shklar into Rorty, *Contingency, Irony, Solidarity*, xv, 74, 89n, 146. See also two recent books not by political theorists: Quint, *Montaigne and the Quality of Mercy: Ethical and Political Themes in the Essais*, and Alexander Nehemas, *The Art of Living* (Berkeley: University of California Press, 1999).

35. For example, Hugo Friedrich, *Montaigne*, Philippe Desan, ed., Dawn Eng, tr. (Berkeley: University of California Press, 1991) usually discusses Montaigne's conception of toleration in a religious context (109-11); a passing remark in another context, however, penetrates to the core: "in the *Essais*, self-knowledge becomes the source of a noble tolerance for any form of being oneself" (210). Unfortunately, Friedrich does not develop this thought. The fundamentally tolerant attitude of the *Essays* is also noted by Martin Dreano, *La religion de Montaigne* (Paris: A.-G. Nizet, 1969), 109-31, and David Schaefer, *The Political Philosophy of Montaigne*, 133-50, but like Friedrich, both discuss Montaigne's tolerance in the context of religion. Dreano presents Montaigne's tolerance as a product of his religious beliefs; Schaefer, more accurately I believe, to show Montaigne's anti-Christianity.

The best account of Montaigne's political involvement in issues of toleration during his lifetime is Geralde Nakam, *Montaigne et son temps: Les événements et les essais; l'histoire, la vie, le livre* (Paris: A-G Nizet, 1982). Also see Arthur Armaingaud, "Étude sur Michel de Montaigne," in *Oeuvres complètes de Michel de Montaigne,* Arthur Armaingaud, ed. (Paris: Louis Conard, 1924-41), vol. I: 1-257; Alphonse Grun, *La vie publique de Michel de Montaigne: Étude biographique* (Paris: D'Amyot, 1855); David Maskell, "Montaigne médiateur entre Navarre et Guise," in *Bibliothèque d'humanisme et Renaissance* 41 (1979): 541-53; and Malcolm Smith, *Montaigne and Religious Freedom: The Dawn of Pluralism*, Étude de philologie et d'histoire, no. 45 (Geneva: Droz, 1981).

36. Lecler, *Toleration and the Reformation*, II: 168.

37. Lecler, *Toleration and the Reformation*, II:168. Montaigne is one of the few figures who prompt such a judgment from Lecler.

38. Henry Kamen, *The Rise of Toleration*, 23-24. Kamen's rationale for omitting Montaigne is curious in light of another of his remarks. He says that Montaigne's thought led him "to naturalism and tolerance, and his approach arouses suspicions about the religious basis of his beliefs; but he remained fundamentally Catholic in outlook" (131). Montaigne's "Catholicism" landed his one book, the *Essays*, on the Church's *Index Librorum Prohibitorum* (*Index of Prohibited Books*). Kamen does better by excluding Montaigne because of irreligiosity rather than defending him as a believer, but either way he does not do

Montaigne justice.

39. Tuck, "Skepticism and Toleration in the Seventeenth Century," in *Justifying Toleration: Conceptual and Historical Perspectives*, Susan Mendus, ed. (Cambridge: Cambridge University Press, 1988), 21-36.

40. Tuck, "Skepticism and Toleration in the Seventeenth Century," 23. For a somewhat fuller account of Tuck's position on Montaigne, see his *Philosophy and Government, 1572-1651*, 45-64.

41. Quentin Skinner, *The Foundations of Modern Political Thought* (Cambridge: Cambridge University Press, 1988), II: 279. See II: 275-84 generally.

42. The most succinct explanations of the limits of this neo-stoical interpretation of Montaigne are found in Armaingaud, "Étude," 107-28 and 158; Friedrich, *Montaigne* (1991), 56-66; and Laursen, *The Politics of Skepticism*, 97-98. They persuasively argue that Montaigne adopts and omits elements of Stoicism when incorporating it into his own unique thought.

43. Judith Shklar, "The Liberalism of Fear," in *Liberalism and the Moral Life*, Nancy Rosenblum, ed. (Cambridge: Harvard University Press, 1989), 23. See also Shklar, *Ordinary Vices*, especially chapter 1, "Putting Cruelty First."

44. Influence of Shklar's use of Montaigne may be seen in Richard Rorty, *Contingency, Irony, Solidarity*, xv: 74, 89n, and 146. See also Bernard Yack, ed., *Liberalism Without Illusions: Essays on Liberal Theory and the Political Vision of Judith N. Shklar* (Chicago: University of Chicago Press, 1996).

45. Because Montaigne emphasizes the self's body and celebrates its corporeality and sensuality, he also sometimes expresses cruelty to animals as well. See the section on pity in chapter 5 below.

46. Rorty writes, "For purposes of social theory, we can put aside such topics as an ahistorical human nature, the nature of selfhood, the motive of moral behavior, and the meaning of life. We treat these as irrelevant to politics as Jefferson thought questions about the Trinity and about transubstantiation" (Rorty, "The Priority of Democracy to Philosophy," 261-62).

47. I share Shklar's concerns about the danger inherent in trying to institute a political system whose primary aim is to promote virtue or self-perfection. However, I do not have that fear in the case of Montaigne, because the primary knowledge on which he insists is negative. It is knowledge of human ignorance, human inabilities, human lacks.

48. Schaefer, *The Political Philosophy of Montaigne*, 340 and 375, but see 340-86 generally.

49. Schaefer, *The Political Philosophy of Montaigne*, 309.

50. Schaefer, *The Political Philosophy of Montaigne*, 308 and 340-41.

51. Schaefer, *The Political Philosophy of Montaigne*, 332 (emphasis added).

52. Although I disagree with the way that Schaefer rejects the idea of natural limits in Montaigne, he partially cedes the point by acknowledging that "it would be misleading to say that Montaigne leaves the question of the good life entirely open-ended: only some ways of life—that is, those that aim at earthly pleasure

rather than glory or immortality—are fully compatible with an uncritical tolerance of other people's ways" (Schaefer, *The Political Philosophy of Montaigne*, 332). I present my argument for the idea of natural limits in Montaigne in chapter 3 below.

53. Schaefer, *The Political Philosophy of Montaigne*, 145-50; Michel Butor, *Essais sur les Essais* (Paris: Gallimard, 1968), 131-39; and Michael Platt, "In the Middle of Montaigne (I.29, II.19, III.7)," and Schaefer, "Let Us Return to Our Temporal Greatness *Essais*," both found in *The Order of Montaigne's Essays,* Daniel Martin, ed. (Amherst, Mass.: Hestia, 1989), 124-43 and 144-52, respectively.

54. Different commentators have different motives, and the renewed interest in Montaigne might be nothing other than a new fad or reflect the inevitable ups and downs which every historical figure undergoes. However, I believe there is an underlying concern generating the renewed interest in Montaigne. While Shklar explicitly focuses on Montaigne in order to emulate his sane moderation and worldly tolerance, other scholars discuss Montaigne for reasons of historical and academic scholarship. Nonetheless, I would argue that the recent emphasis on the origins of liberalism and its main conceptions and institutions is also driven by the desire, on the part of the researchers, to help us today clarify and justify these ideas and institutions. If this is so, Montaigne is exceedingly relevant to the political projects that Shklar explicitly acknowledges but in which all are engaged.

55. Richard Rorty makes a similar analogy in the conclusion, indeed in the very last paragraph, of his celebrated *Philosophy and the Mirror of Nature* (Princeton: Princeton University Press, 1979). Rorty suggests that twentieth-century philosophy might come to be perceived "as sixteenth-century philosophy now seems to us," i.e., as "a stage of awkward transitional backing and filling" (394). Earlier in the book he describes the sixteenth century's crisis (as I do below) as "a crisis of confidence in established institutions, a crisis expressed paradigmatically in Montaigne" (139). However, I emphasize the intellectual aspects of these crises more than Rorty does, and I am more anxious about our current one than he is.

56. For fuller accounts of the crises that led the old truths to be doubted, see Popkin, *The History of Scepticism from Erasmus to Spinoza* (Los Angeles: University of California Press, 1988.), ch.1, as well as his essay "The Skeptical Origins of the Modern Problem of Knowledge," in *Perception and Personal Identity*, Norman Care and Robert Grimm, eds. (Cleveland: Case Western, 1969), 3-24.

57. In interpreting Montaigne as a protoliberal, that is to say as supremely important in the development of liberalism while not being a liberal himself, I concur most closely with Judith Shklar. David Schaefer goes too far in describing Montaigne as a full liberal.

58. Indeed, it would be hard to point to a political system that has fallen solely because its principles were refuted or no longer believed, although the former Soviet Union is probably the best example of this.

59. Most Montaigne scholars accept this claim about Montaigne's Jewish origins, but a dissenting view is found in Roger Trinquet, *La jeunesse de Montaigne: ses origines familiales, son enfance et ses études* (Paris: A.-G. Nizet, 1972). The best biographies of Montaigne include Donald Frame, *Montaigne: A Biography* (New York: Harcourt, Brace & World, 1965) and Géralde Nakam, *Montaigne et son temps: les événements et les essais; l'histoire, la vie, le livre* (Paris: A.-G. Nizet, 1982). See also Jean Plattard, *Montaigne et son temps* (Paris: Boivin & Co, 1933). On Montaigne's Jewish background, see Frame, 16-28 and Nakam, 30-33; 31, n.72 lists an excellent set of sources of the Jews of Bordeaux and the so-called New Christians, generally. An excellent historical overview of the sixteenth century is J. H. M. Salmon, *Society in Crisis: France in the Sixteenth Century* (New York: St. Martin's, 1975).

60. Navarre is alleged to have uttered these words when, having been kept from his crown by a virulently Catholic Paris that refused to have a heretical king, he decided to convert.

61. However, Montaigne speaks of *"conscience"* over 125 times in numerous essays at every stage of his writing process, including the important essay "Of Freedom of Conscience" (II.19). Roy E. Leake, *Concordance des Essais de Montaigne*, 2 vols. (Geneva: Droz, 1981), 265-66, 1249.

62. Good accounts of the *"arrière boutique"* image are found in Nannerl Keohane, *Philosophy and the State in France: The Renaissance to the Enlightenment* (Princeton: Princeton University Press, 1980), 111-16 and Keohane, "Montaigne's Individualism," *Political Theory* 5 (August 1977): 363-90.

Chapter One

1. Most of the studies of Montaigne's skepticism focus on his "The Apology for Raymond Sebond," because it is the essay in which he most clearly lays out his skeptical arguments. Ironically, this essay on the impotence of reason is also Montaigne's longest and most systematic. Textually systematic studies of the "Apology" include Schaefer, *The Political Philosophy of Montaigne*, chs. 2-4; Zbigniew Gierczynski, "Le Scepticisme de Montaigne, principe de l'équilibre de l'esprit," in *Kwartalnik Neofilologiczny*, 14 (1967): 111-31; Zbigniew Gierczynski, "La Science de l'ignorance de Montaigne," in *Roczniki Humanistyczne,* 15 (1967): 5-85; and, Zbigniew Gierczynski, "Le 'Que sais-je?' de Montaigne: Interpretation de l'Apologie de Raimond Sebond," in *Roczniki Humanistyczne*, 18 (1970): 5-103. For a systematic overview of Montaigne's skepticism not primarily based on the "Apology," see Laursen, *The Politics of Skepticism*, chs. 4-5. In this book, I both follow the "Apology's" clear method and agenda (in this chapter) and explore the argument's implications as discussed elsewhere in the *Essays* (in chapters 2 through 5).

2. Commentators who find the "Apology" to be lacking a coherent structure include Villey, *Les sources et l'évolution des Essais de Montaigne* (Paris: Hachette,

1908), II: 172, who finds it to be "capricious" and "brusque"; and Grace Norton, "A Handbook to *The Essays* of Michel de Montaigne," in *The Essays of Montaigne*, George B. Ives, tr. (New York: Heritage Press, 1946), III: 1787-89.

3. While there is a clear structure to the essay overall, many of its parts are less clearly organized. More specifically, the sections on the animals, the philosophers, and God are characterized by extensive lists of stories, arguments, and examples occasionally interrupted by digressions or reflections. Because these asides are often more interesting than the lists, it is impossible coherently to present the argument simply as it unfolds. Instead, I will generally examine the overarching argument first and then the asides.

4. See Quentin Skinner, *Foundations of Modern Political Thought.*

5. Both Rawls and Rorty explicitly acknowledge the tradition of political theory that grew out of the sixteenth century's religious wars as the tradition in which they operate. On Rawls, see, for example, "Justice as Fairness: Political not Metaphysical:" 225. On Rorty, see ch.1, n. 55 above. See the introduction to this book for a more extensive discussion of the numerous crises that led to skepticism emerging at this time.

6. For a brief account of the fifteenth- and sixteenth-century Christian humanists' accounts see Lecler, *Toleration and the Reformation*; and Kamen, *The Rise of Toleration,* 22-29.

7. Charles Schmitt's excellent studies detail the little that was known about skepticism throughout Medieval times prior to Stephanus' publishing of Sextus Empiricus. See his *Cicero Scepticus* (The Hague: Nijhoff, 1972); *Studies in Renaissance Philosophy and Science* (London: Variorum reprints, 1981); and *Reappraisals in Renaissance Thought* (London: Variorum reprints, 1989).

8. On Montaigne's linguistic training and expertise in ancient languages, see Donald Frame, *Montaigne: A Biography*, 39-40.

9. Montaigne's view of natural man is most fully presented in "Of Cannibals" (I.31) and "Of Coaches" (III.6) and is discussed systematically in chapter 2 below.

10. The non-Latinized version of Stephanus' name is Henri Estienne. The pagination from his edition of the complete works of Plato is used as the standard scholarly reference even today.

11. Other skeptical works such as Cicero's *Academica*, accounts of skeptical movements recorded in Diogenes Laertius' *Eminent Lives of the Philosophers*, and two earlier Latin manuscripts of Sextus had been brought back to Europe as early as the thirteenth century but had only limited influence. See Charles Schmitt's comprehensive studies cited in note 7 above.

12. Bayle quoted in Popkin, *History of Skepticism from Erasmus to Spinoza*, xvii. Julia Annas and Jonathan Barnes, eds., *The Modes of Skepticism: Ancient Texts and Modern Interpretations* (Cambridge: Cambridge University Press, 1985), 5.

13. J. B. Schneewind, "The Divine Corporation and the History of Ethics," in *Philosophy in History*, Richard Rorty, J. B. Schneewind, and Quentin Skinner, eds.

(Cambridge: Cambridge University Press, 1984), 174. Schneewind further recognizes Montaigne's importance in his edited book *Moral Philosophy from Montaigne to Kant* (Cambridge: Cambridge University Press, 1990).

14. Popkin, *The History of Skepticism from Erasmus to Spinoza*, 4.

15. Annas and Barnes, *The Modes of Skepticism*, 6.

16. Myles Burnyeat, "The Skeptic in his Place and Time," in *Philosophy in History*, Richard Rorty, Malcolm Schneewind, and Quentin Skinner, eds. (Cambridge, Cambridge University Press, 1984), 231.

17. Burnyeat, "The Skeptic in his Place and Time," 231.

18. These terms will be discussed at length below but a provisional definition is in order. Fideists believe that human beings cannot possess knowledge by natural or human means alone but can possess it through, and only through, faith in the revealed word of God. Pyrrhonists argue that they do not know whether they know anything or not. Unlike Academic skeptics, they do not know that they know nothing, because this would be knowing something. Rather, they argue that they might know something or might not. Every claim, no matter how trivial, is disputable. From this radical uncertainty, they propose to suspend their judgment on all things.

19. Frieda Brown, *Religious and Political Conservatism in the Essais of Montaigne* (Geneva: Librarie Droz, 1963).

20. Jacob Zeitlin, ed., *The Essays of Michel de Montaigne*, 3 vols. (New York: Alfred Knopf, 1935).

21. Herman Janssen, *Montaigne Fideiste* (Utrecht: Nijmegen, 1930), 78.

22. Hugo Friedrich, *Montaigne,* Robert Rovini, tr. (Paris: Gallimard, 1968), 109.

23. Armaingaud, *Montaigne pamphlétaire L'énigme de contr'un.* (Paris: Hachette, 1910) and André Gide, *Montaigne,* Dorothy Bussy, tr. (New York: McGraw-Hill, 1964).

24. Schaefer, *The Political Philosophy of Montaigne*, chs. 2-4; Zbigniew Gierczynski, "Le Scepticisme de Montaigne, principe de l'équilibre de l'esprit," in *Kwartalnik Neofilologiczny,* 14 (1967): 111-31; Zbigniew Gierczynski, "La Science de l'ignorance de Montaigne," in *Roczniki Humanistyczne,* 15 (1967): 5-85; and, Zbigniew Gierczynski, "Le 'Que sais-je?' de Montaigne: Interpretation de l'Apologie de Raimond Sebond," in *Roczniki Humanistyczne*, 18 (1970): 5-103.

25. Popkin, *The History of Skepticism from Erasmus to Spinoza*, 44-66; and Burnyeat, "The Skeptic in his Place and Time," 231.

26. I am one of the few scholars to argue this point. The only other scholar who argues this is Elaine Limbrick, "Was Montaigne Really a Pyrrhonian?" *Bibliothèque d'humanisme et renaissance* 34 (1977): 67-80. Frederick Kellerman offers a view of Montaigne as a partial Academic skeptic. See his articles: "*The Essais* and Socrates," in *Symposium* 10 (1956): 204-16 and "Montaigne's Socrates," in *The Romanic Review* 45 (1954): 170-77. Laursen, *The Politics of Skepticism*, 102, argues that Montaigne was a skeptic and that Sextus' distinction

between Academic and Pyrrhonian skepticism "is not likely to have much of a differential effect on Montaigne's politics." Indeed, Laursen even doubts whether this "distinction can be maintained" at all. Laursen is right that many aspects of these two schools of thought are shared and other aspects get blurred, both in their followers generally and in Montaigne himself, so his emphasis on a skeptical "politics of human fallibility" is helpful and gets at the nub of the issue (94, 102). However, as we shall see below, there are important—and politically relevant—aspects to the distinction.

27. Forty percent equals fifty-three of one hundred thirty pages in the Frame translation.

28. R. A. Sayce, *The Essays of Montaigne: A Critical Exploration* (London: Weidenfeld and Nicolson, 1972) is eloquent on this point.

29. Finally, at the end of this attack, he suggests a remedy, in the form of some kind of "obedience"; if our problem is that we don't know, then we should follow some external authority. However, Montaigne cites several different kinds of authority to follow, which indicates the fundamental problem with this suggestion: doesn't it matter which authority one follows? It does, and we shall see that Christianity is not Montaigne's top choice.

30. On Sebond, consider Philip Hendrick, *Montaigne et Sebond: L'art de la traduction* (Paris: Honoré Champion, 1996) and Donald Frame, "Did Montaigne Betray Sebond?," in *Romanic Review* XXXVIII (1947): 297-329.

31. Villey, *Les sources*, II: 173.

32. Grace Norton, "A Handbook to *The Essays* of Michel de Montaigne," in *The Essays of Montaigne*, George B. Ives, tr., III: 1788. Remarks about Montaigne being confused are on 1787 and 1789.

33. Donald Frame, *The Complete Works of Montaigne*, 319.

34. Friedrich, *Montaigne* (1991), 103.

35. Schaefer, *The Political Philosophy of Montaigne*, cites Charles Sainte-Beuve, Port-Royal (Paris, 1952), III, iii: 849. See also Frame, "Did Montaigne Betray Sebond?" and Armaingaud, Gierczynski, and Gide.

36. Schaefer, *The Political Philosophy of Montaigne*, 48-49. Schaefer further argues that using Sebond as a stand-in for St. Thomas Aquinas "will actually have revealed the need for a revision of fundamental principles that were long regarded as authoritative in the Christian world, and perhaps in post-Socratic Western thought generally" (49).

37. And in addition to the sense of self-protection that Schaefer emphasizes as Montaigne's motive, I believe that Montaigne's use of Sebond involves a sense of ironic play. Montaigne says that philosophers insincerely advance certain ideas for one of three reasons: to be useful, for protection, and in play. Schaefer emphasizes self-protection; I agree that this is a factor in Montaigne's case, but I emphasize play.

38. This issue is less of a problem for those who consider Montaigne to be a sincere believer. For them, it is only natural that Montaigne should cite another

religious thinker; their only question concerns why Montaigne leaves Sebond behind. For those who believe that Montaigne is not a sincere believer, the issue is more complex. They have to explain both why Montaigne begins with Sebond, and why he is left behind.

39. For example, Sebond argued "by human and natural reasons to establish and prove against the atheists all the articles of the Christian religion," including the trinity and the incarnation of God (II.12, 417 [320]). Thomas Hobbes, *Leviathan,* Michael Oakeshott, ed. (New York, Simon & Schuster, 1962), "Author's Introduction,"19-20, uses the analogy of the "world as book," but, of course, with a radically different intention.

40. Note also that Bunel is said to arrive at his conclusions "by rational inference" (II.12, 416 [320]), which Montaigne goes on to belittle and blame for most human ills. Thus, despite his recognition of Bunel's great "reputation," Montaigne has as little respect for him as he does for Sebond, the author Bunel recommends.

41. Popkin, *The History of Skepticism*, 45. Popkin cites Jacob Zeitlin, *The Essays of Michel de Montaigne*, II: 481-87, especially 485, as the basis for his claim.

42. D. J. Kennedy, "Thomism," in *The Catholic Encyclopedia* (NY: Robert Appleton, 1913), XIV: 702, specifically lists Sebond as a Thomist.

43. On the medieval Islamic philosophers, see Ralph Lerner and Muhsin Mahdi, eds., *Medieval Political Philosophy* (New York: Free Press, 1963).

44. Montaigne decries Christianity's brutal and systematic book burnings and censorship. See II.18, 650[506]) and II.19, "Of Freedom of Conscious" (entire).

45. On this point, see, for example, Thomas Aquinas, *Summa Theologica*, Questions 90-97 on the different kinds of law, eternal, human, natural, and divine. In particular, Aquinas argues that "to his supernatural end man needs to be directed in a yet higher way. Hence the additional law given by God" (Q.91, A.4, R.O.1) and that it is not enough "to proceed from principles imparted by nature, which are the precepts of natural law . . . but there is need for certain additional principles, namely, the precepts of the divine law" (Q.91, A.4, R.O.2). Quotations from Dino Bigongiari, ed., *The Political Ideas of St. Thomas Aquinas* (New York: Hafner, 1953), 18.

46. Friedrich, *Montaigne* (1991), 97. There is scholarly disagreement about whether the doctrine of the double truth was advocated with pious sincerity or subversively, as a first means of undermining Christianity. Friedrich takes the former position, but its classic statement is Etienne Gilson, "La doctrine de la double verité" in *Études de philosophie médievale* (Strasburg: Commission des publications de la faculté des lettres, 1921); Paul O. Kristeller also vociferously advocates this position. See his "The Myth of Renaissance Atheism and the French Tradition of Free Thought" in *The Journal of the History of Philosophy*, 6 (1968), 241-43. The irreligionist argument is forcefully made by Pintard, *Le Libertinage Érudit*, 39-48 and passim. Settling this debate is beyond the scope of this work. For

our purposes, it does not matter whether the doctrine of the double truth was advocated sincerely or not. We are concerned with the reaction against this doctrine.

47. See II.12, 486-94 [375-81].

48. Donald Frame's translation of Montaigne is astoundingly admirable in the way it catches the flavor of the flux and flow of Montaigne's thought. However, from time to time, he uses an unfortunate anachronism. His use of Nietzsche's image of the masses as the "common herd" is one such instance. For the sake of consistency, I use Frame's translations throughout, occasionally correcting them.

49. Madison, *Federalist* 49, was arguing against Jefferson's famous argument for having a new constitution every generation. Only such explicit consent, Jefferson argued, was legitimate. Madison argued that society depends on having the "prejudices" of the community on its side. See Jefferson's Letter to Madison, "The Earth Belongs in Usufruct to the Living" (September 6, 1789) in Jefferson, *Political Writings*, Joyce Appleby and Terence Ball, eds. (Cambridge: Cambridge University Press, 1999), 593-98.

50. Montaigne's views on political and social reform are examined in chapter 4 below.

51. See II.12, 467 [359] and II.12, 541 [419]).

52. Castellio is discussed by Montaigne at I.35, 220[165]. Bruno was burned in 1600—after Montaigne's death—but I cite him as one of the best-known victims of excessive Christian zeal.

53. According to Montaigne, Sebond says, "They instruct us, if we are capable of understanding" (II.12, 424 [326]).

54. Indeed, later in the essay, Montaigne shows the dubiousness of this claim by reciting long lists of the numerous philosophers who have inquired into God, the soul, and the human body and come up with wildly different conclusions.

55. The limits of Sebond's usefulness are seen in the group he is said to be able to help. Montaigne disparages the judgment of both the ladies and the masses throughout the *Essays*.

56. Montaigne says that those who make this argument "seem" to have "pious zeal" (II.12, 417 [321]), and therefore he proposes to treat them gently. Montaigne also says it is not a topic that he should address: "This would be rather the task for a man versed in theology than for myself, who know nothing about it" (II.12, 417 [321]). Nonetheless, like Machiavelli gingerly discussing the revealed basis of Moses' actions in *The Prince*, ch.6, he boldly proceeds to give his opinion.

57. Even if reason cannot reveal divine truth, he begins, it is an agreeable task to use our natural tools in the service of faith: "There can be no doubt that this is the most honorable use that we could put them to, and that there is no occupation or design more worthy of a Christian man than to aim, by all his studies and thoughts, to embellish, extend, and amplify the truth of his belief" (II.12, 418 [321]).

58. Note Montaigne's confidence in the abilities of the ancient pagans, who

according to Sebond must have had inferior intellects to have failed to see the light: "I do not think that purely human means are at all capable of this; if they were, so many rare and excellent souls, so abundantly furnished with natural powers, in ancient times, would not have failed to arrive at this knowledge through their reason. It is faith alone that embraces vividly and surely the high mysteries of our religion" (II.12, 417-18 [321]). Also note that this position corresponds to the fideistic belief that so many commentators attribute to Montaigne. But what it surely does not do is defend Sebond.

59. Louis Cons, *Anthologie littéraire de la Renaissance française* (New York: Holt, Rinehart, and Winston, 1931), 143, cited in Frame, *Montaigne's Essais: A Study*, 27.

60. Even here Montaigne had just previously agreed with Plato's views about those most susceptible to and in need of religion, and he also argues that people as virtuous and wise as Plato, Socrates, and Cato could not be damned for their ignorance of revelation.

61. Compare to the discussion of Montaigne's anti-ecstasy in M.A. Screech, *Montaigne and Melancholy: The Wisdom of the Essays* (London: Duckworth, 1983).

62. He does not mention Moses, Jesus, or Mohammad here, those most often cited as exceptions to his claim.

63. Like the Averroists—and unlike Sebond, whose position has been totally discredited—Montaigne radically separates reason and revelation, and this separation largely accounts for the differences among interpreters about Montaigne's religious beliefs. The interpreters who believe that Montaigne thinks that revelation successfully stands without reason consider Montaigne to be fideistic. Those who think that Montaigne thinks the separation dooms revelation consider him to be atheistic. I agree with Judith Shklar that Montaigne abandoned Christianity and probably any other form of deity, too. Shklar, *Ordinary Vices*, 10. But if he does have a deist outlook, it is one that, as we shall see, has no earthly or political consequences. Either way it makes Montaigne speak to those in a post-Nietzschean godless age.

64. Schaefer, *The Political Philosophy of Montaigne.*

65. Compare this with Machiavelli's famous condemnation of Christian priests, who, he says, "give [the populace] to understand that it is evil to say evil of evil, and that it is good to live under obedience to them [the priests] and, if they make an error, to leave them for God to punish. So they do the worst they can because they do not fear the punishment that they do not see and do not believe." Niccolò Machiavelli, *Discourses on Livy*, Harvey C. Mansfield and Nathan Tarcov, trs. and eds. (Chicago: University of Chicago Press, 1997), III. 1, 212.

66. The normative "ought" here, I believe, merely refers to the claims that Christianity advances on its own behalf, not to what Montaigne himself thinks.

67. Machiavelli, *Discourses*, III. 1, 212.

68. Montaigne also challenges the nature of Christian belief in other more

fundamental ways. He does this by posing questions from two ancient pagan philosophers. Antisthenes, when told by a priest of Orpheus that his believers would receive "eternal and perfect blessings" after their death, asked, "Why, then, do you not die yourself?" (II.12, 421 [324]). When a proselytizing priest argued that members of his sect would attain all the goods of the other world, Diogenes replied, "Do you want me to believe that Agesilaus and Epaminondas, such great men, will be miserable, and that you, who are only a calf, will be blessed because you are a priest?" (II.12, 422 [324]). Perhaps Montaigne is merely criticizing pagan hubris, but he proceeds to draw a comparison unfavorable to Christianity. Christians "say" they are with Jesus, but, believing his teachings on the afterlife, some of Plato's followers actually committed suicide. By contrast, Montaigne implies, Christianity lacks power over its disciples. Undoubtedly, many Christians have died and risked death for their beliefs, which makes Montaigne's assertions all the more astounding. Either he is purposely exaggerating his attack or he might be discussing the impotent, corrupt Christianity of his own time. Either way, Montaigne is implying that the questions posed by these ancients have no good answer in Montaigne's own Christian times.

69. Like Montaigne, John Stuart Mill argues that religion is held as a custom: "the same causes which make him a Churchman in London, would have made him a Buddhist or a Confucian in Pekin." John Stuart Mill, *On Liberty*, David Spitz, ed. (New York: Norton, 1975), 19.

70. Perigordian, after Montaigne's region of France, east of Bordeaux.

71. Popkin, *The History of Skepticism*, 46, cites this passage as evidence of Montaigne's sincere belief.

72. Montaigne criticizes atheism, but he does so only on pragmatic grounds: atheism collapses when one is faced with death. Atheists claim to have disproved "by the reason of their judgment" what is said about hell and punishments in an afterlife (II.12, 423 [325]). But Montaigne argues that as old age or sickness bring atheists toward death, the terror of its nearness creates horror. "And because such impressions make hearts fearful," Plato forbade the teaching of it (II.12, 423 [325]). Plato does this not because atheism is untrue, but because of the bad consequences such an opinion has on the living. Montaigne's objection to atheism seems to be based on similar grounds. Atheism is "a proposition as it were unnatural and monstrous, difficult too and not easy to establish in the human mind," which is professed outwardly by many people due to vanity and pride, even though they "are not strong enough nevertheless to have implanted it in their conscience" (II.12, 423 [325]). Thus, "they will not fail to clasp their hands to heaven if you stick them with a good sword-thrust in the chest" (II.12, 423 [325]). The failure of atheism seems to be its practical difficulty, not a theoretical one. Montaigne concludes: "A doctrine seriously digested is one thing; another thing is these superficial impressions, which, born of the disorder of an unhinged mind, swim about heedlessly and uncertainly in the imagination" (II.12, 423 [325]). Atheism, Montaigne says, is acceptable if it is compatible with tranquility of mind.

This is not the position of a believer. It might be objected that Montaigne does not in fact think that atheism is practicable. This may be true, but it is an empirical, not a religious, objection.

73. Jean-Jacques Rousseau, "The Second Discourse," in *The First and Second Discourses*, Roger D. Masters, ed., tr. (New York: St. Martin's, 1964), 103. On the debate over Latin Averroism, see note 46 above.

74. Montaigne cites Augustine a few times and passages from the Bible on how human beings are empty and but dust.

75. No doctrine has probably ever argued that human beings created the physical world that we inhabit. However, several doctrines have argued that human beings create the mental or spiritual world in which they live.

76. A possible exception of this, however, would be the various romantic thinkers, from Shelley to Wilde to Nietzsche and the postmoderns, who argue that everything in the world is a human creation, that there is no reality except for how human beings make or interpret the world.

77. Rousseau makes a similar claim. See *Second Discourse*, Part 1.

78. Montaigne also digresses to argue that "[t]he souls of emperors and cobblers are cast in the same mold" (II.12, 454 [350]). In other words, "The same reason that makes us bicker with a neighbor creates a war between princes; the same reason that makes us whip a lackey, when it happens in a king makes him ruin a province. Their will is as frivolous as ours, but their power is greater" (II.12, 454 [350]). Montaigne argues the equality of all human beings just as he is here arguing the equality between species. Neither is his last word on equality.

79. Montaigne distinguishes between three types of desires: those that are natural and necessary, like eating and drinking; those that are natural and not necessary, like sexual intercourse; and those that are neither natural nor necessary. "Of this last type are nearly all those of men; they are all superfluous and artificial" (II.12, 450 [346]). It is these false opinions and the zealous pursuit of them that creates the specifically human ills. Montaigne laments that "[t]hese extraneous desires, which ignorance of the good and a false opinion have insinuated into us, are in such a great number that they drive out almost all the natural ones" (II.12, 450 [346]).

80. Our self-serving judgment of the animals is but a specific case of a very human syndrome: "Everything that seems strange to us we condemn, and everything that we do not understand; as happens in our judgment of the animals" (II.12, 446 [343]). This same phenomenon applies equally to foreigners, whose unfamiliar ways are often condemned. And it explains why Montaigne declares that "God himself," to make himself appreciated, must resemble us (II.12, 465 [358]). Our imagination and reason get in the way of and filter everything; they prevent us from seeing the underlying unity of things. The opinion of our nearness to God and our distance from the "condition and society" of the other animals (II.12, 465 [358]) is a result of our foolish pride and hubris. One source of this foolish pride that Montaigne mentions here only in passing but that he shortly

examines in depth is "the poets" (II.12, 463 [356]).

81. Despite the similarity here to the Bible's Garden of Eden account of man's Fall, Montaigne's own account of natural man (I.31) presents mankind as this way from the beginning without any devilish downfall. This is our natural condition to be understood and dealt with, not a "fallen" condition for which we should or could atone. For a statement in the spirit of Montaigne's comparison of man and the animals, see Walt Whitman's "Song of Myself," stanza 32 [1855].

82. Montaigne's vision of the human good closely resembles the tranquility of mind championed by the Epicureans. Although Lucretius, the chief Epicurean poet, is approvingly quoted throughout the *Essays*, Montaigne explicitly disagrees with Lucretius over a few key points. First, Montaigne never mentions or he explicitly rejects the Epicurean belief in science. Second, Lucretius argues that by nature man is "naked and empty" and born into a hostile world where all animals are provided for except man. The Epicurean position is noted for its harsh assessment of reality. In arguing against the view that man alone is ill-equipped by nature, Montaigne outdoes the Epicureans. In order to make man's natural condition no different from the other animals', Montaigne makes it even harsher than the Epicureans understand it to be. The Epicureans are wrong to accept the traditional distinction between nature and art: "the skill to fortify and protect the body by acquired means, we possess by a natural instinct and precept"; "it is just as natural to arm ourselves with wood and iron" (II.12, 435 [335]). Montaigne here claims that acquisition and armaments, usually attributed to civilization and art, are natural. This could be mere rhetorical excess. Montaigne might have fudged the line between nature and art only to allay Epicurean objections. On the other hand, it is consistent with the unification of the human and animal realms. He argues that animals use tools, too. But if skepticism destroys all outside sources of authority, what assurance is there that our natural tendency to arm ourselves will be restrained? What is the difference between the natural inclinations of humans and the other animals? Does the law of the jungle naturally rule both kingdoms? Despite the problems raised here about our natural condition, it is still our artificial condition that Montaigne laments most. Montaigne's critique of the Epicureans, however, questions the very definition of artificiality.

83. Montaigne affirms that if he is sick he wants to know it. The human realm, like the realm of the animals, we might add, is the realm of pleasure and pain. "In truth, he who would eradicate the knowledge of evil would at the same time extirpate the knowledge of pleasure, and in fine would annihilate man" (II.12, 473 [364]). In attacking one perversely learned sect, Montaigne asserts that he wants to know things, the simple phenomenological and corporeal aspects of life: pleasure and pain. This emphasis on bodily feeling is not only anti-Stoical, but anti-Biblical.

84. On Calvin and Luther's skepticism about human capacities, see Joshua Mitchell, "Through a Glass Darkly," in *Early Modern Skepticism and the Origins of Toleration*, Levine, ed., ch. 2. On this tradition in general, see Jean Delumeau,

Sin and Fear: the Emergence of a Western Guilt Culture, 13th-18th Centuries, Eric Nicholson, tr. (NY: St. Martin's, 1990), especially ch. 5, "Fragile Humanity." See also John Edwards, *A Free Discourse Concerning Truth and Error, especially in matters of religion* (London, 1701), especially chapters 10 and 11. An English Calvinist and a fairly confused thinker, Edwards runs through numerous skeptical arguments at the same time that he defends Calvinist orthodoxy. Though late in date, it reflects things that had long been repeated.

85. This line from Epicurus on cannibalism is the only one referred to twice in this essay. See also II.12, 541 [419], where Montaigne also attributes a similar statement to Plato. Both times it is mentioned, Montaigne is emphasizing the need for law.

86. These quotations come from a later passage in the "Apology," referred to by Frame as Montaigne's "warning to the princess" (II.12, 540-42 [418-20]). I consider it here, because it reinforces the two claims that human beings should follow authority and that authority has no ultimate basis. The warning, which advises caution and moderation in the reader's opinions, speech, and deeds and the avoidance of all novelty and strangeness, is addressed only to "Vous," but it is read by all of us. It is clearly intended for a lady with power, and Frame suggests that it is "almost certainly" addressed to Montaigne's friend, Margaret of Valois (Frame, *The Complete Works of Montaigne*, 418). Margaret was also the daughter of Henry II and Catherine de' Medici (the power behind the Catholic throne) and wife of Henry of Navarre (leader of the Huguenots and future Henry IV). Montaigne feels the need to make this warning perhaps because the preceding section of the "Apology" impugned the status of all existing otherworldly authority. Whatever the reason, Montaigne emphasizes the necessity of law.

87. See chapter 4, Section II below.

88. Alexis de Tocqueville, *Democracy in America*, J. P. Mayer, ed., George Lawrence, tr. (Garden City, N.Y.: Doubleday, 1969), vol. I, pt. II, ch. 9, 290 and vol. II, pt. I, ch. 2, 433-34. Of course, this is not Tocqueville's only statement on the benefits of religion. He is also concerned with its genuine effects on the soul and how it answers to the deepest longings of human beings. See, for example, vol. I, pt. II, ch. 9, 294-301.

89. The first paragraph of "The Apology," which serves as an introduction to the essay as a whole, begins: "In truth, knowledge is a great and very useful quality" (II.12, 415 [319]). Not only does it raise the essay's major theme, the status of knowledge, but it does so in a surprising way. Montaigne begins his most skeptical essay with a truth claim: "in truth" [c'est, à la vérité], which he will repeat in numerous other places (II.13, 420 [323], for example). One does not expect this from a skeptic. And whereas the general thrust of the essay's argument is that nothing can be known by human beings, Montaigne here asserts that knowledge is a very useful and great thing. Useful for what? How is it so? And how does Montaigne know this? What standard is he using? It is an indication right from the start that Montaigne's skepticism is not all-encompassing.

90. This line is quoted from Cicero. On the importance of Montaigne's Latin quotations, see Mary McKinley, *Words in a Corner: Studies in Montaigne's Latin Quotations*, French Forum Monographs 26, R. C. La Charité and V. A. La Charité, eds. (Lexington: French Forum Publishers, 1981).

91. These names come from Sextus Empiricus' *Outlines of Pyrrhonism*, which had its first printed edition (1562) during Montaigne's lifetime.

92. See notes 20-21 above.

93. He cites Plato and Cicero to defend this claim. Socrates tells Timaeus, in Montaigne's words, "it is enough if his reasons are as probable as another man's" (II.12, 487 [375]). Cicero says that man is only capable of "pursuing probabilities by conjecture" (II.12, 487 [375]). See the whole section, II.12, 487-89 [375 and 377].

94. Undoubtedly, Montaigne has an ulterior motive for emphasizing the skeptical nature of all philosophers, and of Aristotle in particular. Aristotle was the philosopher of the Church. If he was tentative in what he said, he could not serve as authority for the religious fanatics of Montaigne's time.

95. Montaigne anticipates the critiques later made by Derrida and others. Despite having produced a wealth of evidence that these dogmatists knew that their dogmas simply were not true, and despite not having made any effort to prove the contrary, Montaigne raises a question about their motives: they could have written as they did "either on purpose, to show the vacillation of the human mind around all matters, or unwittingly, forced by the mobility and incomprehensibility of all matters" (II.12, 490 [378]). But whereas Derrida dogmatically asserts the pre-eminence of the "unwitting" gaps and contradictions, Montaigne—at least in his discussion of the great philosophers—assumes intentionality.

96. The term "fideism" was coined only in the nineteenth century, but the epistemological position represented by the word certainly was well known in the sixteenth century. Thus, the absence of the word cannot be considered grounds for his omission of the idea. Even if lacking a label, Montaigne could have described the phenomenon.

97. Montaigne's account of "natural man" has nothing to do with Eden. Instead, he attributes it to the "cannibals" of the New World (see I.31).

98. When Montaigne criticizes divine "cuckoldries" and virgin births, he attributes such claims to the "religion of Mohammed," but these are, of course, among the central miracles of Christianity.

99. II.12, 584 [453]: "[T]he bread we eat: it is only bread, but our use makes of it bones, blood, flesh, hair, and nails."

100. Montaigne argues that God has nothing to do with our realm or with our choices. Our life consists in choosing between good and evil, but this is irrelevant to God since evil never touches Him. "Power," "truth," "justice," "fear," "anger," and "love" do not apply to Him. "These are all feelings and emotions that cannot be lodged in God in our sense, nor can we imagine them according to his" (II.12, 479 [369]).

101. On the significance of this point, see David Wootton, "New Histories of Atheism," in *Atheism from the Reformation to the Enlightenment*, Hunter and Wootton, eds. (Oxford: Oxford University Press, 1992), 27 and Wootton, "Unbelief in Early Modern Europe," in *History Workshop Journal* 20 (1985): 82-100.

102. According to Montaigne, "justice" is a human concern, and it is wrong to assume that it concerns God or that God is concerned with our petty affairs. "It is for God alone to know himself and interpret his works" (II.12, 479 [369]). Several things must be said about this conclusion. First, it is exactly the opposite of Sebond's central claim that we can know God by interpreting his works. Second, in contrast to Montaigne's God, the God of the Bible is jealous, angry, or loving. Montaigne's conception is much more Greek (philosophic, not Homeric) than Jewish or Christian. Indeed, although he once here quotes Saint Augustine—"God is better known by not knowing"(II.12, 478 [369])—all the other quotations are from pagans. Third, and most important, there is a striking rift between the docility and obedience that is necessary for the preservation of society and religion on the one hand, and the impossibility of grounding this necessity in a true knowledge of God on the other. To get around this problem, Montaigne articulates a fideistic position, but he also mentions several other, better, solutions.

103. This is consistent with what we know of Montaigne's own life. Montaigne's contemporary, Etienne Pasquier, wrote that Montaigne "would not send for a priest, and in his last illness (i.e., on his deathbed) did not depart from this custom." But he goes on to say that when a priest came anyway, Montaigne did not send him away or refuse him, but "raised himself as well as he could in bed with joined hands" (cited in U. Benigni, "Montaigne," in *The Catholic Encyclopedia*, vol. 10: 512-13). Montaigne's outward conformity to Church rules is also seen in his handling of the criticism made of his book by the official Church censors in Rome, who in 1581 approved his book, requesting only that he make some changes (which he describes in his *Travel Journal*). Despite writing in later editions that he wanted to do everything the Church recommended on this point, he made no substantial changes. (His *Travel Journal*, which was not intended for publication, also mentions that he went to mass several times, but it reveals that he visited the services of several Protestant and Jewish sects as well.)

104. See notes 15 and 16 above.

105. Philosophers interested in the history of Pyrrhonism tend not to perceive how Montaigne uses and alters Pyrrhonism for his own purposes. See, for example, the otherwise excellent book by Annas and Barnes, *The Modes of Skepticism*, 6.

106. Unlike with fideistic skepticism, however, Montaigne does acknowledge Academic skepticism as one of the epistemological possibilities.

107. Note that this is Montaigne's second innovation on typical Pyrrhonist ideas. Just as he uses the Pyrrhonist method of listing incompatible claims but—originally—claims to find the hidden motives underlying these vain attempts, so here he uses Pyrrhonist arguments about the fallibility of reason and the senses

but—originally—shows the truth claims about the subjective self that he argues underlie these claims.

108. Schaefer dismisses these arguments as mere "diversion" for vulgar readers, saying that Montaigne's "extended transcription of the Pyrrhonian doctrines at this point is a kind of rhetorical window-dressing, designed to mitigate the shocking effect of the attack on Christianity and conventional morality that preceded it" (Schaefer, *Political Philosophy of Montaigne*, 144). He also cites Zeitlin and Brush, who downplay the significance of these arguments. I argue, however, that the significance of this section is less the Pyrrhonist arguments themselves, than the innovative way in which Montaigne, unlike the Pyrrhonists, claims to prove them based on his own phenomenological and experiential knowledge claims.

109. Schaefer's claim on Montaigne's behalf is clear: "I argue that this new conception of science was fully, not just partly, in accordance with Montaigne's teaching" (Schaefer, *The Political Philosophy of Montaigne*, 118, n. 8). See 114-33 for his full argument.

110. This is reiterated at II.12, 527-28 [408] and II.12, 538 [417].

111. Note the religious analogy for what is primarily a religious phenomenon.

112. The distinction between religious and natural simplicity is clear evidence for our earlier claim that simplicity need not be understood as a simply religious ideal. In any case, we have already seen that the first way amounts to nothing for Montaigne. Divine intervention can be either direct or indirect. The Bible had already been available for 1,500 years without anyone's gleaning indisputable principles from it, and Montaigne has argued that there is no evidence that divine intervention has ever occurred directly (II.12, 417-18 [321-22]). Indeed, Montaigne makes no effort to even elaborate, let alone argue, for this possibility here. This alternative is rhetoric. Attaining knowledge based upon our natural impressions is an equally problematic option. Montaigne raises the possibility of being in "our natural state, receiving external impressions as they present themselves to us through our senses, and . . . follow[ing] our simple appetites, regulated by the condition of our birth" (II.12, 522-23 [404]), which is the solution he urged in his discussion of the animals and the cannibals. Indeed, he here says that this would work for "all the animals, and everything over which the domination of natural law is still pure and simple" and for "cannibals, who enjoy the happiness of a long, tranquil, and peaceable life without" being corrupted by "the precepts of Aristotle" or "the name of physics" (II.12, 523 [405 and 404], respectively). But "civilized" human beings cannot regain such a state, at least as long as they remain culturally sophisticated. It is also a question of whether this would constitute knowledge in a scientific way or only phenomenologically. Perhaps science is on the wrong track and phenomenological knowledge is all that is available to human beings. This possibility has difficulties, as we shall see in the next chapter, but Montaigne here leaves it open.

113. See Schaefer, *The Political Philosophy of Montaigne*, 114-33.

114. I agree with Schaefer that "the ultimate intent of [Montaigne's] skepticism is not to convince us that the pursuit of knowledge is futile but to direct and encourage us to seek an attainable kind of knowledge that will promote the good of humanity (129), but I disagree with Schaefer's characterizations of this good: "human beings should take the place of God in another sense, by achieving the *creative* power that the Bible attributes to the Deity" (126), that Montaigne thinks that "Our proper posture towards nature is one of mastery" (126), and that this is intended to "awaken and serve" all sorts of earthly good (127). I agree with Jules Michelet and the more conventional view that Montaigne's skepticism "is but the provisional doubt that renders science possible"—without going so far as to assert that modern science is already there in Montaigne. (Michelet quoted in Schaefer, 130, from Sayce, *Essays*, 185.) In my reading, Montaigne's emphasis on experience and phenomena is for the conquest of oneself, not the conquest of all of nature. See chapter 3 below.

115. This quotation echoes Aristophanes' parody of Socrates in *The Clouds*.

116. In a digression in his section on the soul, Montaigne chose to bare his soul: "My behavior is natural," he says, "I have not called in the help of any teaching to build it. . . . What rule my life belonged to, I did not learn until after it was completed and spent. A new figure: an unpremeditated and accidental philosopher!" (II.12, 528 [409]). Montaigne's self-description—dare we say 'ideal'?—emerged: the unpremeditated and accidental philosopher. Montaigne identifies himself as a philosopher, but he is not engaged in a laborious chore. He does so spontaneously out of a love for and curiosity about life. He has no vested interests and clings tenaciously to nothing. He only inquires into the wonder of it all.

117. It is in this context that Montaigne discusses how time and place affect reason and the senses. This allows him to take yet another implicit swipe at Christianity, arguing that "all beliefs" have "their season, their birth, their death, like cabbages . . . what magisterial and permanent authority are we attributing to them" (II.12, 559 [433]).

118. John Locke, "Epistle to the Reader," *An Essay Concerning Human Understanding*, Peter Nidditch, ed. (Oxford: Oxford University Press, 1982), 7.

119. Immanuel Kant, *Critique of Pure Reason*, F. Max Muller, tr. (New York: Anchor Books, 1966), "Preface to the First Edition," xxiv.

120. Kant, *Critique of Pure Reason*, xxiv.

121. See Annas and Barnes, *The Modes of Skepticism,* 4.

122. *Essays*, II.7, 359 [274]. Montaigne laments "this airy medium of words."

123. Popkin, *The History of Scepticism,* 54. Popkin refers to "Pyrrhonism," which does not adequately describe the nature of Montaigne's skepticism.

124. The best general accounts of Montaigne's influence on modern skepticism include René Pintard, *Le Libertinage Érudit dans la première moitié du XVIIe siècle*; Popkin, *The History of Scepticism*; and Horowitz, "French Free-Thinkers in the First Decades of the Edict of Nantes," in *Early Modern Skepticism and the*

Origins of Toleration, Levine, ed. For particular studies detailing Montaigne's connection to a host of later thinkers, see the bibliographic references in the endnotes for the Introduction above.

Chapter Two

1. Bernadette Bucher, *Icon and Structure*, Basia Miller Gulati, tr. (Chicago: University of Chicago Press, 1981), 5, declares Montaigne to be "the first true anthropologist." James Slotkin, ed., *Readings in Early Anthropology* (Chicago: Aldine, 1965), devotes twelve of the forty-one pages in his section entitled "The Fifteenth and Sixteenth Centuries" to Montaigne. See also Margaret Hodgen, *Early Anthropology in the Sixteenth and Seventeenth Centuries* (Philadelphia: University of Pennsylvania Press, 1964), and James Boone, *Other Tribes, Other Scribes* (Cambridge: Cambridge University Press, 1982). Hodgen speaks for the group when she says that Montaigne "strove mightily really to understand the condition of savagery as it was then found in the New World" (185). In support of this position, they correctly point out that Montaigne talks at length about and reflects on the reliability of his sources, speaks with as many travelers as possible, insists on seeing Indian artifacts to support travelers' reports, and actually meets (and converses through a translator) with several Indians at Rouen. In his discussion of the Indians' tangible things, such as tools, houses, clothing, and food, Montaigne often cites evidence to support his claims.

2. When discussing the cannibals' beliefs and *moeurs*, Montaigne stops offering anthropological proof for his claims, and they start resembling other previously published accounts. Gilbert Chinard, *L'exotisme américain dans la littérature française au XVI siècle* (Geneva: Slatkine Reprints, 1978), demonstrates Montaigne's borrowing, especially from Jean de Léry. Several excellent publications of Frank Lestringant trace the literary and worldy influences on Montaigne's cannibals, including: "L'Amérique de 'Coches', fille du Brésil des 'Cannibales': Montaigne à la rencontre de deux traditions historiques" in *Montaigne et l'histoire*, ed. Claude-Gilbert Dubois (Paris: Klincksieck, 1991), 143-57; *Cannibals: The Discovery and Representation of the Cannibal from Columbus to Jules Verne*, Rosemary Morris, tr. (Berkeley: University of California Press, 1997), especially 94-96; "'Des Cannibales' et le 'corpus huguenot' sur l'Amerique," in *Le huguenot et le sauvage* (Paris: Klincksieck, 1990), especially 143-45; and, "Le Cannibalisme des 'Cannibals,'" in *Bulletin de la Société des amis de Montaigne*, 9-10 (1982): 27-40. See also Geoffroy Atkinson, *Les nouveaux horizons de la Renaissance française* (Paris: Droz, 1935); Harry Levin, *The Myth of the Golden Age in the Renaissance* (Bloomington: Indiana University Press, 1969), 74-81, 125-27; Gérard Defaux, "Un Cannibale en haut chausses: Montaigne, la différance et la logique de l'identité," in *Modern Language Notes* 97 (1982), 919-57; and Géralde Nakam, *Les 'Essais' de Montaigne: Miroir et procès de leur temps* (Paris: A-G Nizet, 1984), 329-51. Others who have noted Montaigne's anti-

European emphasis include Stephen Greenblatt, *Marvelous Possessions: The Wonder of the New World* (Chicago, University of Chicago Press, 1991), 150, and Anthony Grafton, *New Worlds, Ancient Texts: The Power of Tradition and the Shock of Discovery* (Cambridge: Belknap Press of Harvard University, 1992), 157.

Just as important in demonstrating the fictitious character of Montaigne's account is the way his descriptions of the cannibals' *moeurs* and character parallel what he says of several other peoples and individuals. See, for example, his accounts of the two Catos (I.52, 295-96 [224], II.2, 324 [246], II.8, 375 [286], II.28, 680-82 [531-32], II.37, 745 [581], III.3, 796 [621], & III.13, 1089 [851]), the Theban general Betis (I.1, 13-14 [5]), the numerous examples at II.29, 689-90 [537-38] and II.32, 700-03 [546-48], and his descriptions of the Lahontans (II.37, 758-60 [591-92]) and Dioscorides (I.56, 307-8 [233]).

3. Schaefer, *The Political Philosophy of Montaigne*, 196 and 194, respectively.

4. Contrast Schaefer, who says Montaigne "regards the essential features of this society as capable of being actualized because they are derived from the most basic and universal human instincts." Because he misses the "tranquility" component of what the cannibals represent, Schaefer is too optimistic and exaggerates Montaigne's ambition: "Montaigne's intention to reconstitute human moral and political life," he says, "may amount to the almost literal re-creation of the world, the creation of a world more truly 'new' (in the sense of being unprecedented) than America itself." Schaefer, *The Political Philosophy of Montaigne*, 196 and 198.

5. John H. Elliott, *The Old World and the New: 1492-1650* (Cambridge: Cambridge University Press, 1970), 8-9.

6. John Hooker and Raphael Holinshed. *The Chronicles of England, Scotland, and Ireland* (London: 1586), IV: 898-927; Jacques Auguste de Thou, *Histoire de son Temps* [1604] in *Histoire universelle* (Basel: 1742), I: 21-22; Myron P. Gilmore, "The New World in French and English Historians of the Sixteenth Century," in *First Images of America*, Fredi Chiapelli, ed. (Berkeley: University of California Press, 1976), 524.

7. Machiavelli, *The Discourses*, Bk. I, preface, 5.

8. See Jean Bodin, *Method for the Easy Comprehension of History*, Beatrice Reynolds, tr. (New York: Octagon Books, 1966) and Gilmore, "The New World," 520.

9. See Christopher Columbus' writings in Cecil Jane, ed., tr., *The Journal of Christopher Columbus* (New York: Bonanza, 1989) and Cecil Jane, ed., tr., *The Four Voyages of Columbus: A History in Eight Documents* (New York: Dover, 1988). From Las Casas' *History of the Indies*, (1527), cited in Aldo Scaglione, "A note on Montaigne's 'Des Cannibales' and the Humanist Tradition" in *First Images of America*, Chiapelli, ed., 64.

10. Wayland D. Hand, "The Effect of the Discovery on Ethnological and Folklore Studies in Europe," in Chiapelli, ed., *First Images of America*, 46. For a complete list of the publication dates of travel books in Spain, see Anthony Pagden, *The Fall of Natural Man: The American Indian and the Origins of Comparative*

Ethnology (Cambridge: Cambridge University Press, 1982), 57-59.

11. See Gilbert Chinard, *L'exotisme américain dans la littérature française au XVI siècle*, ch.1; and Myron P. Gilmore, "The New World in French and English Historians of the Sixteenth Century," in *First Images of America: The Impact of the New World on the Old*, 519-21, for complete lists of what was published in French and English and when.

12. Quantitatively speaking, only a small fraction of all the books published in English or French during the sixteenth century concerned travel or geography. See Gilmore, "The New World," 519-20, and Rudolph Hirsh, "Printed Reports on the Early Discoveries and Their Reception," in *First Images of America*, Chiapelli, ed., 550.

13. Gilmore, "The New World," 520.

14. Montaigne details his efforts in "Of Cannibals" (I.31, 200-13 [150-59]), but several commentators have doubted the sincerity of Montaigne's account for among other reasons, his stated preference here for evidence from "a simple, crude fellow" rather than from shrewd observers, claiming "clever people observe more things and more curiously, but they interpret them" (I.31, 202-3 [151-52]). It puts Montaigne in the odd position of defending dull-witted observers. On this point, see, for example, Schaefer, *Political Philosophy of Montaigne*, 178-83.

15. Of all the newly "discovered" peoples, more thought was invested in defining the nature of the inhabitants of the New World, due to moral questions surrounding the Spanish Crown's right to rule, than on any other people.

16. Columbus speaks of converting the Indians on 10-16-1492, 33; 11-6-1492, 57; 11-12-1492, 58; 11-27-1494, 76 and 78; 12-15-1492, 100; and 12-21-1492, 112. He speaks of enslaving them on 10-14-1492, 28; 11-12-1492, 60; and 1-14-1493, 151 (Jane, ed., *The Journal of Christopher Columbus*). See also Columbus' famous "First Letter" written immediately upon his return to Europe, especially pages 192, 194, 196, and 201 in Jane, ed., *The Journal of Christopher Columbus*.

17. The most fascinating example of these uniquely flavored histories is Bernal Diaz, *History of the Conquest of New Spain* (1568). It is available in English as *The Conquest of New Spain*, J. M. Cohen, tr. (New York: Penguin, 1963).

18. Tzvetan Todorov, *The Conquest of America: The Question of the Other*, Richard Howard, tr. (New York: Harper and Row, 1984), "Dedication."

19. These myths are nicely traced and documented by Richard Bernheimer, *Wild Men in the Middle Ages: A Study in Art, Sentiment, and Demonology* (Cambridge: Harvard University Press, 1952) and Hodgen, *Early Anthropology in the Sixteenth and Seventeenth Centuries*, 17-107.

20. Columbus, "First Letter," in Jane, ed., *The Journal of Christopher Columbus*, 198 and 200. See also Jane, ed., *The Journal of Christopher Columbus*, 11-4-1492, 52; 11-6-1492, 74; 11-23-1492, 68; 12-5-1492, 85; 12-17-1492, 102; 1-6-1493, 140 and 147; 1-9-1493, 143; and, 1-16-1493, 152.

21. This idea is nicely expressed in Edmundo O'Gorman, *The Invention of America: An Inquiry into the Historical Nature of the New World and the Meaning*

of History (Bloomington: Indiana University Press, 1961). Also of interest on this point is Tzvetan Todorov, *The Conquest of America*.

22. Anthony Pagden, *The Fall of Natural Man: The American Indian and the Origins of Comparative Ethnology* (Cambridge: Cambridge University Press, 1982), 29.

23. This story is recounted by Las Casas, who might have witnessed it and was later moved to agitate for the humane treatment of the Indians. The story is found in his *History of the Indies*, Bk. III, chs. 4-5 found in English in Bartolomé de Las Casas, *A Selection of His Writings*, George Sanderlin, ed. (New York: Knopf, 1971), 80-85. See also, Venancio D. Carro, "The Spanish Theological-Juridical Renaissance and the Ideology of Bartolomé de Las Casas," in *Bartolomé de Las Casas in History*, Juan Friede and Benjamin Keen, eds. (DeKalb: Northern Illinois University Press, 1971), 245.

24. Crediting Spain for this moral soul searching, twentieth-century Spanish scholars are quick to note that debates of this sort were never held in France or England, neither in the sixteenth century nor in the seventeenth when their colonial activities intensified. See, for example, the works of Juan Gil and the article by Venancio Carro cited above. One wonders, however, just how searching these tribunals were. They did little to prevent the brutalization of the Indians.

25. Pagden, *The Fall of Natural Man*, 38-41. Pagden's account of Aristotle's theory of natural slavery, unfortunately, is insufficient. By introducing the idea of slavery "by nature" as opposed to conventional slavery, Aristotle is setting out the grounds when slavery is legitimate and when it is not. Aristotle is clear that natural slaves do not correspond with any known class of people who were sometimes labeled as slaves; as a class, they are neither barbarians nor women. Far from justifying the slavery that existed in his time, Aristotle's distinction implicitly condemns it all. See Aristotle, *The Politics*, Book I: chs. 4-7, 1253b23-1255b40.

26. Sepúlveda's writings no longer exist. The fullest account of his position comes from Las Casas, who argued with Sepúlveda in the Spanish court. See Lewis Hanke, *All Mankind Is One: A Study of the Disputation between Bartolomé de Las Casas and Juan Gines Sepúlveda in 1550 on the Intellectual and Religious Capacity of the American Indians* (DeKalb: Northern Illinois University Press, 1974). See also Pagden, *The Fall of Natural Man*, 39.

27. Pagden, *The Fall of Natural Man*, 47.

28. Other main figures of the Salamanca school include the Dominicans Domingo de Soto (1494-1560) and Melchor Cano (1509-60) and the Jesuits Francisco Suárez (1548-1617) and Luis de Molina (1535-1600).

29. See Aristotle, *The Politics*, Book I: ch. 2, 1252b27-1253a40, where he says that the uniquely human characteristic is *logos* (reason/speech). Human beings who possess logos come together first to make a household for the sake of securing the necessities of life, and then several households form a city for the sake of securing the good life.

30. On cannibalism, see Francisco de Vitoria, "On Dietary Laws, or Self-

Restraint" in *Political Writings*, Anthony Pagden and Jeremy Lawrance, eds. (Cambridge: Cambridge University Press, 1991), 207-30. On the Indians' religious shortcomings, see Vitoria, "On the American Indians" in *Political Writings*, 233-92.

31. Vitoria, "On the American Indians," Q.1, conc., 251.

32. Vitoria, "On the American Indians," Q.1, A.6, 250 and Q.3, A.8, 290.

33. Vitoria, "On the American Indians," Q.1, A.6, 250.

34. Las Casas, *A Selection of His Writings*, 200. The editor unfortunately puts Las Casas' discussion under the anachronistic title of "A Declaration of Human Rights." Las Casas asserts human equality, not the existence of universal rights. On the Indians' religious shortcomings, see the fourth of Las Casas' four definitions of "barbarous" (142-46).

35. On Las Casas, see Pagden, 142-43 and Carro, 273-75. On Acosta, see Pagden, 167.

36. Aldo Scaglione, "A Note on Montaigne's 'Des cannibales' and the Humanist Tradition," in *First Images of America*, 65.

37. A statue of Bruno stands in Campo Di Fiore on the spot where he was burned to death in Rome. In the constant Church-state battles of nineteenth-century Italy, Bruno had emerged as a symbol of the Church's vices and a martyr for freedom of thought and speech. The statue was built for political reasons by the Socialists as their power grew around 1900, and was threatened as political power reversed, with the Church asking the statue to be destroyed as it rose to power following the signing of the Lateran Pact. Fortunately, Mussolini did not consent to this request. February 17, 2000 was the 400th anniversary of the death of Giordano Bruno. In remembrance of the event there was a large rally that continued all weekend and included speeches by various "oppressed groups," celebrating Bruno as a martyr for freedom of speech. Atheists, unions, socialists, communists, gay and lesbian organizations, and several freedom-of-thought groups from around the world sponsored various parts of the event. Ironically for a celebration of someone who was burned to death, candles were also lit in prayer and remembrance.

38. Two partial exceptions are Peter Martyr and Jean de Léry. Although both went so far as to say that the Indians lived in a kind of Golden Age, both severely qualified their praise by denouncing the Indians for lacking civilization as manifested in such things as clothing and, most importantly, for not possessing the true religion, Christianity. Their concomitant praise and criticism uneasily coexist, but ultimately and on balance, they condemn the Indians on grounds similar to Vitoria's. These two are the only ones before Montaigne to say anything substantially positive about the Indians, but animated by a strong faith in the legitimacy of their own world, neither could question core beliefs in making his judgments.

39. Rousseau read and knew Montaigne's works well. Rousseau's critique of civilization, as presented in his *First and Second Discourses*, draws heavily on

Montaigne.

40. For a comprehensive analysis of the idea of seeds of virtue and natural law, in both Montaigne and throughout Western history, see Maryanne Cline Horowitz, *Seeds of Virtue and Knowledge* (Princeton: Princeton University Press, 1998).

41. I have not seen the phrase *habitude naturelle* (II.12, 470 [362]) in any of the literature on Montaigne's account of natural man. As far as I am aware, I am the first to make the connection between this phrase, which Montaigne uses in his "Apology for Raymond Sebond," and the extensive literature on Montaigne's natural man, which is, unfortunately, based almost entirely on the two essays in which Montaigne speaks extensively about the native inhabitants of the New World, "Of Cannibals" and "Of Coaches."

42. Montaigne does not here explain what these laws of nature are. In other places, however, as we see in chapter 1, section IV above, Montaigne denies that such laws exist. To the extent that he upholds them, he describes them as, first and foremost, "[t]he care every animal has for its own preservation and the avoidance of what is harmful, the affection that the begetter has for his begotten ranks second" (II.8, 365 [279]).

43. Montaigne is followed in this argument by Hobbes, Locke, and Rousseau, but Montaigne first equated America, the Indians, and primitive peoples generally with natural man. Before Montaigne, this view was heresy. After him, it was commonplace. Montaigne changes the debate from the definition of nature to an evaluation of it. After him, the argument is whether nature is an innocence to recapture or a brutishness to overcome, but everyone agrees with John Locke's famous assertion that "in the beginning all the world was America." Locke, *Second Treatise*, paragraph 49.

44. Compare II.12, [333] and I.31, 204 [152-53].

45. Anacreon is mentioned only one other time in the rest of the *Essays*. In "On Some Verses of Virgil" (III.5, 870 [680]), which is really about love, Anacreon is said to have benefitted from love's "biting agitation." Does this imply that the cannibals might experience this agitation, or does their poetry derive from a wholly serene love? In either case, the "youth, vigor, and gaiety" it gave to him is consistent with cannibal behavior. Anacreon is also quoted once to the effect that he does not care about useless knowledge (I.26, 159 [118]). Montaigne's comparison of the Indians' poetry to that of Anacreon is discussed by John O'Brien, *Anacreon Redivivus: A Study of Anacreontic Translation in Mid-Sixteenth-Century France* (Ann Arbor: University of Michigan Press, 1995).

46. Edwin Duval shows that Montaigne includes five different perspectives in "Of Cannibals." Despite his wonderful sensitivity to the structure of the essays he considers, the substantive conclusions he draws at the end of his discussions are nonetheless somewhat overstated and unwarranted. Edwin M. Duval, "Lessons of the New World: Design and Meaning in Montaigne's 'Des cannibales' (I:31) and 'Des coches' (III.6)," in *Montaigne: Essays in Reading*, Defaux, ed., Yale French Studies, issue 64 (New Haven: Yale University Press, 1983), 95-112.

47. The essay concludes with the line "All this is not too bad—but what's the use? They don't wear breeches" (I.31, 213 [159]). While some have held this to be Montaigne's last ironic twist, a revocation of all that went before, it is more likely a jab at those defenders of civilization who equate it with artificial standards such as clothing. This line is an implicit swipe at Léry, who, despite his praise of many features of Indian life, withholds his final approval of them on the grounds that they go naked (and do not have the Christian religion). Which is to be preferred, Montaigne forces us to ask: noble characters in naked bodies or corrupt souls in clothed ones? Montaigne's difference from Léry can easily be inferred from the essay as a whole, his skepticism and in particular his continuous criticism of Christianity, and the essay "Of the Custom of Wearing Clothes" (I.36), which appears only a few pages after "Of Cannibals," in which he argues that clothes exist only by custom and that human beings are equipped by nature to survive perfectly well without them. For a discussion of "breeches" in other essays, see Schaefer, *The Political Philosophy of Montaigne*, 188-94.

48. In attempting to uncover nature, he knows that biases and prejudices, the socially inculcated values which lead people to reject all "other" possible ways of life as unworthy, are his enemies. Self-love leads people to praise their own. "Each man," says Montaigne, "calls barbarism whatever is not his own practice; for indeed it seems we have no other test of truth and reason than the example and pattern of the opinions and customs of the country in which we live. *There* is always perfect religion, the perfect government, the perfect and accomplished manner of all things" (I.31,203 [152]). Like all good skeptics, Montaigne attempts to get beyond this barrier. Unlike every other sixteenth-century thinker who discussed the Indians, Montaigne does not blame them for not being Christian. In fact, Montaigne's only mention of the Bible in the essay is in support of bigamy (I.31, 211 [158)]). None of the others thinkers we have discussed had been able to get over their religiocentrism.

49.Girolamo Cardano, in *De rerum varietate* (*On the Variety of Things*, 1557), XVII, in a chapter called "The Rites of People," "reduces the ritual to an expression of bestial hunger." Cited in Lestringant, *Cannibals: The Discovery and Representation of the Cannibal*, 116. See also Vitoria, "On Dietary Laws, or Self-Restraint."

50. Consider also Montaigne's assertion of "a general duty of humanity, that attaches us not only to animals, who have life and feeling, but even to trees and plants. We owe justice to men, and mercy and kindness to other creatures that may be capable of receiving it. There is some relationship between them and us, and some mutual obligation" (II.11, 414 [318]). Although Montaigne makes this argument in jest, some people, such as Peter Singer, argue this position seriously. See Peter Singer, *Animal Liberation* (New York: Avon Books, 1991) and the critical review of his work by Peter Berkowitz, "Other People's Mothers," in *The New Republic*, (10 January 2000): 27.

51. As if to suggest that there are universal standards for judging from the

outset, Montaigne begins his exploration of natural man by relating three anecdotes from antiquity where the "civilized" are confronted with armies of unknown peoples. Despite the newness and oddity of the never-before-seen formations, the "civilized" observers immediately recognize the military sense behind the alignments. Montaigne's choice of the military examples is shrewd, because military confrontation offers about the clearest universal criterion that exists anywhere in human affairs. Victory is the same everywhere. Different cultures may or may not be willing to do what is necessary to win a particular battle. Some might want their armies to do anything to win, while others insist that they fight "well," either with élan or bravely, but the criterion for victory is always the same. Montaigne concludes that "we should beware of clinging to vulgar opinions, and judge things by reason's way, not by popular say" (I.31, 200 [150]). The question is what is reasonable and what is the standard to decide.

52. Montaigne does not even attempt to specify the exact nature and substance of these "rules of reason." Indeed, his analysis of reason in the "Apology" suggests that they cannot be fully articulated (although Montaigne might think he can cite violations of "reason" without being able to articulate the essence of its rules). In any case, Montaigne uses Europe's standard against itself, appealing, as he often does, to a kind of ordinary-language, enlightened common sense. In the sixteenth century the word *reason* also had the meaning of common sense, but this begs the question of common to whom—all human beings, all sensible human beings, or only to those of his culture? On seventeenth-century meanings of "reason," see Jeanne Haight, *The Concept of Reason in French Classical Literature, 1635-1690* (Toronto: University of Toronto Press, 1982).

53. He cites two ancient philosophers (Chrysippus and Zeno, heads of the Stoic school) who thought there was nothing wrong with using carcasses for any purpose in cases of need, including getting nourishment from them; he cites an example from ancient history where "our ancestors" the Gauls ate people who were useless for fighting when a town was under siege; and he cites medical authority from his day that does not fear to use human flesh if it would help restore health (I.31, 208 [155-56]).

54. Cited in Horowitz, *Seeds of Virtue*, 219. Scholars are wont to note that there is a tradition of natural law dating from antiquity through the seventeenth century in which cannibalism had a place in nature. See also Lestringant, *Cannibals: The Discovery and Representation of the Cannibal* and Bernheimer, *Wild Men in the Middle Ages*.

55. In support of this conclusion, Montaigne seems to argue that aggression is part of human nature: "Nature herself, I fear, attaches to man some instinct for inhumanity" (II.12, 412 [316]). Montaigne also praises martial virtue generally. See, for example, III.13, 1075-76 [841].

56. Not only does Montaigne not use the word "essay" to describe this martial process, but he does not use it in this essay at all. This reflects, I believe, a fundamental defect in the nature of this "ideal."

57. This may be seen as other than the usual criterion for victory (see note 49 above). The fighting described here seems more about testing themselves than defeating the enemy. While Montaigne seems to suggest that this is the noblest reason to fight, it abstracts from the need to protect one's village, which is not an urgent or ongoing need in the cannibals' world.

58. The main exception to their social equality is that each sex has its unique role: men fight, women prepare and heat the drinks. This leads to what strikes the modern reader as the main inequality in their society: men can have multiple wives depending on their valor. According to Montaigne, however, this arrangement is wholly consensual by all parties involved, based on merit, and its effects are mitigated by the complete communism of children (perhaps another reference to Plato's *Republic*). Interestingly, the only mention of the *Bible* in this chapter is used to defend the cannibals' bigamy (I.31, 211 [158]). Montaigne picks and chooses from all past traditions to support his ideal.

59. Jean-Jacques Rousseau, "The Second Discourse," in *Basic Political Writings*, tr. Donald Cress, 81.

60. Montaigne does in fact claim this to be the case in "The Apology," Cf. chapter 1, above.

61. Lestringant, *Cannibals*, 95-96, traces this topos of praiseworthy absences to Book I of Ovid's *Metamorphoses*. It had powerful expressions in the sixteenth century in Ronsard's *Complainte contre fortune* and an anonymous pamphlet translated into French under the title *Les louanges de la folie* (1566). After Montaigne, this idea appeared in a letter by Pasquier, and Shakespeare puts an almost identical speech into the mouth of the noble advisor Gonzalo, who also says this would "excel the Golden Age" in *The Tempest*, Act II: Scene 1.

62. See, for example, "Of Cruelty," II.11. As one among several statements that might be cited from the latter half of the essay, consider this one: "We owe justice to men, and mercy and kindness to other creatures that may be capable of receiving it" (II.11, 414 [318]). While European misapplication of pardons might well have contributed to the acceptance and multiplication of its "ordinary vices," to abandon pardon altogether is at least as bad. On the cruelty and negative consequences that follow from these lacks, see Quint, *Montaigne and the Quality of Mercy*, 75-101, and Schaefer, *The Political Philosophy of Montaigne*, 181-88.

63. An excellent comparison of the cannibals' society to the numerous appearances of such simple cities in the work of Plato is found in Schaefer, *The Political Philosophy of Montaigne*, 181-86.

64. Hobbes, *Leviathan*, ch. 13: 100.

65. The cannibals' simplicity is further reflected in an offhand phrase in which Montaigne refers to "*leur naifveté originelle*" (I.31, 204 [153]).

66. Excepting its brief but important introduction, "Of Coaches" is arranged in three concentric circles around a comparison between Europe's cruelty and New World virtue. Before the central point, Montaigne discusses Roman coaches, Roman pomp and magnificence especially as displayed in its amphitheaters, and

Roman conceptions about the age of the world. After the central point, Montaigne compares each of these to its counterpart in the New World but in reverse order. To make sure we do not miss his point, Montaigne uncharacteristically highlights the comparisons for us: "they judged, as we do, that the universe was near its end" (III.6, 892 [698]); "As for pomp and magnificence, whereby I entered upon this subject" (III.6, 893 [698]); and, "Let us fall back to our coaches" (III.6, 894 [698]). By reminding the reader of the earlier discussions, Montaigne invites him to compare the Indians' views and behavior to Rome's. These comparisons highlight the Indians' problems. See Duval, "Lessons of the New World," in *Montaigne Essays in Reading*, Gerald Defaux, ed., 104-6.

67. The Conquistadors represent "treachery, lewdness, avarice, and every sort of inhumanity and cruelty, after the example and pattern of our ways" (III.6, 889 [695]). Montaigne rejects them as follows: "So many cities razed, so many nations exterminated, so many millions of people put to the sword, and the richest and most beautiful part of the world turned upside down, for the traffic in pearls and pepper! Base and mechanical victories! Never did ambition, never did public enmities, drive men against one another to such horrible hostilities and such miserable calamities" (III.6, 889 [695]).

68. See, for example, Olive Patricia Dickason, *The Myth of the Savage* (Edmonton: The University of Alberta Press, 1984).

69. References to astonishment, its causes and effects, recur throughout Montaigne's writings and would make an interesting study in itself. See, for example, I.11, 45 [29]; II.21, 660-61 [515]; II.32, 703 [548]; II.37, 741 [578]; III.6, 877-78 [686]; and, III.12, 1024 [801]. Since overcoming astonishment is clearly a key ingredient of Montaigne's conception of the good life, it is all the more ironic that Montaigne himself takes such obvious delight in astonishing and shocking his readers.

70. An excellent comparison between the Indian and ancient "worlds" is Dain Trafton, "Ancients and Indians in Montaigne's 'Des coches'" *Symposium* 27:1 (Spring 1973): 76-90.

71. Montaigne does give one example of an unnamed Indian people who deter attack with a prudent speech. The fact that they are unnamed may suggest that this is how Montaigne wishes they would have reacted but that no actual example can be cited. The Indians who are identified fight bravely but uselessly. Not only can they not deter attack, but they even hasten their ruin by their untutored curiosity and their childish simplicity that gives the newcomers everything they want. They are brave once they understand what is happening to them, but by then it is too late.

72. The story of Socrates' retreat is told by Alcibiades in Plato's *Symposium*.

73. Montaigne himself is the paradigm of "sophisticated simplicity" both in his life and his writing. His rhetoric claims that he is simple and straightforward, writing only what pops into his mind, yet he is a very artful writer who carefully plans, adds, subtracts, rewrites, and edits his *Essays*. Montaigne wants to seem simple, but his is an artful and sophisticated simplicity.

74. See, for example, Frame's footnotes to his edition of the *Essays* on pages 4-5, 7, 68, 84, 144, 145, 266, 286-87, 530, 576, 588-89, 678, 702, 752, 772, 809, and 814.

75. Montaigne never calls himself a great author, but he does advance himself together with the great Socrates as the corrective figures for what the Indians lack. In any case, if Montaigne's rule of interpretation is true for anyone, it seems that it would be true for him.

76. Montesquieu, *The Spirit of the Laws*, Bk. XI, ch. 6, "Of the Constitution of England." Montaigne's attribution of this ideal to an actually existing place, unlike Thomas More in his *Utopia*, is intended only to lend a hint of practicality to his vision, for he had no illusions about it having been realized in the New World.

77. Montaigne writes: "And in these new lands discovered in our time, still pure and virgin compared with ours, this practice is to some extent accepted everywhere: all their idols are drenched with human blood, often with horrible cruelty. They burn the victims alive, and take them out of the brazier half roasted to tear their heart and entrails out. Others, even women, are flayed alive, and with their bloody skins they dress and disguise others" (I.30, 199 [149]). Montaigne notes that the Mexicans alone claimed to "sacrifice to the gods fifty thousand men a year" (I.30, 199 [149]). Schaefer and Screech both note this cruelty, but Screech is wrong to conclude from it that "Montaigne's 'primitivism' (his respect for barbarous peoples and his admiration for much of their conduct, once their motives are understood) has little in common with the 'noble savages' of later centuries. These people are indeed cruel; but so are we" (Screech, tr., Montaigne, *The Complete Essays* [London: Penguin, 1993], 228, and Schaefer, *The Political Philosophy of Montaigne*, 187). Rousseau attributes just such cruelty to his "golden age" (*Second Discourse*, 65).

78. On the origin and early history of the idea of the Noble Savage, see Hayden White's insightful "The Forms of Wildness: Archaeology of an Idea," in *The Wild Man Within: An Image in Western Thought from the Renaissance to Romanticism*, Edward Dudley and Maximillian E. Novak, eds. (Pittsburgh: University of Pittsburgh Press, 1972), 3-38; Stelio Cro, *The Noble Savage: Allegory of Freedom* (Waterloo, Canada: Wilfrid Laurier University Press, 1990); William M. Hamlin, *The Image of America in Montaigne, Spenser, and Shakespeare* (New York: St. Martin's, 1995)—as well as the scholars listed in note 2 above.

79. The French Enlightenment thinkers imitate Montaigne's ideal of *habitude naturelle*, a balance of nature and social institutions. Rousseau cannot give a single example of people living according to his hypothesized natural state of man living all alone but calls humanity's "middle position" of development "between the indolence of our primitive state and the petulant activity of our egocentrism . . . the happiest and most durable epoch." Furthermore, of all the simple peoples found around the world, he says that "almost all of whom have been found in this [happy, middle] state" (*Second Discourse*, 65). Voltaire's Huron's and Diderot's Tahitians similarly embody the happy combination of nature and social institutions. They

have developed their reason, but it is—and they live—in accordance with nature.

80. John Locke, *Second Treatise of Government*, §49.

Chapter Three

1. We have seen in chapter 1 that Montaigne deduces the ideal of tranquility from the philosophers, too: "Philosophers and rustics, concur in tranquility and happiness" (III.10, 998 [780]).

2. Nature, for Montaigne, is what is left at the end of his skeptical doubting. As we have seen, he doubts everything until he can no longer doubt. He is sure of man's inability to know the essence of anything, especially anything, such as metaphysics, outside a subjective self. He thus turns inward, into the self—"I study myself more than any other subject. That is my metaphysics, that is my physics" (III.13, 1050 [821])—to ground his starting point and to serve as his point of departure. Whereas Descartes begins his discovery of nature in a similar fashion, they make different discoveries: Descartes finds reliable tools, which when applied in accordance with proper method, can uncover the mysteries of the universe; Montaigne finds only enough to begin to unravel the mysteries of the self.

3. Alexander the Great and Caesar are great men and praised by Montaigne, but they are insufficiently reflective for Montaigne, who criticizes them for this. Thus, just as Plato in Book II of the *Republic* tries to replace Achilles with Socrates as the social role model *par excellence*, Montaigne wants to replace Alexander, Caesar, Luther, Calvin (and the like) with his Socrates and himself.

4. I am not arguing that Montaigne's conception of the self is the only thing that can prevent moral skepticism from degenerating into nihilism. But something that plays the same role of limiting will is needed.

5. Montaigne himself remarks about this reception several times in Book III. See also Boase, *The Fortunes of Montaigne*; Villey, ed., *Les Essais de Michel Montaigne*, vol. III, appendix I: 1199 and 1200; and Friedrich, *Montaigne*, 1991, 224-27.

6. Hugo Friedrich, *Montaigne*, 1991, 208.

7. Karl Joachim Weintraub, *The Value of the Individual: Self and Circumstance in Autobiography* (Chicago: University of Chicago Press, 1978), 167.

8. Charles Taylor, *Sources of the Self: The Making of the Modern Identity* (Cambridge: Harvard University Press, 1989), 178, 181 and 182. It is noteworthy that these opinions transcend nationality and the disciplinarian lines of contemporary academia. Friedrich is German; Taylor Canadian; Weintraub American. Moreover, Friedrich is trained in literature; Weintraub, history; Taylor, political theory and philosophy. Friedrich, the recognized dean of Montaigne scholarship, is the key here. The others are explicitly influenced by him. Starobinski also calls Friedrich the best scholar on Montaigne, *Montaigne in Motion*, 311, n. 31.

9. On Heraclitus, see W. K. C. Guthrie, *A History of Greek Philosophy*, 2 vols.

(Cambridge: Cambridge University Press, 1962); G. S. Kirk, *Heraclitus: The Cosmic Fragments* (Cambridge: Cambridge University Press, 1954); and James Olney, *Metaphors of Self: The Meaning of Autobiography* (Princeton: Princeton University Press, 1972), 4-9.

10. For a discussion of Plutarch, Seneca, and other Roman thinkers, see Craig Brush, *From the Perspective of the Self: Montaigne's Self-Portrait* (New York: Fordham University Press, 1994), 173-74.

11. Augustine, *The Confessions*, Edward Bouverie Pusey, tr., in *Augustine*, Great Books of the Western World, vol. 18, Robert Maynard Hutchins, ed. (Chicago: Encyclopedia Britannica, 1952), Bk. X, 5-7, 72-73.

12. For Montaigne's differences from the confessional and autobiographical writings of Augustine, Petrarch, Cellini, Cardano and others, Weintraub has the fullest account. Taylor is very good on Augustine, and Friedrich, ch. 5, secs. 3 and 4, gives a short but comprehensive overview. See also Olney, *Metaphors of the Self*.

13. For Montaigne's differences from an array of later figures, consult James Olney, *Metaphors of Self: The Meaning of Autobiography* (Princeton: Princeton University Press, 1972) and P. Mansell Jones, *French Introspectives: From Montaigne to André Gide* (Cambridge: Cambridge University Press, 1937).

14. Malcolm Smith, *Montaigne and Religious Freedom: The Dawn of Pluralism*, 54.

15. Nicolas Malebranche, *De la Recherche de la Vérité* in *Oeuvres* (2 vols.) Geneviève Rodis-Lewis and Germain Malbreil, eds. (Paris: Gallimard, 1979 [1674]), Bk. II, part II, ch. V, vol. I: 278-79. Malebranche cites three editions of the *Essais*. There are references, however, to two other printings, one of which has been lost. For a succinct account of the year, place, and publisher of each edition, see Donald Frame, *Montaigne: A Biography*, 145-46. For a comprehensive account, see Richard A. Sayce and David Maskell, *A Descriptive Bibliography of Montaigne's Essais, 1580-1700* (London: The Bibliographical Society & The Modern Humanities Research Association, 1983).

16. Rousseau is the notable exception to this. In his *Confessions*, he accuses Montaigne of revealing only lovable ("aimables") vices and goes so far as to put Montaigne at the head of the false sincere: "Je mets Montaigne à la tête de ces faux sincères qui veulent tromper en disant vrai." In his *Rêveries*, he is equally harsh. He says, "Je fais la même entreprise que Montaigne, mais avec un bout contraire au sein: car il n'écrivoit ses essais que pour les autres, et je n'écris mes rêveries que pour moi." Jean-Jacques Rousseau, Première Préface aux *Confessions*, manuscrit de Neuchâtel, and *Les Rêveries du Promeneur Solitaire* in *Oeuvres complètes*, Gagnebin, Raymond, and Osmont, eds. (Paris: Pléiade, 1959), vol. I: 1149-50 and 1001, respectively.

A more extreme dissent is Schaefer's view that Montaigne "aspires to become a kind of super-ruler of generations of human beings, extending into the indefinite (if not infinite) future, thereby achieving a glory rivaling or surpassing that of the greatest founder-lawgivers" (395-96).

17. While self-knowledge is necessary for the happiness of complicated or reflective people, it is not necessary for the unreflective masses. They can achieve mental tranquility by relying on habit.

18. Scholars who appreciate the universal aspects of Montaigne's self-descriptions include R. A. Sayce, *The Essays of Montaigne: A Critical Exploration* (London: Weidenfeld and Nicolson, 1972), 117, and André Gide, *Montaigne*, 3.

19. Francis Bacon, *The New Organon*, I:51.

20. When first published, the *Essais* included only two Books. Book III and several additions to Books I and II were added in 1592 and after. On this topic see Pierre Villey's classic work, *Les sources et l'évolution des Essais de Montaigne*; and compelling criticisms by Arthur Armaingaud, "Étude sur Michel de Montaigne," in *Oeuvres complètes de Michel de Montaigne*, I: 1-257; and David Schaefer, *The Political Philosophy of Montaigne*, ch.1.

21. An interesting account of Montaigne's first essay is Robert Eden's "The Introduction of Montaigne's Politics." *Perspectives on Political Science* 20:4 (Fall 1991): 211-20.

22. See the works of Jacques Derrida, particularly *Writing and Difference*, Bass, tr. (Chicago: The University of Chicago Press, 1978) and Gilles Deleuze, *Différence et répétition* (Paris: PUF, 1968). On Derrida's account, see Vincent Descombes, *Modern French Philosophy* (Cambridge: Cambridge University Press, 1980), 36-39 and 136-67. For an account of Gilles Deleuze on themes similar to Montaigne's, see Todd May, "Difference and Unity in Gilles Deleuze," in *Gilles Deleuze and the Theater of Philosophy*, Boundas and Olkowski, eds. (New York: Routledge, 1994), 33-50. Montaigne differs from poststructuralist thinkers in thinking that there are some relevant universal qualities that human beings possess.

23. Montaigne also speaks of a "ruling pattern" ("*maistresse forme*") at II.32, 703 [548] and of "pattern and rule" at I.49, 284 [215].

24. On Montaigne's use and the history of this phrase, see Erich Auerbach, "La Condition Humaine" in *Mimesis: The Representation of Reality in Western Literature*, Willard Trask, tr. (Princeton: Princeton University Press, 1953), 285-311.

25. For comments on the corruption of his own times, see: I.37, 225-26 [169-70]; II.18, 650 [505-6]; (III.8, 920 [719]); (III.9, 923, 933, 971 [722, 729, 759]) and (III.10, 999-1000 [782]). For other derogatory judgments on the political *moeurs* of his century, see (I.23, 116-19 [85-87]) & (II.17, 642-43 [500]).

26. For diverse statements on the importance of freedom to Montaigne, see (I.21, 105 [76]); (II.17, 637-38, 641, 642 [496, 499, 500]); (III.3, 801 [625]); (III.10, 981 [767]); and all of II.19, "Of Freedom of Conscience."

27. Montaigne's conception of judgment is one of his most difficult topics to pin down. Interesting discussions of it can be found in Raymond La Charité, *The Concept of Judgment in Montaigne* (The Hague: Martinus Nijhoff, 1968) and Etienne Gilson, *Modern Philosophy: Descartes to Kant* (New York: Random

House, 1963), "Part One: The Dawn of Modern Times," 7-16.

28. Hence the work's title: *Essays*.

29. Montaigne's concept of judgment also differs from the Pyrrhonnists' conception. Like the Pyrrhonists, Montaigne emphasizes that variety exists and cannot be destroyed, but he differs from them in thinking that if a reflective person is to be happy, refining his judgment and incorporating its lessons must be among his chief occupations. To Montaigne, judgment should be honed not suspended.

30. Human beings are thus revealed as fundamentally weak creatures unable to know what they most desire to know. It is this fundamental weakness that serves for Montaigne as the basis for his calls for toleration. If man accepts his natural limits, toleration will follow. But we are getting ahead of our story.

31. On Montaigne's view of natural law, see Horowitz, *Seeds of Virtue and Knowledge*, 206-22. An excellent illustration of the importance of Cicero in the sixteenth century is Gary Remer, *Humanism and the Rhetoric of Toleration* (University Park: Penn State University Press, 1996). For an interesting study of Montaigne's use of quotations, see Mary McKinley, *Words in a Corner: Studies in Montaigne's Latin Quotations*.

32. In altering Montaigne's chosen method of presentation, I somewhat excuse myself by recollecting his view that one can do violence when necessary but that one should feel bad about doing it (III.1, 777 [607]).

33. Just as Montaigne's account of the cannibals emphasizes the things they do without, so Montaigne's conception of the reflective life emphasizes the things to be avoided: metaphysics and fear of death. To be healthy and whole, one must also accept one's fundamental ignorance.

34. Similarly, both the Academic and Pyrrhonist skeptics reject troubling oneself over issues of God or the beyond.

35. The Frame edition of the *Essays* has 856 pages, the Pléiade edition has 1,088.

36. On the lack of correspondence between the true and the useful according to Montaigne, see: II.12, 492 [379]; III.6, 876 [685]; III.8, 904-5, 909 [707 and 711]; III.9, 929 [726]; III.11, 1003-4, 1011-12 [785 and 791]; and, III.13, 1056 [826].

37. Montaigne is thus "no longer amazed" that people are "hoodwinked by the monkey tricks" of religious prophets (III.10, 991 [775]) and observes that "men stunned by their fate will throw themselves back, as on any superstition, on seeking in the heavens the ancient cause and threats of their misfortune" (I.11, 45 [29]).

38. See also II.29, 688 [537]; II.37, 761-62 [594]; and, III.11, 1004-5 [786].

39. For more on Montaigne's views of comedy and tragedy, see "Of Democritus and Heraclitus" (I.50).

40. See, for example, (I.20, 83-84 [59] and (III.9, 956 [747]).

41. On suicide, see II.3 (entire) and II.35, 728-29 [568]. On funeral rites, see (I.3, 23 [12]). On Montaigne's own brushes with death, see (II.6, 352-53 [268-69]), and his account of when he was captured and held prisoner. Death is also

thematically treated in essays such as the "Apology." I.20 includes a three-page speech on death which Montaigne puts into the mouth of "Nature" herself. (While attributed to nature, the views expressed in the speech rely heavily on Seneca and Lucretius.) On other topics related to death, see (I.22, 105 [77]); (III.12, 1037 [811]); and II.35 (entire).

42. Although this is qualified by Montaigne's sometimes praise of the acceptance of death demonstrated by simple peasants and statements asserting that Nature will teach men how to die if they give her the chance (see, for example, I, 20, 88-89 [63] and III.12, 1016 [794]), Montaigne also criticizes the peasants' acceptance of death for two reasons. First, because it is unthinking, done without reflection, he says that they are open to manipulation by people who confront them with (false) ideas about an afterlife. Second, this option is simply unavailable to more reflective people.

43. See also II.6, especially the examples of Canius Julius (II.6, 350-51 [267]) and of Montaigne himself (II.6, 352-53 [269] et passim).

44. I am here speaking only about "natural" deaths, not accidents, murders, etc., for which one can never totally plan.

45. See, for example, (I.20, 88 [62]).

46. U. Benigni, "Montaigne." *The Catholic Encyclopedia*, vol. 10: 512-13.

47. Jean Starobinski, *Montaigne in Motion*, Goldhammer, tr. (Chicago: University of Chicago Press, 1985) speaks eloquently on this relationship.

48. On occasion, Montaigne almost makes death seem to be welcome, which is why he says, "Most philosophers have either deliberately anticipated or hastened and abetted their own death" (I.14, 51 [34]), but it is important to note that Socrates only provoked his death when he was seventy years old. He avoided politics his entire life, he says, to avoid a premature death (Plato, "The Apology," 31d-32a).

49. Starobinski, *Montaigne in Motion*, 74.

50. This claim that "there is nothing evil" is, as we shall see later in this chapter, overstated. Suffering pain, while not exactly "evil," is nonetheless described by Montaigne as horrible and to be avoided.

51. This emphasis on knowledge of ignorance seems to put Montaigne squarely in the Academic camp, not in the Pyrrhonist, because the latter never know if they know anything or not. However, noting many similarities between the two schools, Laursen says that "the principle justification for treating them as different movements is the historiographical tradition" (*Politics of Skepticism*, 52). This may be so, but at least with respect to the traditional distinctions as Sextus presents them—which have analytical significance—Montaigne is an Academic, not a Pyrrhonist, skeptic.

52. II.12, 487-94 [375-80]. By contrast, Schaefer, *The Political Philosophy of Montaigne*, 308-9, asserts that Montaigne is not only a mythmaker but an exponent of "philosophic propaganda." Schaefer's claim that Montaigne advocates *divertissement*, as argued below, however, is unpersuasive. Montaigne takes his self-exploration much more seriously than Schaefer allows.

53. "It is not in Montaigne, but in me, that I find all that I see there." Blaise Pascal, "Pensée number 64," in *Pensées de Pascal,* Léon Brunschvicg ed. (Paris: Éditions de Cluny, 1934); "Pensée number 689," (according to Pascal's own text) in *Oeuvres Complètes*, Louis Lafuma, ed. (Paris: Éditions de Seuil, 1963), 591.

54. "He painted human nature." Voltaire, *Remarques sur les Pensées de M. Pascal* in *Oeuvres Complètes de Voltaire* (Garnier Frères: Paris, 1879), vol. 22: 27-64. Ironically, Voltaire's praise of Montaigne is coupled with attacks on Pascal and all the Port Royal school.

55. For a different comparison between Montaigne and Socrates, see Frederick Kellermann, "Montaigne's Socrates," *The Romanic Review* 45:3 (October 1954): 170-77. Kellermann's Montaigne is well presented, and he makes many important comparisons, but his Socrates is more religious than mine or Montaigne's.

56. Montaigne's putting words in Socrates' mouth raises the same issue as it does when Plato and Xenophon do the same thing: the relation of Socrates to the author. Do the authors, Montaigne included, accurately portray Socrates or use him to make their own points? Comparisons of the different portrayals reveal more about the authors than about Socrates himself.

57. Montaigne discusses the art of seeming artless in many contexts but especially with respect to education and courtly life. For an important earlier discussion of this, see Baldesar Castiglione, *The Book of the Courtier* (1528). Castiglione describes ideal court manners as "to practice in all things a certain nonchalance which conceals all artistry and makes whatever one says or does seem uncontrived and effortless" and says that "true art is what does not seem to be art" (Castiglione, *The Book of the Courtier*, George Bull, tr. [London: Penguin, 1967], Bk. I: 67). Similarly, Montaigne says, "my plan in speaking is to display extreme carelessness and unstudied and unpremeditated gestures, as if they arose from the immediate occasion" (III.9, 940 [735]).

58. People have been arguing over the proper interpretation of Plato's Socrates for millennia and Montaigne was acutely aware that more books are written on books than on any other topic (III.13, 1045 [818]). Nonetheless, to see how Montaigne reads Plato, see, for example: I.25, 142 [106]; I.30, 195-96 [146]; I.47, 276 [209]; II.11, 401-2 [307]; II.12, 487-95 [375-81]; III.2, 795-96 [620]; and, III.8, 906 [708].

59. Kellermann sees it as the reverse. He considers Socrates to be the correction of Montaigne's excessive anthropocentrism ("Montaigne's Socrates," 177). Whether Montaigne's interpretation of Socrates clarifies the Socratic project or does injustice to it is a question beyond the scope of this book.

60. On Montaigne's alleged accidental nature, see also II.27, 677 [528]; II.33, 710 [553]; I.20, 82-83 [58]; and I. 23, 108-9 [79].

61. On Montaigne's rhetoric, see Frank Lestringant, ed., *Rhétorique de Montaigne* (Paris: Champion, 1985), especially the preface by Marc Fumaroli, and Schaefer, *The Political Philosophy of Montaigne*, ch.1.

62. Plato, *The Republic*, 372d; and *Symposium*, 210b-c.

63. On Pascal's discussion of *divertissement*, see *Pensées*, Lafuma, ed., section VIII: numbers 132-39, and 414. In Brunschvicg, ed., numbers 170, 168, 169, 469, 139, 142, 166, 143, 171. Schaefer claims that Montaigne promotes *divertissement*. Schaefer is correct that Montaigne insists that the mind have a goal, and it is true that he says that any goal is better than no goal, but how can it be doubted that Montaigne prefers self-discovery over all other goals?

64. It is for exactly this reason that Montaigne says he began to write his *Essays*. He turned his attention to himself to tame the "chimeras and fantastic monsters" which "one after another, without order or purpose" troubled his mind (I.8, 34 [21]).

65. Montaigne delights in the perverse contrariness of human desire. On this paradox, see: II.17, 633-34 [493]. For similar paradoxes, see, for example: I.10, 42 [27]; I.21 (entire); I.37, 226-27 [170]; I.39, 239 [180]; II.15 (entire); II.20 (entire); II.31 (entire); III.5, 855-60 [669-72]; and III.9, 925 [723].

66. Many people have written on Montaigne's conception of self-exploration, and it is not necessary to give an exhaustive account of it here. Among these accounts, Starobinski, *Montaigne in Motion,* is the most psychologically attuned; Frederick Rider, *The Dialectic of Selfhood in Montaigne* (Stanford: Stanford University Press, 1973) is interesting; and Ermanno Bencivenga, *The Discipline of Subjectivity: An Essay on Montaigne* (Princeton: Princeton University Press, 1990), pays particular attention to the image of the double self.

67. On Montaigne's passive and active natures of the self, see: Starobinski, *Montaigne in Motion*; Ermanno Bencivenga, *The Discipline of Subjectivity: An Essay on Montaigne* (Princeton: Princeton University Press, 1990); and Friedrich, *Montaigne* (1991), 208.

68. "It takes management to enjoy life" (III.13, 1092 [853]), and Montaigne thinks that a happy person will order and regulate himself.

69. Jacques Lacan, "Propos sur la causalité psychique," in *Écrits* (Paris: Le Seuil, 1966), 179.

70. An illuminating discussion of the paradoxical connection between self-acceptance and self-empowerment is Marianne Noble, *The Masochistic Pleasures of Sentimental Literature* (Princeton: Princeton University Press, 2000).

71. Montaigne names discussion with "talented gentlemen" as one "Of Three Kinds of Association" (III.3) that he praises. He also favors associations with "beautiful and well-bred women" and books.

72. See for example the descriptions on (III.8, 917 [717]) and (III.3, 802 [625-26]).

73. Rousseau accuses Montaigne of revealing only lovable ("*aimables*") vices. Jean-Jacques Rousseau, "Première Préface" aux *Confessions*, manuscrit de Neuchâtel, in *Oeuvres complètes*, vol. I: 1149-50. Not all readers, of course, share this judgment of Montaigne. For a list of readers who found Montaigne to be vulgar, one might consult Boase, *The Fortunes of Montaigne*; Donald Frame, *Montaigne in France: 1812-1852* (New York: Columbia University Press, 1940);

and Pierre Villey, *Montaigne devant la postérité* (Paris: Boivin, 1935).

74. This does not mention Montaigne's political discretion. He was sent on weighty political missions by both Henry III and Henry of Navarre, which he teasingly alludes to but declines to discuss. Because of his extensive and unique participation in events, the historian de Thou, a contemporary of Montaigne's, encouraged him to write a political history of his times. Cited in Malcolm Smith, *Montaigne and Religious Freedom*, 174 and 224.

75. David Quint, *Montaigne and the Quality of Mercy*, 57, makes a parallel observation about the importance of accepting the body, noting that for Montaigne an absence of cruelty toward oneself is linked to an absence of cruelty toward others: "those who cannot forgive themselves—particularly those that cannot forgive their own bodies that doom them to mortality—will not be apt to show clemency toward others."

76. For the full story, see (I.33, 216-17 [162]).

77. Stoics deny the reality of pain; Pyrrhonists refuse to decide whether it is good or bad.

78. Montaigne counsels the essaying of pain (II.37, 740 [577]), just as he counsels the "essaying" of death (I.19, 78-79 [55]). It is no accident that in dealing with these matters of supreme importance, Montaigne uses the word "essay" (I.23, 107 [78] & III.9, 946 [740]). By using this word, he is confirming the importance of the confrontation with these subjects for life.

79. Nannerl Keohane, *Philosophy and the State in France*, 99.

80. On Descartes' debt to Montaigne, see Léon Brunschvicg, *Descartes et Pascal: Lecteurs de Montaigne*; Michael G. Paulson, *The Possible Influence of Montaigne's "Essais" on Descartes' "Treatise on the Passions*;" and Boase, *The Fortunes of Montaigne*, ch. 25.

Chapter Four

1. On the importance of this positioning in Montaigne, see Schaefer, *Political Philosophy of Montaigne*, chs. 1 and 4; Arthur Armaingaud, *Montaigne pamphlétaire: L'énigme du Contr'un* (Paris: Hachette, 1910); and Michael Platt, "In the Middle of Montaigne (I.29, II.19, III.7)" in *The Order of Montaigne's Essays*, Daniel Martin, ed. (Amherst: The University of Massachusetts and Hestia Press, 1989), 124-43. On the importance placed on "the center" in Renaissance writing generally, see the several publications of Alastair Fowler, particularly *Triumphal Forms: Structural Patterns in Elizabethan Poetry* (Cambridge: Cambridge University Press, 1970), chs. 4 and 5.

2. III.9, 941 [736].

3. Montaigne never published La Boétie's work as part of the *Essays*. He did, however, publish his original intention and states his second intention to replace *La Servitude Volontaire* with some of La Boétie's sonnets. Montaigne published some of La Boétie's sonnets in the first editions of the *Essays* but later removed

them, leaving the center of Book I virtually blank. Does his omission of La Boétie's work signify a breaking with La Boétie's radical views, which Montaigne never states in his own name in the *Essays*, or is Montaigne simply being more cautious than La Boétie, whose work, Montaigne writes (I.28, 193 [144]), was being used to justify revolution? For a complex, politically oriented discussion of Montaigne's relation to La Boétie, see David Schaefer, ed., *Freedom over Servitude: Montaigne, La Boétie, and On Voluntary Servitude* (Westport, Conn.: Greenwood Press, 1998). François Rigolot, "Montaigne's Purloined Letters," in *Montaigne: Essays in Reading*, Gérard Defaux, ed., 145-66, explains Montaigne's relationship to both La Boétie and these textual changes as playful.

4. Just as Montaigne juxtaposes his ideal in "Of Cannibals" with a description of the cannibals' cruelty at the end of the preceding chapter (I.30), so his vision in "Of Freedom of Conscience" draws on examples from the end of II.18.

5. To appreciate the depth of Montaigne's hatred for Christianity's crude censorship, one must appreciate the importance of the example. While Montaigne says that he normally cannot spend an hour on a book, he claims to have read Tacitus—at least what's left of his writing—in one sitting (III.8, 919 [718]). This is a function both of what was destroyed and Montaigne's deep appreciation for this writer.

6. Locke, *Second Treatise of Government*, §§ 9 and 13 similarly calls his doctrines strange. Machiavelli and Hobbes call theirs new. While Montaigne joins them with his self-consciously "novel and strange" doctrine, he does so by attempting to resurrect an ancient practice—although for radically modern reasons.

7. For more on Montaigne's views of Epaminondas, see (III.1, 779-81 [608-10]) and "Of the Most Outstanding Men," (II.36, 734-36 [572-74]).

8. Ammianus Marcellinus, *Rerum Gestarum Liber* XXII.5: 2-4, quoted in Lecler, *Toleration and the Reformation*, vol. I: 43. Marcellinus, mentioned several times in "Of Freedom of Conscience," is probably Montaigne's main source on Julian.

9. In his *Travel Journal* (March 20, 1581), Montaigne mentions five other heresies with which he was charged: overuse of the word "fortune," praising heretics as poets, demanding that people be free of evil impulses while praying, blaming as cruelty any punishment more severe than death, and wanting children to be able to do both good and bad, so they can freely choose to do good. Montaigne added a statement explaining how he meant no offense and would, of course, change all the errant passages. Other than adding this disclaimer, however, he made no significant alterations.

10. The issue of naturalness here parallels the discussion of nature as both merely descriptive versus nature as normative that we explored in chapter 3.

11. The astonishment that Montaigne condemns, with the limited foresight and the inability to adapt which is implied by it, is exactly the fault that, according to Montaigne, led to the cannibals' destruction.

12. See Nakam, *Montaigne et son temps*.

13. Unlike other moderns, who strive only to institute the effectual truth, Montaigne also makes room for philosophical speculations about moral ideas. The "exercise of our minds," he says, is not totally vain; he just relegates it to the private sphere of essaying (III.9, 934 [730]). Unlike many modern political philosophers, Montaigne celebrates the philosophical activity in itself.

14. Many scholars emphasize Montaigne's conservatism. See, for example, Frieda Brown, *Religious and Political Conservatism in the Essais of Montaigne*; Sayce, *The Essays of Montaigne*, 233-59; and, Edward Williamson, "On the Montaigne: A Remonstrance," *French Review,* 23 (1949): 92-100.

15. Montaigne's conservatism applies to religious affairs, too. He is against the vernacularization of the Bible (I.56, 306 [232]) and often states that humans must submit completely to authority or do without it. By yielding on some points of dogma, Montaigne thinks Catholics have thrown everything into doubt (I.27, 180 [134] and II.12, 416 [320]). However, he approvingly cites Plato's model of only allowing old people (when not in the presence of the young) to search for the reasons behind religious requirements (I.56, 307 [233]).

16. On the benefits and weaknesses of democracy, consider some of Montaigne's remarks on the most celebrated democracies: Athens, which he once condemns as "*domination populaire*" for murdering its great generals (but, oddly, he does not here mention its murder of Socrates) (I.3, 23 [12]); Venice, then regarded as the greatest republic of modern times, about which Montaigne says that La Boétie "would rather have been born in Venice than in Sarlat, *and with reason*" (I.28, [144], my emphasis); and Rome, which made Montaigne an honorary citizen—a fact he immodestly trumpets for four pages (III.9, 762-66]). (Montaigne's vanity about this honor occurs in his essay "Of Vanity"—a playful and demonstrative illustration of the vice at issue.)

17. Thus, far from denying the importance of regime type in affecting the views of ordinary citizens, Montaigne argues that regime type is so important that changing it is a process doomed to many, perhaps insurmountable, difficulties and disasters.

18. In an essay entitled "Of the Inequality that is between us" (I.42), Montaigne describes monarchs as we might describe the wizard in Oz: The stage and pomp create an illusion; "the emperor, whose pomp dazzles you in public . . . see him behind the curtain: he is nothing but an ordinary man" (I.42, 253 [191]). Montaigne often says that the differences between human beings are like costumes in a play: take off the uniforms and we are all the same underneath. Monarchs' powers do not protect them from illnesses or anxieties. Indeed, he says in the book's memorable closing passage: "there is no use mounting on stilts, for on stilts we must still walk on our own legs. And on the loftiest throne in the world we are still sitting only on our own rump" (III.13, [857]).

19. On the need for veneration of law, consider the debate between Madison in *Federalist* 49 and Jefferson's Letter to Madison, "The Earth Belongs in Usufruct to the Living" (September 6, 1789) in Jefferson, *Political Writings*, 593-98.

20. Aristotle, *The Politics*, 1253a1-40. Politics, he says, is necessary for reason to fully develop in human beings. Those without the city are either beasts (no reason) or gods (reason without the city).

21. Montaigne also says that "custom and length of time are far stronger counselors than any other compulsion" (I.14, 54 [36]).

22. Montaigne acknowledges that laws are sometimes made by wise men, such as Solon, but he considers this the exception, not the rule. And while laws are made by people who happen to live in constructed cultures, they might be "reasonable" relative to the context; laws can be arbitrary but not wicked. All of this acknowledged, Montaigne nonetheless thinks that laws are a particular facet of human life in which exploitation rears its ugly head.

23. Montaigne's "natural men" are cannibals.

24. In one place Montaigne notes how vice can be channelled to produce virtuous actions. "Ambition can teach men valor, and temperance, and liberality, and even justice. Greed can implant in the heart of a shop apprentice, brought up in obscurity and idleness, the confidence to cast himself far from hearth and home . . . it also teaches discretion and wisdom. Venus herself supplies resolution and boldness to boys" (II.1, 321 [244]). While this perhaps suggests that prudent laws could channel these desires into fruitful and useful activities, Montaigne considers this to be an "arduous and hazardous undertaking" and wishes that "fewer people would meddle with it" (II.1, 321 [244]). He has little confidence in man's ability to foresee the results of such "meddling" and does not advise it. If law can secure peace and stability, Montaigne seems to be content.

25. Although Montaigne once distinguishes "justice in itself, natural and universal" from "that other, special, national justice, constrained to the need of our governments" (III.1, 773 [604]), he never defines "justice in itself," probably because he cannot. Such a pure concept exists outside the human sphere, if it exists at all. Montaigne's aim is not to dwell on the undefinable but to think through the implications of the crookedness of public life and political affairs.

26. Montaigne catalogues these bad effects in several places. See, for example: I.23, 117-20 [86-89]; I.37, 225-27 [169-70]; II.17, 638-39 [497]; II.18, 648-50 [505-6]; III.2, 788 [615]; III.8, 918-21 [719]; III.9, 923-24 [722]; III.9, 938-39 [734]; III.9, 943-44 [738]; III.9, 970-72 [759-60], and, III.10, 999-1000 [782].

27. For example, Mill lists three freedoms that must be secured if a society is to be considered free: "the inward domain of consciousness," which Montaigne demands, the "liberty of tastes and pursuits," i.e., the right to act based on one's opinion, which is the point in dispute here, and the right "of combination" with others in pursuit of one's ideas and life plan (*On Liberty*, ch.1, 13-14).

28. Montaigne uses the role-playing metaphor throughout the *Essays*. See: I.14, 55 [37]; I.19, 78 [55]; I.20, 80 [56]; I.20, 87 [62]; I.20, 92 [65-66]; I.20, 94-95 [68]; I.42, 252-53 [191]; I.50, 291-92 [220-21]; II.3, 330 [251]; II.6, 357 [273]; II.16, 605-7 [471-2]; II.17, 618 [481]; II.17, 630 [491]; II.17, 639 [497]; II.31, 696 [543]; II.36, 732 [571]; II.37, 739-40 [577]; II.37, 764 [596]; III.1, 769-70 [601];

III.2, 785-86 [613]; III.3, 803 [626]; III.5, 860 [672]; III.7, 896 [700]; III.8, 913-14 [714]; III.9, 957 [748]; III.10, 980-81 [766-67]; III.10, 989-90 [773-74]; III.10, 997 [780]; III.11, 1004 [785]; III.12, 1023 [800]; and, III.13, 1089-90 [851-52]. Montaigne's most frequent references along these lines are to the world as a stage, human beings as actors, and masks. Montaigne did not invent this imagery; it was common in ancient Rome. Montaigne did bring it forcefully into the modern era. For example, it is believed that Shakespeare was greatly influenced by Montaigne on this point.

29. The relation between being in the world and essaying oneself is a complicated one in Montaigne's thought. Paradoxically, he says that he pulls into himself when in a crowd and "I throw myself into affairs of state and into the world more readily when I am alone" (III.3, 801 [625]). Moreover, he himself personally always did both; he retreated from the life at the court in order to essay himself on his relatively isolated estate, but he nonetheless stayed in touch with the world through his political advising and negotiating and his service as mayor.

30. Derrida, "Structure, Sign and Play in the Discourse of the Human Sciences" in *Writing and Difference*, Alan Bass, tr. (Chicago: University of Chicago Press, 1978), 278.

31. Butler argues that human beings have no choice but to play roles that are handed to them at birth and that the only agency available to an individual is to say her or his lines badly, ironically, or as parody. See Judith Butler, *Gender Trouble: Feminism and the Subversion of Identity* (New York: Routledge, 1990).

32. The best attempt at such a critique is Michael Walzer, *Interpretation and Social Criticism* (Cambridge: Harvard University Press, 1987). Walzer's critique assumes divergent moral strands in a society; from the point of view of one, the others can be criticized. But suppose the whole scope of debate within a society is repulsive? In such a case, Walzer's critic would have only undesirable ground on which to stand.

33. Thus, despite the fact that Defaux and Duvall, two poststructuralist readers of Montaigne, note clear patterns in particular essays that they study, they conclude that Montaigne had no discernable intention in or reason for making them. Their perceptive observations about the text are overridden by the methodological assumptions with which they began.

34. Derrida, quoted in Butler, *Bodies that Matter: On the Discursive Limits of "Sex"* (New York: Routledge, 1993), 1.

35. See Butler's *Gender Trouble: Feminism and the Subversion of Identity* as well as *Bodies that Matter*, intro.

36. Foucault, "Nietzsche, Genealogy, History," 87-88.

37. Foucault, "Nietzsche, Genealogy, History," 85.

38. Foucault, "Nietzsche, Genealogy, History," 88.

39. Montaigne speaks, for example, of preserving "freedom of choice" and his "free will not to enslave my belief easily" (II.17, 637 [496] and II.17, 641 [499]).

40. "What fear has once made me will, I am bound still to will when without

fear" (III.1, 779 [608]).

41. For more on Montaigne's views of Epaminondas, see (III.1, 779-81 [608-10]) and II.36, "Of the Most Outstanding Men," (II.36, 734-36 [572-74]).

42. A friend, being another self, is extremely important to Montaigne. In his essay "Of Friendship" (I.28), Montaigne cites several examples of friends who, out of allegiance to each other, fought and killed tyrants who infringed on their relationship. Friendship, a seemingly private activity, thus has strong political implications for Montaigne.

43. Mill, *On Liberty*, ch.1, 13-14.

44. Among the limits that Montaigne says the state should accept is the rule of law, as opposed to the sovereign's whim: "I hold that we should live by right and authority, not by reward or favor" (III.9, 944 [738]); "What I owe, I owe to the ordinary and natural obligations" (III.9, 945 [739]), what he terms "common obligation" (III.9, 944 [738]); and he wants his obligation to be "relative to" and "restricted" by law (III.1, 772 [603]). Montaigne's emphasis on law aims to remove zeal from the public sphere: "We owe subjection and obedience equally to all kings, for that concerns their office; but we do not owe esteem, any more than affection, except to their virtue" (I.3, 19 [9]).

45. See Stephen Holmes, "Jean Bodin: The Paradox of Sovereignty and the Privatization of Religion" in *Nomos* XXX (1988): 5-45. Foucault argues that the state's surrendering of political power does not lead to more freedom on the part of individual citizens, because the relinquished power of the state is more than increased through the domination of the modern disciplines.

46. See Plato, *Republic*, 496d-e, where Socrates says a philosopher in an unjust city "keeps quiet and minds his own business—as a man in a storm, when dust and rain are blown about by the wind, stands aside under a little wall. Seeing others filled with lawlessness, he is content if somehow he himself can live his life here pure of injustice and unholy deeds, and take his leave from it graciously and cheerfully with fair hope." Montaigne also says that he would not have stayed in Athens as Socrates did. He might also agree with the philosopher Theodorus' view that "it is unjust for a wise man to risk his life for the good of his country, and endanger wisdom for the sake of fools" (I.50, 292 [221]).

47. Keohane, *Philosophy and the State in France*, 111. For some of Montaigne's wittier comments debunking royal pomp, see (I.42, 250-53 [189-91]); (III.2, 787 [614]); and (III.13, 1096 [857]).

48. Plato, *Republic*, 376c-417b and 555b-563e.

49. Plato, *Republic*, 557c-558a.

50. Plato, *Laws*, see Books X and XII. For different statements on the composition of the Nocturnal Council, see 951d-e, 961a-c, and 964b.

51. See, for example, Aristotle's account of the unnamed virtue resembling sociability (*Nichomachean Ethics*, 1126b11-1127a14), how even mundane associations are based on friendship rather than tolerance (*Ethics*, 1161b11-16), and his account of goodwill (*Ethics*, 1166b29-1167a20).

52. Matt. 22: 21. For background and the influence of Lactantius and Tertullian, see Lecler, *Toleration and the Reformation*, I: 32-64.

53. Matt. 13: 24-30, 13: 6-43.

54. Eph. 4: 15.

55. Augustine, *Ad Donatistas*, 10. On faith not being forced, see *Joannem*, xxvi, n. 2.

56. Thomas Aquinas, *Summa Theologica*, II, II, q. 10, art. 8, ad. 2.

57. Thomas Aquinas, *Summa Theologica*, II, II, q. 10, art. 8, c.

58. Lecler, *Toleration and the Reformation*, I: 88.

59. Ficino, "Of the Christian Religion," ch. 4, cited in Lecler, *Toleration and the Reformation*, I: 111.

60. Nederman, *Worlds of Difference: European Discourses of Toleration, 1100-1550*, makes compelling arguments for more toleration in Medieval and Renaissance philosophy than is conventionally acknowledged.

61. Cited in Roland Bainton, "Sebastian Castellio and the Toleration Controversies of the Sixteenth Century," in *Persecution and Liberty: Essays in Honor of George Lincoln Burr* (New York: Century, 1931), 183-209. On the toleration controversies in general, a concise account is J. W. Allen, *A History of Political Thought in the Sixteenth Century* (London: Methuen, 1928), 73-102.

62. Erasmus is generally considered to be the most tolerant and most creative of all the Christian humanists. See Johan Huizinga, *Erasmus and the Age of Reformation*, F. Hopman, tr. (New York: Harper and Row, 1975).

63. Bodin sometimes exceeds the typical scope of the *politiques'* arguments. In his *Heptaplomeres*, for example, which was not published until well after his death, he treats all religions as equals, considers argument and disputation about religious affairs to be futile, and wants everyone regardless of religious persuasion to live together in peace.

64. Montaigne does not compare his arguments for toleration to those of his predecessors; the comparisons are my own. For background, see Lecler, *Toleration and the Reformation*, vol. I: 11-113 and Kamen, *The Rise of Toleration*, 7-110.

65. See Kamen and Pintard.

Chapter Five

1. See also Michael Gillespie, *Nihilism Before Nietzsche* (Chicago: University of Chicago Press, 1995).

2. Nietzsche, *Assorted Opinions and Maxims*, aphorism 408. See also the introduction, note 27 above.

3. While Montaigne here speaks of "desires," he holds the same to be true of the will.

4. Nietzsche, *On the Genealogy of Morals*, "Second Essay," Aphorism 12, 79. Unlike Nietzsche, Montaigne does not deem the will to be irresistible. He agrees that "[w]ill and desires are a law unto themselves," but he nonetheless says that

"actions must receive their law from public regulation" (III.1, 772 [603]).

5. For Nietzsche's views on Napoleon, see *On the Genealogy of Morals*, I.16, 54. Montaigne says this of Alexander's conquests had he lived longer. And in few peaks of enthusiasm Montaigne represents Alexander as "the utmost achievement of human nature"(571) and, in contrast to Jesus, he is "the greatest man that was simply a man" (58). Of Caesar, Montaigne writes: "when I consider the incomparable greatness of that soul, I excuse victory for being unable to shake free of him, even in that very unjust and very iniquitous cause." He adds that Caesar's excessive vanity, "this single vice, in my opinion, ruined in him the finest and richest nature that ever was, and has made his memory abominable to all good men, because he *willed* to seek his glory in the ruin of his country and the subversion of the most powerful and flourishing republic that the world will ever see" (II.33, [553 and 554], emphasis added). Montaigne's ultimate judgment of Caesar might differ from Nietzsche's, but the point is that Montaigne appreciates the same qualities as Nietzsche.

6. Montaigne agrees with Nietzsche that struggle is inevitable in human life, that pain and suffering come with the human condition. Both also deem struggle to be good for mankind; they just advocate struggle for different things.

7. See Mark Warren and Alexander Nehemas. Also, Derrida, and the book *The New Nietzsche*.

8. Nietzsche, *On the Genealogy of Morals*, I.11, 40. Among such destructive types, Nietzsche includes: "the Roman, Arabian, Germanic, Japanese nobility, the Homeric heroes, the Scandinavian Vikings—they all shared this need" (I.11, 41).

9. Nietzsche, *On the Genealogy of Morals*, II.17, 86-87.

10. See Nietzsche's account of the Homeric heroes (I.11, 41). Interestingly, Montaigne praises Homer in very similar terms. In an essay entitled, "Of the Most Outstanding Men" (II.36), which praises Homer, Alexander the Great, and Epaminondas, Homer is praised by Montaigne as "a source of wonder to me, almost above man's estate," because "his authority created and brought into credit in the world many deities." He is described as "the first and the last of poets" (which might seem to be a difference with Nietzsche except that Montaigne thinks that all philosophers are poets, too) and praised for having "created the most excellent production that can be": "Is it not a noble drama in which kings, commonwealths, and emperors keep playing their parts for so many ages, and for which this whole great universe serves as a theater?" (II.36, 730-32 [569-71]).

11. Nietzsche, *On the Genealogy of Morals*, II.18, 87.

12. Nietzsche, *On the Genealogy of Morals*, II.6, 67; II.7, 67; and, II.24, 95.

13. In this sense, Nietzsche, Montaigne, and perhaps all philosophers, are alike: they want to persuade the world of their visions.

14. Passages in which Alexander is described in terms that imply his possession of self-knowledge or mental tranquility include I.20, 83 [58]; I.42, 253-54 [192]; I.44, 262 [198]; and III.13, 1088 [850]. Despite these passages, Montaigne's claim that Alexander and Caesar "sought unrest [*l'inquietude*] and difficulties"—not

"security and repose"—fundamentally contradicts the idea of their having achieved tranquility (I.14, 61 [42]). On Alexander's lack of contentedness, see also III.13, 1093 [854].

15. Despite the coinage of the word only in 1895, the fact that Montaigne—and Seneca—wrote on this point shows that *schadenfreude* is no recent phenomenon.

16. Montaigne follows this statement with a famous quotation from Lucretius: "Tis sweet, when the sea is high and winds are driving/To watch from shore another's anguished striving" (III.1, 768 [599]). For Lucretius on *schadenfreude*, see *De Rerum Nature*, W. H. D. Rouse, tr., Martin Ferguson Smith, ed. (Cambridge: Harvard University Press, 1982), especially the opening lines of Bk. II, 95. See also Bk. V, lines 1-12, 379; Bk. V, lines 999-1010, 457; Bk. V, lines 1412-35, 489.

17. Montaigne's attitude towards women is complicated. On the one hand, his work is littered with pejorative statements about women, often lumping them with children and the elderly as enfeebled classes. On the other hand, in "On Some Verses of Virgil" (III.5), his most systematic exploration of the relations between the sexes, he argues: "Women are not wrong at all when they reject the rules of life that have been introduced into the world, inasmuch as it is the men who have made these without them" (III.5, 832 [649]). Moreover, Montaigne concludes: "I say that males and females are cast in the same mold; except for education and custom, the difference is not great" (III.5, 875 [685]). Education and custom account for the enfeeblement of women that he observes around him. Also, Montaigne's closest student, to whom he bequeathed his literary papers, was a woman, Marie de Gournay. See Maryanne Cline Horowitz, "Marie de Gournay: A Case Study of the Mentor-Protegee Friendship," in *Sixteenth Century Journal* 17:3 (1986): 271-84 and Cecile Insdorf, *Montaigne and Feminism* (Chapel Hill: University of North Carolina Press, 1977).

18. Montaigne also traces the source of cruelty to cowardice in the doer's soul at II.27, 678 [528]; II.27, 678-79 [529]; and, II.5, 348-49 [266].

19. Montaigne's notion of pity may very well have Christian roots. Rousseau uses pity in a way similar to Montaigne. Both ascribe it only to those who are healthy. But whereas Montaigne thinks that the healthy are relatively rare, Rousseau, in his *Second Discourse*, credits it to all men in his description of the original state of nature.

20. While pointing out that "[p]ity and commiseration are mingled with some esteem for the thing we pity" (I.50, 291 [221]), Montaigne does in this context advise against feeling pity for human beings generally. As we saw in chapter 3, he prefers to mock the inanity of the human condition rather than pity it. This is by no means inconsistent with his commiseration for the suffering, however, because mocking the silliness of man's actions and his sensitivity to pain and suffering both result from his awareness of human frailty.

21. Rousseau, "Discourse on the Origin of Inequality," in *Basic Political Writings*, 35.

22. Adam Smith, *The Theory of Moral Sentiments* (Oxford: Clarendon Press, 1976 [1759-90]), part I, section I, chapter 1, paragraph 5, 10. In fact, for Smith the empathetic connection between sufferer and observer runs both ways. (See, for example, I, I, 2, 1, 13).

23. David Hume, *A Treatise of Human Nature* (London: J. M. Dent and Sons, 1936 [1739-40]), Book II, part II, section VII (vol. II: 86).

24. Smith, *The Theory of Moral Sentiments*, part VII, section III, chapter 3, paragraphs 1-17, 321-27, nicely explains the differences between the two accounts of the origin of sympathy and gives a brief but powerful analysis of them.

25. Anthony Ashley Cooper, 3rd Earl of Shaftesbury, *Characteristicks of Men, Manners, Opinions, Times* (Oxford: Clarendon Press, 1999 [1711]), I. III. 3, 215.

26. Hume, *A Treatise of Human Nature*, Book II, part II, section VII (vol. II: 88).

27. Smith, *The Theory of Moral Sentiments*, 12 and 9. Hume, *A Treatise of Human Nature*, II: 88.

28. Hume, *A Treatise of Human Nature*, II, I, IV (II: 10); Smith, *The Theory of Moral Sentiments*, part I, section I, chapter 5, paragraph 9, 26.

29. Montaigne's condemnation of torture is another one of the reasons why his book was criticized by the Church's censors in Rome.

30. Elaine Scarry, *The Body in Pain: The Making and Unmaking of the World* (New York: Oxford University Press, 1985), is a thorough exploration of bodily pain, how it manifests itself, and how it is manipulated by others. Like Montaigne, she says, "physical pain is so incontestably real" (27). By contrast, Montaigne does not seem to consider psychic or spiritual pain to be as bad. While this might seem shocking, he thinks people have a remedy at hand for noncorporeal pain: essaying themselves.

31. In addition to the Scottish Enlightenment, the concept of shared human emotions is a major topic of scholarship in the study of eighteenth-century European literature through the cult of sensibility that lionized "the man of feeling" in England, the *Sturm und Drang* in Germany, and *sensibilité* in France. See R. S. Crane, "Suggestions Toward a Genealogy of the 'Man of Feeling,'" in *English Literary History*, 1.3 (1934): 205-6; Donald Greene, "Latitudinarianism and Sensibility: The Genealogy of the 'Man of Feeling' Reconsidered" in *Modern Philology* (November 1977): 159-60; Janet Todd, *Sensibility: An Introduction* (London: Methuen, 1986), 6-31; David J. Denby, *Sentimental Narrative and the Social Order in France*, 1760-1820 (Cambridge: Cambridge University Press, 1994), 3-6; and John K. Sheriff, *The Good-Natured Man: The Evolution of a Moral Ideal, 1660-1800* (Tuscaloosa, Ala.: University of Alabama Press, 1982), 1-18.

32. For the traditional account that traces the origins of compassion in political theory to the 3rd Earl of Shaftesbury, see C. A. Moore, "Shaftesbury and the Ethical Poets in England, 1700-1760" in *PMLA*, 31 (1916): 264-325. The influential critique that traces the origins of this movement to the Latitudinarian movement earlier in the seventeenth century is found in Donald Greene,

"Latitudinarianism and Sensibility: The Genealogy of the 'Man of Feeling' Reconsidered," in *Modern Philology* (November 1977): 159-83.

33. Francis Hutcheson, *A System of Moral Philosophy* (New York: Augustus M. Kelley, 1968 [1755]), 37; Smith, *The Theory of Moral Sentiments*, part V, ch. 1 & 2, 194-211; Hume, *A Treatise on Human Nature*, Book II, part III, section V (II: 133).

34. Shaftesbury, *An Inquiry Concerning Virtue*, Philip Ayres, ed. (Oxford: Oxford University Press, 1999 [1699]), vol. I, part III, section 1, 210, passim. Shaftesbury also says it might result from "the wrong sense or false imagination of right and wrong" (211).

35. Smith, *The Theory of Moral Sentiments*, part I, section I, chapter 1, paragraph 2, 2.

36. Smith, *The Theory of Moral Sentiments*, part I, section III, chapter 1, paragraph 5, 45.

37. Hobbes, *Leviathan*, Oakeshott, ed., Bk. I, ch. 11, 80. Based on this conception of a natural limit for desire, one can see that Montaigne is not as "modern" as Schaefer makes him out to be.

38. For a contrasting interpretation of Montaigne's view of acquisition, see Schaefer, *The Political Philosophy of Montaigne*, 340-86. Schaefer argues that Montaigne is a bourgeois individualist who advocates unlimited acquisition.

39. *Leviathan*, Bk. I, ch. 11, 80. Despite a difference of only some decades, Montaigne is thus revealed as much more "ancient" than Hobbes. However, Montaigne shares with Hobbes their jesting proof of human equality. Montaigne says, "It is said that the fairest division of her favors Nature has given us is that of sense; for there is no one who is not content with the share of it that she has allotted him. Is that not reasonable? If anyone saw beyond, he would see beyond his sight" (II.17, 641 [499]). "Whoever thought he lacked sense? That would be a proposition implying its own contradiction . . . . To accuse oneself would be to excuse oneself in that subject, and to condemn oneself would be to absolve oneself" (II.17, 640 [498]). For further elaboration see II.17, "Of Presumption," especially circa (II.17, 640-42 [498-99]).

40. Scholars who relate Montaigne to bourgeois individualism include Schaefer, who says that Montaigne teaches it (*The Political Philosophy of Montaigne*, ch. 7, especially 340-46), and Max Horkheimer, who says that Montaigne is bourgeois himself ("Montaigne and the Function of Skepticism" in Horkheimer, *Between Philosophy and Social Science: Selected Early Writings*, John Torpey, tr. [Cambridge: MIT Press, 1993], 265-311).

41. On the moderate enjoyment of wealth and pleasure, see also (II.2, 328 [250]); (II.33, 712-13 [555-56]); (III.10, 980 [767]); and (III.13, 1080-81 [845]).

42. Consider Machiavelli: "truly it is a very natural and ordinary thing to desire to acquire, and always, when men do it who can, they will be praised or not blamed" (*The Prince*, ch. 3, 14). An excellent account of the development of the arguments praising wealth is found in Albert O. Hirschman, *The Passion and the*

Interests: Political Arguments for Capitalism before Its Triumph (Princeton: Princeton University Press, 1977).

43. Montaigne also denounces the greedy rich via political analogy: "According to this way of using things, the men richest in money are those who have charge of guarding the gates and walls of a good city" (I.14, 65-66 [45]).

44. Machiavelli, *The Prince*, ch. 3, 14.

45. Montaigne also remarks, "In general, greatness has this evident advantage, that it can step down whenever it pleases, and that it almost has the choice of both conditions" (III.7, 894 [699]). But why would someone want to pursue something so that he could have the option of renouncing it?

46. "Of the Inequality that is Between Us" (I.42) humorously rails along these lines.

47. III.7, 897 [701]. See also the amusing anecdotes about Favorinus and Asinus Pollio (III.7, 899 [702-3]).

48. Judith Shklar, *Ordinary Vices*, ch. 1, agrees with my contrast between Montaigne and Machiavelli. Those who disagree include Schaefer, 347-51, and Alexandre Nicolaï, "Le Machiavélisme de Montaigne, 1-4" in *Bulletin de la société des amis de Montaigne* 3:4-7 (1957-1958). For a balanced comparison, see also Nakam, *Les Essais*, 245-51.

49. These arguments are derived principally from "Of Glory" (II.16, especially 610-13 [475-77]).

50. The four sons of Aymon were Charlemagne's main rivals. That this reference is probably lost on most readers today illustrates Montaigne's point about the role of fortune in securing glory.

51. Raul Hilberg, *Perpatrators, Victims, Bystanders: The Jewish Catastrophe, 1933-1945* (New York: Aaron Asher Books, 1992).

52. Montaigne reinforces these fears when he tells us that as a child he was thought to be prone toward acquiescence: "The danger," he was apparently told, "was not that I should do ill, but that I should do nothing" (I.26, 175 [130]).

53. Machiavelli, *The Discourses*, III. 1.

54. Both of these people were strong advocates of toleration.

55. Montaigne says that "I hate every sort of tyranny" and that he has a "distaste for mastery." Moreover, he says that everyone, even servants, should be treated as full human beings, because "it is inhuman and unjust to make so much of this accidental privilege of fortune" (III.8, 910 [711]; III.7, 896 [700]; and III.3, 799 [623], respectively).

56. Rawls, "Justice as Fairness," 224.

57. Rawls, "Justice as Fairness," 225.

58. Rawls, "Justice as Fairness," 228.

59. Rawls, "Justice as Fairness," 228.

60. As we saw above, Rorty's "prevention of cruelty" criterion for judging regimes comes from Montaigne via Judith Shklar. See Introduction, 19 (especially note 44).

61. Rorty, "The Priority of Democracy to Philosophy," 261-62.

Bibliography

Acontio, Jacopo. *Satan's Strategems, Books I-VIII*. Unknown publisher, 1565; reprint, English Series, no. 5. San Francisco: Suotro Branch California State Library, 1940.

Allen, J. W. *A History of Political Thought in the Sixteenth Century*. London: Methuen, 1977.

Annas, Julia, and Jonathan Barnes, eds. *The Modes of Skepticism: Ancient Texts and Modern Interpretations*. Cambridge: Cambridge University Press, 1985.

Aristotle. *Nicomachean Ethics*. Translated by Hippocrates G. Apostle. Grinnell, Iowa: Peripatetic Press, 1984.

Aristotle. *The Politics*. Translated by Carnes Lord. Chicago: University of Chicago Press, 1984.

Armaingaud, Arthur, ed. *Oeuvres complètes de Michel de Montaigne*. Paris: Louis Conard, 1924-41.

Armaingaud, Arthur. *Montaigne pamphlétaire: L'énigme du contr'un*. Paris: Hachette, 1910.

Ashcraft, Richard. "Leviathan Triumphant: Thomas Hobbes and the Politics of Wild Men." In *The Wild Man Within: An Image in Western Thought from the Renaissance to Romanticism*, edited by Edward Dudley and Maximilian Novak, 141-81. Pittsburgh: University of Pittsburgh Press, 1972.

Atkinson, Geoffroy. *Les nouveaux horizons de la Renaissance française*. Paris: Librarie Droz, 1935.

Auerbach, Erich. "La Condition Humaine." In *Mimesis: The Representation of Reality in Western Literature*, translated by Willard Trask, 285-311. Princeton: Princeton University Press, 1953.

Augustine. *The Confessions*. Translated by Edward Bouverie Pusey. In *Augustine, Great Books of the Western World*, vol. 18, edited by Robert Maynard Hutchins. Chicago: Encyclopedia Britannica, 1952.

Bacon, Francis. *The New Organon*. Edited by Lisa Jardine and Michael Siverthorne. New York: Cambridge University Press, 2000.

Bainton, Roland. "Sebastian Castellio and the Toleration Controversy of the Sixteenth Century." In *Persecution and Liberty: Essays in Honor of George Lincoln Burr*, 183-209. New York: Century, 1931.

Barnes, Jonathan. "Ancient Skepticism and Causation." In *The Skeptical Tradition*, edited by Myles Burnyeat, 149-204. Berkeley: University of California Press, 1983.

Barnes, Jonathan. "The Beliefs of a Pyrrhonist." *Proceedings of the Cambridge Philological Society* 28 (1982): 1-29.

Baumer, Franklin. *Religion and the Rise of Scepticism*. New York: Harcourt Brace, 1960.

Bencivenga, Ermanno. *The Discipline of Subjectivity: An Essay on Montaigne*. Princeton: Princeton University Press, 1990.

Benigni, U. "Montaigne." In *The Catholic Encyclopedia*, vol. 10: 512-13. New York: Robert Appleton, 1913.

Berkowitz, Peter. "Other People's Mothers." *The New Republic* (10 January 2000): 27.

Berlin, Isaiah. *Four Essays on Liberty*. Oxford: Oxford University Press, 1969.

Bernheimer, Richard. *Wild Men in the Middle Ages: A Study in Art, Sentiment and Demonology*. Cambridge: Harvard University Press, 1952.

Berven, Dikka, ed. *Montaigne: A Collection of Essays*. 5 vols. New York: Garland, 1995.

Bettinson, Christopher. "France and Europe, 1559-1598." In *Montaigne and His Age*, edited by Keith Cameron, 97-106. Exeter: University of Exeter Printing Unit, 1981.

Bigongiari, Dino, ed. *The Political Ideas of St. Thomas Aquinas*. New York: Hafner, 1953.

Bloom, Harold, ed. *Michel de Montaigne*. Modern Critical Views Series. New York: Chelsea House, 1987.

Boas, George. *Essays on Primitivism and Related Ideas in the Middle Ages*. Baltimore: Johns Hopkins Press, 1948.

Boase, Alan. *The Fortunes of Montaigne: A History of the Essays in France, 1580-1669*. New York: Octagon Books, 1970.

Bodin, Jean. *Method for the Easy Comprehension of History*. Translated by Beatrice Reynolds. New York: Octagon Books, 1966.

Bodin, Jean. *The Six Books of a Commonwealth*. Edited by Kenneth Douglas McRae. Cambridge: Harvard University Press, 1962 [1576].

Bomer, John. *The Presence of Montaigne in the Lettres Persanes*. Birmingham, Ala.: Summa, 1988.

Bonadeo, Alfredo. "Montaigne on War." *Journal of the History of Ideas* 46:3 (1985): 417-26.

Bond, R. Warwick. *Montaigne*. London: Henry Frowde, 1906.

Boone, James. *Other Tribes, Other Scribes*. Cambridge: Cambridge University Press, 1982.

Bots, W. J. A. "Montaigne et l'écriture, l'écriture de Montaigne." *Bibliothèque d'humanisme et Renaissance* 45:2 (1983): 301-15.

Boudou, Bénédicte. "Montaigne et l'interprétation des écritures saintes." *Bulletin de la société d'histoire du protestantisme français* 132:1 (1986): 5-22.

Boundas, Constantin, and Dorothea Olkowski, eds. *Gilles Deleuze and the Theater of Philosophy*. New York: Routledge, 1994.

Boutaudou, Christiane. *Montaigne: Textes et débats*. Paris: Le Livre de Poche, 1984.

Bowen, Barbara. "Montaigne's anti-Phaedrus: 'Sur des vers de Virgile.'" *Journal of Medieval and Renaissance Studies* 5 (1975): 107-22.

Bowman, F. P. *Montaigne: Essays*. London: Edward Arnold, 1965.

Brody, Jules. "'Du repentir' (III.2): A Philological Reading." In *Montaigne: Essays in Reading*, edited by Gérard Defaux, 238-72. Yale French Studies Series, edited by Liliane Green, no. 6. New Haven: Yale University Press, 1983.

Brown, Frieda. *Religious and Political Conservatism in the Essais of Montaigne*. Geneva: Librarie Droz, 1963.

Bruhlmeier, Daniel. "Connaissance and Présence." *Civitas* 33:1-2 (1977): 785-90.

Brunel, Pierre, Yvonne Bellenger, Daniel Couty, Philippe Sellier, Michel Truffet, and Jean-Pierre Gourdeau. *Histoire de la Littérature Française*. 2 vols. Paris: Bordas, 1986.

Brunschvicg, Léon. *Descartes et Pascal: Lecteurs de Montaigne*. New York: Brentano's, 1944.

Brunschvicg, Léon. *Le progrès de la conscience dans la philosophie occidentale*. 2 vols. Paris: Librairie Félix Alcan, 1927.

Brush, Craig. *From the Perspective of the Self: Montaigne's Self-Portrait*. New York: Fordham University Press, 1994.

Brush, Craig. *Montaigne and Bayle: Variations on the Theme of Skepticism*. The Hague: Martinus Nijhoff, 1966.

Bucher, Bernadette. *Icon and Structure*. Translated by Basia Miller Gulati. Chicago: University of Chicago Press, 1981.

Burke, Peter. *Montaigne*. Past Masters Series. Oxford: Oxford University Press, 1981.

Burnyeat, Myles. "Can the Skeptic Live His Skepticism." In *The Skeptical Tradition*, edited by Myles Burnyeat, 117-48. Berkeley: University of California Press, 1983.

Burnyeat, Myles, ed. *The Skeptical Tradition*. Berkeley: University of California Press, 1983.

Burnyeat, Myles. "The Skeptic in his Place and Time." In *Philosophy in History*, edited by Richard Rorty, Malcolm Schneewind, and Quentin Skinner, 225-54. Cambridge: Cambridge University Press, 1984.

Busson, Henri. *La pensée religieuse française de Charron á Pascal*. Paris:

Librairie Philosophique J. Vrin, 1933.

Busson, Henri. *Le rationalisme dans la littérature française de la Renaissance.* Paris: Librairie Philosophique J. Vrin, 1957.

Butler, Judith. *Bodies that Matter: On the Discursive Limits of "Sex."* New York: Routledge, 1993.

Butler, Judith. *Gender Trouble: Feminism and Subversion of Identity.* New York: Routledge, 1990.

Butor, Michel. *Essais sur les Essais.* Paris: Gallimard, 1968.

Calder, Ruth. "Montaigne and Customary Law: Some Precisions on Certain Financial Dispositions within the Montaigne Family." *Bibliothèque d'humanisme et Renaissance* 47 (1985): 79-85.

Calder, Ruth. "Montaigne as Satirist." *Sixteenth Century Journal* 17:2 (1986): 225-35.

Cameron, Keith. "Montaigne and 'De la liberté de conscience.'" *Renaissance Quarterly* 26 (1973): 285-94.

Cameron, Keith, ed. *Montaigne and His Age.* Exeter: Exeter University Printing Unit, 1981.

Campbell, Blair. "Montaigne and Rousseau's First Discourse." *Western Political Quarterly* 28 (1975): 7-31.

Carro, Venancio. "The Spanish Theological-Juridical Renaissance and the Ideology of Bartolomé de Las Casas." In *Bartolomé de Las Casas in History*, edited by Juan Friede and Benjamin Keen. Dekalb: Northern Illinois University Press, 1971.

Cave, Terence. "Problems of Reading in the *Essais.*" In *Michel de Montaigne*, edited by Harold Bloom, Modern Critical Views Series, 79-116. New York: Chelsea House, 1987.

Château, Jean. *Montaigne: psychologue et pédagogue.* Paris: Librairie Philosophique J. Vrin, 1964.

Chiapelli, Fredi, J. B. Allen, and Robert Benson, eds. *First Images of America: The Impact of the New World on the Old.* 2 vols. Berkeley: University of California Press, 1976.

Chinard, Gilbert. *L'exotisme américain dans la littérature française au XVI siècle.* Geneva: Slatkine Reprints, 1978.

Cixous, Hélène. *Three Steps on the Ladder of Writing.* Translated by Sarah Cornell and Susan Sellers. New York: Columbia University Press, 1993.

Clark, Carol. "Montaigne and Law." In *Montaigne and His Age*, edited by Keith Cameron, 49-68. Exeter: University of Exeter Printing Unit, 1981.

Clark, Carol. "Montaigne and the Imagery of Political Discourse in Sixteenth-Century France." *French Studies* 24:4 (October 1970): 337-55.

Clive, H. Peter. *Bibliographie annoteé des ourvrages relatifs á Montaigne.* Paris: Librarie Honoré Champion, 1990.

Coates, Willson, Hayden White, and J. Salwyn Schapiro. *The Emergence of Liberal Humanism: An Intellectual History of Western Europe.* New York:

McGraw-Hill, 1966.

Coleman, James. "Montaigne and the Wars of Religion." In *Montaigne and His Age*, edited by Keith Cameron, 107-20. Exeter: University of Exeter Printing Unit, 1981.

Columbus, Christopher. *The Journal of Christopher Columbus*. Edited and translated by Cecil Jane. New York: Bonanza Books, 1989.

Compagnon, Antoine. "A Long Short Story: Montaigne's Brevity." In *Montaigne: Essays in Reading*, edited by Gérard Defaux, 24-50. Yale French Studies Series, edited by Liliane Green, no. 64. New Haven: Yale University Press, 1983.

Compayré, Gabriel. *Montaigne and Education of the Judgment*. Translated by J. E. Mansion. New York: Thomas Y. Crowell, 1908.

Conche, Marcel. "La méthode pyrrhonienne de Montaigne." *Bulletin de la société des amis de Montaigne* 5:10/11 (1974): 47-62.

Cons, Louis. *Anthologie littéraire de la Renaissance française*. New York: Holt, Rinehart, and Winston, 1931.

Cons, Louis. "Montaigne et Julien L'Apostat." *Humanisme et Renaissance* 4 (1937): 411-20.

Copleston, Frederick. *A History of Philosophy*. Garden City, N.J.: Image Books, 1964.

Costa-Lima, Luiz. *The Limits of Voice*. Stanford: Stanford University Press. 1996.

Cottrell, Robert. *Sexuality/Textuality: A Study of the Fabric of Montaigne's Essais*. Columbus: Ohio State University Press, 1981.

Couissin, Pierre. "The Stoicism of the New Academy." In *The Skeptical Tradition*, edited by Myles Burnyeat, 31-64. Berkeley: University of California Press, 1983.

Crane, R. S. "Suggestions Toward a Genealogy of the 'Man of Feeling.'" *English Literary History* 1.3 (1934): 205-30.

Cro, Stelio. *The Noble Savage: Allegory of Freedom*. Waterloo, Ontario: Wilfrid Laurier University Press, 1990.

Croquette, Bernard. *Pascal et Montaigne: Étude des réminiscences des Essais dans l'oeuvre de Pascal*. Geneva: Librarie Droz, 1974.

Daly, L. J. *The Political Theory of John Wyclif*. Chicago: Loyola University Press, 1962.

David, Jean. "Quelques aspects démocratiques de la philosophie de Montaigne." *Modern Language Notes* 61:7 (November 1941): 485-93.

Davis, Natalie. "A Renaissance Text to the Historian's Eye: The Gifts of Montaigne." *The Journal of Medieval and Renaissance Studies* 15 (1985): 47-56.

Defaux, Gérard, ed. *Montaigne: Essays in Reading*. Yale French Studies Series, edited by Liliane Green, no. 64. New Haven: Yale University Press, 1983.

Defaux, Gérard. "Readings of Montaigne." In *Montaigne: Essays in Reading*, edited by Gérard Defaux, 73-94. Yale French Studies Series, edited by Liliane

Green, no. 64. New Haven: Yale University Press, 1983.

Defaux, Gérard. "Un Cannibale en haut chausses: Montaigne, la différance et la logique de l'identité." *Modern Language Notes* 97 (1982): 919-57.

Deleuze, Gilles. *Différence et répétition.* Paris: Presses Universitaires de France, 1968.

Delumeau, Jean. *Sin and Fear: the Emergence of a Western Guilt Culture, 13th-18th Centuries.* Translated by Eric Nicholson. New York: St. Martin's, 1990.

Demure, Catherine. "The Paradox and the Miracle: Structure and Meaning in 'The Apology for Raymond Sebond.'" In *Michel de Montaigne*, edited by Harold Bloom, 135-54. Modern Critical Views Series. New York: Chelsea House, 1987.

Denby, David J. *Sentimental Narrative and the Social Order in France, 1760-1820.* Cambridge: Cambridge University Press, 1994.

Dent, Nicholas. "Rousseau and Respect for Others." In *Justifying Toleration: Conceptual and Historical Perspectives*, edited by Susan Mendus, 115-36. Cambridge: Cambridge University Press, 1988.

Derrida, Jacques. "Force de Loi: Le 'Fondement Mystique de l'Autorité.'" ["The Force of Law: 'The Mystical Foundations of Authority.'"] Found in French and English in *Cardozo Law Review*: 11 (5-6) (July-Aug. 1990): 919-1045.

Derrida, Jacques. *Politics of Friendship.* Translated by George Collins. London: Verso, 1997.

Derrida, Jacques. *Writing and Difference.* Translated by Alan Bass. Chicago: University of Chicago Press, 1978.

Desan, Philippe. *Naissance de la Méthode: Machiavel, La Ramée, Bodin, Montaigne, Descartes.* Paris: A.-G. Nizet, 1987.

Descartes, René. *The Passions of the Soul.* Translated by Stephen Voss. Indianapolis: Hackett, 1989.

Descombes, Vincent. *Modern French Philosophy.* Cambridge: Cambridge University Press, 1980.

Diaz, Bernal. *The Conquest of New Spain* [1568]. Translated by J. M. Cohen. New York: Penguin, 1963.

Dickason, Olive Patricia. *The Myth of the Savage.* Edmonton: University of Alberta Press, 1984.

Donnellan, Brendan. *Nietzsche and the French Moralists.* Bonn: Bouvier, 1982.

Dostoyevsky, Fyodor. *The Brothers Karamazov.* Translated by David McDuff. New York: Penguin, 1993.

Dow, Neal. "The Concept and Term Nature in Montaigne's Essays." Ph.D. Diss., University of Pennsylvania, 1940.

Dreano, Mathurin. "La pensée religieuse de Montaigne." Ph. D. Diss., University of Paris, 1936.

Dreano, Mathurin. *La religion de Montaigne.* Paris: A.-G. Nizet, 1969.

DuBruck, Edelgard. "Montaigne on Cruelty." *Michigan Academician* 11 (1979):

297-306.

Dudley, Edward, and Maximillan Novak, eds. *The Wild Man Within: An Image in Western Thought from the Renaissance to Romanticism.* Pittsburgh: University of Pittsburgh Press, 1972.

Duhamel, Roger. *Lecture de Montaigne.* Ottawa: Éditions de l'université d'Ottawa, 1965.

Dunn, John. "The Claim to Freedom of Conscience." In *From Persecution to Toleration,* edited by Ole Grell, Jonathan Israel, and Nicholas Tyacke, 171-93. Oxford: Oxford University Press, 1991.

Durkan, John. "John Rutherford and Montaigne: An Early Influence?" *Bibliothèque d'humanisme et Renaissance* 41 (1979): 114-22.

Duval, Edwin. "Lessons of the New World: Design and Meaning in Montaigne's 'Des cannibales' and 'Des coches.'" In *Montaigne: Essays in Reading*, edited by Gérard Defaux, 95-112. Yale French Studies Series, edited by Liliane Green, no. 64. New Haven: Yale University Press, 1983.

Eden, Robert. "The Introduction of Montaigne's Politics." *Perspectives on Political Science* 20:4 (Fall 1991): 211-20.

Edwards, John. *A Free Discourse Concerning Truth and Error, especially in matters of religion.* London, 1701.

Eliot, T. S. "The '*Pensées*' of Pascal." In *Selected Essays,* 355-68. New York: Harcourt Brace, 1950.

Elliott, John H. "The Discovery of America and the Discovery of Man." The Raleigh Lecture on History (February 2, 1972). *Proceedings of the British Academy* 58 (1972): 101-25.

Elliott, John H. *The Old World and the New: 1492-1650.* Cambridge: Cambridge University Press, 1970.

Elliott, John H. "Renaissance Europe and America: A Blunted Impact?" In *First Images of America: The Impact of the New World on the Old*, edited by Fredi Chiapelli, vol.1: 11-23. Berkeley: University of California Press, 1976.

Ellrodt, Robert. "Self-Consciousness in Montaigne and Shakespeare." *Shakespeare Studies* 28 (1975): 37-50.

Emerson, Ralph Waldo. "Montaigne; Or, The Skeptic." In *Representative Men.* Boston: Houghton Mifflin, 1930.

Erasmus, Desiderius. *The Immense Mercy of God* [1524]. Reprint, English Series, no. 6, part 1. San Francisco: Suotro Branch California State Library, 1940.

Feis, Jacob. *Shakespeare and Montaigne.* London: Kegan, Paul, Trench, 1884.

Ferguson, Wallace K. "The Attitude of Erasmus Toward Toleration." In *Persecution and Liberty: Essays in Honor of George Lincoln Burr*, 171-82. New York: Century, 1931.

Ferguson, Wallace K. *Facets of the Renaissance.* New York: Harper and Row, 1963.

Flathman, Richard. *Reflections of a Would-be Anarchist.* Minneapolis: University of Minnesota Press, 1999.

Foucault, Michel. *Discipline and Punish*. Translated by Alan Sheridan. New York: Vintage, 1979.

Foucault, Michel. "Nietzsche, Genealogy, History." In *The Foucault Reader,* edited by Paul Rabinow. New York: Pantheon, 1984.

Fowler, Alastair. *Triumphal Forms: Structural Patterns in Elizabethan Poetry*. Cambridge: Cambridge University Press, 1970.

Frame, Donald, ed. *The Complete Works of Montaigne*. Stanford: Stanford University Press. 1957.

Frame, Donald. "Did Montaigne Betray Sebond?" *Romanic Review* XXXVIII (1947): 297-329.

Frame, Donald. *European Writers in the Middle Ages and the Renaissance*. New York: Scribner's, 1983.

Frame, Donald. *Montaigne: A Biography*. New York: Harcourt, Brace, and World, 1965.

Frame, Donald. *Montaigne in France: 1812-1852*. New York: Columbia University Press, 1940.

Frame, Donald. "Montaigne on the Absurdity and Dignity of Man." In *Renaissance Men and Ideas*, edited by Robert Schwoebel, 121-35. New York: St. Martin's, 1971.

Frame, Donald. *Montaigne's Discovery of Man: The Humanization of a Humanist*. New York: Columbia University Press, 1955.

Frame, Donald. *Montaigne's Essais: A Study*. Englewood, N.J.: Prentice Hall, 1969.

Frame, Donald. "What Next in Montaigne Studies?" *The French Review* 36:6 (May 1963): 577-87.

Frame, Donald. "The Whole Man, 1586-1592." In *Michel de Montaigne*, edited by Harold Bloom, 11-28. Modern Critical Views Series. New York: Chelsea House, 1987.

Françon, Marcel. "Montaigne et les Brésiliens." *Bulletin de la société des amis de Montaigne* 5:16 (1975): 73-74.

Françon, Marcel. "On the Cannibals." *The Modern Language Review* 48 (1953): 443-45.

Françon, Marcel. "Sur Montaigne et les chansons populaires des Brésiliens." *Bulletin de la société des amis de Montaigne* 5:9 (1974): 64-65.

Frank, Joseph. *The Levellers: A History of the Writings of Three Seventeenth Century Social Democrats: John Lilburne, Richard Overton, William Walwyn*. Cambridge: Harvard University Press, 1955.

Franklin, Julian. *Jean Bodin and the Rise of Absolutist Theory*. Cambridge: Cambridge University Press, 1973.

Friede, Juan, and Benjamin Keen, eds. *Bartolomé de Las Casas in History*. Dekalb: Northern Illinois University Press, 1971.

Friedrich, Hugo. *Montaigne*. Edited by Philippe Desan, translated by Dawn Eng. Berkeley: University of California Press, 1991.

Friedrich, Hugo. *Montaigne*. Translated to French by Robert Rovini. Paris: Gallimard, 1968.

Fumaroli, Marc. *L'Age de l'éloquence*. Geneva: Librairie Droz, 1980.

Fumaroli, Marc. "Preface." In *Rhétorique de Montaigne*. Edited by Frank Lestringant. Paris: Champion, 1985.

Galland, René. "Montaigne et Shakespeare." In *Quatrième Centenaire de la Naissance de Montaigne, Conférences organisées par la ville de Bordeaux*, 333-71. Geneva: Slatkine Reprints, 1969.

Gascudo, Luis da Camara. "Montaigne et l'indigène du Brésil: Le chapitre 'Des cannibales' lu et annoté par un Brésilien." *Bulletin de la société des amis de Montaigne* 5:14/15 (1975): 89-102.

Gerbi, Antonello. "The Earliest Accounts of the New World." In *First Images of America: The Impact of the New World on the Old*, edited by Fredi Chiapelli, vol.1: 37-44. Berkeley: University of California Press, 1976.

Gerbi, Antonello. *The Dispute of the New World: The History of a Polemic, 1750-1900*. Translated by Jeremy Moyle. Pittsburgh: University of Pittsburgh Press, 1973.

Gide, André. *Montaigne*. Translated by Dorothy Bussy. New York: McGraw-Hill, 1964.

Gierczynski, Zbigniew. "Le 'Que sais-je?' de Montaigne: Interprétation de l'Apologie de Raymond Sebond." *Roczniki Humanistyczne* 18 (1970): 5-103.

Gierczynski, Zbigniew. "Le Scepticisme de Montaigne, principe de l'équilibre de l'esprit." *Kwartalnik Neofilologiczny* 14 (1967): 111-31.

Gierczynski, Zbigniew. "La Science de l'ignorance de Montaigne." *Roczniki Humanistyczne* 15 (1967): 5-85

Gillespie, Michael. "Montaigne's Humanistic Liberalism." *Journal of Politics* 47 (1985): 140-59.

Gillespie, Michael. *Nihilism Before Nietzsche*. Chicago: University of Chicago Press, 1995.

Gillespie, Michael. "The Structure of the Essays: Montaigne's Notion of Friendship, Politics, and the Self." Paper delivered at the American Political Science Association Annual Meeting, 1-4 September, 1983.

Gilmore, Myron P. "The New World in French and English Historians of the Sixteenth Century." In *First Images of America: The Impact of the New World on the Old*, edited by Fredi Chiapelli, vol. 2: 519-27. Berkeley: University of California Press, 1976.

Gilson, Étienne. "La doctrine de la double verité." In *Études de philosophie médievale*. Strasburg: Commission des publications de la faculté des lettres, 1921.

Gilson, Étienne, and Thomas Langan. *Modern Philosophy: Descartes to Kant*. A History of Philosophy Series, edited by Étienne Gilson, no. 3. New York: Random House, 1963.

Goumarre, Pierre. "La hiérarchie du mérite selon Machiavel et Montaigne." *Revue belge de philologie et d'histoire* 55 (1977): 785-90.

Grafton, Anthony. *New Worlds, Ancient Texts: The Power of Tradition and the Shock of Discovery.* Cambridge: Belknap Press of Harvard University, 1992.

Gray, Floyd. *La Balance de Montaigne.* Paris: A.-G. Nizet, 1982.

Gray, Floyd. "The Unity of Montaigne in the Essais." *Modern Language Quarterly* 22 (1961): 79-87.

Green, Jeffrey. "Montaigne's Critique of Cicero." *Journal of the History of Ideas* 36 (1975): 595-612.

Greenberg, Mitchell. "Montaigne at the Crossroads: Textual Conundrums in the *Essais.*" *Stanford French Review* 6:1 (1982): 21-34.

Greenblatt, Stephen. "Learning to Curse: Aspects of Linguistic Colonialism in the Sixteenth Century." In *First Images of America: The Impact of the New World on the Old,* edited by Fredi Chiapelli, vol. 2: 561-80. Berkeley: University of California Press, 1976.

Greenblatt, Stephen. *Marvelous Possessions: The Wonder of the New World.* Chicago: University of Chicago Press, 1991.

Greenblatt, Stephen. *Renaissance Self-Fashioning: From More to Shakespeare.* Chicago: University of Chicago Press, 1980.

Greene, Donald. "Latitudinarianism and Sensibility: The Genealogy of the 'Man of Feeling' Reconsidered." *Modern Philology* (November 1977): 159-83.

Greene, Thomas. "Dangerous Parleys—*Essais* 1.5 and 6." In *Michel de Montaigne,* edited by Harold Bloom, 155-76. Modern Critical Views Series. New York: Chelsea House, 1987.

Greene, Thomas. "Montaigne and the Savage Infirmity." *The Yale Review* 46:2 (December 1956): 191-205.

Greenwood, Thomas. "L'éclosion du scepticisme pendant la Renaissance et les premiers apologistes." *Revue de l'université d'Ottawa* 17:1 (1947): 69-99.

Grell, Ole, Jonathan Israel, and Nicholas Tyacke, eds. *From Persecution to Toleration: The Glorious Revolution and Religion in England.* Oxford: Clarendon Press, 1991.

Grun, Alphonse. *La vie publique de Michel de Montaigne: Étude biographique.* Paris: Libraire D'Amyot, 1855.

Grun, Alphonse. *Montaigne: Magistrat.* Paris: Dubuisson, 1854.

Guthrie, W. K. C. *A History of Greek Philosophy.* 2 vols. Cambridge: Cambridge University Press, 1962.

Gutmann, Amy. "Communitarian Critics of Liberalism." *Philosophy and Public Affairs* 14 (Summer 1985): 319.

Gutwirth, Marcel. "By Diverse Means." In *Montaigne: Essays in Reading,* edited by Gérard Defaux, 180-87. Yale French Studies Series, edited by Liliane Green, no. 64. New Haven: Yale University Press, 1983.

Hahn, Thomas. "Indians East and West: Primitivism and Savagery in English Discovery Narratives of the Sixteenth Century." *The Journal of Medieval and Renaissance Studies* 8 (1978): 77-114.

Haight, Jeanne. *The Concept of Reason in French Classical Literature, 1635-1690.* Toronto: University of Toronto Press, 1982.

Hale, J. R. *Renaissance Europe: Individual and Society, 1480-1520.* Berkeley: University of California Press, 1971.

Hamlin, William M. *The Image of America in Montaigne, Spenser, and Shakespeare.* New York: St. Martin's, 1995.

Hand, Wayland D. "The Effect of the Discovery on Ethnological and Folklore Studies in Europe." In *First Images of America: The Impact of the New World on the Old,* edited by Fredi Chiapelli, vol.1: 45-55. Berkeley: University of California Press, 1976.

Hanke, Lewis. *All Mankind Is One: A Study of the Disputation between Bartolomé de Las Casas and Juan Gines Sepúlveda in 1550 on the Intellectual and Religious Capacity of the American Indians.* DeKalb: Northern Illinois University Press, 1974.

Hanke, Lewis. "The Theological Significance of the Discovery of America." In *First Images of America: The Impact of the New World on the Old,* edited by Fredi Chiapelli, vol.1, 363-89. Berkeley: University of California Press, 1976.

Hartranft, Chester, and Elmer Johnson. *Corpus Schwenckfeldianorum.* Leipzig: Breitkopf and Hartel, 1927.

Hendrick, Philip, J. *Montaigne et Sebond: L'art de la traduction.* Paris: Honoré Champion, 1996.

Hendrick, Philip, J. "Montaigne, Lucretius and Skepticism: An Interpretation of 'L'Apologie de Raimond Sebond.'" *Proceedings of the Royal Irish Academy* 79 (1979): 139-52.

Henry, Patrick. "Montaigne: Censorship and Defensive Writing." *Proceedings of the Annual Meeting of the Western Society for French History* 8 (1980): 90-102.

Henry, Patrick. *Montaigne in Dialogue: Censorship and Defensive Writing; Architecture and Friendship; The Self and the Other.* Stanford French and Italian Studies Series, edited by Alphonse Juilland, no. 57. Saratoga, Calif.: ANMA Libri, 1987.

Heyd, David, ed. *Toleration: An Elusive Virtue.* Princeton: Princeton University Press, 1996.

Hilberg, Raul. *Perpetrators, Victims, Bystanders: The Jewish Catastrophe, 1933-1945.* New York: Aaron Asher Books, 1992.

Hirsch, Rudolph. "Printed Reports on the Early Discoveries and Their Reception." In *First Images of America: The Impact of the New World on the Old,* edited by Fredi Chiapelli, vol. 2: 537-59. Berkeley: University of California Press, 1976.

Hirschman, Albert O., *The Passion and the Interests: Political Arguments for Capitalism Before Its Triumph.* Princeton: Princeton University Press, 1977.

Hobbes, Thomas. *Leviathan.* Edited by Michael Oakeshott. London: Collier Macmillan, 1962.

Hodgen, Margaret. *Early Anthropology in the Sixteenth and Seventeenth Centuries.* Philadelphia: University of Pennsylvania Press, 1964.

Hooker, Elizabeth Robins. "The Relation of Shakespeare to Montaigne." *Publications of the Modern Language Association of America*, vol. xvii (1902).

Hooker, John, and Raphael Holinshed. *The Chronicles of England, Scotland, and Ireland.* 6 vols. London: 1586.

Horkheimer, Max. "Montaigne and the Function of Skepticism." In Horkheimer, *Between Philosophy and Social Science: Selected Early Writings*, translated by John Torpey. Cambridge: MIT Press, 1993.

Horowitz, Maryanne Cline. "Marie de Gournay: A Case Study of the Mentor-Protegee Friendship." *Sixteenth Century Journal* 17:3 (1986): 271-84.

Horowitz, Maryanne Cline. *Seeds of Virtue and Knowledge.* Princeton: Princeton University Press, 1998.

Horton, John, and Susan Mendus, eds. *Aspects of Toleration: Philosophical Studies.* London: Methuen, 1985.

Huizinga, Johan. *Erasmus and the Age of reformation.* Translated by F. Hopman. New York: Harper and Row, 1975.

Hume, David. *A Treatise of Human Nature.* London: J. N. Dent and Sons, 1934.

Humphries, Jefferson. "Montaigne's Anti-Influential Model of Identity." In *Michel de Montaigne*, edited by Harold Bloom, 219-30. Modern Critical Views Series. New York: Chelsea House, 1987.

Hunt, Carew. "Montaigne and the State." *Edinburgh Review* (1927): 259-72.

Hunter, Michael Cyril William, and David Wootton, eds. *Atheism from the Reformation to the Enlightenment.* Oxford: Oxford University Press, 1992.

Hutcheson, Francis. *A System of Moral Philosophy* [1755]. New York: Augustus M. Kelly, 1968.

Insdorf, Cecile. *Montaigne and Feminism.* North Carolina Studies in the Romance Languages and Literatures, no. 194. Chapel Hill: University of North Carolina Press, 1977.

Jane, Cecil, ed. *The Four Voyages of Columbus: A History in Eight Documents.* New York: Dover, 1988.

Jane, Cecil, ed. *The Journal of Christopher Columbus.* New York: Bonanza, 1989.

Janssen, Herman. *Montaigne fidéiste.* Utrecht, The Netherlands: Nijmegen, 1930.

Jefferson, Thomas. *Political Writings.* Edited by Joyce Appleby and Terence Ball. Cambridge: Cambridge University Press, 1999.

Jones, P. Mansell. *French Introspectives: From Montaigne to André Gide.* Cambridge: Cambridge University Press, 1937.

Jones, Robert. "On the Dialogic Impulse in the Genesis of Montaigne's Essays." *Renaissance Quarterly* 30 (1977): 172-80.

Kamen, Henry. *The Rise of Toleration.* New York: McGraw-Hill, 1967.

Kaminsky, Howard. *A History of the Hussite Revolution.* Berkeley: University of California Press, 1967.

Kant, Immanuel. *Critique of Pure Reason.* Translated by F. Max Muller. New

York: Anchor, 1966.

Kateb, George. "Utopia and the Good Life." In *Utopias and Utopian Thought*, edited by Frank Manuel, 239-59. Boston: Beacon Press, 1966.

Keller, Abraham. "Montaigne on the Dignity of Man." *Proceedings of the Modern Language Association* 72 (1957): 43-54.

Keller, Abraham. "Optimism in the Essays of Montaigne." *Studies in Philology* 54 (1957): 408-28.

Kellerman, Frederick. "*The Essais* and Socrates." *Symposium* 10 (1956): 204-16.

Kellerman, Frederick. "Montaigne's Socrates." *The Romanic Review* 45:3 (October 1954): 170-77.

Kennedy, D. J. "Thomism" in *The Catholic Encyclopedia*, XIV: 702. New York: Robert Appleton, 1913.

Keohane, Nannerl. "Montaigne's Individualism." *Political Theory* 5 (August 1977): 363-90.

Keohane, Nannerl. *Philosophy and the State in France: The Renaissance to the Enlightenment*. Princeton: Princeton University Press, 1980.

Keohane, Nannerl. "The Radical Humanism of *La Boétie.*" *Journal of the History of Ideas* 38:1 (1977): 119-30.

King, Preston. *Toleration*. New York: St. Martin's, 1976.

Kirk, G. S. *Heraclitus: The Cosmic Fragments*. Cambridge: Cambridge University Press, 1954.

Kirsh, Arthur. *Shakespeare and the Experience of Love*. Cambridge: Cambridge University Press, 1981.

Kirsh, Arthur. "Virtue, Vice, and Compassion in Montaigne and The Tempest." *SEL* 37 (1997): 337-52.

Kojève, Alexandre. "The Emperor Julian and His Art of Writing." In *Ancients and Moderns*, edited by Joseph Cropsey. New York: Basic Books, 1964.

Kraynak, Robert. "John Locke: From Absolutism to Toleration." *The American Political Science Review* 74 (1980): 53-69.

Kristeller, Paul O. "The Myth of Renaissance Atheism and the French Tradition of Free Thought." *The Journal of the History of Philosophy* 6 (1968): 241-43.

La Charité, Raymond. *The Concept of Judgment in Montaigne*. The Hague: Martinus Nijhoff, 1968.

Lablénie, E. *Essais sur Montaigne*. Paris: Société d'édition d'enseignement supérieur, 1967.

Lacan, Jacques. "Propos sur la causalité psychique." In *Écrits*. Paris: Le Seuil, 1966.

Las Casas, Bartolomé de. *History of the Indies* [1527].

Las Casas, Bartolomé de. *A Selection of his Writings*. Edited by George Sanderlin. New York: Knopf, 1971.

Laursen, John Christian. *The Politics of Skepticism in the Ancients, Montaigne, Hume, and Kant*. Leiden: Brill, 1992.

Laursen, John Christian, and Cary Nederman, eds. *Beyond the Persecuting Society:*

Religious Toleration Before the Enlightenment. Philadelphia: University of Pennsylvania Press, 1998.

Laursen, John Christian, ed. *Religious Toleration: "The Variety of Rites" from Cyrus to Defoe*. New York: St. Martin's, 1999.

Leake, Roy E. *Concordance des Essais de Montaigne*. 2 vols. Geneva: Librarie Droz, 1981.

Lecler, Joseph. *Toleration and the Reformation*. 2 vols. Translated by T. L. Westow. New York: Association Press, 1960.

Leigh, Ralph Alexander. *Rousseau and the Problem of Tolerance in the Eighteenth Century*. Oxford: Clarendon Press, 1979.

Lerner, Ralph, and Muhsin Mahdi, eds. *Medieval Political Philosophy*. New York: Free Press, 1963.

Léry, Jean de. *History of a Voyage to the Land of Brazil, Otherwise Called America*. Translated by Janet Whatley. Berkeley: University of California Press, 1990.

Lestringant, Frank. "L'Amérique de 'Coches,' fille du Brésil des 'Cannibales': Montaigne à la rencontre de deux traditions historiques." In *Montaigne et l'histoire*, edited by Claude-Gilbert Dubois. 143-57. Paris: Klincksieck, 1991.

Lestringant, Frank. *Cannibals: The Discovery and Representation of the Cannibal from Columbus to Jules Verne*. Translated by Rosemary Morris. Berkeley: University of California Press, 1997.

Lestringant, Frank, ed. *Le huguenot et le sauvage*. Paris: Klincksieck, 1990.

Lestringant, Frank. "Le Cannibalisme des 'Cannibals.'" *Bulletin de la Société des amis de Montaigne* 9-10 (1982): 27-40.

Lestringant, Frank, ed. *Rhétorique de Montaigne*. Paris: Champion, 1985.

Levin, Harry. *The Myth of the Golden Age in the Renaissance*. Bloomington: Indiana University Press, 1969.

Levine, Alan, ed. *Early Modern Skepticism and the Origins of Toleration*. Lanham, Md.: Lexington Books, 1999.

Limbrick, Elaine. "Was Montaigne Really a Pyrrohonian?" *Bibliotheque d'humanisme et renaissance* 34 (1977): 67-80.

Locke, John. *An Essay Concerning Human Understanding*. Edited by Peter H. Nidditch. Oxford: Oxford University Press, 1982.

Locke, John. *Two Treatises of Government*. Edited by Peter Laslett. New York: Mentor, 1965.

Logan, John. "Montaigne et Longin: Une nouvelle hypothese." *Revue d'histoire littéraire de la France* (1983): 355-70.

Logan, George. "Relation of Montaigne to Renaissance Humanism." *Journal of the History of Ideas* 36 (1975): 613-32.

Lowenthal, Marvin, ed. *The Autobiography of Montaigne*. London: George Rutledge and Sons, 1935.

Lucki, Emil. *History of the Renaissance: 1350-1550*. 5 vols. Salt Lake City: University of Utah Press, 1964.

Lucretius. *De Rerum Nature*. Translated by W. H. D. Rouse, edited by Martin Ferguson Smith. Cambridge: Harvard University Press, 1982.

Luthy, Herbert. "Montaigne, or the Art of Being Truthful." In *Michel de Montaigne*, edited by Harold Bloom, 11-28. Modern Critical Views Series. New York: Chelsea House, 1987.

Lutri, Joseph R. de. "L'humour de la déception dans le chapitre 'Des cannibales.'" *Bulletin de la Société des Amis de Montaigne* 5:14/15 (1975): 103-7.

Lyotard, Jean-François. "Answering the Question: What Is Postmodern?" Translated by Régis Durand. In Jean-François Lyotard, *The Postmodern Condition: A Report on Knowledge*. Translated by Geoff Bennington and Brian Massumi. Minneapolis: University of Minnesota Press, 1984.

Machiavelli, Niccolò. *Discourses on Livy*. Translated and edited by Harvey C. Mansfield and Nathan Tarcov. Chicago: University of Chicago Press, 1997.

Majer, Irma. "Montaigne's Cure: Stones and Roman Ruins." In *Michel de Montaigne*, edited by Harold Bloom, 117-33. Modern Critical Views Series. New York: Chelsea House, 1987.

Major, J. Russell. *The Age of the Renaissance and Reformation*. Philadelphia: Lippincott, 1970.

Maneli, Mieczyslaw. *Freedom and Tolerance*. New York: Octagon Books, 1984.

Mansfield, Harvey C., Jr. *Taming the Prince: The Ambivalence of Modern Executive Power*. New York: Free Press, 1989.

Manuel, Frank, and Fritzie Manuel. *Utopian Thought in the Western World*. Cambridge: Belknap Press of Harvard, 1979.

Manuel, Frank. *The Enlightenment*. Englewood Cliffs, N.J.: Prentice Hall, 1965.

Manuel, Frank, ed. *Utopias and Utopian Thought*. Boston: Beacon Press, 1966.

Marchi, Dudley. *Montaigne Among the Moderns*. Providence, R.I.: Berghahn, 1994.

Marin, Louis. "Montaigne's Tomb, or Autobiographical Discourse." In *Michel de Montaigne*, edited by Harold Bloom, 61-78. Modern Critical Views Series. New York: Chelsea House, 1987.

Martin, Daniel. *The Order of Montaigne's Essays*. Amherst, Mass.: Hestia Press, 1989.

Maskell, David. "Montaigne médiateur entre Navarre et Guise." *Bibliothèque d'humanisme et Renaissance* 41 (1979): 541-53.

Mattingly, Garrett. *Renaissance Diplomacy*. New York: Dover Publications, 1988.

May, Todd. "Difference and Unity in Gilles Deleuze." In *Gilles Deleuze and the Theater of Philosophy*, edited by Constantin Boundas and Dorothea Olkowski. New York: Routledge, 1994.

McFarlare, I. D., and Ian Maclean, eds. *Montaigne*. Oxford: Clarendon Press, 1982.

McGowan, Margaret. *Montaigne's Deceits: The Art of Persuasion in the Essais*. Philadelphia: Temple University Press, 1974.

McKinley, Mary. *Words in a Corner: Studies in Montaigne's Latin Quotations*.

French Forum Monographs, edited by R. C. La Charité and V. A. La Charité, no. 26. Lexington, Ky.: French Forum Publishers, 1981.

Mehlman, Jeffrey. "La Boétie's Montaigne." *The Oxford Literary Review* 4:1 (Autumn 1979): 45-61.

Meijer, Marianne. "De l'honnête, de l'utile, et du repentir." *Journal of Medieval and Renaissance Studies* 12:2 (1982): 259-74.

Meijer, Marianne. "Guesswork or Facts: Connections between Montaigne's Last Three Chapters (III:11, 12, and 13)." In *Montaigne: Essays in Reading*, edited by Gérard Defaux, 167-79. Yale French Studies Series, edited by Liliane Green, no. 64. New Haven: Yale University Press, 1983.

Ménager, Daniel. *Introduction á la vie littéraire du XVI siècle*. Paris: Bordas, 1968.

Mendus, Susan, and David Edwards, eds. *On Toleration*. Oxford: Clarendon Press, 1987.

Mendus, Susan, ed. *Justifying Toleration: Conceptual and Historical Perspectives*. Cambridge: Cambridge University Press, 1988.

Mendus, Susan. *Toleration and the Limits of Liberalism*. Atlantic Highlands, N.J.: Humanities Press, 1989.

Merleau-Ponty, Maurice. "Reading Montaigne." In *Michel de Montaigne*, edited by Harold Bloom, 47-60. Modern Critical Views Series. New York: Chelsea House, 1987.

Mermier, Guy. "L'essai 'Des cannibales' de Montaigne." *Bulletin de la société des amis de Montaigne* 5:7/8 (1973): 27-38.

Mill, John Stuart. *On Liberty*. Edited by David Spitz. New York: Norton, 1975.

Miner, Earl. "The Wild Man Through the Looking Glass." In *The Wild Man Within: An Image in Western Thought from the Renaissance to Romanticism*, edited by Edward Dudley and Maximilian Novak, 87-114. Pittsburgh: University of Pittsburgh Press, 1972.

Mitchell, Joshua. "Through a Glass Darkly." In *Early Modern Skepticism and the Origins of Toleration*, edited by Alan Levine. Lanham, Md.: Lexington Books, 1999.

Montaigne, Michel de. *Oeuvres complètes*. Edited by Albert Thibaudet and Maurice Rat. Paris: Gallimard, 1962.

Montaigne, Michel de. *The Complete Works of Montaigne*. Translated by Donald Frame. Stanford: Stanford University Press, 1957.

Montaigne, Michel de. *The Complete Essays*. Translated by M. A. Screech. London: Penguin, 1993.

Montesquieu, Charles de Secondat, baron de. *Oeuvres complètes*, edited by Daniel Oster. Paris: Éditions de Seuil, 1964.

Moore, C. A. "Shaftesbury and the Ethical Poets in England, 1700-1760." *PMLA* 31 (1916): 264-325.

Morsy, Zaghlowl, ed. *La Tolérance*. Paris: UNESCO, 1988.

Moussat, Émile. "De Montaigne à Montesquieu." *Bulletin de la société des amis de Montaigne* 5:12 (1974): 2-4.

Nakam, Géralde. *Les 'Essais' de Montaigne: Miroir et procès de leur temps*. Paris: A.-G. Nizet, 1984.

Nakam, Géralde. *Montaigne et son temps: Les événements et les essais; l'histoire, la vie, le livre*. Paris: A.-G. Nizet, 1982.

Nederman, Cary, and John Laursen, eds. *Difference and Dissent: Theories of Tolerance in Medieval and Early Modern Europe*. Lanham, Md.: Rowman & Littlefield, 1997.

Nederman, Cary. *Worlds of Difference: European Discourses of Toleration, 1100-1550*. State College, Pa.: Penn State University Press, 2000.

Nehemas, Alexander. *The Art of Living*. Berkeley: University of California Press, 1999.

Nelson, Ernest. "The Theory of Persecution." In *Persecution and Liberty: Essays in Honor of George Lincoln Burr*, 3-20. New York: Century, 1931.

Nichols, James H., Jr. *Epicurean Political Philosophy: The 'De Rerum Natura' of Lucretius*. Ithaca, N.Y.: Cornell University Press, 1972.

Nicolaï, Alexandre. "Le Machiavélisme de Montaigne, 1 et 2." *Bulletin de la société des amis de Montaigne* 3:4 (1957): 11-21.

Nicolaï, Alexandre. "Le Machiavélisme de Montaigne, 3." *Bulletin de la société des amis de Montaigne* 3:5/6 (1958): 3-47.

Nicolaï, Alexandre. "Le Machiavélisme de Montaigne, 4." *Bulletin de la société des amis de Montaigne* 3:7 (1958): 2-8.

Nicolaï, Alexandre. *Montaigne intime*. Paris: Aubier, 1947.

Nietzsche, Friedrich. *On the Genealogy of Morals*. Translated by Walter Kaufmann. New York: Vintage, 1967.

Nietzsche, Friedrich. *The Portable Nietzsche*. Edited and translated by Walter Kaufmann. New York: Viking, 1954.

Nietzsche, Friedrich. *Untimely Meditations*. Translated by R. J. Hollingdale. New York: Cambridge University Press, 1983.

Nietzsche, Friedrich. *Joyful Wisdom*. Translated by Thomas Common. New York: Frederick Ungar, 1960.

Nietzsche, Friedrich. *Human, All Too Human*. Translated by R. J. Hollingdale. New York: Cambridge University Press, 1986.

Nietzsche, Friedrich. *On the Advantage and Disadvantage of History for Life*. Translated by Peter Preuss. Indianapolis: Hackett, 1980.

Noddings, Nel. *Caring*. Berkeley: University of California Press, 1984.

Norton, Grace. *The Early Writings of Montaigne and Other Papers*. New York: Macmillan, 1904.

Norton, Grace. "A Handbook to *The Essays* of Michel de Montaigne." In *The Essays of Montaigne*. Translated by George B. Ives. New York: Heritage Press, 1946.

Norton, Glyn. *Montaigne and the Introspective Mind*. Paris: Mouton, 1975.

O'Brien, John. *Anacreon Redivivus: A Study of Anacreontic Translation in Mid-Sixteenth-Century France*. Ann Arbor: University of Michigan Press, 1995.

O'Gorman, Edmundo. *The Invention of America: An Inquiry into the Historical Nature of the New World and the Meaning of Its History*. Bloomington: Indiana University Press, 1961.

O'Neill, John. *Essaying Montaigne: A Study of the Renaissance Institutions of Writing and Reading*. London: Routledge and Kegan Paul, 1982.

Olney, James. *Metaphors of Self: The Meaning of Autobiography*. Princeton: Princeton University Press, 1972.

Ozment, Steven. *The Age of Reform, 1250-1550: An Intellectual and Religious History of Late Medieval and Reformation Europe*. New Haven: Yale University Press, 1980.

Pagden, Anthony. *The Fall of Natural Man: The American Indian and the Origins of Comparative Ethnology*. Cambridge: Cambridge University Press, 1982.

Pagden, Anthony, and Jeremy Lawrance, eds. *Political Writings of Francisco de Vitoria*. Cambridge: Cambridge University Press, 1991.

Parker, Patricia, and David Quint, eds. *Literary Theory/Renaissance Texts*. Baltimore: Johns Hopkins University Press, 1986.

Parry, John H. "A Secular Sense of Responsibility." In *First Images of America: The Impact of the New World on the Old*, edited by Fredi Chiapelli, vol.1: 287-304. Berkeley: University of California Press, 1976.

Pascal, Blaise. *Pensées de Pascal*. Edited by Léon Brunschvicg. Paris: Éditions de Cluny, 1934.

Pascal, Blaise. *Oeuvres Complètes*. Edited by Louis Lafuma. Paris: Éditions de Seuil, 1963.

Paulson, Michael. *The Possible Influence of Montaigne's Essais on Descartes' Treatise on the Passions*. Lanham, Md.: University Press of America, 1988.

Penelhum, Terence. "Skepticism and Fideism." In *The Skeptical Tradition*, edited by Myles Burnyeat, 287-318. Berkeley: University of California Press, 1983.

Persecution and Liberty: Essays in Honor of George Lincoln Burr. New York: Century, 1931.

Pintard, René. *Le Libertinage Érudit*. Paris: Boivin, 1943.

Plato. *The Laws*. Translated by Thomas Pangle. New York: Basic Books, 1980.

Plato. *The Republic*. Translated by Allan Bloom. New York: Basic Books, 1968.

Platt, Michael. "In the Middle of Montaigne." In *The Order of Montaigne's Essays*, edited by Daniel Martin, 124-43. Amherst: University of Massachusetts Press, 1989.

Plattard, Jean. *Montaigne et son temps*. Paris: Boivin, 1933.

Popkin, Richard. *The History of Skepticism from Erasmus to Spinoza*. Los Angeles: University of California Press, 1985.

Popkin, Richard. "The Sceptical Origins of the Modern Problem of Knowledge." In *Perception and Personal Identity: Proceedings of the 1967 Oberlin Colloquium in Philosophy*, edited by Norman Care and Robert Grimm, 3-24. Cleveland: Case Western Reserve University, 1969.

Potter, G. R., ed. *The Renaissance*. In *The New Cambridge Modern History*, vol.

l. Cambridge: Cambridge University Press, 1957.

Quint, David. *Montaigne and the Quality of Mercy: Ethical and Political Themes in the Essais*. Princeton: Princeton University Press, 1998.

Rabb, Theodore. *The Struggle for Stability in Early Modern Europe*. New York: Oxford University Press, 1975.

Rainbow, Paul, ed. *The Foucault Reader*. New York: Pantheon, 1984.

Rawls, John. "Justice as Fairness: Political not Metaphysical." *Philosophy and Public Affairs* 14 (1985): 223-51.

Rawls, John. *A Theory of Justice*. Cambridge: Harvard University Press, 1971.

Rawls, John. *Political Liberalism*. New York: Columbia University Press, 1993.

Regosin, Richard. "Recent Trends in Montaigne Scholarship: A Post-Structuralist Perspective." *Renaissance Quarterly* 37 (1984): 34-54.

Reiss, Timothy. "Montaigne and the Subject of Polity." In *Literary Theory/Renaissance Texts*, edited by Patricia Parker and David Quint, 115-49. Baltimore: Johns Hopkins University Press, 1986.

Remer, Gary. *Humanism and the Rhetoric of Toleration*. University Park: Penn State University Press, 1996.

Rendall, Steven. *Distinguo: Reading Montaigne Differently*. Oxford: Clarendon Press, 1992.

Rendall, Steven. "On Reading the Essais Differently." *Modern Language Notes* 100:5 (December 1985): 1080-85.

Rendall, Steven. "Reading Montaigne." *Diacritics: A Review of Contemporary Criticism* 15:2 (Summer 1985): 44-53.

Rider, Frederick. *The Dialectic of Selfhood in Montaigne*. Stanford: Stanford University Press, 1973.

Rigolot, François. "Montaigne's Purloined Letters." In *Montaigne: Essays in Reading*, edited by Gérard Defaux, 145-66. Yale French Studies Series, edited by Liliane Green, no. 64. New Haven: Yale University Press, 1983.

Riveline, Maurice. *Montaigne et l'amitié*. Paris: Librairie Félix Alcan, 1939.

Robe, Stanley. "Wild Men and Spain's Brave New World." In *The Wild Man Within: An Image in Western Thought from the Renaissance to Romanticism*, edited by Edward Dudley and Maximilian Novak, 39-53. Pittsburgh: University of Pittsburgh Press, 1972.

Robertson, John. "La moralité de conflit militaire dans les *Essais* de Montaigne." *Bulletin de la société des amis de Montaigne* 5:10/11 (1974): 79-82.

Robertson, J. M. *Montaigne and Shakespeare*. London: A. and C. Black, 1909[1897].

Robinet, André. *La philosophie française*. Vendôme: Presses Universitaires de France, 1966.

Romier, Lucien. *A History of France*. Translated by A. L. Rowse. New York: St. Martin's, 1953.

Rorty, Richard. *Contingency, Irony, and Solidarity*. Cambridge: Cambridge University Press, 1989.

Rorty, Richard. "The Historiography of Philosophy." In *Philosophy in History*, edited by Richard Rorty, J. B. Schneewind, and Quentin Skinner, 49-76. Cambridge: Cambridge University Press, 1984.

Rorty, Richard. *Philosophy and the Mirror of Nature*. Princeton: Princeton University Press, 1979.

Rorty, Richard. "The Priority of Democracy to Philosophy." In *The Virginia Statute for Religious Freedom*, edited by Merrill Peterson. Cambridge: Cambridge University Press, 1988.

Rorty, Richard, J. B. Schneewind, and Quentin Skinner, eds. *Philosophy in History*. Cambridge: Cambridge University Press, 1984.

Rosenblum, Nancy, ed. *Liberalism and the Moral Life*. Cambridge: Harvard University Press, 1989.

Rousseau, Jean-Jacques. *The First and Second Discourses*. Edited and translated by Roger D. Masters. New York: St. Martin's, 1964.

Rousseau, Jean-Jacques. *Oeuvres complètes*. Edited by Bernard Gagnebin and Marcel Raymond, 4 vols. Paris: Pléiade, 1959.

Russell, Bertrand. *A History of Western Philosophy*. New York: Simon & Schuster, 1945.

Sabine, George H. "The *Colloquium Heptaplomeres* of Jean Bodin." In *Persecution and Liberty: Essays in Honor of George Lincoln Burr*, 271-309. New York: Century, 1931.

Salingar, Leo. *Dramatic Form in Shakespeare and the Jacobeans*. Cambridge: Harvard University Press, 1959.

Salmon, J. H. M. *Renaissance and Revolt*. New York: Cambridge University Press, 1987.

Salmon, J. H. M. *Society in Crisis: France in the Sixteenth Century*. New York: St. Martin's, 1975.

Samaras, Zoé. "Le rôle de la fortune dans la pensée de Montaigne." *Bulletin de la société des amis de Montaigne* 5:10/11 (1974): 71-77.

Sanderlin, George, ed. *Bartolomé de Las Casas: A Selection of His Writings*. New York: Knopf, 1971.

Sanders, Sylvia Griffith. "The Political Thought of Montaigne." Ph.D. Diss., Yale University, 1971.

Sayce, Richard A. *The Essays of Montaigne: A Critical Exploration*. London: Weidenfeld and Nicolson, 1972.

Sayce, Richard A., and David Maskell. *A Descriptive Bibliography of Montaigne's Essais, 1580-1700*. London: The Bibliographical Society and The Modern Humanities Research Association, 1983.

Scaglione, Aldo. "A Note on Montaigne's 'Des cannibales' and the Humanist Tradition." In *First Images of America: The Impact of the New World on the Old*, edited by Fredi Chiapelli, vol.1: 63-70. Berkeley: University of California Press, 1976.

Scarry, Elaine. *The Body in Pain: The Making and Unmaking of the World*. New

York: Oxford University Press, 1985.

Schaefer, David. "The Good, the Beautiful, and the Useful: Montaigne's Transvaluation of Values." *The American Political Science Review* 73 (1979): 139-54.

Schaefer, David. "Let Us Return to Our Temporal Greatness *Essais.*" In *The Order of Montaigne's Essays,* edited by Daniel Martin. Amherst, Mass.: Hestia, 1989.

Schaefer, David. "Montaigne's Political Reformation." *Journal of Politics* 42 (1980): 766-91.

Schaefer, David. "Montaigne's Political Skepticism." *Polity* 11 (1979): 512-41.

Schaefer, David. *The Political Philosophy of Montaigne.* Ithaca, N.Y.: Cornell University Press, 1990.

Schiffman, Zachary. "Montaigne and the Problem of Machiavellism." *The Journal of Medieval and Renaissance Studies* 12 (1982): 237-58.

Schiffman, Zachary. "Montaigne and the Rise of Skepticism in Early Modern Europe: A Reappraisal." *Journal of the History of Ideas* 45 (October-December 1984): 499-516.

Schmitt, Carl. *The Crisis of Parliamentary Democracy.* Translated by Ellen Kennedy. Cambridge: MIT Press, 1985.

Schmitt, Charles B. *Cicero Scepticus.* The Hague: Nijhoff, 1972.

Schmitt, Charles B. *Reappraisals in Renaissance Thought.* Edited by Charles Webster. London: Variorum Reprints, 1989.

Schmitt, Charles B. "The Rediscovery of Ancient Skepticism in Modern Times." In *The Skeptical Tradition,* edited by Myles Burnyeat, 225-52. Berkeley: University of California Press, 1983.

Schmitt, Charles B. *Studies in Renaissance Philosophy and Science.* London: Variorum Reprints, 1981.

Schneewind, J. B. "The Divine Corporation and the History of Ethics." In *Philosophy in History,* edited by Richard Rorty, J. B. Schneewind, and Quentin Skinner, 173-91. Cambridge: Cambridge University Press, 1984.

Schneewind, J. B., ed. *Moral Philosophy from Montaigne to Kant.* Cambridge: Cambridge University Press, 1990.

Schofield, Malcome, Myles Burnyeat, and Jonathan Barnes, eds. *Doubt and Dogmatism: Studies in Hellenistic Epistemology.* Oxford: Clarendon Press, 1980.

Schonberger, Vincent. "La conception de l'honneste homme' chez Montaigne." *Revue de l'université d'Ottawa* 45:4 (1975): 491-507.

Scodel, Joshua. "The Affirmation of Paradox: A Reading of Montaigne's 'De la Phisionomie.'" In *Montaigne: Essays in Reading,* edited by Gérard Defaux, 209-37. Yale French Studies Series, edited by Liliane Green, no. 64. New Haven: Yale University Press, 1983.

Screech, M. A. *Montaigne and Melancholy: The Wisdom of the Essays.* London: Penguin, 1983.

Seaton, A. A. *The Theory of Toleration Under the Later Stuarts.* New York:

Octagon Books, 1972.

Sedley, David. "The Motivation of Greek Skepticism." In *The Skeptical Tradition*, edited by Myles Burnyeat, 9-30. Berkeley: University of California Press, 1983.

Shaftesbury, Anthony Ashely Cooper 3rd Earl of. *Characteristicks of Men, Manners, Opinions, Times*. 2 vols. Edited by Philip Ayres. Oxford: Clarendon Press, 1999.

Shakespeare, William. *The Tempest*. Edited by Robert Langbaum. New York: Signet, 1964.

Sheriff, John K. *The Good-Natured Man: The Evolution of a Moral Ideal, 1660-1800*. University, Ala.: University of Alabama Press, 1982.

Shklar, Judith. "The Liberalism of Fear." In *Liberalism and the Moral Life*, edited by Nancy Rosenblum, 21-38. Cambridge: Harvard University Press, 1989.

Shklar, Judith. *Montesquieu*. Past Masters Series. Oxford: Oxford University Press, 1987.

Shklar, Judith. *Ordinary Vices*. Cambridge: Belknap Press of Harvard University, 1984.

Shklar, Judith. "The Political Theory of Utopia: From Melancholy to Nostalgia." In *Utopias and Utopian Thought*, edited by Frank Manuel, 101-15. Boston: Beacon Press, 1966.

Singer, Peter. *Animal Liberation*. New York: Avon Books, 1975.

Skinner, Quentin. *The Foundations of Modern Political Thought*. 2 vols. Cambridge: Cambridge University Press, 1978.

Skinner, Quentin. "Political Philosophy." In *The Cambridge History of Renaissance Philosophy*. Cambridge: Cambridge University Press, 1988.

Slavin, Arthur. "The American Principle from More to Locke." In *First Images of America: The Impact of the New World on the Old*, edited by Fredi Chiapelli, vol.1, 139-64. Berkeley: University of California Press, 1976.

Slotkin, James, ed. *Readings in Early Anthropology*. Chicago: Aldine, 1965.

Smith, Adam. *The Theory of Moral Sentiments*. Oxford: Clarendon Press, 1976.

Smith, H. F. Russell. *The Theory of Religious Liberty in the Reigns of Charles II and James II*. Cambridge: Cambridge University Press, 1911.

Smith, Malcolm. "Lost Writings by Montaigne." *Bibliothèque d'humanisme et Renaissance* 49 (1987): 309-18.

Smith, Malcolm. *Montaigne and Religious Freedom: The Dawn of Pluralism*. Études de philologie et d'histoire, no 45. Geneva: Librarie Droz, 1991.

Smith, Malcolm. *Montaigne and the Roman Censors*. Études de philologie et d'histoire, no 37. Geneva: Librarie Droz, 1981.

Smith, Norman Kemp. *The Philosophy of David Hume: A Critical Study of Its Origins and Central Decrees*. London: Macmillan, 1960.

Solomon, Robert, and Kathleen Higgins. *A Short History of Philosophy*. Oxford: Oxford University Press, 1996.

Spencer, Theodore. "Montaigne in America." *The Atlantic Monthly* 177 (March

1946): 91-97.

Starobinski, Jean. "The Body's Moment." In *Montaigne: Essays in Reading*, edited by Gérard Defaux, 273-305. Yale French Studies Series, edited by Liliane Green, no. 64. New Haven: Yale University Press, 1983.

Starobinski, Jean. "Montaigne's Illusion: The Denunciation of Untruth." *Daedalus* 108:3 (1979): 297-306.

Starobinski, Jean. *Montaigne in Motion*. Translated by Arthur Goldhammer. Chicago: University of Chicago Press, 1985.

Starobinski, Jean. "And Then, for Whom Are You Writing." In *Michel de Montaigne*, ed. Harold Bloom, 177-218. Modern Critical Views Series. New York: Chelsea House, 1987.

Stock, Irvin. "Our Friend Montaigne, or the Revolt Against Culture." *Southern Humanities Review* 11:2 (Spring 1977): 162-74.

Strauss, Leo, and Joseph Cropsey, eds. *History of Political Philosophy*. Chicago: University of Chicago Press, 1987.

Strauss, Leo. "Notes on Lucretius." In Leo Strauss, *Liberalism Ancient and Modern*. Ithaca, N.Y.: Cornell University Press, 1968.

Strowski, Fortunat. *Montaigne*. Paris: Librairie Félix Alcan, 1934.

Supple, James J. *Arms Versus Letters*. Oxford: Clarendon Press, 1984.

Symcox, Geoffrey. "The Wild Man's Return: The Enclosed Vision of Rousseau's Discourses." In *The Wild Man Within: An Image in Western Thought from the Renaissance to Romanticism*, edited by Edward Dudley and Maximilian Novak, 223-47. Pittsburgh: University of Pittsburgh Press, 1972.

Symon, J. D., and S. L. Bensusan. *The Renaissance and its Makers*. New York: Dodge, 1953.

Tavéra, François. *L'idée d'humanité dans Montaigne*. Paris: Librairie Ancienne Honoré Champion, 1932.

Taylor, Charles. *Sources of the Self: The Making of the Modern Identity*. Cambridge: Harvard University Press, 1989.

Taylor, George Coffin. *Shakespeare's Debt to Montaigne*. New York: Phaeton Press, 1968.

Telle, Emile. "Montaigne et le procès de Martin Guerre." *Bibliothèque d'humanisme et Renaissance* 37 (1975): 387-419.

Tetel, Marcel. *Montaigne*. New York: Twayne, 1974.

Thibaudet, Albert. *Montaigne*. Paris: Gallimard, 1963.

Thibaudet, Albert, and Maurice Rat, eds. *Oeuvres complètes de Michel de Montaigne*. Paris: Gallimard, 1962.

Thorslev, Peter, Jr. "The Wild Man's Revenge." In *The Wild Man Within: An Image in Western Thought from the Renaissance to Romanticism*, edited by Edward Dudley and Maximilian Novak, 281-307. Pittsburgh: University of Pittsburgh Press, 1972.

Thou, Jacques Auguste de. *Histoire de son Temps* [1604]. In *Histoire universelle*. 11 vols. Basel, 1742.

Tocqueville, Alexis de. *Democracy in America*. Edited by J. P. Mayer, translated by George Lawrence. Garden City, N.Y.: Doubleday, 1969.

Todd, Janet. *Sensibility: An Introduction*. London: Methuen, 1986

Todorov, Tzvetan. *The Conquest of America: The Question of the Other*. Translated by Richard Howard. New York: Harper and Row, 1984.

Todorov, Tzvetan. "L'être et l'autre: Montaigne." In *Montaigne: Essays in Reading*, edited by Gérard Defaux, 113-44. Yale French Studies Series, edited by Liliane Green, no. 64. New Haven: Yale University Press, 1983.

Tong, Rosemarie. *Feminine and Feminist Ethics*. Belmont, Calif.: Wadsworth, 1993.

Toulmin, Stephen. *Cosmopolis: The Hidden Agenda of Modernity*. New York: Free Press, 1990.

Tournon, André. "Self Interpretation in Montaigne's *Essais*." In *Montaigne: Essays in Reading*, edited by Gérard Defaux, 51-72. Yale French Studies Series, edited by Liliane Green, no. 64. New Haven: Yale University Press, 1983.

Trafton, Dain. "Ancients and Indians in Montaigne's 'Des coches.'" *Symposium* 27:1 (Spring 1973): 76-90.

Trinquet, Roger. *La jeunesse de Montaigne: ses origines familiales, son enfance et ses études*. Paris: A.-G. Nizet, 1972.

Tripet, Arnard. *Montaigne et l'art du prologue*. Paris: Librairie Honoré Champion, 1992.

Tronquart, G. "Montaigne et la gloire." *Bulletin de la société des amis de Montaigne* 3:7 (1958): 17-22.

Tuck, Richard. *Philosophy and Government, 1572-1651*. Cambridge: Cambridge University Press, 1993.

Tuck, Richard. "Scepticism and Toleration in the Seventeenth Century." In *Justifying Toleration: Conceptual and Historical Perspectives*, edited by Susan Mendus, 21-36. Cambridge: Cambridge University Press, 1988.

Upham, A. H. *The French Influence in English Literature*. New York: Octagon Books, 1965 [1911].

Villey, Pierre, ed. *Les Essais de Michel de Montaigne*. Paris: Presses Universitaires de France, 1924.

Villey, Pierre. *L'influence de Montaigne sur les idées pédagogiques de Locke et de Rousseau*. Paris: Hachette, 1911.

Villey, Pierre. *Les livres d'histoire moderne utilisés par Montaigne: Contribution à l'étude des sources des Essais*. Paris: Hachette, 1908.

Villey, Pierre. *Les sources et l'évolution des Essais de Montaigne*. 2 vols. Paris: Hachette, 1908.

Villey, Pierre. "Montaigne et François Bacon." *Revue de la Renaissance* 11 (July-September 1911): 122-58.

Villey, Pierre. *Montaigne devant la postérité*. Paris: Boivin, 1935.

Villey, Pierre. "Montaigne and Shakespeare." In *A Book of Homage to*

Shakespeare, edited by Israel Gollancz. Oxford: University Press, H. Milford, 1916.

Vinet, Alexandre. *Histoire de la littérature française au dix-huitième siècle.* Lausanne: Payot, 1960 [1854].

Vitoria, Francisco de. *Political Writings,* edited by Anthony Pagden and Jeremy Lawrance. Cambridge: Cambridge University Press, 1991.

Voltaire, Francois Marie Arouet de. *Oeurves Complètes de Voltaire*, 52 vols., edited by Louis Moland. Paris: Garnier Frères, 1877-1885.

Waldron, Jeremy. "Locke: Toleration and the Rationality of Persecution." In *Justifying Toleration: Conceptual and Historical Perspectives*, edited by Susan Mendus, 61-86. Cambridge: Cambridge University Press, 1988.

Walwyn, William. *Toleration Justified.* Unknown publisher, 1646; reprint, English Series, no. 6, part 3. San Francisco: Suotro Branch California State Library, 1940.

Walzer, Michael. *Interpretation and Social Criticism.* Cambridge: Harvard University Press, 1987.

Walzer, Michael. *On Toleration.* New Haven: Yale University Press, 1997.

Warren, Mark. *Nietzsche and Political Thought.* Cambridge: MIT Press, 1988.

Weale, Albert. "Toleration, Individual Differences and Respect for Differences." In *Aspects of Toleration*, edited by John Horton and Susan Mendus, 16-36. London: Methuen, 1985.

Weintraub, Karl. *The Value of the Individual: Self and Circumstance in Autobiography.* Chicago: University of Chicago Press, 1978.

Weller, Barry. "The Rhetoric of Friendship in Montaigne's Essais." *New Literary History* 9 (Spring 1978): 503-23.

Whatley, Janet. "Food and the Limits of Civility: The Testimony of Jean de Léry." *Sixteenth Century Journal* 15:4 (1984): 387-400.

Whatley, Janet. "Une révérence réciproque: Huguenot Writing on the New World." *University of Toronto Quarterly* 57:2 (winter 1987-1988): 270-89.

White, Hayden. "The Forms of Wildness: Archaeology of an Idea." In *The Wild Man Within: An Image in Western Thought from the Renaissance to Romanticism*, edited by Edward Dudley and Maximilian Novak, 3-38. Pittsburgh: University of Pittsburgh Press, 1972.

White, Hayden. "The Noble Savage Theme as Fetish." In *First Images of America: The Impact of the New World on the Old*, edited by Fredi Chiapelli, vol.1: 121-35. Berkeley: University of California Press, 1976.

Wilden, Anthony. "Montaigne's Essays in the Context of Communication." *Modern Language Notes* 85 (1970): 454-78.

Williams, Bernard. "Descartes' Use of Skepticism." In *The Skeptical Tradition*, edited by Myles Burnyeat, 337-52. Berkeley: University of California Press, 1983.

Williams, George. *The Radical Reformation.* Philadelphia: Westminster Press, 1962.

Williamson, Edward. "On the Liberalizing of Montaigne: A Remonstrance." *French Review* 23 (1949): 92-100.

Wilson, John Laird. *Life of Wycliffe.* New York: Funk and Wagnalls, 1984.

Winter, Ian. *Montaigne's Self-Portrait and its Influence in France, 1580-1630.* French Forum Monographs, edited by R. C. La Charité and V. A. La Charité, no. 3. Lexington, Ky.: French Forum Publishers, 1976.

Wolfe, Don. *Leveller Manifestoes of the Puritan Revolution.* New York: Humanities Press, 1967.

Wootton, David. "New Histories of Atheism." In *Atheism from the Reformation to the Enlightenment,* edited by Michael Hunter and David Wootton. Oxford: Oxford University Press, 1992.

Wootton, David. "Unbelief in Early Modern Europe." In *History Workshop Journal* 20 (1985): 82-100.

Workman, Herbert. *The Dawn of the Reformation.* 2 vols. London: Charles H. Kelly, 1902.

Yack, Bernard, ed. *Liberalism Without Illusions: Essays on Liberal Theory and the Political Vision of Judith N. Shklar.* Chicago: University of Chicago Press, 1996.

Young, Charles Lowell. *Emerson's Montaigne.* New York: Macmillan, 1941.

Zeitlin, Jacob, ed. *The Essays of Michel de Montaigne.* New York: Alfred Knopf, 1935.

Zweig, Stefan. *Montaigne.* Translated by Jean-Jacques Lafaye and François Brugier. Paris: Presses Universitaires de France, 1982.

Index